FALSE PROMISES

The Shaping of American Working Class Consciousness

STANLEY ARONOWITZ

McGraw-Hill Book Company

New York • St. Louis • San Francisco • London • Düsseldorf
Kuala Lumpur • Mexico • Montreal • Panama • São Paulo
Sydney • Toronto • Johannesburg • New Delhi • Singapore

Library of Congress Cataloging in Publication Data

Aronowitz, Stanley.
    False promises.

    Bibliography: p.
    1. Labor and laboring classes—United States—
History. 2. Trade-unions—United States—History.
I. Title.
HD8072.A687   301.44′42′0973   73-5679
ISBN 0-07-002316-6

    3 4 5 6 7 8 9 MU MU 7 9 8 7 6 5

First McGraw-Hill Paperback Edition, 1974

Chapter 4, "Trade Unionism: Illusion and Reality," originally
appeared in *Liberation*, December 1971, under the title "Which
Side Are You On? Trade Unions in America"; Chapter 8, "The
New Workers," originally appeared in *Liberation*, August 1972,
under the title "The Working Class: A Break with the Past."
Both are here included in somewhat altered form by permission
of *Liberation*.

To my father
Nat Aronowitz, 1905–1967,
who showed me words and things,
and helped me find a passion
for justice

Acknowledgments

Writing this book has been the product of a number of intellectual influences as well as personal experiences. I have dealt with the personal in the book itself. My debt to the work of Herbert Marcuse may be obscured by the several occasions that I have differed with him in the text. It seems to me that the line of inquiry pursued by Marcuse and others of the so-called Frankfurt School of philosophy and sociology has been too long neglected by students of American politics and culture. My own efforts have been deeply influenced by them. Similarly, the works of European Marxists such as Karl Korsch and Georg Lukacs are extremely suggestive for understanding working class consciousness and institutions and provide a welcome corrective to the reflex Marxism against which both students and working class militants alike have made justifiable objections. Particularly important for my thinking was the attempt of a number of social theorists after the First World War to locate the production of consciousness not only in the economic conditions of society, but its technology and culture as well.

I wish to acknowledge the significant contribution of several American historians, particularly William Appleman Williams and Gabriel Kolko, to my vision of the past as well as the present. Particularly helpful is the work of Kolko, James Weinstein, Lloyd Gardner and others who have shown that twentieth-century progressivism and liberalism have actually served the corporate order rather than opposing it. Within this judgment, the decline of the unions can be understood without relying for explanation on the perfidy of leadership.

Bruce Brown, Colin Greer, Frank Reissman, Charles Isaacs, and Sol Yurick read the manuscript. Discussions with Greer on the subject of working class immigration were particularly helpful to me. Bruce Brown made substantive contributions to the section on mass culture, and I have learned a great deal about working class play from Ivan Kronenfeld, who read and critized my work on this subject. My gratitude to Carol Lopate is incalculable. She read, criticized, and made valuable suggestions at many points in the writing of the book. Seymour Copstein was much more than a copy-editor. He corrected errors of fact as well as substance. My editor, Joyce Johnson, was a gentle taskmaster who taught me that it was not necessary to do violence to the English language in order to make an argument. Her constant encouragement and acute sense of craft has made this book better. Margaret Wolf typed portions of the manuscript, an unenviable and monotonous job. Of course, these persons have only improved the book. Its weaknesses are solely my responsibility.

The material on Lordstown was gathered in conjunction with a film called *Nuts and Bolts,* on which I served as a part-time member of the crew. I am grateful to Peter Schlaifer and Peter Herman, who granted me the chance to review their video tapes as well as participate in the project.

Contents

Preface

It has been an unfortunate tendency among those who have tried to understand the American working class, its history, institutions, and political consciousness, to treat each of these separately. It is as if a whole person were being cut up into different discrete sections instead of being comprehended as a totality. This book is an attempt to present that totality. Part of the task requires a reinterpretation of American workers' history. Another part of the task is to examine working class consciousness. Among the points argued in the book is that we cannot confine our understanding to the objective events and institutional conflicts that workers have shaped and in which they have discovered or lost their identity as a class. We must examine daily life, for it is in the structures of everyday existence that the social structure is reproduced in the minds of its participants.

Thus, there are really two dimensions to this book. I have spent a good deal of space trying to explain the historical development of the working class, particularly its ethnic, sexual, racial, and skill divisions. I have attempted to chart the relationship between these divisions and working class institutions, particularly the trade unions. Finally, I have linked the events of the recent past with the decline of the historical working class in order to understand what is living and what is dead in its traditions. These questions occupy the substance of Part Two.

Part One discusses the new developments in working class life and labor. I have placed particular emphasis on the emerging culture of the new worker because I believe that this is the decisive element that demarcates the new worker from the old. As will become evident, I have broadened the definition of culture to include all mores and attitudes that characterize a specific psychological as well as political outlook of a class or group. The chapters of Part One on Lordstown and on working class childhood and youth, and on mass culture, are directed toward developing a multidimensional methodology for answering the large question: what role can the working class play as a force for social change or social stability in our country?

Stanley Aronowitz

The Cloakmakers Union is a no good union
It's a company union by the bosses.
The old cloakmakers and the socialist fakers
By the workers are making double crosses.

The Dubinskys, the Hillquits, the Thomases
By the workers are making false promises.
They preach socialism but they practice fascism
To save capitalism by the bosses.

(Old labor song with many variants, attributed to the Needle Workers
Industrial Union, a rival of the ILGWU in the late 1920s)

Introduction

In August 1966 I was sent to Puerto Rico as a representative of the Oil, Chemical, and Atomic Workers. I had been director of organization for the union's region in the Northeastern states until columnist Victor Reisel wrote, in February 1966, that I was among those in the unions most active in pressing for political action against the Vietnam War. His article created a minor ripple within the OCAW and gave the conservatives an occasion for demanding my dismissal and a clear-cut union stand in support of the war. OCAW President Al Grospiron resisted the pressure for a prowar position and for my dismissal as well. But even though I was also supported by my district council, it was hard to keep me at my job. Instead of firing me, Grospiron sent me to help launch an organizing drive in Puerto Rico.

My exile forced me to reexamine my position as a full-time union official, and, eventually, led to a fresh look not only at the union movement but at the working class as a potential force for social and political change. For most of the early 1960s I had walked a fairly thin line between radical activism and trade unionism. I spent a good deal of the period doing two things: helping to create a new left that was both organizationally and ideologically independent of the old Socialist and Communist movements, and working with the more progressive groups in the trade unions that were trying to revive the energy of the CIO. In 1965, I played a minor part in helping to elect Grospiron to succeed O. A. Knight, an old CIO leader who had become increasingly entangled with State-Department- and CIA–sponsored labor activities in Africa and Latin America during the Cold War days, and was steering a fairly conservative course within the union as well. Grospiron was among the younger, more aggressive union leaders who were making successful bids to oust the old-line industrial union leaders at that time. I felt that the atmosphere for more militant, democratic unionism would be improved if he were elected. The circumstances leading to my temporary exile to Puerto Rico were only a last straw in a mounting set of doubts about what I was doing in the labor movement. In March 1967 I decided to take a leave of absence and go back to the United States. My departure in May proved to be permanent. I left not only the OCAW, but the union movement itself.

When I returned to the mainland, the idea of writing a book began to take shape in my mind. It was to be a contemporary analysis of the unions, showing the convergence of liberal and conservative trade union leaders. I believed they both played the same role in giving general support to the policies of the U.S. government, cooperating with the companies against the initiatives of the rank and file, and providing part of the constituency of the Democratic Party. The book was to be written from the point of view of a socialist-minded trade union reformer. I could not write the book: there were too many questions left unanswered and I had not yet attained the distance from my work to deal with them. Instead, I got a job working for a New York City antipoverty agency and went back to school to get a bachelor's degree.

The events of 1968 in France had a profound impact on my thinking. I began to understand that neither the trade unions nor the many left-wing political parties in France were compatible with the incipient revolutionary aspirations of the students or the workers who were straining toward taking control of society. When the 1969–70 wildcat strikes in transportation and among postal workers and auto workers encountered both trade union and government resistance in almost equal measure in this country, a substantial change in my perspective began to congeal for me.

I grew up politically with the orthodox socialist view of radical change. According to this position, workers by themselves could never achieve revolutionary consciousness, since socialism was a science usually brought to the working class by intellectuals from the outside. It was the role of intellectuals to organize a revolutionary political party that would systematically agitate and organize among the industrial working class and other exploited sections of the people. Even though the trade unions could not lead the fight for socialism, they were important as training grounds for the workers. In the trade union struggles, workers learned the value and the techniques of collective action. They became conscious of themselves as a distinct interest group in society that had little in common with the interests of the employers or the capitalist state. To be sure, revolutionary class consciousness—that is, the recognition by workers that their particular interest was identical with the general project of world historical changes and that they alone could propel a transformation in social relations—must await the capitalist crisis that would prove the inability of the economic system to meet the workers' needs. Prior to the crisis, however, political and trade union activity prepared the workers organizationally and ideologically for the conflict that would result in great social changes. Radicals were to enter the trade unions in order to win over workers to the ideas of socialism where possible, but also to encourage militant struggles for immediate demands, to undertake independent political action outside the two major capitalist parties, and to work for the transformation of reactionary trade unions into better instruments for serving workers' interests. The duty of the radicals was to fight for democratic, politically conscious trade unionism as the best first step toward the development of class consciousness.

I came from a working class family and spent nearly fifteen years in the shops and in full-time union work. Even though I never identified with the existing union leadership, and always regarded myself as an oppositionist, I was a firm advocate of building unions—even if conservative—among the unorganized. Implicit in my years as a rank-and-file union member, an activist in caucuses aimed at replacing the existing union leadership in the Steelworkers, and as an organizer, was the idea that the unions played a generally progressive role in U.S. social struggles and that workers could never achieve socialist consciousness until they had learned how to struggle for their immediate demands and take control of their own unions.

This book represents a departure from these views and, indeed, from the way I have spent most of my adult life. During the writing of this book, I have attempted to reexamine all of the ideas that have guided my political and trade union activities. I have also been led to undertake a critique of the methods that are implied by these ideas.

After leaving the trade unions, I began to look at the working class, its institutions and its history, in ways that were radically different from those of most professional social scientists of both left-wing and liberal persuasions. In considering the history and role of the working class in U.S. society, historians and social theorists have characteristically circumscribed the history of the working class by the experience of trade unions and socialist movements. The ideological conflicts among leaders, the relative strength of factions within the unions and political sects, and the events that symbolized the intensity of workers' struggles against capital in the plants or in the political sphere, have become the preoccupation of labor history and theory.

There is a logic to this perspective, if one accepts the view that all history is defined by the conscious, institutionally defined struggles between people. In the United States trade union struggles have been the most overt expressions of worker discontent. But in defining the working class by the evolution of institutions or by episodic struggles, dimensions that can shed light on the configuration of working class consciousness and organizations are ignored. The result of such analysis is, therefore, one-sided and ultimately distorts reality. Implied in this view of working class history is the idea that the origins and development of the institutions themselves can be explained in terms of their internal political struggles and the intelligence or perfidy of the leaders. It refuses to examine the forces that prevented workers from affiliating with these institutions or the alternatives they found to them.

Recently, a number of writers dissatisfied with the limitations of institutional labor history have tried to reconstruct the story of the working class from the fabric of actual mass struggles or, alternatively, the consciousness of rank-and-file workers themselves. The works of Irving Bernstein, Studs Terkel, Jeremy

Brecher, and David Brody have provided welcome antidotes to the prevailing orientation of labor historians.

Bernstein's two massive studies[1] try to connect the circumstances of everyday working class life and trade union development with the political and economic changes of the 1920s and 1930s. His work constitutes a mandatory source for anyone interested in workers' history. But the mass of detail and the many insights provided by him barely touch what should be the starting point of labor studies—the workplace. His history is still written from the outside.

Terkel tries to understand working class life from inside the consciousness of those who live it. As subjective description, his oral history has no parallel in the literature of the American working class. *Hard Times*[2] provides an important corrective to the general tendency of those who look at the working class to ignore how they think. He shows that the anger of workers is not the same as self-recognition of their power and right to control society.

Brecher[3] steps out of institutional controversies to record the important labor struggles of the last one hundred years. He shows that the American working class has acted independently of both the trade unions and the political parties to oppose companies and defend its class interest. His semidocumentary account of some of the epochal struggles of industrial workers reveals their courage, their capacity for self-organization, and their incipient revolutionary awareness despite the vacillations and frequent opposition of organized trade union bureaucracies. It is impossible to come away from a reading of Brecher's book with the consensus view of American workers' history intact.

American workers in all generations have demonstrated that they will fight, with force of arms if necessary, to protect their wages and working conditions. At times, they have been driven to organize the production and distribution of goods on their own, and have taken over cities and whole regions and become the recognized authority regulating both commerce and public services within the community. Brecher concludes that the absence of revolutionary consciousness among workers is less important than the objective conditions that force them to struggle in new ways. In his view, it is the struggles of the workers themselves rather than the agitational activities of organized labor unions or radical groups that compel the development of new forms of consciousness. His book demonstrates that American workers have, upon occasion, taken new political steps out of the imperatives of their own combat. Yet he has fallen short of explaining the failure of the working class to emerge from its odyssey of strike movements and insurrectionary actions with a social tradition and political culture of its own.

Embedded in Brecher's approach is the assumption that since workers constitute the overwhelming force of production in modern capitalism, the question of whether they will take control over production and society as a whole is always a practical issue because all the social conditions are present for historical change. In his view, the subjective conditions, that is, the development of class consciousness, can only be resolved within the experience of working class struggle. It is in the course of the mass strike that revolutionary conditions are created, that workers discover their own power, which remains latent in everyday life. According to Brecher, it is only workers themselves who can bring their struggle forward to new political levels. Neither the trade unions nor radical political parties can lead; the role of conscious radicals is to speak clearly to the workers' needs, to point the lessons of their own efforts, and to participate in their struggles.

The fundamental question to be explored in this book is why the working class in America remains a dependent force in society and what the conditions are that may reverse this situation. In the course of my research I was compelled to abandon explanations that relied exclusively on ideological factors that were not connected to the main forces of the economic and social history of American capitalism. Nor was it possible to accept the romantic view that workers themselves have been able to transcend the institutions of capitalism, including the trade unions and political parties, out of the conditions of their own alienated labor. To be sure, among the sources of their alienation are elements that make protest and contestation a permanent feature of working class life. The struggle between labor and capital is incessant and unresolvable as long as workers are separated from the ownership of the means of production, control over what they produce, and the methods of production. But alienation has other implications that prevent workers from bringing to consciousness their right to control society, to recapture their own labor and to control their own daily lives. The very conditions that produce an acute sense of injustice among workers also obscure the sources of that injustice. The barriers to the ability of the working class to grasp the fact that its own exploitation at the point of production results from systemic causes are not chiefly ideological: they are rooted in the labor process.

Georg Lukacs[4] has shown that explanations for the failure of the working class to develop revolutionary consciousness must be sought within the production and circulation of commodities, not outside of this process. His attempt to locate the production of consciousness within the labor process, and to account for the apparent inability of workers to connect their own individual experience with their social position within capitalist society in the same terms, constitutes a necessary clue to the mystery of working class history.

Lukacs's reading of Marx and Kant provided him with the critical categories for undertaking the study of working class consciousness. A close student of the ideological development of the socialist movement, he rejected the so-called orthodox tendency of Marxism that relied on the strength of the socialist agitation and trade union struggles, on the one hand, and the inevitability of capitalist economic crises, on the other, to reveal to workers the truth of their position within capitalist society. Instead, following Marx's concept of the "fetishism of commodities," Lukacs discovered that in ordinary life the exploitation of labor by capital is hidden from the consciousness of the worker by the fact that the terms on which goods are exchanged in the market appear to be determined by factors independent of the workers' own labor. Commodities appear to assume value in exchange rather than in production and the relations between men are perceived as relations between things. The worker values himself as one values all commodities—by his selling price. Thus all relations appear as object relations. The very existence of the worker is bound up with the sale of his labor power. Individual worth is measured by how much labor can bring in the marketplace. People become identical with their occupations, consumption styles, and social prestige and the self has no autonomy apart from its exchange value. The subordination of the self to the labor process itself takes on the appearance of blind economic law, so that the domination of man by man no longer appears an injustice but a biological or legal necessity. The power of the employer over the worker has the force of economic necessity and its human substance is entirely suppressed. Within the framework of this analysis the crucial ideologies among American workers can be understood.

The "respect for law," "love of country" and the flag, and moral systems that constitute the rules of ordinary behavior assume the status of natural law: they become reified as commands for individual conduct. The institutions of family, school, church, and factory appear in a continuum of experience whose structure and demands on the person are essentially consistent with each other.

Daily life appears as the confrontation between the individual and institutions that exist independently of human intervention. In the contest, the person attempts to individuate himself so that subjectivity can be achieved. But the interventions of human domination masked as objective institutional rules constitute barriers to selfhood. The need to prove one's value for others within the institutions of daily life is always an activity that involves transactional relations. For example, the child agrees to be "good" —that is, to obey parental authority—in return for specific rewards. The high school student agrees to perform in the sports arena in return for partial exemption from the rules of ordinary student conduct imposed by the administration and teachers of the school. The woman agrees to "give love" in return for economic security or the pledge of the man to support her. Even the forms of revolt against the conditions that produce exploitation and oppression are often directed against the appearance of things rather than their essence.

Thus, the early labor struggles were directed against the machine. Workers, recently migrated from the land or artisanship, believed that mechanization itself was the enemy, just as many social theorists today rail against technology as such. The specific conditions under which the individual worker sells his labor power seem to place him in direct opposition to the machine on the one hand, and the employer on the other. The product of his labor is appropriated by the employer and sold in the market according to measures that seem to bear no relation to the fact that it was produced by him.

The circulation of commodities appears to take on a life of its own, independent of social relations. Lukacs's second critical finding was that the commodity form penetrates all corners of the social world. Everything becomes an object of sale in capitalist society, including those activities once considered separate from commercial debasement. The once autonomous elements of working class culture, indeed of all culture, only find their value in the market place and subordinate aesthetic sensibilities to the norms of exchange.

As Herbert Marcuse has shown,[5] the pervasive character of capitalist commodity relations and of the technological rationality upon which they are based tends to reduce social relations and social consciousness to a single dimension: their instrumental value in terms of maintaining the structure of social domination. Not only does the worker lose touch with his congealed labor as the commodity he has produced assumes the form of a material thing, hiding from his view the fact that he produced it, but the particular form of labor constitutes a further alienation. The kind of work performed, e.g., assembly, seems to be related to the wages paid and the position of the worker in the social structure. The divisions in production between skilled and unskilled labor, mental and physical work, men and women, Blacks and whites, and various ethnic groups are significant in the formation of social consciousness. These differences hide the fact that all who work for wages, and the majority of those who are salaried employees of corporations and government, are powerless to determine the basic decisions that affect both their working lives and their private lives.

Labor is divided in society socially as well as technically. The technical division of labor represents the assignment of different tasks to different individuals in an increasingly variegated society. In complex societies it is virtually impossible to reconstruct the "Renaissance person," if indeed such a person ever existed. Not everyone can become a welder or a teacher. Even in the best of situations, we are forced to make choices about the kind of labor we shall undertake. But the technical divisions based on social needs are shaped by the social division of labor—a division based on class position and infused with criteria of power and ownership over the productive forces of society. For example, neither technology nor biological necessity determines the effective exclusion of women from the production of raw materials and heavy machinery in our country. This exclusion is the product not only of efforts by trade unions, employers, and social reformers to enact legislation to protect women and the jobs of men, but of the historical tendencies in the sexual division of labor as well. Thus, sexist ideologies, political and economic interests, and historical tradition must be understood in the convergence of their mutual determination. The effect on consciousness of female exclusion from key production areas becomes a major determinant of future social divisions in the labor process, and the institutions that function within it.

Beginning from an examination of the formation of the working class in terms of the relationship between the industrialization process and the social division of labor that gave it shape, the roles of institutions, ideologies, and cultural influences must be explored as both products of this development and, in turn, determinants of the underlying social relations. The main institutions within and against which the individual confronts society prior to entering the work-world are family, schools, religion, and more recently, mass culture. These institutions mediate between the social relations of production and individual consciousness by communicating to the individual his place in the social division of labor while providing contrary symbols that hold out the possibility of transcending the fate of previous generations. In turn, the ideologies of mobility transmitted by these institutions are in conflict with other ideologies that operate to persuade the person that his failure to transcend his class origins is a product of genetic incapacity or lack of perseverance. The hierarchy of occupations that results from a specific way of organizing social labor tends to give credence to individual mobility aspirations even when mobility between classes is foreclosed. The confusion in America about what constitutes the concept of class arises precisely from the hierarchical organization of labor and of all social institutions. Hierarchy tends to obscure the fundamental relations between members of the same class because of differences within them. At each step of any occupational hierarchy, there are differential economic rewards, degrees of social powerlessness, and variations of consciousness. Although the real subject of this book is the attempt to delineate both objectively and subjectively the divisions within the working class, it is with the purpose of recovering the essential unity of its social position.

The two-class model of orthodox Marxism, according to which capitalist society is divided into an essentially propertyless working class deprived of the ownership of the means of production and a capitalist class holding a monopoly of ownership of productive property, is more apparent today than ever before. The share of large corporations in the total social wealth is larger in the United States than in any other capitalist country. Even though the old middle class of independent shopkeepers, small manufacturers, and farmers has not disappeared, *and* has recently increased in number, its economic and social power continues to diminish. On the other hand, the proportion of wage and salary workers to the total population is now about 80 percent.

But the old model, while correct in its broad outlines, does not constitute an adequate theory of class. At the level of classification this apparent anomaly occurs for two reasons: first, a substantial number of those who work for salaries are not truly part of the working class because of their dependence on the corporate form of economic organization for their existence. These are the managers at various levels of the corporation who neither own nor genuinely control the means of production, but possess power in limited spheres of production and administration. Their interests are those of the corporations and as a social stratum they have no sources of independent power. Second, there has developed a substantial underclass that is not only deprived of property but of participation in the production process. The underclass does not correspond to Marx's notion of a reserve army of labor since it is characteristically not employed in the expansion of capital, but enters the labor market only in the most marginal service occupations or as seasonal agricultural laborers. Nor is the underclass a lumpenproletariat in the classical sense, that is a group without character and potentially "dangerous" to working class interests. The permanently unemployed or marginally employed sectors of the population are formed out of the unevenness of late capitalist development and its chronic inability to absorb ever-larger proportions of the displaced agricultural labor force, older workers, and young school-leavers. The formation of the underclass is a direct result of the disparity between the historical tendency of capitalist production to require less labor for the production of commodities and the urbanization of the whole population, that is, the shrinking of the countryside, owing to the same processes of mechanization.

The underclass is not defined by its income, but by its exclusion from the mainstream of economic life. It is a dependent class in a different way than the managerial class. Essentially, its economic position, although derived from the same processes that determine the formation of other classes, is more closely tied to the expanded role of the state, especially the provision of welfare. Its immediate political thrust is toward the maintenance and nourishment of the state bureaucracy rather than its diminution.

The working class, as here defined, is composed of those engaged in the production and distribution of material goods and services who do not own or control the object of their labor or its uses. The persons grouped within the working class are neither exclusively workers in the production sphere who manipulate things, nor those in the distributive sphere who manipulate symbols and people. The social weight of the former is greater than that of the latter, but their interests are the same.

Beyond problems of classification another critical difficulty concerning the problem of delineating classes must be faced. Contrary to the tendency of both American sociology and some varieties of Marxism to deal with class solely in terms of its definition and mechanical categories, Marx insisted that the working class was not only defined by its objective position within capitalist production as the most exploited class in society, but must be comprehended in terms of its social and political activity. The one-sided analysis that limits an understanding of the worker to his objective position within the prevailing social system and as an object of exploitation may help explain the failure of the working class to transcend its subordinate situation but it cannot explain the conditions necessary for the working class to become a force for social change. The history of the working class is the unfolding of its collective subjectivity as much as of its objectivity. If theory has been forced to consider these aspects separately, it is only a reflection of the splits within the working class movement and in working class consciousness itself. Lukacs has only explained the difficulty of making total the conception of the relationship between personal experience and the social world that includes it: the task of theory is to locate the economic, political, and cultural conditions for transcendence.

This task is made urgent by the condition of humankind itself. The human condition today is marked by a loss of the idea of progress. The capacity of nations to reduce one another to wastelands by technological means is matched by the capacity of capitalist society to reduce its members to objects. One cannot understand the logic of the merciless bombing of Vietnam without understanding the equally relentless exploitation of the miner or of the officeworker, each of whom faces no less serious problems recovering his humanity after the workday than the Vietnamese peasant after the air raids, even if the latter faces a more visible enemy and swifter destruction.

Trade unions and radical political movements reflect aspects of the working class and are only relatively autonomous influences upon it. The trade unions derive both their strengths and their weaknesses from the fact that they operate within the social process of production. The organization of unions by craft and by industry is a reflection of the social divisions of labor and generates ideologies that perpetuate those divisions. On the other hand, socialist movements operating outside production have suffered from a chronic inability to attract the mass of production workers in the United States. Even when American socialism began to approach the proportions of a mass movement in the early decades of the twentieth century, its presentation of itself as an instrument of universal emancipation was in conflict with its practical role as the representative of the more skilled strata within the working class and disaffected members of the middle class. The Socialist Party was committed to its constituency of native-born Americans and those of Northern European origins (chiefly Germany and Great Britain). Their political experience and industrial skill made them formidable combatants against the excesses of advancing capitalism, but they were equally hostile to those who had the least initial resources to conduct their own struggles—the Eastern and Southern European immigrants and the Blacks.

In this book I have concentrated on the issues of ideology and institutional practice that have shaped the radical movements only as they bear on the questions of the development of the class itself. Since, with a few exceptions, socialist ideas have not been organically linked with any substantial sector of the working class in America except those who conducted a rear-guard action against industrialism and the trusts around the turn of the twentieth century, I have limited my treatment of the role of left-wing movements to their bearing on the specific issues raised in the book. This omission should not be interpreted as an attempt to downgrade the role of the left in the formation of working class movements. Radicals have always played an important part in the growth and development of the labor movement, but, with the notable exception of the International Workers of the World, they have rarely played an independent role in the twentieth century. In fact, the consistent retreat of the left from its own fundamental ideas has characterized its activities in the trade unions and working class political movements since the first years of this century.

A sharp separation of theory and practice has marked radical efforts in the trade unions. For the most part, the unions the socialist and the communist left helped to build were conservative.

Always subordinating their ideas to the exigencies of the moment, the left lent its enormous energies, considerable talents, and, at times, financial and organizational resources to this task. Even the opposition of the early socialists to the leadership of the American Federation of Labor was conducted on the basis of accepting the need to work within its framework. For many years, the most important struggle conducted by radicals within the AFL was for industrial rather than craft unions. However, most of them rejected the idea of building revolutionary or industrial unions that directly challenged the conservative craft unions within the AFL and contented themselves with the role of political opposition to the leadership of the Federation. Conservative trade union leaders were often willing to use the services of left-wingers of all political varieties as long as they agreed to keep their politics out of their organizing, but this suicidal collaboration almost always led to the absorption of the left-wingers by the conservatives, or, in more recent years, to their expulsion from the union hierarchies. Nonetheless, radicals entered into it in the sincere belief that the unity of the labor movement was prior to socialist demands, and education was the fundamental condition for the development of advanced consciousness. Despite its accomplishments, the American radical movement, like its European counterparts, has helped to consolidate the power of capital over workers in two ways: it assisted in the organization of unions that have increasingly been instruments for the disciplining and control of workers; and it fought for reforms that strengthened the power of the capitalist state to organize and rationalize the most chaotic features of the socioeconomic system and secure the dependency of larger segments of the underlying population on state welfare measures. The consequences of radical militancy in behalf of unions and social reforms are largely unintended. Socialists and Communists have been unwitting instruments of capitalist rationalization as much as they have been opponents of the most politically authoritarian features of the system.

This present work is an attempt to understand social and political questions from a perspective that embraces both history and culture, politics and everyday life. If the working class is to make a break with the past, this break cannot result from its militancy alone, or simply from the ability of the ideological left to capture a large working class constituency for its ideas. It will arise out of new conditions, rooted equally in new social relations and in the development of a conscious opposition culture generated by the workers themselves. This culture is here defined as the matrix of language, art, and political sensibility that constitutes the world outlook for an entire class. The fundamental condition for its emergence must be located among the sinews of society—not outside it. Since the strength of capitalism depends as much upon its command over the means and the modes of communication as it does on its economic resources, no departure from the past can be realized unless one can envision a challenge to this monopoly that seeks to create an alternative to it.

The distorted communications that are transmitted and received in our society are consequent upon the development of symbols that not only reflect existing social divisions and reify them as the only possible objects of cognition, but construct a new reality that appears eternal. Thus, workers are not only tied to the prevailing system by the everyday material benefits supplied by it as well as its pervasion into all corners of their personal world, but they are linked to it as well by their own perception of themselves as parts of it—the person has become nothing more than another commodity that is exchanged like all other economic goods. To the extent that the social division of labor gives rise to a culture that seems integral to the reproduction of all social life, the sources of a new culture can only be found by conscious understanding of the entire process of social domination, not only its economic aspects.

The appropriation of all culture in the service of commodity production is the distinguishing feature of late capitalism. Nearly all human activity seems directed toward the single end of perpetuating the production-consumption cycle. The vast technical resources mobilized by capital to produce goods demands that no stone be left unturned to assure the conditions for their reproduction, particularly the reproduction of consumers. Culture becomes debased by advertising and finds space for even its most traditional forms only to the extent that it is "sponsored" by a commercial interest. Increasingly, private life and the old arts have gone underground and occupy the invisible margins of the society of "controlled consumption." "High culture," an historical product of the colonization of popular forms by intellectuals, is integrated into the spectacle or relegated to obscurity.

The working class could always be distinguished by its unique language that often clung to it as a stigma, but gave it cultural identity. The appropriation of the production of linguistic forms by mass communications has had a disintegrating effect on the autonomous language of all sectors of the underlying population. The mechanisms of homogenization are more complicated than the flattening of thought and language that Marcuse has described. Uniformity is achieved by the appropriation by mass culture of individual language patterns. Southern dialects, working class Northern speech, and ethnic forms of individuation are all grist for the popular mills. Phrases are incorporated into the speech of all Americans that derive from these specific cultures mediated by mass media. In the process, the old phrases lose their original meaning as a transcendent form of communication appropriate and unique to particular regional or ethnic contexts. They are now integrated unconsciously into speech without the benefit of traditions that imparted a distinct sensibility in their original uses. This process disrupts the meaning-structure of words and phrases, but it forces ordinary people to invent new words and phrases in order to preserve the shreds of autonomy of their culture. Even though all subcultures have capitulated to the assault of mass culture, there remains an impulse toward invention and independence that can be observed every day in the games, language, symbols, that are constantly evolving.

The colonization of private life by the structures of industrial society is revealed most directly in the overwhelming role played by consumption-activity in leisure or unbounded time. The distinctions between the private and the public realm that constitute the real basis for the cultural autonomy of the working class are constantly being undermined. Yet the resistance to such invasion is the fundamental condition for the development of a working class movement capable of charting its own historical course. And to the extent that recent movements spearheaded by young workers against the ordinary aspects of industrial discipline—such as coming to work every day and on time—are propelled by a loosening of the affiliation of workers to the industrial system, these actions may be a harbinger of a new set of cultural values that will become the basis for new forms of social struggle.

NOTES

1. Irving Bernstein, *The Lean Years: A History of the American Worker 1920–1933*, Boston, Mass., Houghton Mifflin Company, 1960.

———, *The Turbulent Years: A History of the American Worker 1933–1941*, Boston, Mass., Houghton Mifflin Company, 1969.

2. Studs Terkel, *Hard Times,* New York, Pantheon Books, 1970.

3. Jeremy Brecher, *Strikes!* San Francisco, Calif., Straight Arrow Books, 1972.

4. Georg Lukacs, *History and Class Consciousness,* London, The Merlin Press, Ltd., 1971.

5. Herbert Marcuse, *One Dimensional Man,* Boston, Mass., Beacon Press, 1964.

PART ONE

New Developments in Working Class Life and Labor

1

Lordstown: Disruption on the Assembly Line

Every day I come out of there I feel ripped off. I'm gettin' the shit kicked out of me and I'm helpless to stop it. A good day's work is being tired but not exhausted. Out there all I feel is glad when it's over.

I don't even feel useful now. They could replace me; I don't even feel necessary.... They could always find somebody stupider than me to do the job."

—Lordstown assembly line worker,
twenty years old

— 1 —

The Lordstown complex of the General Motors Company sprawls along a huge, flat cornfield alongside Route 45 near Warren, Ohio. The facility is called a "complex" because it includes several plants doing different things. The older plants—the Fisher Body shop making subassemblies such as fenders for Chevrolet cars, and the smaller truck plant—are no different from the many similar factories operated by the company in other complexes throughout the United States. The big news is the new Chevrolet assembly plant which rolls out 800 Vega passenger cars a day. This plant is important to the company for two reasons. The Vega is the car counted on to regain GM's slipping position in car sales. Most of the losses have been to small-sized foreign models which, until the devalution of the U.S. dollar in early 1972, cut deeply into the sales and profits of U.S. car manufacturers. The second reason is equally powerful. This factory has become the most productive assembly plant in the world. Its average hourly production of 100 cars or more is at least 40 percent higher than the vast majority of assembly plants of its competitors or within the company itself.

The new plant began to hire workers in 1966, but there was no sign that there was to be anything unusual about the work until the model changeover in the late summer and autumn of 1971. Until then, the 7000 assembly line workers turned out slightly more than 60 cars an hour. In the late summer GM introduced its new production methods and, at the same time, brought in a new management, the GM Assembly Division. A few automatic robot machines were brought into the body shop to replace human labor in welding operations, the number of moving parts in the car was reduced to permit one car to be assembled every 36 seconds, and the parts were made smaller for easier handling.

The General Motors Assembly Division is a tough, no-nonsense outfit charged with the responsibility "of being able to meet foreign competition." GMAD "adopted 'get tough' tactics to cope with increased worker absenteeism and boost productivity." According to *Business Week*, the new division was set up in 1965 to tighten and revamp assembly operations. "The need for GMAD's belt-tightening role was underscored during the late 1960s when GM's profit margin dropped from 10 percent to 7 percent."[1]

At Lordstown, efficiency became the watchword. At 60 cars an hour, the pace of work had not been exactly leisurely, but after GMAD came in the number of cars produced almost doubled. Making one car a minute had been no picnic, especially on a constantly moving line. Assembly work fits the worker to the pace of the machine. Each work station is no more than 6 to 8 feet long. For example, within a minute on the line, a worker in the trim department had to walk about 20 feet to a conveyor belt transporting parts to the line, pick up a front seat weighing 30 pounds, carry it back to his work station, place the seat on the chassis, and put in four bolts to fasten it down by first hand-starting the bolts and then using an air gun to tighten them according to standard. It was steady work when the line moved at 60 cars an hour. When it increased to more than 100 cars an hour, the number of operations on this job were not reduced and the pace became almost maddening. In 36 seconds the worker had to perform at least eight different operations, including, walking, lifting, hauling, lifting the carpet, bending to fasten the bolts by hand, fastening them by air gun, replacing the carpet, and putting a sticker on the hood. Sometimes the bolts fail to fit into the holes; the gun refuses to function at the required torque; the seats are defective or the threads are bare on the bolt. But the line does not stop. Under these circumstances the workers often find themselves "in the hole," which means that they have fallen behind the line.

"You really have to run like hell to catch up, if you're gonna do the whole job right," one operator named Jerry told me when I interviewed him in the summer of 1972. "They had the wrong-sized bolt on the job for a whole year. A lot of times we just miss a bolt to keep up with the line."

In all plants workers try to make the work a little easier for themselves. At Lordstown, as in other automobile plants, there are many methods for making the work tolerable. Despite the already accelerated pace, workers still attempt to use the traditional relief mechanism of "doubling up." This method consists of two workers deciding that they will learn each other's operation. One worker performs both jobs while the other worker is spelled. At Lordstown, a half-hour "on" and a half-hour "off" is a fairly normal pattern. The worker who is on is obliged to do both jobs by superhuman effort. But workers would rather race to keep up with the line than work steadily—in anticipation of a half-hour off to read, lie down, go to the toilet, or roam the plant to talk to a buddy. Not all jobs lend themselves to this arrangement, especially those where a specific part like a front seat must be placed on all models; here the work is time consuming, and full of hassles. But there are many operations where doubling up is feasible, particularly light jobs which have few different movements. Fastening seat belts and putting on windshield wipers are examples.

"The only chance to keep from goin' nuts," said one worker,

"is to double up on the job. It's the only way to survive in the plant. . . ."

The company claims that doubling up reduces quality. The method engenders a tendency for workers to miss operations, especially when they fall behind, according to one general foreman. Some workers believe that the company blames workers for doubling up as an excuse to explain its own quality control failures. There is a widespread feeling among the line workers that the doubling-up "issue" has more to do with the company's program of harrassment than the problem of quality control.

The tenure of the previous management at the Chevrolet division of GM, was characterized by a plethora of shop floor agreements between foremen and line workers on work rules. These agreements were not written down, but were passed from worker to worker as part of the lore of the job. As in many workplaces, a new line supervisor meant that these deals had to be "renegotiated."

When GMAD took over at Lordstown, management imposed new, universally applicable rules, which in fact, were applied selectively. On Mondays, "when there are not many people on the line," the company tolerates lateness. On Tuesdays, when young workers come back from their long weekends, "they throw you out the door" for the rest of the shift for coming in fifteen minutes or a half-hour late. "When the company gets a bug up its ass to improve quality, they come down on you for every little mistake. But then things start goin' good on the cars, so they start to work on other areas. Then you are not allowed to lay down—not allowed to read on the job; no talkin' (you can't talk anyway the noise is so terrific); no doubling up."

Efficiency meant imposing on workers the absolute power of management to control production. GMAD instituted a policy of compulsory overtime at the time of the model changeover. The "normal" shift became ten hours a day and there were no exceptions to the rule. Absenteeism and lateness became the objects of veritable holy crusades for the new management. Nurses refused to grant permission for workers to go home sick. The company began to consider a worker a voluntary quit if he stayed off for three days and failed to bring a doctor's note certifying his illness. Doctors were actually sent to workers' homes to check up on "phony" illnesses in an effort to curb absenteeism.

The average hourly rate for production line workers was $4.56 an hour in mid-1972. In addition, annual cost of living increases geared to the consumer price index had been incorporated into the contract. Gross base weekly earnings for ten hours a day were more than $195. With overtime, some workers had made more than $13,000 a year. Besides, GM workers have among the best pension, health insurance, and unemployment benefits programs in American industry. Certainly, there is no job in the Warren area whose terms compare with the high wages and benefits enjoyed by the GM workers. Equally significant, GM is among the few places in the area still hiring a large number of employees. The steel mills, electrical plants, and retail trades offer lower wages to unskilled workers and less steady employment to low-seniority people. For some, General Motors is "big mother." Many workers echo the sentiment of Joe, a forty-five-year-old assembly line worker who said that GM offered better wages and working conditions than he had ever enjoyed in his life—"I don't know how anybody who works for a living can do better than GM." Compared to the steel mill where he did heavy and dirty jobs, GM was "not near as hard."

Of course Joe has had differences with company policies. The job was "too confining." He didn't like to do the same thing every day. He objected to the company harrassment of the men and had actually voted for a strike to correct some of the injustices in the plant. But, like many others, Joe had "married the job" because he didn't know where else he could get a retirement plan which would give him substantial benefits after thirty years of service, full hospital benefits, and real job security.

GMAD likes workers like Joe too. They know Joe isn't going anywhere. They believe him when he says he is sick and, if he misses installing parts on a car he can "chalk it up." In such cases, he simply tells the foreman about the missing operation and the "repairmen will take care of it."

Yet high wages and substantial fringe benefits have not been sufficient to allay discontent among the young people working on the line. If other area employers paid wages competitive with GM wages, GM would have serious difficulty attracting a labor force. The wages are a tremendous initial attraction for workers and explain why many are reluctant to leave the shop. But even the substantial unemployment in the Warren and Youngstown areas has not succeeded in tempering the spirit of rebellion among young workers or preventing the persistence of turnover among them. The promise of high earnings has not reduced the absentee rate in the plant. One young worker, married with a child, earned a gross income of $10,900 in 1971, a year when overtime was offered regularly to employees. This was a gross pay at least $2,000 below his possible earnings. He had taken at least one day off a week and refused several offers of Saturday work.

GM acknowledges that absenteeism, particularly on Mondays and Fridays, constitutes its most distressing discipline problem. Workers report line shutdowns "for as much as a half hour" on Mondays because there are simply not enough people to perform the operations. But many young people are prepared to sacrifice higher earnings for a respite from the hassles of assembly line work, even for one day.

At Lordstown and other plants where youth constitute either a majority or significant minority of the work force there is concrete evidence that the inducements to hard work have weakened. Older workers in the plant as well as a minority of the youth admit that they have never seen this kind of money in their lives. But the young people are seeking something more from their labor than high wages, pensions, and job security. At Lordstown, they are looking for "a chance to use my brain" and a job "where my high school education counts for something." Even though workers resent the demanding pace of the line, no line job takes more than a half-hour to learn. Most workers achieve sufficient speed in their operation to keep up with the line in about a half a shift. The minute rationalization of assembly line operations to a few simple movements has been perfected by GMAD. One operator whose job was to put two clips on a hose all day long said, "I never think about my job. In fact, I try to do everything I can to forget it. If I concentrated on thinking about it, I'd go crazy. The trouble is I have to look at what I'm doing or else I'd fuck up every time." This worker spent some of his time figuring out ways to get off the line, especially ways to take days off. "I always try to get doctor's slips to take three days if I can." Another worker reported provoking a foreman to give him a disciplinary layoff (DLO) just to avoid the monotony of his tasks.

The drama of Lordstown is the conflict between the old goals of decent income and job security, which have lost their force but are by no means dead, and the new needs voiced by young people for more than mindless labor. The company and the union represent the promise that the old needs can be met on a scale never before imagined for many of the people on the line. The youth are saying that these benefits are not enough.

The picture is complicated by the fact that not all young

people share the same attitudes. Even though the overwhelming majority of workers in the shop are between twenty and thirty years old, they are not all cut from the same cloth. The most disaffected group in the plant are the youth who were raised in the Warren-Youngstown area. Their fathers and mothers were industrial workers, or at least had been part of an urban environment for most of their lives. Since the area has had a long industrial tradition (it lies in the heart of the Ohio valley), high wages and traditional union protections and benefits are part of the taken-for-granted world of a generation brought up in the shadows of the steel mills and rubber factories. These workers share the same upbringing, went to the same schools, frequented the same neighborhood social centers, and speak the same symbolic languages. When they came to General Motors, they brought with them a set of unspoken expectations about their work and their future. Many were high school graduates, a smaller, but significant number were attending college. Although it cannot be denied that the "good money" paid by GM was an important inducement for these young people to choose to work there, few of them considered steady work and good wages sufficient to satisfy a life's ambition.

Another group of young white workers came to Lordstown with entirely different motives. These are the migrants from the coal mining communities of West Virginia and southeastern Kentucky. Twenty-five years ago, bituminous miners were the proud vanguard of the American working class. Their militant traditions were the envy and the beacon of industrial unionists throughout the country. Miners had learned over the years to be self-reliant. In the southern Appalachians, picket lines were formed at rifle point and neither sheriff nor U.S. marshal was inclined to oppose the miners when they shut the pits down.

After 1950 things changed radically in the mining industry. In that year John L. Lewis signed a pact with the coal operators to permit technological innovation in coal production in return for very high wage scales and funds to establish a jointly administered welfare program that included pensions and a number of union-run hospitals which became showplaces for industrial medicine in the 1950s. But as coal prices fell, many of the largest operators began closing the larger mines in union strongholds such as Pennsylvania and West Virginia, and others went out of business or moved into more highly mechanized strip mining. Layoffs in the coal industry reached disastrous proportions in the 1950s and early 1960s. By 1958, nearly the entire coal region of the northern and southern Appalachians was designated a "depressed area" by the federal government in the midst of a fairly high level of economic activity in the country as a whole. In 1964, the union announced the closing of five of its hospitals because of lack of contributions from coal operators who were obliged under the contract to contribute forty cents for each ton of mined coal to the welfare fund, but were avoiding their agreement by ordering coal from nonunion subcontractors.

The hospitals were finally taken over by the Presbyterian Church but not before wildcat strikes forced nearly all mining in West Virginia and eastern Kentucky to a halt in 1964–65. Coal remained a sick industry and the union's power steadily diminished. By the late 1950s youth became the leading export commodity of the coal regions. People began to migrate to industrial centers such as New Jersey, Michigan, Northern Illinois, and the Ohio Valley.

Workers came to Lordstown from the coal regions and hill country with one powerful urge—to find steady work at high wages to support themselves and their families. The natives of the Ohio Valley called them "hillbillies," a pejorative expression which came to mean the same as the names given to previous immigrant groups who had arrived in the area. The hillbillies were the new "honkies," "wops," and "niggers" of the Ohio Valley. They were stereotyped by the natives as people willing to work hard, take all the overtime they could get, and remain on the good side of the company in order to protect their jobs. Socially, they were labeled hard-fighting, hard-drinking fools who hated "hippies" and Blacks with equal venom.

Although it is frequently denied by young Lordstown workers, there has been considerable physical confrontation between white Southerners and white natives at Lordstown. The Southerners have often become the safety valve for the release of frustrations generated by the work situation. They have often found it difficult to get housing except in areas which may be designated "hillbilly" ghettos, especially when they first arrive in the plant. Hillbilly children are snubbed by the native kids in school or are constantly fighting with them.

A curious feature of the hostility toward this new "ethnic minority" is that many young workers, Black and white, who were brought up in the Ohio Valley are from families who migrated here originally from the South. It is not uncommon to find that a youth exhibiting considerable hostility to the recent arrivals is a son of a former mining family or has married a woman whose family is from West Virginia. The evidence of the docility attributed to "hillbillies" in the shop is contradictory. Natives attribute some of the speedup to the readiness of young Southerners to hustle for the company. Yet, during the 1971–72 disruptions inside the plant, it was the Southern workers who were credited with or accused of slowing the line down, performing acts of sabotage, and showing rebellious attitudes toward foremen by refusing direct orders and risking discharge. Even though one worker attributed this militancy to "pep rallies" held by the union during working hours to raise the level of insubordinate activity to a fever pitch, this causal explanation could not account for hillbilly willingness to engage in such struggles if they did not possess a high degree of resentment against the working conditions and an even greater degree of solidarity to permit widespread disruption in the face of company opposition.

The antagonism between white and Black native-born workers and the foreigners demonstrates the persistence of intraworking class conflict, even in a situation where the company has been perceived by all groups to be a common enemy. These divisions extend beyond the shop to cultural and social life. The flareups of fighting within the plant between Southerners and natives are reproduced within the schools, the communities, and in such social centers as bars and bowling alleys.

Yet the Southern youth are no more docile than the native youth. They have demonstrated a capacity for self-organization and militancy that has earned the grudging admiration of the locals. The irrationality of the residue of hostility is recognized by the native young people especially when they are pressed for specific evidence to support their allegations that the Southerner is "dumb and crazy" or oriented toward the company. But the existence of prejudice against the Southerner is undeniable and is an effective means of defusing discontent.

Another subgroup in the plant whose identity is somewhat difficult to describe is the so-called "hippie." A Lordstown hippie bears slight resemblance to his counterpart in St. Marks Place in New York, Haight-Ashbury in San Francisco, or Boulder, Colorado. The Lordstown hippie works fifty hours a week, is typically married, has children, and lives in an apartment or is thinking of buying a house. "Hippie" is a self-definition for a large number of young workers who spend some of their time smoking marijuana or using such psychogenic drugs as LSD or mescaline. Heroin is almost unknown to the "freak" community of Lordstown. The hippies are not the only drug users among the plant's labor force. What distinguishes them is the concept of "acid" and "weed" as integral to their cultural style. This cultural style includes wearing long hair, but here again, one self-designated hippie, Charlie, a twenty-one-year-old with long blond hair and a shaggy beard, complained:

> I have a rule not to rap about politics. Once I almost got the shit kicked out of me. I went up to these dudes who had long hair and shit. Thought they were hippies. They turned out to be hillbillies. I started to rap about the war and shit. They began to call me Commie and I almost got my ass whipped.

The hippies are tremendously involved with rock music, especially white acid rock such as the Rolling Stones, the Jefferson Airplane, Janis Joplin, and Bob Dylan. Some of them play instruments and dream of becoming professionals.

Charlie, a native of the local area, is not well educated by conventional standards but has an acute interest in politics. "Fortunately I dropped out of school early enough to fight brainwashing," he mused. When the strike started in spring 1972, a number of organized radical groups distributed literature about the strike which was mostly ignored by the plant's workers. Charlie made a serious attempt to read the material. He commented:

> The only papers that printed anything good about us were the so-called Communist and Third World papers. During the strike there was so much red-baiting going on it was disgusting. The company blamed the sabotage on Communist agitators and the union did nothing to stop this talk.

Charlie considers himself an anarchist. "I guess I've always been an anarchist but I didn't know it. I don't like to join organizations and don't believe in the government." At the same time he admired George Wallace, "because you know where he's at."

Like many other young native-born workers in the plant, Charlie dislikes the hillbillies and has had bitter experiences of "being jumped by a bunch of hillbilly dudes." But he recognized that the hillbillies are "brainwashed like the rest of us. We need a Radio Free South. Cats down there need more information than the Russians."

Charlie traced his first step on the road to becoming a freak to growing long hair in junior high school. "Growing my long hair was the most important thing in my life. It became a sign of rebellion. When I was in school I used to get into a fight every day just because I looked weird." Charlie was among a few of his classmates in his hometown who were known as troublemakers. His life in the town of Wyndam, a working class suburb of Warren, was a constant series of fights with teachers, policemen, and many of his fellow students. Like many other young workers, he finds striking similarities between plant and school.

For a time, Charlie lived with a group of fellow hippies in an apartment in the center of Warren. Many of them worked in factories such as Packard Electric (which supplies parts to GM) and the rubber mills. The "commune" is disbanded now. Many of its participants have married within the group or have found spouses elsewhere. But they remain friends and constitute a social group during leisure hours. Charlie and his hippie friends at the GM plant have little time for social life, "even to be with our wives." They often smoke a joint of "weed" to help them get through the day. Since they are natives of the area, many of their friends are drawn from among the "straight dudes" whom they grew up with.

Being "straight" differs little from being "hip" among young people of Lordstown. Long hair, marijuana, and rock music is shared by nearly all young workers in the plant. Hillbillies may substitute liquor or beer for drugs, but the hippies are "into" wine and beer almost as much as drugs.

Still there is a definite distinction between the hippies and other young people. They are more aware of alternate political and philosophical ideas. This does not mean that they are intellectuals. But it does indicate an openness to new ways of thinking and living. Charlie does not disdain work. He has even enjoyed some of the jobs he held prior to coming to GM. He would like to slow the line down, and experiment with making the whole car without the intense rationalization of tasks characteristic of the American auto industry. But his critique goes further. He asks why cars are necessary. He wonders about Eastern philosophies. He thinks about reincarnation and how it would be to live without compulsion and arbitrary authority in another life.

He is not alone in his yearnings at Lordstown, even if his

intellectual curiosity is greater. But like many of his generation he is pessimistic about the ability of his fellow workers to make the kind of changes that such ways of life would entail. He thinks it will take a thousand years before humankind will be "ready" to make a new world. Meanwhile he tries to beat the line "by goofing off," missing work, and "fucking up any time I can."

Only 10 percent of the labor force at Lordstown is Black; in other auto plants they compose about one-third of the workers. Taken together, Blacks and Puerto Ricans at Lordstown constitute less than 15 percent of the employees. Smaller numbers have had an important psychological impact on the minorities in the plant. The Black caucus is weaker and less united than similar groups in Detroit and the east coast where the numerical weight of young Black workers has provided the impetus for militant demands upon the company as well as the UAW for relief from dirty, unskilled work, liberalized upgrading to the skilled trades, and access to local union offices. At Lordstown fewer than 5 percent of the skilled-trades workers are Black, but they are to be found in all sections of the assembly line, not just the body shop and among the sweepers, where the work is heavier and somewhat more unskilled than some assembly line jobs. Until recently, the relations between the union and Black workers were more friendly than in many automobile plants. Then an election turned a number of Black officials out of office and left the local union hierarchy almost lily white. There has developed considerable bitterness and disappointment since with what is described by some Black workers as "institutional racism" in a union dominated by the skilled-trades men.

In the past few years, rising race consciousness has been evident among Blacks who were formerly oriented toward the integrationist philosophies of the union leadership. Many Black workers retain shreds of their pro-union feeling and repeat the ideology of "unity" between Black and white workers as the key to taking the company on. In 1969–70, a Black Panther organization made its appearance in Warren, and had a few adherents at the Lordstown plant. Although the Panthers were never strong in the shop numerically, their influence began to be felt in proportion to the disaffection of even middle-of-the-road, older Black workers from both the company and the union. Even though the Panthers disappeared from public view in the area, many younger Black workers have adopted some of their attitudes.

Still, a large number of Black workers have remained loyal to the UAW; their orientation has been toward capturing greater power and consideration inside the union's ranks. Many believe that GM is the best place they can find to work in, despite considerable criticism of its authoritarian supervision and racist hiring and upgrading policies. Rabbit, a Black Vietnam veteran, described his relationship to GM: "Lordstown is about the same as the service, but the service is better because regardless of whether you're absent or late they can't fire you and you get paid." But he quickly added, "We've got a good union. It's mostly young people and we're willing to fight and not let those people [the company] mess over us."

Rabbit's main complaint against the company was that it didn't treat the workers "like men." He thought their policies were "kind of childish" and that the executives exercised their authority for its own sake, "simply because they own the company."

He got along well with most white dudes, "but the hillbillies will take anything from the company because they need money. They've been down all their life."

Although Rabbit would have liked to have more time for himself, he was grateful for his job because of the high wages. He was way behind on bills and "now I got a little time to straighten myself out."

The Black workers at Lordstown have been in the area for many years. Some came over to the plant from the steel mills and rubber factories, where their parents worked as well. They were brought up in Warren and Youngstown and feel like natives, sharing some of the attitudes of younger whites, especially their hostility to the company and mistrust of the hillbillies.

— 2 —

Youth is accented at GM for a couple of reasons. First, young people are the only ones who can keep up to the killing pace of the line. Second, young people get sick less often and use the benefits less frequently. A major exception to this calculation is the rising incidence of mental illness among young people in the plant. According to a union official responsible for taking care of problems arising from illness, accidents, and other work-related health issues, about fifteen workers every week request sick leave for emotional reasons. The company does not acknowledge that the work itself is responsible for the rising incidence of mental illness, but the union official claimed that requests for leaves of absence for psychological disturbances are quite common.

But if young people are essential to the ability of GM to deal with its falling profit margins and foreign competition, the battle to break their spirit is a difficult one for the corporations. On November 10, 1969, Malcolm L. Denise, Vice President of Labor Relations for the Ford Motor Company attributed the problems facing the auto industry to the influx of young workers:

> A few years ago Reuther and his executive board could map the union's course with confidence. Today they seem uncertain. The reason is a big influx of a new breed of union member—a younger, more impatient, less homogeneous, more racially assertive, and less manipulable member—whose attitudes and desires admittedly are not easily read by a sixty-two-year-old labor leader.
>
> For that matter, those attitudes and desires are not always so easily understood by many of us here, either.

Denise proceeded to detail the dramatic changes in the Ford labor force. In 1968 the median age of hourly employees was 35.4 years. "This is the youngest figure we have ever recorded, and it is three and a half years lower than the median age only four years earlier." (In 1972, the average age at Lordstown was about twenty-eight.) In the same year, the number of nonwhite employees had climbed to 35 percent compared to 15 percent in 1960. What did these changes mean for the company?

> From 1960 through 1968 the absentee rate for our hourly employees more than doubled. So did the rate of disciplinary cases per 100 employees. And the turnover rate went up two and a half times.... Such experience is not unique to Ford; it is shared by other employers with comparable work.

The real agony for auto-makers was the fact that this new employee was likely to be a "problem employee."

> These are people who almost habitually violate our plant rules. Although some of them do so with an open attitude of rebellion and defiance, in a great many other cases it is just a matter of the problem employee bringing with him into the plant the mores of his own background. He continues to live

by the loose code he grew up with—and he is generally indifferent to the standards of someone else's society.

Denise was quick to add two other salient points. The presence of the new worker is not merely a reflection of the company's attempt to hire the "unemployables" but has resulted from the normal hiring during recent years. "The other root cause of our present difficulties might be termed a general lowering of employees' frustration tolerance.... Younger [employees] are increasingly reluctant to put up with factory conditions...." The reasons Denise gave for this were their unfamiliarity "with the harsh economic facts of earlier years," the insufficiency of the traditional motivations to work provided by "job security, money rewards, and opportunities for personal advancement," and "a growing reluctance to accept a strict authoritarian shop discipline."

Actually, the history of labor struggles in the auto industry belies some of Denise's implications that prior generations were more docile in their acceptance of the status quo. Auto workers have always protested speedup. The wildcat strike is employed more by auto workers than any other group to fight against poor working conditions such as inadequate ventilation and other health hazards. What is important about the current generation is their "growing reluctance to put up with authoritarian shop discipline." Young workers enter the plant having experienced rebellion in their school lives and in the military service. Their sense of economic imperatives is not sufficient to force subordination to the demand of management for unilateral control of the workplace. The expectations generated by educational ideologies which promise interesting work and the ability to perform socially useful services to the community seem a betrayal at Lordstown, where the object of labor, a car which few plant workers are willing to drive themselves, appears wasteful at best, and even oppressive to some. Denise is right—job security and money rewards "have lost their force as work motivations." GM's strategy to restore motivation seems to rely on the techniques of fear and relentless pressure to produce on lower echelons of supervisors as well as the line workers. Here lies the source of unending conflict at Lordstown.

Denise told his management audience that "the new work force has had a costly and unsettling impact on our operations," by remaining unmoved by attempts to motivate them. In Denise's view, "order in the plants is being maintained with rising difficulty." What is the outlook for industry in view of the trend of the 1970s? There is not much to look forward to from management's point of view. Employees in the 1970s will be even worse than the current crop. They will, as Denise said, continue to protest dirty and uncomfortable working conditions, will "be even less likely to accept the unvarying pace and functions on moving lines," and "even less willing to conform to rules or be amenable to higher authority."

There are some workers at the Lordstown complex rooted in the old ways. They show up every day, take a certain amount of pride in their work, have "clean records," that is, they have not brought upon themselves too many disciplinary layoffs or reprimands; they aspire to join the ranks of supervision, or to retire on a GM pension. But these workers are a minority. For most, the area's young people just out of the armed forces or recently migrated from West Virginia and Eastern Kentucky, the line is "hell."

"When I first got in, the fact that I needed a job and had to be there ninety days before I had any protection, made me come in every day and keep my nose pretty clean," said Ed, a twenty-year-old man whose nineteen-year-old wife had just had a baby. After "serving time," Ed began to find ways to deal with the incessant assembly line. "I don't mind working hard, but when it becomes ridiculous, I slow down.... Constantly doing the same thing over and over kills a person." Ed has begun to let cars go by when he is in the hole. When a new job opens up anywhere else in the plant, he tries to switch to it "any time I can." He tries to arrange doubling-up deals with other workers. "I sing, whistle, throw water at a guy on the line, do anything I can to bust the boredom." When I met Ed, he was out on sick leave and hoped he would never go back "except if I need the money." He admitted the likelihood that economic need would force him back to GM since his wife was pregnant again at the time.

Mary, a young woman of twenty, worked on the motor line, a subassembly operation that is not part of the main line. Mary was also out on sick leave but her ailment was not physical. She was suffering from nervous tension and dreaded the day when she would have to decide whether to go back to Lordstown or quit for another job. Mary's complaints were not focused on the pace of the work but on its content. She wished that she had a job, "where you could use your brain instead of the monotony of just standing there doing the same thing over and over," but she was compelled by the need for money so she remained on the motor line for more than two years. Her main complaint at Lordstown was the men. "Most men out there are perverted, dirty old men." Her special target for criticism was the foremen. "They can be real nasty," she said. Since she had been there, "I had one good foreman." The foreman on her line had sexual designs on her. She told him, "I don't want to hear it." Mary is a pretty woman with a ready smile and a friendly way about her. "People come up and talk to me. He [the foreman] comes up right away. 'What are those men doing here?' he would say. I'd be snotty and missin' work and he'd DLO me and get me kicked out for two weeks." Mary got tired and angry at the men who "slapped me in the rear," or were mad at her for being able to do a job they thought should be reserved for them. She was frustrated because she felt impotent to complain about the problems on the job. "When I get a job I don't complain about it. I hired on sayin' I could do it. If I complain, they say: 'Look you can't ask for special treatment because you're a woman. If you can't do the work we'll get a man to do it.' Most men just don't want the women there. They think they're just comin' out there to miss work and collect money. The older men are the men who are really down on the women." Mary had little confidence that the union could help her. "As for the [union] committeemen it's all men. They should have women committeemen. I don't think the women have too much say-so."

Actually there are about three hundred women at Lordstown working on the production lines. Most of the older women work on first shift. Mary believed they resented her for her youth and her ability to attract young men. The trouble was that the women were not supportive of one another because they were scattered throughout the plant, and there was a considerable amount of friction between the older and the younger women. Mary thought that if she had more women on her line she could have more "say-so" in dealing with her problems on the job. Isolated in a sea of men she felt were lecherous, "cooped up for five or six days a week with nothing to think about except sex," and a boring, repetitive job, Mary's nerves became "shot." "I'd get to the point where I was afraid I would throw something at somebody and hurt them. Sometimes I felt like pickin' up a handful of screws and pointin' them at somebody's eyes."

One maintenance man, a twenty-five-year-old college drop-out, confided: "I have screwed in my mind all the glamorous women and spent a million dollars on them." This worker spent last year practically living in the shop, working seven days a week, twelve hours a day. Sexual fantasies helped sustain him through this ordeal. But, like many other younger workers, he did not intend to "make GM his life's ambition." Fantasies of alternative jobs or professions help sustain many workers. For Eddie, the assembly line worker, "anything is better than this." For Mary, the aspiration was to become a nurse. Bob, the maintenance welder, got a skilled trade from General Motors and intended to save enough money to buy a farm, open a small business, or look for some other less compulsive job to do, "where I am not just a number on the time clock." Scores of young workers "kept a back door open" to another future. One young married line assembler was finishing up at Kent State University and was hoping to become a teacher. He had already done substitute teaching in the Warren area. He had real grievances against the company. "Working ten hours a day five or six days a week, how do they expect you to go to school?" he asked.

GM and the UAW have negotiated an educational program for employees. The company will reimburse tuition for college, provided the worker remains on the job. In rare cases, it grants an educational leave of absence without pay for those who have nearly completed. However, most workers cannot take advantage of this benefit, because they are married with several children before they reach the age of twenty-five. The would-be school teacher, Carl, is particularly angry at the company's new rule against doubling up and reading on the job because it prevents him from doing his homework. And you can't go to school while on sick leave and get a tuition refund from the company.

Carl had been "thrown out the door" several times for being caught reading between jobs. At twenty-three, he has two children and is trying to keep up with a mortgage, car payments, and some appliance bills. Yet he is not afraid of the company or its supervision. Like many other young workers, Carl resents the insistence by the company that it retain absolute control over the production process. The relentless speed of the line, its monotony, and management's contempt for the workers infuriates him and drives him to try, in many small but significant ways to capture a measure of autonomy.

The struggle by the line workers to organize production themselves is a constant motif of daily life. One day Carl and a group of his friends met together to talk about the situation in the plant. They reported several stories which illustrate how workers try to combat the company, particularly its exercise of arbitrary authority. "Once the foreman threw one fella out the door on my line for refusing a direct order to do a job not his own. We just shut the line down for fifteen minutes and simply sat around until they brought the union committeeman over to get us back to work. We told him we would go back to work when they brought the man back. Finally, they went into the washroom and told him to come back and the line started again." When asked why they shut down rather than go through the union grievance procedure, one worker replied with another story: "In my section a foreman once gave a dude a direct order to lift a heavy part even though he had a doctor's note sayin' he couldn't do heavy lifting. The dude called the Man [the union committeeman]. He wrote the foreman up. We never got results from it."

The company's unilateral control is enforced by a method akin to military discipline—the direct order. According to company rules—reinforced by the union's agreement that management has the right to direct the work forces, determine production standards, and make decisions about assignment of workers—the worker must obey a direct order. If he feels the order to be unjust because it violates the collective agreement with the union, he has the right to call the union committeeman, who will write the grievance up. Meanwhile the worker is obliged to do the job under management's direction. As one man put it, "The Man walks away with a piece of paper, but I'm stuck with the job."

Another man related this incident:

The fumes in my part of the shop are so strong, we can't breathe. The foreman keeps sayin' they're goin' to get ventilation in. All the guys can do is call the Man. They can't walk off the job. Sometimes it gets so bad a dude will walk off the job. The foreman gives a direct order to get back to work. If the guy keeps walkin' he gets a DLO if he's lucky. If he's been out too much, he may get canned. Well, we keep puttin' the pressure on to get the ventilation put in. The foreman keeps sayin' the maintenance men don't have time. Before the last strike, the company laid a lot of them off. The union never stands up for anything. They're either scared or paid off. Just before the strike, the union decided to really take on this beef about the air in the area. The committeeman comes around and says: "We're all goin' to take our shirts off and later on the union will bargain with it." I told him, "Let's sit down for an hour—you can take off your shirts, pants, underwear, or anything else you like, but the cars still come off the line." Our union—Miss Goody Two Shoes—never breaks the contract. I was sayin' let's walk and there were a lot of guys ready for it. But the Man refused to back us up. They could afford to knock out twenty-thirty guys—they would have probably throwed us out of the plant. The union would not have stuck up for us. But the members are ready.

The chief grievance man for the union at Lordstown, is a man whose reputation for militancy among the plant workers is fairly secure. As shop chairman, a full-time official in the plant although still on the company's payroll, he works with the shop committee, the key legal instrument for preventing management abuses of the union contract. In this role he tries to deal with everyday problems of health and safety, grievances having to do with work pace or job assignment, transfer rights for workers seeking better jobs in the plant, and disciplinary problems.

A short stocky man whose thirty years have taught him that you don't get anything you don't fight for, he was recently re-elected to his post after a term back on the line. He had been defeated by the chairman of the Fisher Body unit of GM, which had been merged with the Chevrolet Division under GMAD in 1971. But after the 1972 strike was settled, he was back in office. The committeeman is convinced that the big problem in the plant, management's ruthless discipline of workers who question its right to run the shop with a free hand, is a policy handed down from the top rather than the product of capricious acts of lower echelons of supervision. A former Marine prison guard, he is among those who understand GM as a military organization where the chain of command is the prevalent style of supervision and management. According to him: "It's similar to what goes on in the service. The general calls down to the ranks they're goin' to have an inspection. The orders get passed down. The top supervision calls for a crackdown. The word goes down from one level to another—to the production manager, the general superintendent, the superintendents, the general foremen, the foremen—it snowballs down to the bottom."

Some workers believe that during crackdown periods, foremen

receive quotas of how many people to throw out the door. There are times when a worker who leaves the line to get a drink of water is given the rest of the shift off. A worker who reports absent may receive three days DLO during crackdown or simply be reprimanded or receive no discipline at all, depending on orders from the top. "GM is concerned only about people at the point that they affect operations," said the committeeman. "Otherwise supervision uses its powers as a dictatorship."

There are two major issues in the plant over which the union has the right to strike: health and safety, and changes of work pace and work methods. Reflecting the views of a large number of the shop's work force, the committeeman singled out work methods and transfer rights as the two most serious grievances against management, and complained that management is "not totally serious about correcting these problems." Moreover, the company seems to believe that the high wages and benefits it offers are more than sufficient to offset its demand that nobody be "allowed to make a decision other than what they've already been told. Nobody can deviate from the norm. All they want is a robot operation." Even though he admitted that the company offers good benefits, he believed that management encouraged the high rate of turnover in the plant because a man with "one or two years' service" gets no pension and does not get as much vacation pay. "The benefits are geared to loyalty," meaning they went to those who accepted the way things were without complaint.

— 3 —

Shortly after the model and management changeover in fall 1971, it became clear to the union that GMAD sought to roll back some of the basic contract protections against the absolute authority of supervision. Management's tactics were to order frequent crackdowns on absenteeism and lateness, no tolerance by front-line supervision of ways devised by workers to make the job easier and give them some time to read or rest; besides this, there was the introduction of sweeping changes in the work methods which did not alleviate monotony or the swift pace of the line, but simply added more work onto each job assignment. The company's action provoked official grievance procedures initiated by workers in response to these tactics. At the same time, the union and management were engaged in protracted negotiations for a new local agreement since GMAD refused to honor the agreements made with prior management groups. Said Kenneth N. Scott, a GMAD official, "When you have a plant over many years, it is very possible to have developed habits that aren't right: they are outside the agreement."[2]

GMAD sought to eliminate the shop floor agreements between line foremen and workers to allow some flexibility in production methods. It demanded a strict interpretation of the clause in the union contract giving management the right to direct production. Its first dramatic act was to change the speed of the production line to meet the objective of 100 cars an hour. The company claimed that its introduction of "automation" and other stream-lined production methods would make feasible the new line pace without adding to the burdens of the workers.

Emma Rothschild has pointed out that there is little new in the GMAD innovations:

> The Lordstown innovations are based on the same meth-ods of increasing productivity that GM and its competitors use in other auto factories, methods which follow from the earliest techniques of mass production.... The main princi-ple of Lordstown technology is the speedup as developed by Henry Ford.... Of the machines that replace unskilled labor, few incorporate any major technical advances or revolutionize the character of the remaining jobs.[3]

Rothschild's judgment was affirmed by the President of the United Auto Workers, Leonard Woodcock, who judged the Lords-town advances "not as revolutionary" as GM made out and "a development of the same principles used elsewhere."[4]

The "young, aggressive leadership" of the local union was not content to permit hundreds of grievances to pile up while the membership grew increasingly restive. Gary Bryner, the twenty-nine-year-old president of the local representing the Lordstown workers, summarized the union response to the increasing pres-sure of management: "In November and December people re-fused to do extra work. The more the company pressured them, the less work they turned out. Cars went down the line without repairs. The repair lot began to fill up. Soon the company began to retaliate by sending us home early. We had a shorter work week, but we didn't ask for it. We had 1200 disciplinary griev-ances in the procedures."

According to Bryner, the workers were conducting a strike inside the plant during the fall. And it was generally effective. But, he said, the union demands had been relatively modest. All they were asking of GMAD was the same local in-plant agreement they had had in 1970. He believed that the three-week strike waged in March was provoked by the company. On February 1, 97 percent of the plant's workers voted to go out in protest against the speed of the line and the layoff of 350 workers as to an efficiency move of management to cut the number of excess employees. Most important of all, as Bryner remarked, "Many feel that the industry is going to have to do something to change the boring, repetitive nature of assembly line work or it will continue to have unrest in the plant."

Although Bryner claimed that the strike resulted in "total victory" for the union many of the workers were doubtful. One worker commented bitterly: "Before the strike the union was in favor of not working faster than you could. Now people are afraid not to work. The union and the company say everything's settled, but we had a strike. What did we achieve for it? We got the shaft in the last strike. We didn't know what we won and what we lost. When we asked the union we wouldn't get answers."

Another worker described what happened when the vote was conducted to go back to work: "People were at the meeting with their families. One guy had his three kids there and they all voted [by a show of hands]." A Black worker complained, "The union violated its own rules that the skilled trades and the production workers are supposed to vote separately. The skilled trades were all for goin' back, but the dudes on the line would've stayed out forever to slow it down." This worker believed that the $5 million lost by the union members as a result of involuntary short work weeks would never be recovered, although the union claimed that the company has agreed to restore the lost wages.

Bryner admitted that the union had a long way to go before it could win back the confidence of the membership, even though he was reelected to union office overwhelmingly after the strike: "They're angry with the union. When I go through the plant I get catcalls." A Black union official, Tom, lamented, "The union is not about to take management on again for some time. We don't have too much to be proud of. Right after the strike our union (which I speak highly of) went back fifteen years."

Tom, who had been closely identified with the local union leadership in the past, had a litany of complaint about its recent behavior. "The union talks out of both sides of its mouth. On one side it defends the democracy of the UAW. Yet it didn't abide by the constitution during the ratification of the strike settlement. It promised us we would receive back pay for the short work weeks. We'll never get it." But his bitterest criticism was reserved for what he described as the "racist" attitude of the local union officials toward Black workers, who number about 10 percent of the plant. Before the current leadership there were twelve Black representatives in the plant union. "Since Bryner, there are only three left."

A second issue was the demand of the Black caucus, a newly formed group in the plant, for an end to discrimination by the union and the company, which manifested itself very clearly by the fact that there were only five or six skilled Black tradesmen in the plant out of a total of five hundred in these departments. The union had started a training program for the skilled trades some time ago, Tom charged, but dropped it after six months with no visible results. Tom reserved sharp criticism for the local union's attempt to take over the Black-controlled credit union. "They waited for us to accumulate nearly a million dollars before they made their move." He retained a large measure of his antagonism for the company, which, he believes, "uses people as a football, a number, and a puppet."

This judgment was supported by another Black worker who had recently resigned his job as one of the growing number of Black foremen in the shop and returned to the assembly line. Dave had started to work there six years ago, when the men were turning out 40 cars an hour. At that time, the old management was still running the plant, but he was too rebellious to tolerate its rules. "I was on the trim line—one man doin' a seven-man job. They just kept pilin' new duties on me. I called the Man but he couldn't do nothin' anyway except write up a '78' [Article 78 provides that the union can aggrieve changes in work methods]. I kept doin' the job, but told my foreman it was impossible to do. The foreman approached me with an 'attitude' and told me I better do it. I responded tellin' him you can't make me. The next day they took me off the job and put this young white dude on it. He began to fall behind somethin' terrible. After a couple of hours they began strippin' the job of some of its duties until he was doin' a normal job. I got furious. I went up to the foreman and said, 'What kind of shit is this—why did you take me off the job and give him less work?' The foreman gave me a direct order to go back to work. I began to cry, not because I was scared, but because I was so angry. Then I pulled my knife and took my foot and stopped the conveyor. The foreman comes rushin' up to me and I hit him. I couldn't take it no more, I called him prejudiced. They called security, committeeman, and supervision—I didn't get any discipline for this action.

"The next day the foreman started to bug me again. They took me to Labor Relations. I took a swing at him. He started hollering. Labor Relations did nothing. The next day they took the white kid off and put me back on my old job. The foreman walks up to me. 'Dave, somebody wants to talk to you,' he says. I turned around and the assistant plant manager is standing there. 'Have you ever thought about going into salary?' he asked. They told me I had character and ability to handle men. They had asked a lot of Black guys to go into supervision and they were always turned down. I figured if I went on salary I could help—you know. So I took the job. I have come to learn that not all dictatorships are in the Communist countries. Lordstown has its own dictatorship."

Dave went to supervisory school where he learned the techniques of management. "The school was conducted by Labor Relations. They showed us how to handle 'these brainless idiots.' We received instruction on how to get somebody's goat and be cool about it. If you got somebody under you who is hostile, stay on him. Either make him do his job or provoke him to smack you up the side of the head.

"When I went up to the foremen's cafeteria, the conversation was always shoptalk. A bunch of grown men are talkin,' 'You know Joe Doaks. How did you manage to throw him out last time?' I wouldn' have no parts of that kind of talk. I began to eat in the hourly cafeteria. The rest of the foremen stopped talking to me. They thought I was a little strange. Also I couldn't help bein' sympathetic with the men under me. I quit the foreman job twice. GM has worked me into the point where I'm seriously thinking about quitting the company."

Dave had learned that the management and the union "work hand in hand. One hand washes the other." He was back on the line and had regained his acute sense of resentment against the company. "The skilled trades won't teach a Black anything," he explained bitterly. "The reason they give is that the Blacks are lazy. There's plenty of racism in the company and the union. They call me stupid on my job. I'm an ARO, that's an absentee relief operator, but they won't give me enough time to learn the different jobs." He had been shifted around several times against his wishes and felt that the union wouldn't spend "thirty minutes" fighting on transfer rights.

Not all Lordstown workers are down on the union. The skilled trades workers have a sense of control over their work situation, even though they are paid on an hourly basis like unskilled workers. For them, the union represents the "big brother" who steps in when there's a problem. Bob, the maintenance welder, believed that the leadership of the union was young and aggressive and leaned toward the "same ideas I had in college." He had gone to the University of Wisconsin, where he participated in student protests against Dow Chemical Company and other war-related industries and admired the union's stand against the war in Vietnam and its "progressive social policies." Among the skilled trades, most problems are settled on the floor and rarely go into the grievance machinery. Bob had genuine respect for his "Man." "Once they trumped up a charge against the committeeman. Ten men walked out. I guess we went on a wildcat strike. Immediately the skilled trades in the stamping room heard about the strike and we couldn't stay in the plant. We used the excuse that we had to go outside to 'protect our automobiles.' We had to go out otherwise the company would immediately fire the guys who walked. They put our committeeman back after a couple of days."

Bob's fervent pro-union attitude was reflective of an increasing tendency within UAW and other industrial unions to effectively represent the interests of more senior employees, many of whom are in the skilled trades. Many skilled-trades workers within industrial plants make their jobs their life careers, in contrast to semiskilled assembly line workers or machine operators who tend to remain for shorter periods, especially during times when alternate employment opportunities are fairly good. The mobility of the skilled-trades worker within the plant makes him a natural candidate for union office. Many skilled workers have more acquaintances among the line workers than line workers have with one another. Lordstown is no exception to the rule in industry generally or in auto plants. The skilled trades dominate the union structure and articulate a proprietary interest in the union not felt by production workers. Skilled workers refer to the UAW as "our union" while production workers almost always employ the phrase "the union."

Compared to production workers, the sense of solidarity among the trades is greater, reflecting their close contact on a plantwide basis, the frequent occasions on which they work co-operatively on a machine repair job, the relative security born of their pride of craftsmanship (even though this is often over-stated). Most important, they know that the chance of getting fired for battling the company on grievances is reduced by the fact that they know the union will stick up for them because they control great segments of its power. Finally, there is an acute sense of centrality to the operation of the plant not experienced by the relatively isolated production worker locked in by his limited set of operations. The skilled maintenance worker's job is vital for a plant like Lordstown, where management deliberately strains the equipment in the service of productivity. Line break-downs are frequent in the assembly division, and power presses are constantly requiring repair in the subassembly plant. Mainte-nance men who have mastered a large number of machines or are expert electricians have enormous power over production. The assembly line worker knows he can be replaced "by somebody stupider than me," but the maintenance man is sure of his in-dispensability.

When skilled-trades workers are angry at a foreman, they get "awful busy without doin' anything at all. As long as you are in motion GM figures you are working." Bob believed that there was a high degree of unity between the younger and older skilled-trades workers. And militancy was not confined to the younger group. The older guys, secure in their skill and the protection of the union, were likely to battle the company as much as the youth.

Skilled-trades workers have fought direct orders more effec-tively than line workers. Either they refuse an order on the pre-tense that they "didn't hear it" above the din of the machines, or they simply refuse to work by sitting down until the order is rescinded. The "trades" do not depend entirely on the union to settle their problems, even as they retain a high degree of support for it. Bob succeeded in pinpointing a crucial element of the weakness of the union bargaining process. A favorite company tactic is to accumulate for months grievances having to do with such issues as health and safety and work methods without settling them. The plant committeeman previously quoted ad-mitted that the number of unsolved grievances pertaining to these categories was greater since the strike, even though the "union had won a total victory." Union President Bryner's characterization of the company position that it didn't "implement what it has agreed to," seemed to be a definite pattern in union/management relations. "The only way to get anything done," said the committeeman, "is when a whole department gets together."

He saw the object of the company's policy very clearly. "The company waits until some dude fucks up by showin' up drunk or something. The company fires him. The union can only get him back by bargaining away good grievances."

During the last strike Bryner admitted that the union withdrew a great many work-method grievances to get company agreement on the back-pay issue and the reinstatement of the 350 laid-off employees. The union justified its position on the basis of a traditional conception of where the priorities of any union must lie. The tremendous achievement of UAW has been on questions of economic benefits and job security. Even though GMAD brandishes its disciplinary powers in wide strokes at Lordstown there are remarkably few discharges. The objectives of the company's labor relations policy seem to be: (1) to get militant employees to quit the job rather than provoking job actions which disrupt production, (2) to provoke strikes to cool things off rather than risk in-plant strikes which disrupt production, (3) to force the union to bargain away workplace issues to retain its ability to deliver on economic benefits and job security.

This policy has met with a large measure of success. The turnover of young people who are the most rebellious and the least willing to put up with what they perceive to be a GM dictatorship has been fairly high. The three-week strike in the spring of 1972 and smaller wildcat strikes over discipline have been "good for the company." A skilled worker commented: "Everybody gets drunk and has a good time and blows off a lot of steam." He spoke about an alternative to wildcats and other kinds of walkouts: "It would be better to sit down on the job and make them pay our wages. Last night we maintenance welders were given a direct order to repair an electric motor. We refused because that's the job of the electricians. We didn't wildcat because we knew the company wouldn't talk to us if we were on the outside. We simply sat down by the machines. In a few minutes the committeeman was there and the foreman took it up to the upper echelons of supervision. They were embarrassed that they had violated the contract. They took back their direct order to do electricians' work."

Before the three-week strike, the new forms of struggle developed by workers during the winter and spring of 1971–72 produced a sensation in industry as well as in national media. Led by many "hillbillies," the workers passed many cars down the line with bolts and parts missing. Soon repair lots were burgeoning with half-finished cars. Workers even told the story of an engine passed down the line with its shell neatly covering unassembled parts. The company moved swiftly to intensify its disciplinary layoffs for part of the day for the whole plant, but three-day DLO's were common. The situation deteriorated rapidly as workers responded to company pressure by increasing their "sabotage." Under these circumstances the spring walkout was a means to restore the normal processes of bargaining and cool out the fever pitch of protest. The failure of the settlement to address the critical issues behind the rebellion was a product of the complex motives of the various actors in the drama. The union was obliged to concentrate its energies on the problems of the loss of money, wages, and layoffs. This emphasis was a function of its economically oriented ideology as much as its despair at being unable to deal conclusively with the problems of supervisory prerogatives.

The company hoped that the strike at the plant gates would effectively end the strike inside the plant. They were counting on the ability of the union leadership to convince the rebels that it was hopeless to use extralegal means to correct the abuses on the line, and to make them see that they must instead rely on collective bargaining to deal with these issues. As for the workers, many of them came to understand that you can't fight GM in the traditional ways. There is no doubt that they experienced defeat in the spring strike.

Many workers have thought through possible alternatives to the way things are at Lordstown. Everybody is for slowing down the line, at least to the pace of other assembly plants. Some have even gone further in their vision of a different way to work. Many of them favor a shorter work week, "if we have to produce cars." Some are even willing to work ten hours a day if it will result in fewer days in the factory.

Alternate plans for organizing production have also been offered by workers. Many people are aware of the experiment currently under way in Sweden to produce cars differently. They are interested in the attempts at Volvo and Saab to abolish the assembly line and give to a small group the responsibility of making the whole automobile and dividing up the tasks among themselves. Almost everybody would like to see a system of rotation introduced in the Lordstown plant to relieve the boredom of doing the same thing every day. But Eddie expressed the common belief that "the company would never go along with it because it takes time to learn all the jobs enough to get up enough speed and the line would slow down." Actually, the doubling-up system is an attempt by the workers themselves to achieve rotation, but some have expressed the need to go further. "We could do a different job every day during the week," proposed one worker.

Some workers believe that supervision of assembly line and maintenance operations is superfluous. "I know my job," said Bob the maintenance welder. "I'd like to be able to phone my foreman when I had problems on the job. Use him as a kind of technical assistant. I don't need supervision." Assembly line workers expressed similar views, but Eddie disagreed. "If we had no regulation [by a foreman] the stronger guys would take all the good jobs." He strongly believed that people were "not ready" for self-direction, although he favored it abstractly. The belief of many of the Lordstown workers in the possibility of self-regulation of their work is a direct result of the tentative experiences of actually trying to put it into effect on the line.

Still, many workers are not able to visualize a different way of working. They believe that the line is a permanent fixture, which can only be modified by shorter hours, rotation, or a slower speed, but not abolished. If they are going to escape it, they will have to quit. Yet they keep fighting for a better way inside the shop. Most of the time their struggle is underground. It's finding shortcuts to do the job, exchanging jobs with a fellow worker until they are caught by the foreman, finding ways to stop work, or creating grievances. As one worker said: "I get a kick out of watching my foreman and my committeeman hollering at each other. It breaks the day up."

NOTES

1. *Business Week*, "A GM Reorganization Backfires," No. 2221, March 25, 1972, pp. 46–51.

2. *Ibid.*

3. Emma Rothschild, "GM in More Trouble" in *New York Review of Books*, March 23, 1972, p.19.

4. *Ibid.*

2

Colonized Leisure, Trivialized Work

— 1 —

If, as according to traditional Marxist theory, revolution depends upon the inability of the capitalist system to maintain a standard of living consistent with the material needs of the working class, writers like Herbert Marcuse have reminded us that in advanced capitalist societies workers are more likely to remain part of the prevailing system than to turn against it.[1] This phenomenon has been attributed to the success of Western capitalism in providing the material requirements of life. Workers may go so far as to support trade unions and even socialist parties. However, socialism in the West has become a means by which workers obtain a redress of grievances within capitalist society, rather than an instrument for its transformation. Although the rhetoric of revolution serves to provide militant symbols that arouse social action, there is no doubt that the would-be revolutionary elements that are present in all Western countries, including the United States, have failed to connect themselves with decisive sections of the population.

Underlying the view that in the absence of economic crisis

that would affect the material conditions of the working class, capitalism will succeed in maintaining itself for the foreseeable future, is the idea that great historical changes can only occur when the prevailing economic system and the institutions of political power have broken down. Marx himself was persuaded that the necessity of revolution derived preeminently from the structural tendency of mature capitalism toward crisis, since in his own time the crises of capitalism had indeed resulted in the misery of great portions of the working class. In the coming breakdown of capitalism, given the inherent capacity of workers to organize themselves—because of the social character of their labor and their centrality to the capitalist mode of production—they would achieve the consciousness that was denied them in ordinary life and would perceive their historical task as the abolishment of both the prevailing social system and themselves as a class.

Just as daily life is experienced as one of unrelieved subordination, but appears part of the nature of things rather than the product of human activity, so the break in the expanded reproduction of capital would produce a break in consciousness. According to Marx, the revolutionary significance of the crisis would be to provide the space for joining social reality with the subjective experience of alienation and its specific form in the productive process, exploitation.

History has placed severe constraints on Marx's celebrated theory of revolution. Even though, as Lenin shows, the crisis has not been overcome, but has rather been displaced by wars and imperialist conquest and arrested by the interventionist role of the government in stimulating investment in the private sector,[2] the conditions of life in material terms have unquestionably improved for the mass of the working population in the West. Of course, there is still considerable poverty in the United States and other capitalist countries, but the poor represent only a minority and the historical tendency has been toward their numerical diminution rather than increase. It may be objected that poverty is a relative category, and that the unequal distribution of income has actually become more pronounced in the past thirty years. This fact does not obviate the problem posed by Marx. Although Marx spoke about the deterioration of workers' living standards in terms of an historical level of material culture, there was no doubt that he relied on the inability of the system to provide for basic material needs of food, clothing, and shelter at a given level of material culture for the validity of his theory.

To be sure, there is no opposition between the phenomenon of rising levels of real wages and Marxian theory. Contrary to some interpretations, Marx's theory of capitalist accumulation takes specific account of the actual rise in the level of real wages as a barrier to capital formation. The struggle of the working class to obtain a higher price for its own labor power has been incessant, even under totalitarian conditions—bearing out Marx's theory that the upward movement of employment and wages had its limits under capitalism, a limitation imposed by the profit criterion for production and the need for a surplus labor force to be available in periods when capital expands.

The rise in the mass of total capital owing to the rising productivity of labor has made possible the increase of real wages even as the distribution of the total product remains determined by the institutions of social and economic inequality. There is no question that capitalism has been unable to utilize the discoveries of science fully to release workers from arduous labor. Marx's important insight that class society places a fetter on the development of science, technology, and the full application of the skills and knowledge of human labor, has not been obviated by advanced capitalism. What has developed in the twentieth century is the *partial* utilization of knowledge, sufficient to maintain a level of economic growth adequate to the criterion of the profitability of production and to the maintainance of relatively high living standards. In the case of the United States it may be argued that the relative capacity of American capitalism to contain its contradictions has been purchased at the expense of other capitalist countries, particularly Britain, Canada, and, more recently, Japan. Although this stabilized instability has not been successful in all Western countries at all times, it seems clear that if the proletarian revolution awaits the economic crisis it may remain little more than a fantasy.

The theory of revolution as the outcome of the manifest economic crisis of capitalism encounters a second difficulty. There is absolutely no evidence that depressions in themselves lead to a rise of revolutionary activity, much less revolutionary consciousness among the workers. On the contrary, workers tend to become profoundly conservative under conditions of increasing material deprivation. They organize themselves only to fight against wage cuts or to force the government to undertake programs that increase relief payments and job-creating projects such as public works. The economic crisis of the 1930s resulted in the strengthening of the capitalist state, rather than the development of a large revolutionary workers' movement. If there are not enough jobs, competition for the existing jobs increases. Employed workers become fiercely self-protective against the threat posed by the unemployed, who are willing to work for lower wages or to accept more onerous working conditions. Similarly, management is able to use unemployment as a threat against the militancy of those workers who are employed. Despite the revolutionary rhetoric of the Communist and Socialist parties in the 1930s, the truth was that workers became more willing to rally to the radicals' banners precisely because these groups represented the best hope of winning concessions from recalcitrant employers and reforms within the capitalist state. Revolutionary slogans in the thirties served to make legitimate the rising militancy of segments of the underlying population. They provided symbols that were functional to the task of making the system more responsive to the suffering of the underlying population, and contained within them the threat that if concessions were not forthcoming, more drastic action might be undertaken. But in no country were revolutionary goals on the agenda in any practical sense. In fact, it may be said that the revolutionary movement provided a theater of discourse within which the struggle for reform could be waged without being apparent to the actors.

The reasons that large numbers of working people and the revolutionary leadership itself fell easily into the framework of reform politics while believing themselves to be engaged in a quite different process have been debated by historians, sociologists, psychologists, and the actual participants in the social drama. One school of thought chooses to place blame on the ideological and moral perfidy of the leadership. This kind of explanation relies on the phrase "if only . . ." It assumes that social forces can be directed and controlled by the ideology and moral values of individuals. But, as Wilhelm Reich has shown, the question of the politics of the working class and its movement cannot be decided by reference to political and economic leadership alone. Reich argues that it was the authoritarian character structure of the German working class that provides the causal explanation for the revolutionary failure of the 1930s. German society, he asserts, as mediated through the authoritarian family, repressed the instinctual need for freedom. In his view, the working class was predisposed to seek the solution to the world crisis of capitalism in authoritarian institutions because it failed to wage a struggle against authoritarianism within its own organizations. The left-wing parties and the trade unions reflected the hierarchical relations of capitalist society no less than the corporations and the family. Workers were subjected to a consistent pattern of repressed social relations in the entire compass of everyday life. Since workers' consciousness was circumscribed by the problems and the details of ordinary existence, it mattered little that their parties and unions were ideologically committed to resist fascism and to create a new society of equals. As long as the internal life of these organizations did not oppose the pyramidal configuration of the family and the workplace, the crisis of the existing social order could only be resolved by the replacement of the less effective authoritarianism of the Weimar Republic by the more aggressive and overtly domineering Nazi regime. Contradicting those Marxists who asserted that fascism only found its mass basis within the small shopkeeper and professional classes, Reich shows it to have sunk deep roots among the industrial working class.[3]

Reich does not deny that the manifest crisis of capitalism in the 1920s and early 1930s provided the objective possibility for revolution. Nor does he reject the goals of communism. But he is convinced that although crisis provided the necessary condition for revolution, it was not in itself a sufficient condition. Moreover, the existence of radical organizations enjoying the support of masses of workers could constitute a brake on revolutionary activity if they reinforced the system of domination, especially sexual repression, already existing within the culture. Thus the fundamental question for Reich is the transformation of workers' consciousness, not only at the point of production and within political struggle, but also in their daily lives, in the fulfillment or denial of their needs—especially their sexual needs.[4]

Daily life provides clues for both the liberatory and the authoritarian tendencies within the working class as well as all social groups. It is the critical institutions of family, peer groups, school, church and the voluntary association, and the workplace itself that structure the way people respond to events as well as create them. Before proceeding to an account of how individuals and institutions interact to reproduce the working class, we must briefly examine some of the more interesting explanations of the dynamics of this interaction.

Herbert Marcuse has made a serious attempt to supply a theory not only for the persistence of working class integration within the capitalist system, but for the possibilities of liberation.[5] Marcuse understands that the revolutionary movement cannot rely on the imminent breakdown of the capitalist system or the adoption by its leadership of correct scientific principles. His analysis attempts to come to terms with the fact that capitalism has found the mechanism to contain its contradictions and, at the same time, to comprehend that the problem of revolutionary politics must deal with the dynamics of daily life. Finding no Marxist categories to explain the actual psychology of workers, and refusing to be content with the ascription of class consciousness by definition, Marcuse, following Reich and his contemporaries, has made a significant effort to fuse Freudian theory into a revolutionary paradigm. Marcuse proceeds from the argument of Freud's *Civilization and Its Discontents*.[6] In Freud's view, the subordination of the instinctual drives of human beings to the requirements imposed by the conditions for human survival makes inevitable the repressive aspects of society. Marcuse accepts the structure of Freud's argument, but rejects the conclusion. As Anthony Wilden has pointed out, Marcuse assumes the existence of a biologically rooted instinctual structure that provides a material substratum for the liberation of humanity.[7] The repressive civilization that arose out of the necessity to produce the means of subsistence can now be overcome, Marcuse argues. That repression was based on the underdevelopment of the social forces of production in relation to basic material needs. Capitalism, through the socialization of the forces of production, has succeeded in transcending material scarcity. Repression in advanced Western countries has now become socially unnecessary.

According to Marcuse, the ideologies of nascent industrial capitalism that demanded hard work and deprivation as the condition for the salvation of the individual corresponded to the demands of the underdeveloped forces of production. Instinctual repression found its justification in the idea of progress, i.e., economic growth. Deferred gratification, having been overtaken by the fruits of industrial technology, is now maintained by pure domination. Domination no longer relies on ideologies of industrial progress for its hegemony. Now technology has permeated all public and private life to the extent that it has become, itself, a system of domination whose ultimate justification lies in its own logic. In the post-scarcity society, individuals are permitted to experience repressive desublimation. Domination is maintained by the very logic of post-scarcity—consumption becomes ideology as well as a means to survival; sexual needs can be satisfied as long as they do not involve love and human feeling; thought can no longer reach toward transcendence of the prevailing social relations; on the contrary, the idea of an alternative to capitalist society appears absurd, since capitalism itself seems eminently rational when viewed from the point of view of the manipulated needs that it has generated.

Marcuse's optimistic side does not rest on the capacity of workers to organize themselves. On the contrary, he understands fully that in the main the organized working class is aligned with —and not against—the late capitalist system. His faith resides in the ultimate inexorability of the liberatory instincts that provide the substratum of rebellion—rebellion that expresses itself as refusal rather than as a genuine alternative. On occasion, he is convinced, however, that the new repressions engendered by technology (consumption, one-dimensional thought, sexual license without romantic love) have become so pervasive that they have affected the liberatory instincts themselves. Thus soma and gene are united in a new synthesis of surplus repression. Still, for the most part, Marcuse adheres to Freud's energy model. The influence upon daily life of the giant social force of repression seems unmediated by any liberatory potential. Daily life is presumed to be a reproduction in almost mechanical form of the conflict between self and society.

However, Marcuse's model seems to prefigure its results. Hope springs eternal but is never too confident because it ultimately relies on a mechanical-biological presumption of the autonomous self. Parsonian sociology, like the mirror image of Freudian theory, sees the individual as in harmony with the repressive culture, and describes the process by which individuals agree to play out their social roles within capitalism. In Parsonian theory the effective socialization of individuals by the social order seems determined. If Marcuse and others who rely on a bioenergetic model are ultimately defeated in their revolutionary thrust by the inevitable power of a highly rationalized social system of domination, Talcott Parsons, who believes that the individual reproduces perfectly the roles assigned to him by society, celebrates that phenomenon.[8] There is no presumption of autonomy in his view, and his model seems even more scientific than Marcuse's, since the facts of experience appear to verify the proposition that capitalist social structure provides a perfect function both in public and in private life for its participants.

The empirical proof of Parsons' argument resides in the longevity of the social system. It accounts for the subordination of the working class to capitalist organization without appearing to endorse either the conservative or the revolutionary view of this phenomenon. Following the work of Max Weber, the Parsonian theory of capitalist society allows for conflict without struggle.[9] Its presumption of the correspondence between structural requirements and functional roles allows only for discontinuities that are restored by the built-in rational mechanisms of the social order. The Parsonian socialization model is one in which imitation plays a critical role in the learning process.[10] Since what is learned corresponds to the material rewards derived from patterned behavior, Parsons more adequately describes the conditions of stasis than Marcuse, who derives the possibility for deviance not from the activities of individuals, but from their ascribed innate characteristics. The virtue of Parsonian theory is its reliance on social life even if its assertion of equilibrium between the individual and society may prove nothing more than a conservative hope.

The adequacy of a theory of socialization that shows the possibility for liberatory self-activity by workers can neither rely on the pressure of external events nor on the reduction to biological urges. It must show that inside the structure of social life the activity pattern of the subjects (that is, the workers themselves) can produce values, norms, and ways of interacting that depart from the prescribed patterns of capitalist socialization as well as conform to it. It is the contradiction between the autonomous self-activity of workers in the process of their formation as a class both historically and biographically and the social constraints imposed by the capitalist mode of production (or for that matter, any other system) that constitutes the possibility of historical change. If the workers have no elements of their socialization that they can perceive as resistant to the economic role assigned to them by a relatively successful capitalism, neither economic crisis nor biological urges will suffice to change their responses to their life situation.

When Marx asserted the historical role of the working class as the gravedigger of capitalism arising from its unique position in capitalist production, he was only establishing the objective possibility of this process. What is required is to establish its subjective possibility, that is, not the ascribed class consciousness of the working class, but the conditions for its actualization.

— 2 —

According to Parsons and other contemporary sociological theorists, the individual is presumed a function of social roles. Individual choice is circumscribed by those occupations, ideologies, and routes of social interaction prescribed by the requirements of the social whole. Even the most creative of these mechanistic theories, e.g., Piaget's assimilation-adaptation model of child development, presuppose the correspondence between the roles assigned to individuals by the structures and the functions of the ongoing society and the internal system of values and beliefs that become objectivated in patterns of social action. Piaget makes an attempt to integrate a biogenetic orientation with a social interactionist theory. His theory of stages in the sensory-motor and conceptual development of the child provides an apparently dialectical relationship between the self and society.[11] But this dialectic is more apparent than real, since in the last analysis adaptation is equated with the maturation process and assimilation is reduced to the internalization of the structures of legitimate social life. As Brian Sutton-Smith has convincingly shown, Piaget's theory does not grant a creative role to the relationships of children to one another in play, friendships, and other forms of voluntary association.[12] Instead, play is simply the reproduction of social roles and social structure assimilated from the adult world. What Piaget calls individuation is the process by which the person learns, through play, to take the role of the generalized other as part of his self-system.

Sutton-Smith, Kenneth Burke, Hugh Duncan, and others who attempt to ascribe the permutations of consciousness to the characteristic modes of social relationships without reducing them to patterns or "mechanisms," provide much more satisfactory clues for explanation of how it is possible that an autonomous working class movement may emerge. For if domination and hierarchy are so thoroughly integrated into the self-system of individuals and social groups from childhood, then all evidence of rebellion against the essential structure of social hierarchy and authority is epiphenomenal or, at best, no more than temporary instances of deviance which can never congeal into a fundamentally alternative consciousness or structure of social action.

There are two worlds of childhood. The most well understood is the world in which the child is raised by family, school, the working environment, and other institutions that constitute the ideological apparatus of the prevailing social and economic system. Within the symbolic and face-to-face interactions that go on in the everyday sense, and in the overarching ideologies which legitimate them, these institutions reproduce in their structures, the pyramidal configuration of the whole society. Authority relations in capitalist society are hierarchical. These hierarchies correspond to the structures of ownership and domination that underlie the social and technical division of labor in society. As the reproduction of commodities occurs within a specific hierarchically arranged matrix of economic institutions, so the reproduction of the labor force itself takes place within the socializing institutions. Contrary to the reflexive model posited by orthodox Marxism in which all institutions other than the economic base merely copy the requirements of that base, the family, school, mass culture, etc., are absolutely necessary for the production of the economic institutions. Without the socialization of a labor force prepared to enter the workplace and treat it as a "natural" institution that stands over and above the creative action of the workers themselves, it would be necessary to continuously make legitimate to every generation of workers social divisions within the labor process or else to simply control them through force. The importance of the socializing institutions is that they make unnecessary the open use of force, because workers in their earliest experiences find themselves at the bottom of a pyramidal structure within these institutions and come to expect that all social institutions will assign to them the same position. Theories of human nature are constructed that elevate this experience to the level of belief. The superiority and inferiority ratings of human beings based on the criteria of adaptive intelligence justify the hierarchical organization of labor, the domination of political institutions over individual lives, the tracking system in the schools, and the differential treatment accorded members of a person's family by parents.[13]

But there is a second world of childhood. It is a world that is systematically purged from memory, that is symbolically accorded inferior status, that even in adult life is assigned to nonworking time and thereby trivialized. It comes to be viewed by its participants as pleasurable but inessential, except as an interstice bewteen sleep and productive labor. It is the world of play.

Marcuse, following Schiller, appreciates that the substance of human liberation may be realized in the play element. For Marcuse, play represents the flowering of the imagination unfettered by the constraints of material necessity. But he projects play into a utopian nonauthoritarian culture of the future and does not take account of its importance within a historically evolved present.[14]

Play as here defined is the one human activity within capitalist society that is noninstrumental—that is, produced for its own sake. At the same time its rules are not constructed in order to repress freedom, but to repress arbitrary power and thus assure its fairness. The paradoxical character of rules of the game within a noninstrumental and nonhierarchical framework distinguishes play from other human activity. The structure of play is constantly evolving according to the modes of interaction produced by the players, as long as that interaction presupposes their equality.

Nonexploitative love may be defined as play—although "love" has been debased to mean domination, exploitation or objectification of a person; we "love" animals and children to the extent that we make of them degraded images of our own will. The essential relation in this kind of "love" is domination, especially in the case of the relations of adults to children. "Bad" children are those who refuse to submit to society's rules as interpreted by parents and teachers. As they grow up they come to realize that they will receive love in proportion to their willingness to submit to the rules of the adult game. The "rules of the game" in this case stand for the submission to arbitrary power. The distinctions between play, work, and love only appear when each has been degraded to leisure, labor, and alienated sex respectively. Insofar as each involves the use of the imagination as a central faculty for its realization, they are more similar than different. Labor is distinguished by two features: first, it is circumscribed by the realm of necessity, and, second, it is initiated from the outside. Labor requires external authority for its realization. The individual is required to become subordinate to the requirements of the imposed plan. In contrast, creative work is both self-generated and self-revelatory. The individual or group that engages in it must summon imaginative faculties, and achieve the object of work by trial and error, by experiment, by absurd flights of fancy—a process that resembles untrammeled play. The individual experiences the process not as labor but as exhilaration, as a form of erotic activity.

Similarly the sexual act that stems from voluntary love is not engaged in as an exercise in the self-perpetuation of the species. Quintessentially a flight of the creative imagination, sexual love is distinguished from labor by the fact that it is undertaken out of the desire of each partner for participation.

Whereas the person who is forced to sell his labor power to another, subordinate his sensibilities and imagination to the predetermined specifications of the job, understands this sale as the giving up of oneself to the machine, creative work is understood as one understands genuine play—an autonomous expression of the self. In creative work as well as genuine play exhaustion is not deadening. The activity, like deep sexual pleasure, enlivens the senses and elevates the person. When one selects the object of work, determines its method, and creates its configuration, the consciousness of time tends to disappear. While clock-watching is a characteristic disease of those burdened with alienated labor, those engrossed creatively are oblivious of the passage of social time or the dimensions of physical space. We "lose ourselves" and cease to measure our activities in so many units of minutes and hours, just as those enveloped in sexual love begin to lose the sense of spatial limits that separate one person from another.

Play is an activity that human beings create in which the person sees him or herself in the object produced. It presupposes equality. As Hugh Duncan has pointed out, we play neither with inferiors nor with superiors; we play with our equals.[15] Most child's play has embedded within it elements of nonhierarchical and nonauthoritarian relationships.[16] For example, the purest form in which these elements constitute the prevailing mode of the game is "ring around a rosy." Significantly, the circle game is the most universal form of child's play, transcending cultures and social systems. In "ring around a rosy," there are no leaders and there are no followers. The participants join hands and move in a circle, a form of sheer equality. The circle is broken when *all* fall down, whereupon the process is re-created in precisely the same form indefinitely. There are no winners and there are no losers.

The next level of child's play introduces the elements observed by Piaget and others who have understood the relationship to the prevailing structures of daily life of apparently autonomous forms of human interaction and socialization. These games may be called "turn games," as distinct from circle games. In their configuration, they reproduce the hierarchy and authority relations of the family, in particular, as well as those of the whole society. For example, "the farmer in the dell" begins as a circle but has the significant addition of the farmer in the center of it, symbolically representing both the father and the characteristic agricultural base of economic life in nineteenth-century America. The "farmer" chooses the wife, who, in turn, chooses the child, who, in turn, chooses one of the animals, etc. In this game, several elements of the natural and social world are learned. The child learns the characteristic male and female roles; the man is a worker, the woman, a mother. In addition, a classificatory scheme of animal hierarchy down to the inanimate object "knife" or "cheese" is reenacted. But even as social values are inculcated in dramatic form, the children also enact their original egalitarian forms. Everyone gets a turn at playing all the symbolic actors even crossing sexual lines. Everyone gets a chance to choose another, except the inanimate object, which, magically, finally ends the game by running away. Again, there are no winners and no losers. If there is hierarchy, it is within a system of rotation.

Similarly, other rotation games require that everyone have an equal chance at being "it" or "free." The game "hide and go seek" reenacts the hunter/hunted syndrome, with one essential difference from real life; the hunter can only be free if he finds a replacement for himself. Unlike real life, freedom is identified with the role of the oppressed. Here we have a reenactment of what Hegel called the lordship/bondage relationship in which the servant achieves dominance over the master, not as a result of the reversal of their roles, but because the master can only gain recognition of his role as the dominant one by being acknowledged by the servant. The master is a prisoner in "hide and go seek" as much as the servant. Neither is truly free, but the servant can renew his freedom if the master fails to catch him. Here children are saying that although they recognize the structural relationship, they symbolically rebel against the status assigned to the master. In "hide and go seek," the servant has the upper hand. Psychoanalytically, this game may be interpreted as genuine individuation through the creation of the illusion of rebellion against the father.

There is a third type of game, however, that appears in later childhood. It is the game of domination in which the child asks the symbolic parent for permission to move. But even here turns are taken. Domination itself is represented as spatial movement in which the child approaches the position of the parent, but only as the parent accords him or her permission to do so. Such a game is "follow the leader." "Mother may I?" is a direct enactment of the rituals of childhood. "Simon says" has slightly different characteristics in terms of body movement. But they both re-create the structure of authority as well as rebellion. The child must follow the directions of the symbolic parent as long as the parent is watching, but is allowed to move on his own if the Other is not watching.

The fourth type of children's game evolves the social reproductive process more perfectly than any of the other three. It is the game in which children symbolically reenact the actual conditions of family and adult life without rules that symbolically enforce the autonomous and creative activities of childhood. Consistent with the sociological perspectives of those who find in childhood nothing but the reproduction of adult society, such games as "house," "doctor," or "cowboys and Indians" are the ones most studied, for in them the form and content of the adult world become wholly integrated into child's play. In the first three forms described, the rules serve to protect the independence of the participants even when the structure of the game itself is oriented toward re-creating the observed social world. But in the games of "house," "doctor," or "cowboys and Indians" the rituals are determined by cognitive consonance with empirical observation. Deviance means you can't play. For those bold enough to try to change the observed rules of social life imperatives such as "you're supposed to" or "you're not supposed to . . ." are invoked. Within this rigid framework, the fundamental decision concerns who shall assume which roles. Characteristically, the winners of the contests that determine role choice will choose the role of father, doctor, and cowboy, because they know that these roles carry prestige and power. It is also generally true that those who get to play these roles are older than the rest of the children in the play group and are males. Thus girls always play mothers and children, nurses and patients, and Indians within heterosexual groups. There is one caveat to this general model: although predominantly prefigured by age and sex, there is no necessary correlation between these factors and the persons who actually play the roles. There remains an element of chance that the process of decision-making will be democratic, particularly in groups that are homogeneous with regard to age and sex. Here we can observe the distinction between a game which is hierarchical in structure and a selection of roles that may take place on the basis of a democratic ritual, such as choosing with fingers or by numerical counting or by taking turns.

There are two possible interpretations of this distinction. Either children are prone to retain remnants of their own egalitarian forms of social interaction within the authoritarian structure, or they must retain the myth of egalitarianism even though they know they are approaching the adult world. The distinction herein described, nevertheless, constitutes a kind of nostalgia and resistance that we shall see is never quite purged in later life from either institutional or noninstitutional social relationships.

Working-class street games often embody several levels of interaction. Although the popular group game "Johnny on (or ride) the pony" is a turn game, it performs an important additional function. It prepares the child to endure pain, understood to be a certain fate of adulthood. The brutal leap of several members of the opposing team on to the haunches of the defending squad is only relieved when the defenders are able to guess how many fingers are being displayed over their bowed heads. Similarly the children's card game "Knucks" involves the punishment of a full deck of cards being scraped along the knuckles of the vanquished, or being slammed down on them with all possible force. Learning how to lose consists in suffering punishment without showing emotion. The child who cries when punished is understood to be a baby—that is, incapable of withstanding the fortunes of war.

"Kick the can" is an exercise in frustration-tolerance. The person who is "it" is constantly faced with the conspiracy of those who are "out" to perpetuate his condition. After recovering the kicked can the "it" player must prevent the others from repeating the act of kicking it, if he is to be relieved of his burden. A slow runner is almost always perpetually "it," but is expected to keep trying without complaint despite his natural handicaps.

These games reveal the awareness by working class children that play is serious business and a preparation for life. As they grow older, the game becomes increasingly symbolic of actual social life among a group. It represents the actual power relations among children and becomes the enactment of these emergent hierarchies. Yet the group itself retains its integrity and will protect any of its members against the interventions of outsiders, whether adults or other groups. The sense of social solidarity is well developed and represents an incipient attempt to organize a society autonomously.

Even adult games, which are assigned to the relatively trivial realm of leisure-time activities, retain the equality of the forms of child's play. Most games of cards provide for a rotation in the dealership, although the structure of the game is explicitly competitive. In contrast, most children's games only gradually take on the aspects of grim competition. The games of baseball, football, and basketball contain within them the contradictions between cooperation and competition, between equality and authority. These games arose spontaneously from the activities of youth and young adults, but their rules have been solidified by adults. At the core of each is the idea of victory and defeat. However, in contrast to individual sports such as ping-pong or tennis (even though these are modified by "doubles"), baseball and football require a high degree of "teamwork," coordination, and cooperation, in which the individual must subordinate himself to the team in order for the team to win the game. Competition within the team is inimical to the general purpose of winning the game itself. Even though the game results in a victor and a vanquished, "good sportsmanship" consists in a ritual of reconciliation that attempts to reestablish the equality of the process, despite the fact that in reality there is no equality.

In professional sports there is no reconciliation. Victory is rewarded by financial gain. The need for asserting the character of the game as "play" does not spring from the players themselves. They have become wage-workers. Professional sports represent the final perversion of child's play in which the game is reduced to commodity relations. Players are traded as commodities, their exchange value is diminished as their value as box-office attractions is diminished. They know that the wages of victory and defeat can be calculated in the marketplace.

In children's games, one rarely finds large numbers of children acting as spectators, unless they are waiting their turn to play. Their interest in the game resides in the fact that they can learn how to play better through observing the activity of the other players. No such opportunity exists for the spectators of professional sports. For them, that which occurs on the playing field can only be symbolically reenacted in their imaginations. The concrete operations of the game are not nearly as important as the emotional content of what is abstracted from observation. The spectator learns power, the military and political lessons involved in the strategies and tactics of winning. Aesthetic appreciation is embedded in the competitive nature of the game. Sports reinforce the passive character of modern life for the spectator. Just as the worker "observes" the object of his labor passing before him on the assembly line, as if the automobile or television set existed independently of his own activity, the sports fan observes the game as if it existed independently of the fact that a portion of his wages and of his "leisure" time make the whole process possible. Similarly, just as he plays the numbers, bets on horses, or becomes a partisan of a particular professional team, he watches with interest—but sensing his own impotence—the electoral process unfold independently of his determination and he casts his vote as if he were a participant.

There can be no doubt that the process of maturation from childhood/youth to adulthood is signaled by people taking the role of spectator with increasing frequency, so much that they "forget" that their activities produce all of social life. Children also find a world that they never made, but their accommodation to that world is suffused with resistance. They insist not only on re-creating the world made by significant adults, but on creating both an imaginary and real world of their own.

Peer group relationships take place through two modes. The one most characteristic of early childhood is the world of structured play, because this way of relating to one another is an objectified expression of the physical and social difficulties they experience in participating in unmediated interpersonal relations with anyone other than their own parents. Later on, especially as they enter elementary school and make contact with other children routinely, they find the psychic and physical space for relating to one another in unmediated ways. This is the mode of interaction that we call "friendship." Friendship consists of shared perceptions of the adult and peer group world and the tentative exploration of perceptions of each other.

The precondition for friendship is not only space, but also unbound time not structured from without in which people are allowed to find each other voluntarily. As we get older, unmediated peer group relations tend to give way to friendships based on mediations that are contained by institutional life. In adolescence and young adulthood, we choose our friends from among those assigned to the same tracks to which we have been assigned in school and according to the occupational aspirations that these educationally differentiated social positions have generated. In turn, we repress the fact that our friends tend to be from the same social class, race, and sex as ourselves, and that our relationships with them are mediated by the similarity of our backgrounds. Even though the egalitarianism of child's play takes place within the framework of a class-differentiated social system, the contemporary school is characterized by much heterogeneity. Whereas in the early twentieth century large numbers of workers were crowded into urban centers, segmented by class and ethnic affiliation, the possibility of finding working class and middle class kids within the same community and thus in the same educational and religious institutions is greater today than ever before, because of the movement of working class people to the suburbs where they live alongside professionals, managers, and small shopkeepers. It is in very subtle ways that class divisions are maintained within high schools and suburban communities. Children no longer can avoid making the distinctions between themselves and others that were obscured to some extent in homogeneous working class or Black communities. Now the school itself becomes the originator of class differentiation through its method of classifying students according to criteria that apparently have nothing to do with class. The school selects for the higher tracks students who have scored high on IQ tests, who have achieved good grades in elementary school, and who have demonstrated the capacity to observe rules of behavior prescribed by the educational system. Thus friendship and, indeed, the concept of peer, become mediated by the social structure as interpreted by the school.

It may be argued that sports cut across class lines in high school, since persons of different social classes are admitted to the teams based on their abilities rather than their social or educational tracks. But the concept of sports as an equalizer does not carry over into social and occupational relationships. Youths may play together on a formally and bureaucratically constituted high school football team, but this situation is more akin to the professionalization of sports than to child's play. Once off the football field, the players from different classes and educational tracks go their separate ways. By the time a student reaches high school, a sport is no longer regarded in terms of the joy of playing it for itself; it becomes a means to gain admittance to college or, in many cases, a steppingstone toward professional leagues. Working class students, particularly Blacks, regard sports as a chance to transcend their class- and race-determined occupational expectations. For them, sports becomes "serious business" that may spell the difference between having to work in a factory or an office after graduation from high school or going on to a university or a profession. It does not matter that only a minority of the youths who try out for school teams achieve their aspiration; what counts is the motivation that brings them to competition in the first place.

On the other hand, intramural and women's sports in high school still retain some of the joyous characteristics of child's play. They are engaged in expressively rather than instrumentally; there is rarely any particular social status or prestige, much less educational advantage, to be gained from such activities. Here the form of the game often retains the rigidity imposed by professionally generated rules. But its enactment lacks the grimness of institutional sports. Sports engaged in as a genuine leisure activity are voluntaristic, even as they retain socializing features.

It is very interesting that the allocation for intramural sports was among the first cut in school budgets recently. Since extramural games have become an important measure of success and prestige for both school administrations and athletic departments, these activities are considered essential. However, intramural sports gain little power and prestige for anybody. They are engaged in by students for mere enjoyment and can thus be safely cut out if necessary. The fact that they are often a means for students to overcome the fragmented character of the rest of their schooling is of no concern to administrators facing the budget squeeze. For them, learning consists not in the development of modes of interaction among peers that teach equality and fraternity, but in the acquiesence of the individual to hierarchically constituted authority. In fact, "free" play is viewed by many educators as subversive to the general goals of schooling.

— 3 —

In the Middle Ages, at the beginning of modern times, and for a long time after that in the lower classes children were mixed with adults as soon as they were considered capable of doing without their mothers or nannies, not long after tardy weaning (in other words at about the age of seven). They immediately went into the great community of men, sharing in the work and play of their companions, old and young alike. The movement of collective life carried along in a single torrent all ages and classes, leaving nobody any time for solitude and privacy. In these crowded, collective existences there was no room for a private sector. The family fulfilled a function; it ensured the transmission of life, property, and names; but it did not penetrate very far into the human sensibility. . . . Medieval civilization had forgotten the *paideia* of the ancients and knew nothing yet of modern education. That is the main point: it had no idea of education. Nowadays our society depends, and knows that it depends, on the success of its educational system.[17]

It is difficult for us to remember that "childhood" and the "family" are not a state of nature, but are historically evolved conceptions. The predominantly agricultural character of feudal and early capitalist societies left little room for any years that were free of labor. The rise of industrial capitalism was accompanied by the widespread use of child labor in the factories and workshops of city and country alike. In mobilizing children for productive labor, early capitalism was carrying on the traditions of feudal agriculture. The entire family worked in the factories just as they had all worked in the fields.

There were only two kinds of time within the continuum of lower-class life in eighteenth- and nineteenth-century America: work and sleep. The very concept of productive labor was consonant with human existence. The notions "childhood," "play," "leisure"—even the idea of "adulthood"—were reserved for the upper classes, except for "Sunday" rest in which the family was expected to go to church and engage in group recreational activities. As E. P. Thompson has brilliantly shown, time itself was transformed by industrial capitalism.[18] Instead of being oriented to the tasks that were synchronous with the seasons of the agricultural year, labor became subordinated to time. Each motion of work was now measured in microscopic units and thus the relationship between labor and the physical environment was severed in consciousness. Instead workers were apparently dominated, not only by the machine, but also by the clock that suddenly appeared as an autonomous force of production. Internal time consciousness became a function of the industrial system, and punctuality in appearing for work was a requirement that, in highly integrated and rationalized manufacturing processes, became even more fundamental than the possession of manual skills.

In the early United States, even the nascent bourgeoisie was preeminently an agricultural society punctuated with manufacturies directly related to its commercial crops of textiles and tobacco. It was not until the Civil War created the demand for large-scale metallurgical industries to supply the producers of munitions and to expand the production of textiles for army clothing that America entered its belated industrial revolution. The period between 1865 and 1920 witnessed the most explosive years in the development of an industrial economy in world history. By the turn of the century the balance between town and country had shifted in favor of the former and by the end of the First World War the United States had become the leading industrial nation in the world.

In the early years of industrialization, the position of children changed—but for the worse. Contrary to popular belief, industrial capitalism did not bring in its wake the immediate emergence of private life. Instead it made more complete the identification of "life" with "labor." Children were employed in the new coal and metal mines, textile mills, shoe factories, and garment shops to fill the unskilled jobs that abounded in those industries. As men began to shift from agricultural to industrial labor, they left all but the most skilled jobs to women and children within light manufacturing, and became the backbone of heavy industry and transportation. Working life began as early as seven or eight years of age. Since the skills required for such trades as garment and textile machine operation or tending required virtually no reading and writing, the factory was presumed an adequate socializing institution.

With the introduction of electric power, the productivity of labor was vastly increased. As early as 1877 the burgeoning industrial nation revealed the contradictions inherent in its chaotic pattern of industrial growth. In that year, the whole country was rent with labor unrest arising from the decline of employment resulting from the first modern depression. Neither public welfare nor private charity was sufficiently developed to deal with the homeless, starving workers who had been stranded by the economic holocaust. Food riots, mass strikes, growing bands of juvenile gangs, helped create a remembrance of the year as one of unrelieved violence.

From the beginning, U.S. industrial growth was plagued by

hunger, privation, and periodic unemployment for working people, and economic crises for the system as a whole. The frequency of "panics" and depressions accompanying the steep ascent of industrial production after the Civil War reveals a bewilderingly erratic pattern of economic development. Cities were hacked out of the wilderness and erected on the heaped bodies of dead Indians. New cities and old were plagued by a torrent of new social ills arising from industrialism. Despite the expansion westward, there were never enough jobs for those seeking work even as the shortages of workers threatened to stunt the capacity of capital to expand. Thousands of child "urchins" and "ruffians" roamed the streets of major eastern cities in search of food during depressions but were sought after by eager manufacturers, mining companies, and railroads in times of expanding production.

After 1850, the important industrial and commercial states reversed the historical predominance of the family as the basis of the laboring class that was characteristic of agricultural production. In 1836 Massachusetts, the leading textile manufacturing center of the nation, had enacted legislation that required children under fifteen years of age to attend school for three months a year. Rhode Island and Pennsylvania followed suit before 1850. But it was not until the last decades of the century that restrictive child labor legislation and compulsory schooling were able to limit the use of children in mines and mills, although children continued to play an important part in distributive and other non-manufacturing trades. More important than legislation, the development of new machinery and other methods of manufacturing rapidly eliminated the tasks for which children between the ages of ten and fifteen were best suited.

The movement for reforms such as child and female labor restrictions, factory laws that required a minimum standard of health and safety to be maintained by employers, and free compulsory schooling were motivated by both the short-term and long-term interests of the rising capitalist classes. The technological advances that rendered child labor increasingly redundant and politically unfeasible generated a somewhat humanistic ideology. Advancing technology made necessary the production of a literate labor force able to master the simple requirements of more precise machine production. Ordinary lathe operators had to know how to read blueprints and to measure wood and metal in terms of fractions. Technicians, engineers, and scientists were needed on a much wider scale than ever before. It was the consideration of the long-range requirements of industrial society—the need for a labor force that would meet the physical and intellectual requirements of expanding capital—that forced manufacturers and other business leaders to press for the withdrawal of children from the most dangerous and arduous industrial tasks and their conscription into schools. Thus, the expulsion of children from the factories, coincided with the emergence of the movement for extended compulsory schooling beyond the first six grades.

In New England, the school promoters consisted of a coalition of professional educators such as Horace Mann and the philanthropic wing of the manufacturing class represented by such figures as Nathan Appleton and William Ellery Channing. There is little doubt about the motives of these educational reformers. The essence of New England prosperity was the strength of its industrial and commercial enterprises. As Michael Katz has persuasively argued, the protagonists of early school reform were impelled by the desire to accommodate the young to the new industrial civilization through schooling that engendered "respect for authority, self-control, self-discipline, self-reliance and self-respect."[19] These objectives corresponded to the very qualities required of millworkers and clerks in commercial establishments.

Advocates of the extension of schooling to the high school level pointed out that the virtue of education was that it instilled "a better and higher state of morals, more orderly and respectful ... deportment, and more [readiness] to comply with the wholesome and necessary regulations of an establishment" among workers.[20] If left unattended in the jungles of cities and towns, children and youth were likely to fall prey to prostitutes and swindlers and become disruptive to the system, but in schools they could be taught the skills they needed to become efficient laborers and citizens. With this objective in mind, the battle for expanded public support to schools was joined by proponents of the vocational education movement and of the movement to change the emphasis of governmental response to juvenile offenders by viewing them as unfortunate victims of society rather than criminals.

The nineteenth-century education reform movement was suffused with the ideology that schools were essential to economic development to the extent that they produced a perfectly socialized worker. They were also seen as essential to the task of securing society from the ravages that might potentially result from the expression of the unallayed aggressions of young people and the unemployed. On one hand, educators and their allies argued, industrial civilization was a social good that required disciplined and efficient workers in order to flourish. On the other hand, they admitted that despite the economic benefits of commerce, and the rich cultural life possible only in an urban environment, capitalism had brought social decay in its wake. The role of the school was to prevent chaos by providing a way to assist children to adjust to the requirements of machine culture.

In the new civilization, the paths to economic and social advancement for talented working class children would be lubricated by education. Knowledge had begun to replace brawn as the motor of the production process. Since machine technology now lay at the base of society, those capable of mastering its mysteries could rise to the top of the social structure despite humble beginnings. With the new technology there was no longer the same need for the apprenticeship system of artisan crafts or for the existence of as many unskilled jobs; the school would replace these rough-and-ready methods of introducing children to the work-world. Using arguments such as these the early advocates of industrial education advanced their cause by presenting schooling as a means that would enable students to move upward within the prevailing class structure as much as a means of advancing industrial expansion.

But, as Colin Greer has shown, the real achievement of schools consisted in their ability to train children to accept the prevailing class structure and their fate as workers within the industrial system.[21] Contrary to the educational myths propounded by the early school reformers and promoted in our own time, schools are instruments not of social advancement, but of social stasis. What is learned in school—even in vocational school—is rarely related to specific industrial or commercial skills. As in the nineteenth century, the content of industrial and commercial occupations is still taught at the workplace. Rather, students learn the skills needed to accommodate to the first requirement of industrial labor: respect for authority, the self-discipline necessary to internalize the values of the labor process, and the place of the worker within the prevailing occupational hierarchies.

Joseph Grannis has developed a topology to explain the substance of contemporary schools and their social role.[22] The various levels of schooling may be regarded as a small society in which each level can be likened to another institution. In this model, the grammar school is analagous to the family. Characteristically most elementary school teachers until now have been women. The decor of the classroom is fashioned after the home, with windows decorated with curtains, pictures, and other homelike paraphernalia. All learning takes place in one classroom in order to provide an atmosphere of security and intimacy between teacher and child consistent with the explicit conception of the grade school teacher as a surrogate parent.

In contrast to the relative freedom afforded children in early childhood to construct their own play society, the grammar school introduces a new constraint on play. Learning the prescribed curriculum is called "work," and play is assigned to a special time in the day, called "recess" but supervised by adults. Thus the institution simultaneously legitimizes play as one of its regular functions, but rationalizes it as a break from the *real* activity of children within the institution—school "work." Play in this context is meant to rejuvenate the child in order to make it more ready for "learning."[23]

Indeed, the child learns in school. But the content of the curriculum is far less important than the structure of the school itself. The child learns that the teacher is the authoritative person in the classroom, but that she is subordinate to a principal. Thus the structure of society can be learned through understanding the hierarchy of power within the structure of the school. Similarly, the working class child learns its role in society. On one side, school impresses students as a whole with their powerlessness since they are without the knowledge required to become citizens and workers. On the other, the hierarchy of occupations and classes is reproduced by the hierarchy of grade levels and tracks within grades. Promotion to successive grades is the reward for having mastered the approved political and social behavior as well as the prescribed "cognitive" material. But within grades, particularly in large urban schools, further distinctions among students are made on the basis of imputed intelligence and that in turn is determined by the probable ability of children to succeed in terms of standards set by the educational system.

Students placed in lower tracks within the grades learn early in their school careers that these tracks represent their failure. Even if they succeed in terms of the "subject matter," the labels assigned to lower tracks restrict their horizon of future occupations. During the course of schooling these children find themselves in homogeneous groupings based on evaluations of their intelligence that appear to be a function of heredity rather than class. By the time the child reaches junior high school or high school he knows where he is going. His destination is the factory, the office, the retail store, and he will become an operative rather than a manager, a worker rather than an owner. And the school conveys the message, not only in the system of guidance that reinforces the decisions made by educators in the lower grades, but by its structure. In New York City, the junior high school was created overnight when the school leaving age was raised by law. These institutions were nakedly designed as holding pens for those who would have otherwise left school. The junior high school is fashioned neither on the family model of the elementary school nor the factory model of the high school. It is a hybrid with no essential rationale except as a container. Its lack of educational philosophy has produced instances of disorder since students are certain that there is no learning going on and even teachers are not certain why children are there.

By high school the classroom is no longer an attempt to replicate the home; it is rather an attempt to replicate the factory. More men have become teachers than in the lower grades; the decorations are gone and replaced by maps, charts, bulletin boards; the student no longer remains in the classroom the whole day—instead education is now departmentalized, ostensibly to offer a wide range of choices of subjects as well as instructors. The notion of "free time" becomes "study hall." Play is now structured into games that are bureaucratized beyond being put in time slots. The high school has a phalanx of official teams that compete with those of other schools. These are the important, socially recognized forms of play, while the voluntary forms, such as intramural sports, are denigrated.

The classroom has symbolically been represented as the real world, and even large portions of leisure-time activities are organized by the institution. Friendships remain independent of institutions to some extent, but many are now found in various institutionally sponsored activities such as sports, newspapers, and clubs. However, the working class high school students are employed after school and on weekends so that they are unable to participate to much of an extent in extracurricular life. For them, the reality principle organizes life. The centrality of school to work opportunities, the requirement that they work after school in order to help support themselves and their families as a condition for remaining in school, and the confinement of play to Saturday night, make adults of them at an early age.

The curricula of high schools reinforce the three broad tracks to which students have been assigned: academic, vocational, and general diploma students take different classes, develop different friends and other social contacts, and learn that their expectations are limited by the character of their education. Even for those assigned to the academic track, school demands that life consist in continuous work. Homework assignments can occupy most of the afternoon and evening. Parents are mobilized to keep the pressure on students to finish their assignments before they engage in any play, peer relationships, or television watching. Rarely is the substance of the assignments challenged by parents, since the object of their completion is to assure the grades required for admittance to colleges and universities. Just as the reality principle for working class children is represented by the need to work after school, children of professionals, business persons, and skilled workers who are funneled into the academic track learn that their "careers" come first and that autonomy must be subordinated to the goal of college admission.

For the most part, the specter of rejection by college has been sufficient to keep academic-track students in line. They have been introjected with the values of school and parents and engage in other activities when they should be performing their homework tasks only at the price of discomfort and guilt. They know that they should study, even if they are unable to rationalize either the activity or the substance of the homework in terms of the intrinsic worth of the content assimilated. They come to view learning as something outside of themselves—as instrumental to goals that are extrinsic to the questions of interpretation of specific mathematics or literature problems. Children learn in school to become acceptable to others. They know that the bright student is defined in terms of the curriculum, that rewards are given to those who can tolerate its boredom and its demands.

Students unable to tolerate school are those whose earlier life has not been disciplined to the regime of homework and learning "things." Their intelligence is irrelevant to the larger society, at best, and subversive to its values at worst. They are sometimes impatient with school because they are unable to adapt successfully to its demands. If they have broken the linguistic code required for reading, they rebel against the sort of reading required by school. In other cases, learning to read represents a surrender to the school bureaucracy, so some students fail to master the essentials of reading until they have left school and can find a good reason to learn them.

From the point of view of the educational hierarchy, the social legitimation of the school is deeply intertwined with the reading program. It is believed that if children learn nothing else in school, at least they have a chance to master reading. Yet most schools have adopted the empiricist view of language learning, that is, the notion that knowledge of language forms is acquired through the senses and by conditioning. In public schools, reading is typically taught through repetition of atomized pieces of information that are accorded differential status in the knowledge hierarchy and are arranged arbitrarily according to conceptions of child development that assume the progressive character of learning capacity.

The theory of linguistic competence implied by almost all current reading programs in schools is sharply disputed by Noam Chomsky and others who have developed a more rationalist theory of language learning. Chomsky has introduced evidence to show that "taxonomic views of linguistic structure are inadequate and that knowledge of grammatical structure cannot arise by step by step inductive operations (segmentation, classification, substitution procedures, filling of slots in frames, association, etc.)"[24] If Chomsky, following earlier findings by Helmholtz, Leibniz, and others, is right in his assertion that the role of the schools can only be to provide a conducive learning environment within which the deep structures of language embedded in individuals can be developed to their greatest potential, then the current emphasis of schools on segmented, conditioned-reflex, and associative methodologies for teaching reading may be irrational and consequently destructive to learning to read. The implications for education of Chomsky's theory have barely been explored. But his assertion that the capacity for transformational grammars inheres in all children and that these grammars cannot be nourished by current teaching methods, provides a clue to the reasons why children become restless in school when inevitably subjected to these methods.

The implicit content of the school curriculum in almost every instance, has little to do with its explicit educational goals. One need not prove that schools are organized deliberately to thwart learning to recognize the tenuousness of their educational claims. It is remarkable that despite the availability of Chomsky's work and that of others in the structuralist tradition, neither teacher-training institutions nor public educational bureaucracies have shown the slightest interest in the implications of these theories. This "omission" is made even more astounding, considering the anxiety and rage that have enveloped the entire country about the failure of schools to produce literate youth. Educational policy is imprisoned by its empiricist theoretical assumptions. The pressure for more reading programs has resulted in more of the same kind of teaching, albeit more mechanized and segmented than ever before.

For working class children who know that social mobility is an ideology, and that they are probably fated to end up in manual occupations, the effort is to endure school rather than participate. Their energy and their sense of self are preserved by tuning out the rigors of reading and mathematics, since they do not regard these activities as important to their lives. Instead, the curriculum is perceived as a means of pressure to force them to abandon their secret world—to learn to regard their relationships with their peers as less significant than those with teachers. Many children who "fail" in school are trying to cling to childhood because they know it is the moment in their lives, however fleeting, in which authority has least power over them.

The rebellious students' awareness that school represents the end of innocence is quickly transformed into guilt and regret for not having listened to their teachers early in life. By high school the failing students have developed a self-image that corresponds to their class position. They begin to doubt their rejection of mobility, and of school as a significant institution in the process of ascending the class structure. Many working class students become ambivalent about their own choice and live the rest of their lives in simultaneous regret and resentment. The anti-intellectualism prevalent among many workers is wrought of complex motives. On the one hand, they are cynical about the American dream that promises advancement through education. On the other hand, they are not sure that their cynicism is justified. This uncertainty is generated, in part, by the rapidly changing character of the American occupational structure, which has replaced unskilled and semiskilled jobs in manufacturing by unskilled and semiskilled jobs in service industries. In the largest growth areas in the service occupations, public employment and distributive trades, the idea of craft or manual skill is largely eliminated. Persons entering these occupations merely require knowledge of how to read, and how to follow bureaucratic procedures. Most jobs in retailing require the minimum of skills, except "human relations" skills that cannot be learned in school anyway. Public employees are perfectly trained by schools if Grannis is right in his assertion that the curriculum consists chiefly in understanding the structure of domination and hierarchy.

The rise of the service industries has been accompanied by the emergence of an ideology of meritocracy according to which the achievement of credentials actually creates mobility. The reality that the new service sector represents a deterioration of skills rather than their development is obscured by the welter of prerequisites for transition from the blue to the white collar. Another factor contributing to the reinforcement of mobility ideology as the rationale for school attendance is the fact that many children of factory workers are now offered white-collar jobs, a step that seems to signal a fundamental change, even though wages for the new jobs are often significantly lower than for factory or transportation occupations.

Aaron Cicourel has demonstrated that the process of class differentiation is facilitated by decision-makers in the educational process whose image of each child tends to correspond to his or her class background rather than imputed intelligence or academic achievement.[25] His study of administrative attitudes and behavior in an urban high school shows that the key influential staff are not aware of the class criteria upon which they evaluate the chances of students to gain college entrance. On the contrary, their belief that they develop guidance techniques on the basis of evaluation of a student's record of intelligence and achievement is belied by evidence that they have acted on evaluative criteria according to which working class students are *a priori* less able to cope with the demands of colleges.

Thus high school is the critical point in a person's life in terms of probable class and occupational affiliations. The tendency of schools is to strengthen the class structure by assimilating elitist ideologies into the decision-making apparatus while retaining the overarching ideology in which school is seen as the vehicle of class leveling and social mobility. The paradox here parallels the paradox of early school reform: Educational achievement is said to make possible a democratic society freed of class differentiation. However, the promise that educational achievement is a path to social mobility in itself implies the existence of class differences. Schools actually cannot deliver equality of opportunity much less equality *per se*. The IQ test, administered in the second grade, prefigures the differential opportunities that will be offered students, for assignments to different tracks will be made on the basis of the labels derived from test results. These labels attached to students are carried from grade to grade until the student experiences himself as the reflection of the label.

The educational ideologies developed over the past hundred years are more than rationalizations for the role of schools as a traffic police for the prevailing social division of labor and more than the means of justifying the large expenditures of society for school support. They also serve to impress upon the child that his failure to climb the occupational ladder or rise beyond his parents' social class is a function of his own lack of intelligence or effort. The notion of equality of opportunity through universal compulsory schooling places responsibility on the individual for social failure while attributing successes to the institutions.

In grade school, the teacher as the surrogate parent and significant adult in the child's educational experience tells the student daily how he/she is perceived by the school system. In smaller communities where there is only one class to each grade, "bright" children in grammar school are placed in the front of the classroom, are accorded recognition from teachers, and are encouraged to become important actors in aspects of school life such as newspapers, drama groups, and the "monitoring" system where students learn to administer discipline to one another. "Dumb" children or "bad" children are lumped together as the ineducables and are relegated to the back of the classroom and are asked to do nothing except keep quiet. In large urban schools where Black and working class children constitute the majority of the school population the distinctions between the tracks within each grade serve the purpose of selecting out those children for whom school remains chiefly custodial and those who are deemed eligible for possible professional and technical occupations and school experience that may increase the chance of success.

The child may be able to reject these messages through the influence of parents and peers. First, parents' own perception of the child may mitigate the school's label. But often parents are themselves unable to resist the judgments of school officials, which they accept as honest and accurate since they are made by "professionals." In turn, the professional assumes the unwavering accuracy of the intelligence test as a measure of "potential" and a guide for making professional decisions as to the child's future educational experiences.

The strength acquired by becoming recognized as a worthy person by peers is certainly a locus of possible resistance to the imposition from above of the image of failure. Peer interaction, as we have argued, is predicated on the assumption of equality. In play and friendship children experience themselves as persons to be respected and their social environment as characterized by cooperation. Even though factors of geographic and class segregation make reasonable the idea of life chances determined by class the autonomous world of children allows for the process of individuation and the subjectively experienced expectation of dignity.

The child has to assimilate two rather conflicting systems. The battering received by the young from parents and school to force them to adapt to the expected mode of behavior is viewed by them as an imperative to be resisted, but one to which they will ultimately surrender. The form of surrender, however, cannot merely be passive acquiescence, if the social system is to reproduce itself vigorously. Children must make internal, incorporate in their self-system, the ideas of social mobility and social equality. They must learn how to cooperate with authority and with one another, but to compete at the same time for the rewards offered by the adult world. They must retain their "drive" to excel, but this drive must be sublimated by sports, school work, and self-discipline. They must learn to take pleasure in deprivation and reserve their leisure for prescribed periods that are viewed by adults as providing a "release" from the necessary routines of daily life and labor. Under capitalism, as Marx pointed out more than a century ago, the worker only can be allowed to live his own life after labor has been performed. Thus labor must become instrumental for the enjoyment of leisure time, it is not viewed as intrinsically satisfying except by those whose work remains close to the older artisan mode of production where the worker owned his own tools and saw the relationship between his skill and the product resulting from the expenditure of labor time. It is only in artisanship that the aesthetic element of work is preserved.

As we have seen, capitalism forces children to regard play and most adults to regard their leisure as the core of their self-controlled lives. It is here alone that the chance remains to escape domination.

In early adolescence girls have evolved the ritual known as a "slumber" party. It is not a game, but an explicit statement of autonomous relationship that takes the form of a group of girls sleeping at the house of one of their friends. The whole activity consists in being together, sharing with one another their experiences with boys, parents, and teachers. It is a ritual of autonomy because it requires that the parents understand that they are not to interfere with the girls' time together. Boys increasingly spend more time away from home and form peer relationships that are implicitly antiadult and conspiratorial.

Teenagers often adopt popular culture to serve the purpose of strengthening their solidarity. This is especially the case in the era of rock and roll when the music is often raucous and the words refer to such "counter-cultural" phenomena as drugs, political opposition, and other themes that are not socially approved or even understood by their parents. The music of groups such as the Rolling Stones, the Grateful Dead, and the Jefferson Airplane and the lyrics of Bob Dylan and Janis Joplin are particularly illustrative of the contradiction in mass culture between its conservative and radical aspects. The enormous interest by working class high school and college youth in learning how to play guitar, drums, and other musical instruments indigenous to rock music expresses the yearning for participation rather than spectatorship, and the desire for activity that is truly independent of institutional life.

Within schools, both for boys and for girls, the bathroom becomes one of the few places where autonomy can be found. The bathroom is much more than its explicitly intended function would suggest. For high school students it is the place where forbidden activity can be undertaken in relative privacy, except for the occasional raids by teachers. Smoking, horseplay, exchange of pornographic information through graffiti—as well as exchange of novels and other written material and talk about sex and other topics which the classroom has specifically excluded except in their most alienated forms—provide elements of autonomous interaction even in schools that rigidly circumscribe student freedom. The schools are quick to recognize the bathroom as a locus of the resistance of students to total administration. Increasingly, teachers and school guards are assigned to patrol the facility in search of children seeking refuge from the wonders of the classroom. Loitering must be expunged from the daily routine of the school lest students receive information that conflicts with the approved curriculum and learn habits that undermine the ethic of work and subordination.

Yet play is not viewed as serious activity since it is voluntary and is pursued for its own sake. Symbolically its voluntary character makes it "frivolous" in the sense that it neither produces anything that is socially useful nor constitutes a particularly important way to instill values and goals that are consistent with the reproduction of labor. When adults "play" cards, go bowling, or throw a ball around for no particular reason other than pleasurable exercise, they assert their autonomy from institutions that claim their energies in daily life. When games are institutionalized, however, when the players are relegated to the role of spectators of others engaged in the "act" of performing game rituals, one witnesses the perversion of play. As Johann Huizinga has remarked, "Play to order is no longer play: it could at best be a forcible imitation of it."

Within the last decade, higher education has occupied a more crucial position as one of the options available to working-class youth. Post–secondary school education is now more common among working class youth for several reasons. The most important is that, as the productivity of industrial labor has increased because of technological change and the accelerated pace of labor, there are fewer available jobs for which a high school diploma is a sufficient credential. Moreover, the proliferation of the service occupations that have replaced industrial jobs has failed to create jobs requiring new skills. Under these conditions, higher education is one of the alternatives to unemployment or acceptance of a low-paying job (if it can be found) in government and other service industries.

As another option the young person may join the armed forces, and during those years of service learn a trade which may result in a skilled civilian job. However, this decision brings with it the disadvantage of possible active duty in a war zone, and there is no real assurance that voluntary enlistment will result in a marketable skill unless the economy is actually expanding. There is ample evidence, in fact, that the presumption of economic growth is no longer identical with the goal of full employment, especially in manual and technical occupations, since capital investment is concentrated in areas that are both labor- and capital-saving. Nevertheless, many Black and white rural and Southern youths have joined the armed forces rather than face unemployment or dead-end, low-paying jobs in the garment and service industries. In states where free college education is offered only to veterans service in the armed forces becomes for Blacks a prelude to social and occupational advancement.

Other youths enter two-year and four-year colleges precisely to escape the probability of being drafted; others to avoid alienated unskilled labor in a manufacturing or service industry, or the pervasiveness of drugs and petty crime that dominates the streets of some working class and Black neighborhoods.

The armed forces have proven to be no solution for these youths. The promise of learning a trade is often broken by the simple device of flunking students out of mechanical and technical programs using traditional criteria of tests, even when the criterion of aptitude is waived. The hidden history of the Vietnam War, a story only dimly disseminated and understood, is that the termination of U.S. ground fighting resulted as much from the mutinous spirit of the soldiers as it did from international power considerations. The infrequent press reports of refusals by whole companies to engage in combat, widespread use of drugs among both enlisted men and officers, and group desertion from the battlefield, obscured the extent of indiscipline among members of the U.S. armed forces. Combined with the substantial number of young people who refused enlistment and left the country, were excused for mental and physical reasons, or are languishing in jail, the numbers of those rejecting military service in one way or another is huge. I have spoken to veterans attending community college who describe vividly cases where the low morale of American soldiers literally crippled the capacity of U.S. combat forces in the field. Even when the U.S. intensified the air war in Southeast Asia because of its ineffectiveness on the ground, rebellion did not cease. *The New York Times* reported several cases of flight crews and individuals who were "quietly sent home" after declining combat missions.

In late 1972, the rebellion spread to the ships. At first naval officials responded to sailors' protests having to do with racist attitudes of officers and poor food and working conditions; there were promises to improve the situation. But many conservatives in the naval bureaucracy and in Congress were unhappy with this solution. Instead, after conducting a congressional investigation into the rebellion, the chairman of the committee explained that those who participated in the protests were low-IQ, malcontents, mostly Black, unable to master the intricacies of modern naval technology, and recommended that they be released from the service. Shortly thereafter, in early 1973, the naval high command announced that it would discharge "up to 6000" of these men from the Navy and would tighten entrance requirements in the future.

The end of the draft and the national administration's program for an all-volunteer army is directly related to the now open, now hidden, rebellions in the armed forces against the traditional absolute power of the officer corps over enlisted men. The fundamental democratic concept that lay behind the notion of a citizen army, that is, one where all people share the responsibility for national defense, was behind the draft policy during the Civil War. Nixon's program for the professionalization of the armed forces may be welcomed by large numbers of young people who hate the military and have no wish to participate in it. But the impact of the draft on the course of the Vietnam War bears witness to its utility as an instrument of opposition. By making soldiers dependent upon the hierarchy of rank, by transforming the whole military from a "service" to a "profession," a dangerous weapon for suppressing popular movements has been seized by the state. The rebellion in the armed forces has been one of the most important recent manifestations of working class discontent and social actions. Unless understood as part of the same impulse that produced Lordstown and the high school rebellions of 1969–71, an important dimension of its significance is lost. The military revolt attests to the refusal of young people to mindlessly follow the admonition perpetrated by the public school system that citizenship consists in the belief, "My country right or wrong." The ideological role of school in providing the intellectual categories of social cohesion has been seriously questioned by students who have perceived the irrationality of the prevailing authority relations within the institutions.

Beyond the avoidance incentive, the two-year colleges in particular seem to hold out the promise that the ideology of equal educational opportunity can be realized. The past five years have been marked by dramatic expansion in the number of two-year colleges, the enrollment of high school graduates in these institutions, and the expansion of federal and state support for them. In the earlier periods of American higher education these schools were designed to absorb middle and upper class youth who could not qualify for private and state universities; the modern community college movement, however, is aimed at the absorption of working class youth who have been tracked for vocational and general diplomas as well as the lower half of the academic graduates who did not qualify for four-year colleges. Like the armed forces, two-year colleges are institutions of masked unemployment —institutions of containment for youths who cannot be integrated into the labor force in the unskilled and semiskilled job areas, but who nonetheless must be instilled with the ideologies of social advancement.

Community colleges now have an enrollment of nearly two and one-half million, about one third of the total full-time enrollment in post–secondary educational institutions. These schools are the fastest growing sector among all institutions of higher education. Community colleges were first proposed in the late 1950s as training grounds for workers who perform technical labor that requires less than professional credentials. However, in the past few years, with the relatively large unemployment of technical and scientific labor caused by cutbacks in some defense industries and the advancement of technologies, technical training has diminished as the primary focus of these institutions. Instead we can observe a gradual rise in liberal arts curricula, a *de facto* recognition that the community college is no longer a distinct institution providing specific kinds of occupational training.

The rise of liberal arts in the junior colleges can be viewed within the context of the rise of service industries. In the new service sector, workers are required to have no specific knowledge. The important skill required to function within public service bureaucracies is preeminently the toleration of boredom. Community colleges provide ample training for this feature of bureaucratic work. Unlike four-year colleges that prepare students for entrance into graduate schools or for the low-level and middle-level managerial occupations within bureaucracies and industry, community colleges are really an extension of high schools. While the four-year colleges perpetuate the separation of social sciences into a series of discrete disciplines such as sociology, economics, political science, etc., on the presumption that their students are likely to enter teaching occupations or at least require some degree of detailed knowledge of an academic discipline in order to develop the necessary skills of bureaucratic thinking, typically, the two-year colleges avoid the separation of the social sciences and languages. But the integration of the social sciences or the physical sciences is not an expression of any intellectual realization that such fragmentation is theoretically and educationally unsound. Rather, the "social studies" department of the community college is characterized by a plethora of survey courses in which theory is subsumed by historical empiricism, where issues are not sharpened, and where the object is to provide students with the most superficial information to be regurgitated on end-term examinations.

The basis of the community college curriculum (and the first two years of state university) is the task of maintaining the educational experience as alienated activity. The student is further socialized to the work-world by such means as lecture halls containing four hundred students for a course in psychology in which various approaches to the "subject" are handed down by the teacher in bewildering succession. The successful student is the one who endures the massification of his education and manages to pass the exam. The others are either academically dismissed on the basis of their short tolerance or placed on probation and advised to take courses that are oriented exclusively to the practical applications of the sciences, social sciences, or humanities.

The job of the community colleges and the first two years of state and city universities is to screen out those students who are deemed academically unfit. The dreadful curriculum may be a product of the limited intellect of school planners, the large classes may reflect the impoverishment of the school budget, but the objective role of the school is not unrelated to these phenomena. The success of the community college and junior college may be measured by the number of students who have dropped out of college and have internalized their decision as a failure to measure up to academic standards. Since higher education is presumed to be qualitatively different from secondary school insofar as it claims to provide concrete professional or preprofessional training, its standards are held determined by the criteria that are external to its institutional decision-making process.

The life of the university is understood to consist in the content of the curriculum, a program normally divided into specialized fields of inquiry corresponding to the division of technical and intellectual labor. Typically, teaching is an activity engaged in by a person of no particular pedagogic skills since his employment is ordinarily dependent on the acquiring of credentials and the publication of books and of papers in recognized professional and scientific journals. In contrast to lower schools, colleges and universities accord ambivalent status and powers to the administration, often considered a necessary evil rather than a source of academic authority. This tendency to hold to the ideology of the university as a "community of scholars" has suffered some erosion in recent years with the entrance of a large number of Blacks, veterans, and other groups ordinarily deemed unfit for higher learning. "Compensatory" education has asserted the importance of teaching as opposed to meticulous scholarship and lecturing methods. But the old guard will not abandon the image of the university as the repository of objective knowledge independent of all political and bureaucratic considerations. This myth is maintained in the midst of the most comprehensive transition in the role of the universities since their inception.

The curious alliance between minority students, including women, and college administrations has resulted from the perception of formerly excluded groups that the old academic standards are maintained, to a large degree, to perpetuate their exclusion. Thus the "Black Power" revolt in the colleges has had the anomalous effect of strengthening anti-intellectual currents in American life even as it asserts democratic values. Movements for loosening entrance requirements and effecting curriculum reform within higher education are profoundly important means of challenging elitism. Yet the danger is real that they will become instruments for battering down the last ramparts of serious scholarship within colleges and help accelerate the tendencies toward mass education. Increasingly, the broad objective of critical thinking has been submerged in liberal arts curricula, and students are advised that these disciplines must be viewed from the standpoint of their occupational utility. Even in areas such as humanities and social sciences that have no direct links to the prevailing technical division of labor within corporations and public agencies, these disciplines are still understood, in part, as training grounds for teachers and research workers.

The instrumental character of American higher education has been engendered by its massification and its specific economic role as an institution of deferred labor. As a consequence the stratification of higher education parallels the tracking system within elementary and secondary schools that, in turn, reflects the social and technical division of labor in capitalist society as a whole. The elite universities from which corporate and political managers are drawn are institutions that permit the widest range of cultural and intellectual choices and experiences available in capitalist educational institutions. Like the "academies" of ruling class socialization (e.g., Exeter, Andover, Groton), the real curriculum is not the specific subject matter offered in the classroom, but the social and political networks established among peers who understand that they are destined to occupy positions at the pinnacle or at least on the higher levels of corporate/political hierarchies. Radical ideas are given the widest possible range for expression because the assumption is that these ideas are functional to training persons who are required to possess a flexibility sufficient to integrate a broad range of alien views within the dominant culture. The condition of success of capitalist culture is its ability to thwart the development of alternatives. This task can only be achieved by exposing the new elites to their negations and assisting them to find ways to make any negation an instrument of domination.

The community college, in contrast, is typically bereft of liberal culture. Where the play element is particularly stressed at ruling class universities in order to train elites for occupational and social roles that demand the widest degree of imagination and invention, even if these qualities are put to questionable uses, imagination is held in low esteem in the state schools and community colleges, where training replaces education and programmed response overcomes thought.

The community college student becomes aware that he is receiving an inferior training, much less education, by the content of the courses, the cultural poverty of campus life, and the dreary physical surroundings. Many urban colleges are located in storefronts, converted office buildings, trailers, barracks, and makeshift facilities of varied assortment. Since a preponderance of students hold part-time jobs provided directly by the college through federally aided programs such as "work/study" or sling hamburgers in chain restaurants like McDonald's and Burger Chef, there is little time for reflection. The lecture character of many courses, the limited opportunity for interaction between students and faculties created by the heavy teaching loads and large number of students in each class, all contribute to the sense of futility shared by many who may have entered these schools with some expectations of learning something.

The student does learn that he has been deceived once more. The endless waiting in the lower grades for a different education that was supposed to be fulfilled by college is followed by the recognition that college is not meant to be a fount of wisdom, but is, at best, a credential for a job. When this illusion too is smashed by the high levels of unemployment among those who have completed four-year colleges, the student realizes that college beats working at McDonald's and that its main value consists in postponing for a while the bleak job prospects that lie ahead. At best, the community college graduate may become a manager at McDonald's rather than a short-order cook, who is typically only a high school graduate.

The radical separation of the public and the private realms in late capitalism, that is, the distinctions made in ordinary life between work and leisure owing to the long-range tendency of working hours to diminish, has contrary implications for working class consciousness. The worker's home and friends provide a retreat from the world of authority and domination, a world in which the worker is required to surrender his labor to another, where labor is understood to be that aspect of daily life given over to necessity as opposed to freedom. In this context, leisure becomes the refuge from dehumanization. The family, an institution that can only be experienced by children as a microcosm of the arbitrariness of social authority in general, is welcomed by adults as a protection against the insecurities of modern life. As the family represses children, so it constitutes the chance for adults to achieve the mastery denied them in the workplace. Leisure becomes a chance for the working man to locate himself as a significant actor in the private world, even as in the public world, particularly work, his identity is being whittled away toward extinction.

The last decade has revealed the ambivalent position of women in the family. Like the schoolteacher, the woman participates in the process by which children learn to repress their own needs and their autonomous activity in the service of institutional solidarity (experienced by children as the whim of adults). She believes that her children can succeed in the world to the extent that they learn to submit to the reality principle and her role is to help make this socialization to the necessities of life and labor as painless as possible. She protects the child from the arbitrary power of the father, from the dangers that lurk in the streets, the pains of childhood and youth, but she knows that it must learn how to survive and that paternal authority and the school represent the best chance for climbing the long hill to adulthood. In growing up, the child suffers the almost inevitable denouement of self-concept—the realization that the dream of success and fortune will elude him, even though the hope of deliverance from working class hardships is never fully extinguished.

The working class woman herself is a victim of paternal authority. Hers is a life of unrelieved labor in which the workplace, the factory or office, has no separate character from the home because subordination is the chief feature of both. The working class woman attempts to escape from her oppression by finding interstices between private household labor and public labor where she can individuate her own needs. Parents' associations, religious women's organizations, bingo, bowling, and extended family relationships are the characteristic avenues taken by women in their search for autonomy. These forms of voluntary association and activity provide the outlets for friendship for its own sake, recreation and even play. However, the introjection of domination finds its way into consciousness to the extent that even the object chosen for the expression of autonomy is connected with a socially approved activity, such as schools and religion. Here the woman is unable to leave the home except by telling herself and her family that she is still serving them and is not engaging in anything that can be described as "sheer" fun. The impulses toward friendship are complicated by feelings of guilt for abandoning the home even for a single evening.

Although there are distinct cultural differences between the forms of self-activity chosen by working class and middle class women, the motivations are not so far apart. Working class women raise their consciousness about their life situation in the course of developing friendships with women who share similar problems. Their conversations center upon the problems of children, husbands, and shared work environments, and they are less confident than middle class women that their predicament is subject to alteration by their own efforts. But the church groups or bowling teams are symbolic forms that legitimate their need to establish communication with one another just as the isolated wives of professionals seek therapy groups or the feminist movement or engage in charity or political activities to make contacts with other women and to ascertain that their own oppression and solitude are shared by others.

Men play with one another in bars around a few beers, a game of darts or a game of pool. Others go to the races or play cards. As among women, social contact is mediated by a common activity that resembles the play of childhood but is presented in the form of "games" in which the object is to win money, since there are few other circumstances in which men are prepared to confess that an activity is, in itself, engrossing. They cannot admit the legitimacy of play, even as they enact this need spontaneously in barroom encounters or the formation of voluntary social clubs. Some of these social clubs exist as veterans' organizations, civic groups, or fraternal groups of ethnically homogeneous persons who require support in the transition to the new society. In these instances, the need for fraternity is masked as participation in public life, but its real substance is the hunger for communication and social interaction.

Historically, working men have combined political and social action with private needs. Many local unions function most of the time as barrooms and social clubs; union business is transacted, in part, to provide legitimacy for the real activity of the membership—play. In the nineteenth century, a large number of "secret societies" of working men were formed under religious, fraternal, or purely social guises. Labor historians and others who have studied the period have traditionally interpreted the secrecy as purely a response to the certain repression an avowed trade union or group of political dissenters would encounter during the period when the employers in conspiracy with the courts regarded the self-organization of laborers as tantamount to a restraint of trade and economic expansion. There can be no doubt about the accuracy of these interpretations. But they miss a crucial dimension of secret societies. Just as children spontaneously create secret clubs that are barred to adults and other children who do not give the proper secret word to gain entrance, the rituals surrounding adult social and fraternal clubs are more than carryovers from the bygone days of overt repression of labor organizations. They are signs that workers still require a shield to protect their private lives beyond the family.

Secret societies exist today. Their exclusivity is sometimes perverted in elitist or racist forms. But the driving force of these groups is the demand for an underlife that cannot be penetrated by the employer, the spouse, or mass culture. The social club, notwithstanding its contradictory features when subsumed under the rubric of a reactionary veterans organization or religious group, remains a major institution that workers control. Although workers bring the values of the everyday world into the clubhouse, they still enact there the relatively egalitarian practices of child's play. Parents' associations rarely "elect" their officers from among competing factions. Anyone who wishes to serve becomes an officer by volunteering for a committee. Officers are selected by succession rather than competition and the analogy is to the turn-taking in the games of childhood. This practice is characteristic of all working class voluntary groups at the local level. Social clubs cannot engender fierce competition for leadership lest the prerequisite for the existence of the organization itself, group solidarity, be rent by electoral contests. Since the stakes of these organizations are not intimately linked with political power —that is, the alienated forms of social life encapsulated within the critical institutions of schools, religious organizations, unions, and the state—their members are interested neither in profits nor in the allocation of resources that constitutes the real business of large-scale public institutions. Instead, differences among members that might be interpreted as "political," that is, differences surrounding those issues that are understood as of a public character, are either consciously suppressed by the group or repressed by each individual.

Trade unions often occupy a difficult ground between the public and the private realms. Where the local union represents a single plant and is located in a geographic center easily accessible to the membership, it tends to remain preeminently a social center, that is a place to "spend" leisure time (often defined by men as the time away from both home and work). The trade union function is relegated to working hours and is viewed as distinctly public activity that rarely interferes with the ordinary course of private life, except in times of strikes and other crises, when the active members who use the union hall for meeting their play needs, agree to suppress these needs in the service of public issues. In contrast, unions that are formed of a number of small plants or workplaces spread over a large geographic area rarely assume a social play character. They bear a resemblance more to business organizations that have regular office hours; sometimes they assume the functions of a welfare agency, and may powerfully influence members' political views. But they rarely are organically linked to the everyday world of their membership except to the extent that they affect working time. Thus, even though the play role of local unions is grounded in the community of interest derived from a single work situation (or labor skill as in the craft unions), its significance resides not in the identification of the members with the union, but with the similarity of their lives. Adults rarely consciously attach significance to play except as an interlude between the responsibilities of labor and family life. And yet it is in these situations that the person achieves the status of equal to other persons in contrast to the subordination in the shop and his abstracted domination of the home.

— 4 —

Capitalist development during the post–World War II period has transformed the character of everyday life for the working masses of the Western nations in two fundamental respects. First, there has been a pronounced tendency under the impact of social and technological change for the traditional institutions of private life, especially the traditional working class family, to disintegrate. Not that the family itself has disappeared; it indeed persists, but only in the face of the progressive loss of one after another of the functions that traditionally supplied its *raison d'être*. In particular, the key function of the family as the principal context for the early socialization of children has been continually undermined as the schools and the mass media progressively take over this role.

This, in turn, is related to a second tendency, toward the replacement of all the traditional forms of proletarian culture and everyday life—which gave working class communities their coherence and provided the underpinnings for the traditional forms of proletarian class-consciousness—with a new, manipulated consumer culture which for convenience's sake we will call mass culture. More generally, the formation of such a mass culture reflects the further development of the internal tendency of capitalism to increasingly give relationships between *people* the character of relationships between *things*. Commodity production intrudes into all corners of the social world. Its province is no longer restricted to meeting economic needs at a given level of material culture; it penetrates the sphere of cultural needs as well if profit can be gained by this intervention. The institutions of mass culture have in this way become central to the process of reproducing the labor force in proportion to the weaknesses of family, church, and school. Mass culture arises as part of the same development of advanced technologies that released workers from labor. It springs from the replacement of mechanical with electric power and the application of wave theory to communications at the turn of the century. The confluence between the simultaneous development of the public school and the machine technologies that supplanted children in the factories was repeated in the relationship between the emergence of mass communications and the increased leisure resulting from the rising productivity of labor. In each case, institutions intervened to fill the space created by the development of the forces of production lest the underlying population develop its own forms of social life independent of these provided from above. In the case of the replacement of the factory and the farm by the school and the character of deliberate planning; in the case of mass communications, an industry emerged out of the need to find new fields for capital investment, on the one hand, and a means of rapid transportation and communications, on the other, in order to facilitate the distribution of goods. The condition of capital expansion is its ability to complete the circular process of production-consumption. From the beginning, mass communications have had a twofold character: through advertising they stimulate the circulation of capital and commodities. Newspaper, radio, and later television were vital means of assuring that markets were created under conditions of enormous acceleration in the productivity of labor as a result of technical innovation and the dissemination of knowledge.

Mass communications in the twentieth century have become an intermediary between the sphere of production and the sphere of consumption, that is, a technologically more advanced means not only of transporting goods, but providing information about the goods themselves to potential consumers by symbolic as well as literal representations. But in the process of symbolization, the symbols themselves become significant. The character of advertising has been transformed by visual media. No longer are consumers simply made aware of commodities. The commodities take on a significance that is independent of material wants. One no longer buys a car merely for the purpose of getting from one place to another. The car assumes value beyond its practical utility. It represents a matrix of economic achievement and social status.

The social importance of advertising goes beyond its obvious economic function. It becomes a means of creating new needs. These subjectively perceived needs are only partially related to the new material culture that has been created by advanced capitalism. The needs generated by mass communications are compensatory for the failure of work and the family to provide the satisfactions derived from the sense of the intrinsic worth of human activity. It is for the sake of consumption rather than production itself that persons learn to sell their labor power in our society. Mass communications provide the values and norms for consumption that make labor tolerable. But it would be an error to view mass communications in functional terms alone. They create a basis for the production of ideologies that have become a universe of discourse in themselves. The work of McLuhan and Andre Bazin is particularly helpful in this connection. They have insisted that mass communications and the culture products must be understood as part of social reality rather than simply as a reflection of other structures. A new world is created in the media of mass culture. This is not merely a world of representation of reality. Its pervasive character in contemporary society makes it constitutive of social reality. McLuhan, however, goes too far in claiming that the power of mass communications is greater than that of other institutions of social life just as those who reduce mass culture to its commercial or ideological functions severely underestimate its import upon society. But there is no doubt that the influence of mass communications on human action makes the notions of mass society and mass culture serious conceptions with which social theory must contend.

It remains for us to investigate in what way mass culture becomes constitutive of social reality, especially in terms of our analysis of the reproduction of the working class by the institutions of daily life. We return to early childhood because it is here that the play element in culture is most affected. Children no longer draw on their unmediated experience of family and other aspects of social life to derive the forms and substance of play. Child's play is no longer exclusively self-reflexive and self-generated. Television-watching has become a major form of child activity that is undertaken both with other children and alone. Inevitably the relations between children are mediated by the values and perceptions suggested by television, and the very activity of watching itself. Elements of mass culture are incorporated into the modes of child's play, which becomes more imitative of mediated patterns of adult interaction and social relations in general. The creative aspect is significantly diminished. In relation to the influence of television culture on early childhood in particular, the tube takes on the function of surrogate parent and teacher both intentionally and unintentionally so that the child has less of a concept of its own space than ever before.

In the new types of games that are engendered by mass culture, one need mention only a few to illustrate how they differ from earlier games. The game "cowboys and Indians," a product of the late nineteenth- and early twentieth-century mythologizing of the heroic character of capitalist expansion, has become more powerful in the era of radio and television. Not unexpectedly, the role of cowboy is coveted by children since the Indian is always killed in the ritual. Unlike the earlier hide and go seek, where the master-slave relationship is essentially ambiguous, the cowboy is clearly on the side of right and justice, and his inevitable domination of the Indian, as enacted in the chase and murder, ends the game. Not all egalitarian aspects of play are purged in this game: turns are still taken and the initial selection of roles is often the result of chance determination. But we learn that the Indians are evil, must be exterminated, and that the myth of domination is just.

The games of Black children conform very closely to the everyday life of ghetto residents. They are imitative in content insofar as they describe the conditions of home life in the slum buildings. They concern rats and roaches, police and junkies. But they are also profoundly reflective of the visual images generated by mass culture. These children play war, "cops and robbers" in which the desired roles are the American army or the police against the criminal "gooks," or Communists or the dope pushers and thieves. The socialization functions of these games are startling. In the first place they are stark representations of approved social values and social roles, little mediated even by the child's creative symbols. Second, Black children take the role of their own oppressors uncritically. Most important, fantasy tends to be obliterated on the altar of the reality principle. Children learn that the dream of rebellion is futile. It cannot even be tolerated in "play." Through these games, ghetto children are able to objectivate the frustrations and violent impulses generated by the social environment in a scenario that is eminently respectable.

This is not to say that traditional children's games disappear among Black children in the wake of mass culture. Girls still play turn games such as jump rope, and boys still play together in school yards and on the streets in ways that are cooperative and resistant to competitiveness. Kick the can, ring-a-levio, and Johnny on the pony are turn games and widely played in working class white and Black neighborhoods. But games among both white and Black children have also increasingly contained the aggressive content provided by television and conditions of everyday life. The messages sent by both family and school that non-goal-oriented childhood play is a waste of time and that children are obliged at an early age to get on with the business of survival have been made powerful by the representation of these values by such television shows as "Sesame Street." This government-sponsored educational program reinforces the growing movement toward an early childhood education in which frivolity is replaced by "hard knowledge," albeit presented in an entertaining manner, or as play itself in day care centers and nurseries. The cooperation of parents, educational institutions, and the mass media is tantamount to a conspiracy against childhood—it corresponds to the attempt to narrow the space afforded children by the advance of technologies that replace the need for human labor in the production of goods. The emergence of alternative forms of peer-group social life is severely thwarted, forcing it more and more to assume an underground existence. The creative element of play, imagination, is restricted by the powerful images of social roles and social values presented by mass culture. The dramatic visual forms in which these values are communicated tend to command adaptation because their symbolic and ideological content is masked as objective reality in which the condition of communication is the absorption of the spectator in the "play" as a vicarious participant. As in spectator sports, television- or movie-watching is not social activity in which the participant is able to see himself in the outcome of the activity, or the activity as a product of his own effort. Mass media is stark. Its values can only be inferred by achieving distance from the action presented on the screen or radio because these images appear to be real. One "forgets" in the darkness of the movie theaters, the semilit room that is the location of television viewing, or the anonymity of the sports arena that what is viewed is not real. Emotional distance, the condition of critical thinking, can only be established after the fact or by distraction. But the trivialization of culture produced by the conditions of its mechanical reproduction on the one hand, and its ephemeral character on the other, render critical thought extraordinarily difficult. The fleeting instant of visceral experience permitted by modern visual culture contrasts sharply with the durability of the painting, the mural or sculpture. Characterisically, high culture never had a popular audience. Its aesthetic conditions have always been delimited by its class-specific audience. But even under these conditions the work of art is not only expressive of the individual sensibility of the artist, but can communicate its values, its aesthetic priorities, to diverse audiences, who possess the time to reflect on the artistic intention. The world of high culture is one where the relationship of the artist to the audience is dialectical, at least potentially. Artist and audience are known to each other to a much greater degree than in mass arts.

Mass art is a one-way communication and thus takes on the character of domination. The social impact of its production consists not only in its ideological content (a property it shares with high culture), but in its pervasive intervention into the existential time and consequently the psychic space of the person. Thus television, movies, and popular music, like sports, must be understood in the dimension of their significance as forms of life activity as well as ideological apparatuses.

In the past half century, Americans have all but lost their capacity to produce popular arts. The nostalgia for the self-production of art lives among the urban middle class, but this class lacks the imagination to create its own forms. Just as the white-dominated commercial music business absorbed Black music, so have the educated strata within cities attempted to connect themselves to the country music of the agricultural era, undertaking folksinging and dancing in a purely imitative manner.

Even within the Black communities, jazz has become esoteric —an art form adopted by intellectuals and separated radically from working class life. It could be argued, however, that in contrast to gospel or blues, jazz has always been more a medium of the Black intelligentsia than a mass form—in effect, it represents a component of Black "high culture." As jazz became a profitable business in the 1930s and 1940s, it began to develop avant garde channels among Black musicians. Not only did Black musicians, attempting to escape from the cooptation of commercial music, create their own groups that played music outside of established markets, but they consciously made their music less and less amenable to commercial debasement, evolving styles that were increasingly atonal. The rhythmic links to the older jazz forms were retained, but the developments introduced into twentieth-century classical music by Schoenberg, Stravinsky, Berg, Webern, Varese and others were integrated into the melodic line and the counterpoint of instruments. In the process of demarcation between commerical and serious jazz, the music itself became separated from its audience, and the measure of the authenticity of the new music became its resistance to popular culture. In essence, modern jazz and some kinds of blue-grass and folk music have attempted to become forms of high culture, notwithstanding their lower-class origins.

In the 1960s young whites, many of whom were of British working class origin, attempted to effect a synthesis of older Black blues, popular and folk melodies, and rhythmic patterns borrowed from gospel and jazz music. As early as the late 1940s rock and roll was a well-established kind of popular music among Black people. Such artists as Ruth Brown, Bo Diddley, and many others had already pioneered in the development of this music when Bill Haley, Chubby Checker, Chuck Berry, Kay Starr, and other commercial singers and instrumentalists brought the music into the mainstream of white popular music in the late 1950s. But the Beatles, the Rolling Stones, and the Animals were qualitatively different from their predecessors. Their music was highly individual but they spoke an international musical language whose imitative aspects were by no means as apparent as the music of Americans like Elvis Presley. It was not merely more vital. It attempted to break out of the straitjacket of banal lyrics that had placed constraints even on great singers such as Billie Holiday, Sarah Vaughan, Dinah Washington, and Ella Fitzgerald.

The lyrics of the new rock were difficult to assimilate into traditional popular culture and its media outlets. Subjects such as drug use, revolution, and even the class-conscious songs of John Lennon, The Grateful Dead, the Rolling Stones—such as "Salt of the Earth," "Factory Girl"—did not find receptivity among disc jockeys of leading rock stations. The social protest music of Bob Dylan was only played commerically as a retrospective view of Dylan's career. Commercially he was best known for his more banal songs such as "Tambourine Man" or "Blowing in the Wind," a sentimental, whining lyric that pales next to his existential ballad "Like a Rolling Stone," which addresses the inevitable separation of children from their families and the agony of individuation in a hostile culture.

Underground stations sprang up to give voice to the less popular rock music. Within a few years, these were purchased by the major radio network that attempts to reach young audiences, ABC. Similarly, the number of arenas for concerts that first gave hard rock the opportunity for live performances dwindled as large ball parks and sports stadiums were procured for the performance of the music. Unable to compete with the fees offered by large promoters to once-obscure performers, the smaller clubs and auditoriums were no longer viable in commodity terms.

The fate of the new rock music parallels the fate of jazz. There are still underground musicians with a relatively small group of devoted followers. But the main drift has been toward the debasement of the art form. The 1970s have witnessed the final denouement. The music has become more slick and cool. Its rhythms are distinctly less vigorous than those of the 1960s. And the lyrics have reverted to the gross teen-age love themes of the earlier pop forms, combined with a strain of nihilism and privatization that reflects the sense of isolation shared by musician and audience amid the commercial success of the once-despised music.

At the same time as mass culture and the mass communications media tend toward the destruction of traditional working class or popular cultures and the manipulative integration of the working masses into a bureaucratic consumer capitalism, the "products" of this culture reflect these very processes in an inverted, ideologically refracted form. The most popular family show on television, a series begun in 1971, shortly after the right-wing protests of construction workers, is "All in the Family." Archie Bunker, the hero of the series, is a middle-aged, vaguely ethnic man whose life revolves around his family. He is a strongly authoritarian personality, but completely ineffectual in controlling the lives of the members of his family, even though he requires their approval and needs to sense power over them. Archie's political views are slightly to the right of the Republican Party and his social morality is directly descendant from the Victorian era. He is a profoundly ignorant and suspicious man, whose lack of middle class manners is as ubiquitous as the narrowness of his aesthetic culture. Archie oppresses his wife, who, like other women of her genre, conducts the liberation struggle underground. Archie's wife actually has some control over the situation, but she must perpetuate the sham of acknowledging her husband's power over the family domain. She presents herself as totally unthreatening, as befits the wife of a working class tyrant, even as she manages to assert her autonomy. When her children goad her into making explicit her fight against Archie's oppressiveness, she is unable to rise to the occasion. Her style is antithetical to any effort demanding articulation. She operates entirely in the *sub rosa* world of daily activity. Rhetorical struggle is as foreign to her life as are public issues generally.

The overriding theme of the television series is the generation gap—specifically the resistance of the old, blue-collar world to the new values and life styles of the young. Naturally, Archie's children share neither his blue-collar work-world nor his concepts of appropriate home life. The next generation is integrationist, mildly sympathetic to feminism, and, accordingly, headed for middle class occupations. An important theme of the series is the conflict between Archie and his student son-in-law. Archie loses all the battles; he simply cannot match the reasoned liberal arguments of the college-trained youth. Yet Archie retains his authority. He pays the bills and is presented as a down-to-earth person whose concern for the wellbeing of the family is unquestionable. We come away from the television set admiring Archie's struggle to preserve traditional society against the buffeting of a new world he never made.

The subject of a recent film, *Joe*, is a balding, aggressive and somewhat vituperative man. Archie is lovable, but Joe is a man to be feared. His hatred of the new generation's departures is so passionate that it drives him to murder. In Joe, we witness the struggle of the blue-collar worker striving to become middle class. Archie is locked into the private house. The decor of his home is more typical of the 1940s and 1950s than the present. While Archie remains stereotypically working class, Joe exhibits the ambiguity of the upwardly mobile blue-collar suburbanite. Superficially his home resembles those of his more affluent neighbors, but he is painfully aware of the persistent class cleavage. His speech is riddled with proletarian sounds and he cannot communicate a system of shared values to his upper class acquaintance.

Archie is confused and annoyed by the new world, but is ultimately tolerant of it. Joe's whole *raison d'être* is threatened. For him, opposition to the next generation's adoption of countercultural life style cannot be contained in argument: it must be exorcised as one destroys a witch. Joe understands the new life style as an existential challenge even as he yearns to be part of it. Everything he aspires to in the world is thrown into question by the decision of the younger people to break from his values.

Many Americans accept these portraits. In contrast to the common beliefs of the 1950s, the myth of the complacent worker with the middle class life style is constantly belied by the discontent revealed by these new popular images. The split-level home cannot obscure the deeply felt insecurity of the older blue-collar worker. This insecurity is not so much a product of economic vicissitudes as it is generated by the breakup of family life and other institutions and ideologies. For the older workers who have achieved a measure of seniority in their jobs, there are fewer layoffs. Even the shocks of plant removal that transformed whole regions into depressed areas in the 1950s have subsided. Having become stable in economic terms, older workers came to rely on the home for a source of spiritual renewal denied them by the banality of their work. But by the 1960s, under the weight of social forces they were ill prepared to understand or cope with, the few economic gains they had made seemed to be eroding.

Even working class youth were breaking away from the values and life styles of their parents. Respect for the authority of the father was harder to maintain in a world in which the ethic of "ripping off the system" replaced the work compulsion. Young people sensed that the work-world held little promise for fulfillment so they resolved to do as little as they could in the public realm and reserve their real lives for "leisure." But now the family was no longer sufficient to provide the "heart" denied in the heartless world. Children no longer were able to find role models in their blue-collar parents. In the first place, it was highly unlikely that most of them could end up in the factory or even on trains or trucks, supposing they wanted such occupations. Second, young people had become skeptical that "society" would make good its promises in return for hard work and the performance of citizenship duties. Society, that is, the corporations, was evidently "ripping off" the consumers, had a stranglehold on the government, and was now unworthy of support. The denouement did not necessarily create the actual revolt among working class youth, but constituted a basis for resisting the old institutional ideologies. "All in the Family" shows the struggle between a generation locked into the consciousness of material scarcity and authoritarian values and its offspring, confused and rebellious but without alternative values or ideologies to provide coherence to its opposition.

In the 1950s popular culture found little reason to be overly concerned with working class life. The political and social behavior of the factory worker was presumed a function of the stability of the economy; the prevailing view was that workers, as predictable as the drone of the machine, were safely ensconced within rules of conduct prescribed by capitalist culture. They accepted the inevitability of the prevailing social system. Sociologists of the left lamented the passivity of the underlying population, while the liberal sociologists celebrated the citizenship workers had achieved. Unions made them strong, but non-revolutionary. Lacking the ideologies of class struggle, workers were devoted to the nonideological world of incremental consumption. The affluent worker was interested not in change but in "progress." Consonant with technocratic notions of social development, the fate of the working class was thought to be dependent upon the ability of social organization to generate techniques adequate to the general goals of economic growth, of which the working class was a beneficiary. Thus the problem of working class power was subsumed by the parameters of capitalist accumulation. The happy worker was prototypically a successful consumer of goods. The radical aura of the trade unions of the 1930s gave way to an image of conservatism, even if this alleged difference was more a product of the disappointment of the romantic left-winger than a reflection of actual changes in the institutions. The picket line was perceived as an outmoded weapon in comparison to the new technique of professional collective bargaining, complete with its array of "experts" on both sides who eschewed any kind of violence. Class struggle was to be conducted by means of statistics and compromise. Workers were narrowly self-interested, and this self-interest made them allies in the great liberal consensus that dominated American politics. If their unions were something less than a force for social change, it was a reflection more of the stunning success of capitalism than of the venality of leadership.

On the Waterfront and *Marty,* two films of the 1950s that dealt with aspects of working class life, illustrate the requirements of the changing times. In *Marty,* the agony of the protagonist is a product of his inability to shape his life according to the norms of his social environment, even though he accepts them. Marty is the antithesis of the Hollywood image of what a young man is supposed to be. He is heavily built, somewhat inarticulate; he makes a good living but in a trade considered less than prestigious. Yet to women Marty applies Hollywood standards of attractiveness and finds himself alone as a result. As he works out his conflict, he rejects neither the goals of the outer society nor its essential values. It is only the surface values that must be abandoned. Marty seeks marriage and family life and agrees to the prevailing separation of work and leisure activity. His adjustment consists in self-recognition. "I'm ugly," he admits. Consequently, happiness must be achieved with a woman who will accept the superficial truth of the statement because she is herself a victim of the same social stigma. *Marty* is a story of private persons seeking happiness. Behind the simple tale of an East Bronx butcher boy is the theme of the times. Persons must "adjust" their dreams to the constraints imposed by their life situations. Each of us, we are told, can overcome the loneliness of modern life only if he abandons his childhood fantasies. Maturity consists in the acceptance of ourselves as limited persons whose expectations cannot exceed our own abilities. Marty decides to jettison his artificial and unrealistic notions of love and romance, and settle for companionship in a relationship where he is accepted for what he is.

Elia Kazan's *On the Waterfront* is a film that teaches similar, yet curiously contradictory, lessons. Terry is an ex-prizefighter whose dream of success was shattered by his loyalties to the underworld. Even though he considered himself a possible "contender" for the championship, the mob demands that he throw a fight and his pugilistic career as well. His loyalty is rewarded by an easy longshore job on the waterfront. The film depicts Terry's struggle to free himself from his Old World beliefs in the sanctity of the "family" of crime as well as the essential invincibility of blood ties. His crisis occurs only when he learns that his fierce loyalties are not shared by his "family" and discovers that he is able to break from this strange moral system. The idea of conjugal love opens the way for the adoption of new moral codes. Terry learns that personal ambition and other personal interests are not to be despised, that the ego has its own legitimacy and need not be subordinated to the interests of his subculture.

On the Waterfront and *Marty* depict the final assimilation of first-generation ethnic Americans to the new world. There is dignity in the acceptance of the limitations of the self and in the alienation of that self from the community. The separation of the person from the neighborhood subculture's rules of conduct, illustrated by Terry's abandonment of the Old World ties, or Marty's ultimate rejection of the abstract ideal of social acceptibility as internalized by his peers, expresses the individualist bias of popular culture in the era. Yet each of these protagonists moves closer toward society's ideals. The 1950s witnessed the breakup of the old ethnic neighborhoods. Terry and Marty are transitional figures insofar as they are located in the heart of the city, even as they are being prepared ideologically to make a successful break with it. Suburban life cannot be sustained on ethnic or neighborhood relationships. The "significant others" are now the immediate family, particularly one's mate. Neither friends on the block nor the parental home are sufficient to the task of survival in the shifting modern world. The message of the working class movies of the fifties is, "You're on your own, young man." These films instruct us about the validity of private goals, the ephemeral quality of communal values and social ties, the legitimacy of the individual against the mob. Terry becomes an "enemy of the people" even though his testimony against the corrupt waterfront bosses is, in part, designed to destroy their power over the lives of working longshoremen. But, having disturbed the equilibrium of the prevailing corrupt system under which he and his workmates are obliged to suffer, he finds them predictably ungrateful. Yet there is no remorse for Terry. He has chosen his course. His own sense of justice, validated by a socially marginal liberal Catholic priest and his upwardly mobile lover, a longshoreman's daughter who attends college to escape the fate of her father, is sufficient to effect Terry's separation from his old life and comrades.

The political interest of this film cannot be underestimated. It was made during the McCarthy period, when the informer had been elevated to a cultural hero and had become an important source for the government's attack on left-wing groups. At first Terry represents the traditional antipathy of working class people to cooperating with the police or any other agency of law enforcement. His final decision to become a government witness paralleled the decision of the director of the film, Elia Kazan, to do the same with respect to his former associations with the Communist movement. In its attack against group solidarity as a form of cretinism a theme that has agonized twentieth-century intellectuals and has been especially relevant to their relationship to the Communist and labor movements, *On the Waterfront* raises more sharply than any recent American film the issue of the relationship of the individual to society. Terry's decision to fight the mob and become autonomous is mediated by a different conception of family, not a rejection of it. He can bring himself to testify only after his blood relation has been violated by the corrupt "mob," so that a new conception of group solidarity is introduced to replace the old one. He learns that both the "mob" and his fellow workers rob him of his individuality. In the end, the principle of the charismatic leader replaces the principle of terror: the workers are not elevated to leaders; they remain the led as Terry now becomes the symbol of power.

Joe and Archie are Terry and Marty grown to middle age. Having successfully adapted to the new society that demanded privatization of goals and daily life, they find themselves in the 1970s in a world that is changing again. They are being forced to make adjustments once more but rebel against that demand. Terry and Marty were men in the late twenties and early thirties in 1950. In the 1960s they are replaced on the screen by college students, professional and technical workers. To make popular the image of a young industrial worker would undermine the myth of mobility; it would be tantamount to the admission that social class transcended social time, hardly consonant with the notion of economic and social progress. Obviously, a young person who works in a factory or drives a truck could not provoke identification among the members of the audience. The young industrial worker, if glimpsed at all, must be a failure, someone incapable of grasping the opportunities presented by the educational system. Clearly, society assigns only the least able, those who show the least initiative and intelligence, to the blue-collar world. If a person of obvious intelligence and glamour is presented as a blue-collar worker, we soon learn that this role is taken as a sign of rebellion from another life. Such a figure is the oil-field hero of *Five Easy Pieces,* who, it turns out, is really a talented but confused pianist of upper class origins. Clearly, his entry into the blue-collar world is temporary and somewhat capricious.

The class ethos of the mass media has been consistent despite stylistic differences from previous eras. With few exceptions, the factory worker is a failure, ignorantly committed to a private world without richness, accepting a system of beliefs devoid of genuine intelligence and compassion. The factory worker is a man without qualities capable of universal admiration. He is a comic and pathetic figure at best, an irrationally violent man at worst.

What do the films and television shows teach us about women? When women are allowed to be shown in work situations, it is almost always in the role of office wives. Such a figure is Ingrid Bergman of *Cactus Flower,* a lonely spinster who works as assistant to denist Walter Matthau. Only Candice Bergen, the modernistically cool-hip heroine of *TR Baskin,* is presented in her work situation with its oppressive monotony. Yet we are assured that Bergen has more on the ball than the job in the impersonal large corporate office would suggest. She, like the hero of *Five Easy Pieces,* is merely a turned-off young woman who has taken the job in order to further remove herself from life's commitments. No serious person could tolerate such a routine job is the message of the movie, certainly nobody as Beautiful as the heroine.

The contrast between the American movie heroine and a recent working class portrait by a Swiss director, Alain Tanner, is instructive. *La Salamandre* concerns a woman who is unable to find meaning in her life either in the boring work she is obliged to perform or as a courtesan for her intellectual friends. She finds exhilaration only in her freedom from labor with its accompaniment of male, supervisory authority. Her rebellion against her condition is individual. At no time is she aware of collective solutions to the situation. Contrary to the images possessed by the two men in her life who can only comprehend her as a simple sex-object, she experiences both her joys and her sufferings intensely. She cannot resolve the problems posed by her condition, but is constantly engaged in a struggle for freedom that has a spontaneous and poignant quality.

American movie heroines are blessed with esoteric occupations or none at all. In her two films of the early 1970s, Barbra Streisand has played successively a prostitute and a professional student drop-out. Jane Fonda joined the small circle of professional prostitutes in *Klute,* but neither Fonda nor Streisand enjoys the tragic grandeur of a Greta Garbo in *Anna Christie.* There is only *angst;* prostitution for them is a way of being involved. In the end they fall in love and experience their "normality" once more. One wonders what happens to their economic base once this occurs. One may assume perhaps that they will revert to being supported by their respective lovers.

The tendency to regress to the earlier film characterizations of the woman who does absolutely nothing is somewhat fudged by the "youth" trends evident among film stars and movie themes. Brilliant and talented young men like Dustin Hoffman are connected to college trained women who, despite their implied erudition become housewives and follow their husbands around. Such is the fate of Hoffman's screen wife in *Straw Dogs* and his girlfriends of the *Graduate* and *Harry Kellerman.* In fact, women remain objects for most of the "new wave" heroes. In its frantic efforts to re-create the excitement of Humphrey Bogart crime stories, Hollywood has made haste to re-create the objectification of women as well. They remain "things" for Nicholson in *Five*

Easy Pieces and *Carnal Knowledge.* In *The French Connection* Gene Hackman can't even get it together enough to sleep with a woman for more than one night. In this context, the portrayal of women as self-determined prostitutes appears ennobled in comparison to the nonpersons who are presented to us in an increasing proportion of Hollywood films.

Since the new generation of industrial workers has no place in the presentations of mass culture because it cannot provide quaint or romantic role models, the young television hero must be a doctor or a lawyer, since these remain the most acceptable routes from working class bondage. Young doctors shown as giving "service" to patients and young lawyers struggling for social justice are eminently acceptable images to be presented to the alienated attenders of school. They create goals that seem to justify the toleration of boredom. Moreover, the "Bold Ones," "Dr. Kildare," and other professionals attest to the viability of the service institutions and prepare large numbers of new workers for these roles. In these series the old doctor and the old lawyer are persons of high principle whose loyalties to professional codes are as fierce as their devotion to justice and service. The young lawyer must learn how to be coolly professional, while remaining totally subordinate to socially useful work. Crass commercialism, reserved to station breaks, is strictly excluded in the lives of the new professional heroes and heroines.

As the young television heroes engaged in service institutions proliferate, there is a simultaneous growth of programs depicting a "different kind of cop," who simultaneously fights criminals generally considered socially heinous, and engages in a life that is revealed to be suffused with all the weaknesses of ordinary people. The police are now young, sometimes Black, and always hip.

The new criminal, almost invariably working class, is often a victim of a bureaucratically wrought miscarriage of justice, and is portrayed more sympathetically than in the simple environmental or biological explanations for criminality of earlier films. Mass culture has discovered the new art of advocacy, an occupation designed to protect the individual from the power of impersonal forces. There are few executioners remaining in the media; only organizations and procedures that oppress the victim. But the young worker who in real life participates in the protest against his working life as well as the poverty of his leisure does not exist for mass culture. He is an anachronism in this stereotypical world. As the new interest in workers has both the object of understanding and containing the new phenomenon of working class discontent with the fragmentation of modern life, so it must expurgate its full dimension.

The subcontent of the messages of popular culture remains intact. The old working class norms must give way in the wake of the new service society. Working class recalcitrancy as exhibited by Archie consists in ignorance of the new world of hip and cool. It is a middle-aged, archaic revolt against the technocratic world of expertise, one where work itself becomes once more socially useful and personally satisfying. The fluidity of the new morality serves the transition from the old society of production of goods to the new consumer society of services.

— 5 —

To fully understand the ideological impact and manipulative functions of current media presentations, it is necessary to appreciate the multilayered character of contemporary mass culture. In addition to the *overt* ideological content of films and television— transmitting new role models, values, life styles to be more or less consciously emulated by a mass audience—there is also a series of *covert* messages contained within them which appeal to the audience largely on the unconscious level. These messages have not so much an ideological as an affective content. Typically, they define the character of the spectator's experience of the spectacle in terms of the repressed gratification of his or her unconscious desires. In this sense, they reinforce the overt ideological messages inasmuch as they provide a sphere of vicarious or substitute gratification for impulses prohibited by the prevailing ideologies. Sexually explicit or violent films provide frameworks for the vicarious gratification of erotic or aggressive drives which individuals are unable to pursue consciously. Advertising, too, increasingly appeals less to the conscious and rational judgment of the consumer than to his or her unconscious (and, especially, sexual) needs and desires. Sports serve similar functions.

In this regard, it is clear that by creating a system of pseudo-gratifications, mass culture functions as a sort of social regulator, attempting to absorb tensions arising out of everyday life and to deflect frustrations which might otherwise actualize themselves in opposition to the system into channels which serve the system.

More specifically, these tensions include those generated by the contradictions between the promises of the mass consumption system and the reality of the gratification provided and between the increasing socialization of production and the atomization of individuals within the mass society. They manifest themselves typically in the yearning for community and authentic human relationships, in the violent refusal of institutionally defined roles and values.

The media attempt to defuse the explosive potential of such desires in two ways essentially. The first way involves the redirection of these impulses into channels functional to the system's ends. The classic pattern for this sort of ideological mobilization is, of course, that of Nazism, which in films and symbols sought to redirect the authentic desire of the German masses for community into the pseudo-collectivity of the racial nation, whose inauthentic solidarity could only be sustained by the myth of the leader and the creation of internal or external enemies against which the mass was mobilized. This sort of stereotypical art and the scapegoating processes one associates with it are, of course, not restricted to fascism but can be seen clearly not only in the typical American war movie but also in the more recent attempts to stigmatize groups like "hippies" or "radicals" within contemporary American society. In this regard, the scapegoating processes and the redirection of aggression toward the stigmatized group, as, say, in the film *Joe,* has a psychologically purgative function.

In contrast, a second type of media presentation seeks the more modest end of simply neutralizing these dissident impulses. That is, it seeks the maximum passive isolation of the spectator, rather than his or her mobilization within a pseudo-community. Toward this end, this sort of media production typically plays off the spectator's conscious systems of self-integration, generally organized in the interests of self-preservation, against those repressed impulses toward freedom or revolt which are normally censored from consciousness. While denying their legitimacy on the overt, conscious level, the repressed themes of rebellion, community, etc., are allowed to emerge in covert, distorted forms in the guise of the aggressive or violently transgressive themes which are so prominent in current films and TV.

The typical crime drama, for example, aims on a subliminal level at a temporary resolution of psychic tensions resulting, on the one hand, from the individual's belief in the necessity of "law and order," and, on the other, the suppressed desire of the same individual to rebel against the constraints and frustrations imposed by this system. Thus, on the subconscious level the individual can vicariously identify with the criminal, and on the conscious level with the forces of law and order. Inasmuch as the latter generally triumph, the crime drama, while releasing some of the tensions built up in the law-abiding individual, ultimately serves to reinforce adherence to the law and order ideologies as the only posture consistent with self-preservation.

Underlying the demobilizing tendencies of these productions in current films and TV is an anti-utopian, intrinsically conservative image of human nature. Whereas during the fifties and early sixties the typical form of anti-utopian imagery presented in the media involved the identification of fundamental social change and egalitarian demands with an external enemy such as the "Communist menace," today the search for a new "enemy" with which to identify and thus discredit utopian demands has shifted from the international arena to the psyche itself. Thus, the new anti-utopian animus is based less and less upon the fear of external forces subverting the "American way of life" and more and more upon each individual's fear of the submerged destructive forces lying just beneath consciousness. Essentially, the doctrine of original sin has been revived with the aid of pseudo-biological or behaviorist theories of human nature; man is seen as inherently incapable of democratic self-determination and constitutionally in need of social restraints to prevent the unleashing of submerged bestial drives. Thus, in the most recent media presentations, this most degraded possible view of man is presented. It is not the psyche alone that has come under the camera's eye, but the beast himself. In *Clockwork Orange* and *Straw Dogs* the lower class is shown in unrelieved bestiality. Yet the split between mind and body is preserved according to social class criteria on the one hand, but healed by a gross biological reduction on the other. In both films, what is left of man's specifically human character seems to be embodied in the man of ideas and law. Yet in the end even the intellectual reveals himself a prisoner of his own aggression, so that violence itself becomes the admission that there are no solutions to problems, which ultimately cannot be reduced to economic or political causes. Violence is simultaneously the symbolic expression of man's defeat in the struggle against his own animal nature and yet presented as the only means of controlling this nature. Law and order, having been deprived of their peaceful regulatory functions implied by the social contract, must now be achieved by means that may spell man's own destruction.

The new films reflect no universally recognized solutions to social and personal ills. The pervasiveness of degradation defies psychotherapy, traditional justice, altered social arrangements. In contrast to the relative optimism of the social film of the 1960s, the underlying content of film in the 1970s is profoundly conservative. The task of society is to curb the beast. Here we can see an essential parallel to the images of man depicted in many films of the pre-fascist period of the 1920s and into the 1930s. Siegfried Kracauer has shown how the German film was prophetic of the coming of fascism. From the *Cabinet of Dr. Caligari* to Leni Reifenstahl's *Triumph of the Will*, a veritable hymnal to the Nazi party and its godlike leader, Adolph Hitler, the individual is told that he is powerless to deal with the large impersonal forces that control his life.

According to Kracauer, the psychological propensities of the German film from Versailles to the 1934 Nazi congress were toward a reification of society in the forms of pervasive machine power, despair and ultimate surrender of the person to the superior force and wisdom of authority. Only the leader representing the collective human will could harmonize the growing complexity of civilization with the needs of the individual. Kracauer shows how the German film reflected the exquisite sense of powerlessness of ordinary persons in the modern world. The themes of the film were duplicated in the biting satire of George Grosz's drawings, the horrific novels of Franz Kafka, the early plays of Brecht and Georg Kaiser. German art of the 1920s was dominated by the theme of modern technology as a Frankenstein. The impersonal bureaucracies of the state and the large corporations have reduced the individual to impotence. The human being is not only incapable of effectively controlling these forces that he, himself, has created, but is imbued with irrational impulses that must be curbed if the race is to survive. Sexual passions and aggressive instincts are essentially uncontrollable; even the middle class is unable to apply its rational faculties to either suppressing or sublimating them. Even if the Enlightenment relied on science and reason to deliver mankind from pestilence and scarcity, the scientist has been proven incapable of preventing the machine from emerging as dominant over man. Clearly, the message of the German film was that people must surrender their autonomy, since they are driven by deeply destructive forces that lie beyond their power. The authoritarian core of the German film was its attack on bourgeois culture, particularly its optimistic reliance on the ability of man to find reasonable solutions to the human predicament. More specifically, a basic theme running through the German films of this period is an image of the world as characterized by a precarious balance between submission to despotic authority and Hobbesian chaos. Within such a world a radical assault on authority borders on insanity while authority itself comes increasingly to be identified with the imperative of preserving society.

If the film reflects the collective psychological propensities of human society and cannot be understood either as pure propaganda or as the private production of the film-maker whose awareness is independent of social determinants, then recent American films may indeed be reflective of things as they are as well as prophetic of things to come. The contemporary emphasis of both films and TV shows on violence and law and order, reflecting the apparent powerlessness of humans to control their institutions, augurs badly for the future of our social and political life. Even social themes, those that are not content to depict the relationship between the individual and society as a purely private affair, have been subtly transformed.

The heroes of *Clockwork Orange, Carnal Knowledge, Five Easy Pieces,* and *Straw Dogs* are men who seem unable to control their aggressions. Their "primal" violence asserts itself and is no longer human. Instead, the beast has taken over. It is important to understand that these films reflect an important current in recent popular sociological and anthropological literature. The work of Robert Ardrey, Desmond Morris, Tiger, and Fox, and the later writing of Konrad Lorenz, have painted a collective portrait of the human race that is profoundly pessimistic. Beneath the veneer of culture that purports to distinguish man from his ancestors, lie instincts of territoriality, aggression, and competitiveness that account for the apparent inevitability of wars, capitalist civilization, mass destruction and the exploitation of man by man. Enter B. F. Skinner. The only solution to the inexorability of human misery is for society to agree to make behavior consistent by the use of social engineering. Applying the technologies of behavioristic psychology, Skinner would introduce even more authoritarian methods of social control than the relatively unplanned methods of human socialization have hitherto permitted. For Skinner, freedom is a luxury reserved for civilizations less complex, less vulnerable to the destructiveness that man's mastery over nature has inadvertently wrought. Given the infinite manipulability of human nature, only a programmed society can hope to avoid the coming holocaust. Individualism and dignity must surrender to behavioral planning if the human race is to survive.

This theme, reflected almost perfectly in Kubrick's *Clockwork Orange*, a movie written as if it were a commentary on the work of Lorenz and Skinner, has resonated beyond the fantasies of social scientists and purveyors of mass culture. We are now faced with the prospect that government, assessing the weakness of those social institutions relied upon for integrating people into the requirements of technological society and mass politics, is turning to totalitarian solutions for the reconstruction of the values and norms that constitute the adhesive of the prevailing culture. Toward this end, moreover, the capitalist class is increasingly mobilizing all the unprecedented technical resources at its disposal, and in particular its techniques of mass communications, and is employing them in such a way as to promote the greatest possible passive isolation of individuals, on the one hand, and the imposition over this fragmented "mass" of the most direct possible forms of control by means of the permanent one-way transmission of directives to it from above.

The passivity of the spectator is facilitated by the very conditions of film presentation. Most contemporary Hollywood films provide little or no space for the audience to supply their own insights. It is not only the content of the film—the plot and the action—that limits the participation of the observer. The techniques of film-making embody these limitations as well. Rarely do recent films allow the characters to portray ordinary activities. Unlike the important efforts of Japanese and European filmmakers to fix the camera directly on the action and permit the scene to work "itself" out, American films are characterized by rapid camera work and sharp editing whose effect is to segment the action into one- or two-minute time slots, paralleling the prevailing styles of television production. The American moviegoer, having become accustomed in TV watching to commercial breaks in the action of a dramatic presentation, is believed to have become incapable of sustaining longer and slower action. Therefore the prevailing modes of film production rely on conceptions of dramatic time inherited from the more crass forms of commercial culture.

The film-maker who subordinates the action and the characters to his concept of dramatic time, reveals a politics inside technique that is far more insidious than "reactionary" content. When viewed from this perspective, the film-maker, such as Howard Hawks, who refuses to subordinate art to the requirements of segmented time, becomes more resistant to authoritarianism than the liberal or left-wing film-makers who are concerned with the humanitarian content of film, but have capitulated to techniques that totally reduce the audience to spectators. Some specific examples may serve to illustrate this point.

The Japanese film *Tokyo Story* depicts the relationship between an aging small-town couple and their children, who have left both house and town for big-city life. The director, Ozo, takes pains to simulate the rituals of daily life by focusing the camera on the minute details of such activities as packing a suitcase with the folding of linen and clothes shown in careful, deliberate movements. Similarly, John Huston's *Fat City*, a tale of a fallen prize-fighter deteriorating into insentient anonymity, shows this development by paying as much attention to such comparatively mundane activities as drinking a cup of coffee in a greasy-spoon restaurant as it does to angry scenes of a degenerating love affair. Huston is not completely faithful to his project; the film sometimes lapses into the techniques of compressed space and time. But it is clear that *Fat City*, albeit without political content, embodies an attempt to reverse the tendency of Huston's contemporaries to cut out the reality of daily life in the swift continuum created by the editor's scissors. There is time in these films of Huston and Ozo to reflect on the meaning of events, on the peculiarities of the characters, on the infinite oppressiveness of social time. Contrast this orientation with the never-ending whirl of *The French Connection, Straw Dogs,* and *Clockwork Orange,* where the content is matched perfectly by the authoritarian, one-dimensional quality of a technique that reinforces the feeling that reality has completely unfolded before the eyes, completely enveloping the senses, with little space or need for exercise of the mind.

There is no intention here to argue for a Brechtian view of the didactic function of drama. Indeed, Brecht's genius for engagement of the audience on the emotional as well as the intellectual plane persists despite his own intention of creating distance in order to allow for thought. Yet, without the distantial element in plays or films, the control of communication remains in the hands of those who produce the films. And the immediacy by which the consumption of the film or television show occurs militates against the participation of the audience unless the presentation offers an opportunity for participation within its own structure. This opportunity can be provided by the self-consciousness of the producer—his commitment to subordinate the camera to the characters and the action rather than making the montage a handservant of the director as *auteur*.

— 6 —

Fortunately, despite the present tendency toward the increasing employment of the media in the interests of creating a totally closed ideological universe and an increasingly programmed totalitarian society, there are contradictions inherent in the very nature of the mass media and the culture industry, which ultimately place limits on their capacity as instruments of integration and which may even, under certain circumstances, operate so as to transform them into disruptive forces undermining an existing consensus. Above all, these constraints on the ability of late capitalism to transform culture into an instrument of adaptation arise from the fact that in addition to its ideological content, culture is also a *praxis* and in the broadest sense a means of production (that is, in the sense that the conception of production encompasses not only the production of capital and of commodities but also the production of social relations and of individuals). This implies that culture is not a mere derivative factor in social development but an active force in the historical process by which human beings produce their own modes of existence. It also implies that there is a necessary feedback between the instrumental activities (for example, social labor in the context of a specific system of production relations) by which the material substructure of society is produced and the symbolically mediated activities (for example, creativity, play, imagination, and so on) by which the human beings in a particular society organize their everyday life and give meaning to their existence. What this means is that while a ruling class can appropriate existing cultural forms and symbols and to a certain extent convert them into means of legitimizing its hegemony, it cannot *create* culture any more than it can create means of production. It thus depends in the last analysis on the exercise of creativity by others as they attempt to adapt their everyday lives under the impact of socio-economic changes.

This appropriation of social creativity, as Gramsci and others have pointed out,[27] is in part accomplished through the mediation of intellectuals, of artists, and of specialists who in a sense function, on the one hand, as mediators between the summits of institutional power and the various spheres of everyday life, and, on the other, as "organizers" of culture who elaborate the structures which lend it a legitimate appearance of unity or coherence and give institutional authority its apparent universality. In this way, such intellectual or cultural workers fulfill a vital need for the ruling class. Without overt creativity it would be impossible for a ruling class to maintain the ideological domination which in the last analysis is vital to the reproduction of its power. Herein, however, lies a crucial contradiction: In order to provide the functions so essential to the legitimation of power, it is essential for the cultural producers to remain distinct from power. As Henri Lefebvre has shown, creativity can only be provided by groups that are simultaneously *social* and *extra-social*. "Poets, artists, creative intellectuals derive their inspiration from a marginal situation [for only] marginal groups can perceive and grasp society in its totality through the elaboration of significant representations."[28] Nevertheless, the very society that depends on the exercises of creative artists and intellectuals, in the act of appropriating their expressions, tends to undermine their marginality by subjecting them to the norms and imperatives of the ruling class and state apparatus. As pressure, repression, seduction, or compensation are employed to make creation *functional* to the system, the creative groups are reintegrated or destroyed. As a result, even contemporary mass culture cannot reduce art totally to propaganda without placing itself in peril. To put it another way, we may say that mass culture contains a contradiction between the ideological need for stability, equilibrium, and integration, on the one hand, and a latent need for creativity and innovation, on the other. The former calls for the degradation of the artist and the intellectual into a mere functionary; the latter demands that he or she retain a degree of independence and a capacity for critical thinking. Thus, even though the work of artists or film-makers may remain strongly tied to the norms of the dominant consensus and of the system of class domination, it also may to some extent contain a critique of reality.

Such critical content is, to some degree, presented in Bogdanovich's *The Last Picture Show*. The quality of life in Bogdanovich's small town in mass society is far from the idyllic sweetness of Thornton Wilder's *Our Town* or even the crass, bourgeois comfort of Peyton Place. Even the film *Superfly*, which in many ways attempts to parrot white films of the same genre, retains an understanding of the Black underworld figure as a person seeking to find autonomy and self-determination in a world that is monopolized by white businessmen. The hero of the film, a cocaine dealer, is a sympathetic figure, a person who lives by a serious moral code and who, while forced to play a game dictated from above is never so involved in it that his critical sensibility is dulled.

Film comedy has revealed flashes of social satire in recent years. Woody Allen's portrayal of the congenitally unsuccessful lover whose fantasy life is the only aspect of his existence that has ontological status in *Play It Again, Sam* can be seen as a comment on the vacuousness of daily life in our society. His ultimate criticism of this way of life is vitiated by the triumph of his romantic fantasies borrowed from the renunciations of Humphrey Bogart's last scenes in *Casablanca*. However, the marvelous spoof on the compulsively ambitious lawyer-husband of his confidante is the high point of the film and successfully retains its critical orientation. Other satirical attempts such as *The Ruling Class* are less successful, but illustrate the contradiction between creativity and conformity in commercial film.

To be sure, if it were simply a matter of isolating, neutralizing, or taking over those critical or radical themes which might appear in contemporary films or media presentations, the repressive system would be in no way threatened. However, the contradictions between creativity and the fixed forms of the existing culture are not confined to the specifically "cultural" institutions and media or to particular artistic and intellectual milieux. Rather, creative expression on this level is closely linked to impulses arising out of the everyday life and activity of the working masses who form the "public" for the culture industry. More specifically, the cultural producer does not work in a vacuum nor is he or she necessarily responsive only to the demands emanating from the summits of institutional power. On the contrary, despite the attempt by the ruling class to use its centralized control over the societal means of communication to restrict all public communication to one-way transmissions between centralized "transmitters" and fragmented or massified "receivers," in fact the imperatives of authentic creation—inasmuch as they require the achievement of new forms of intersubjectivity and the elaboration of new language in which to convey them—necessitate some form of two-way communication between artist and public.

It follows that innovative art or cultural productions with a content that transcends the parameters of existing social relations arise not only out of the exercise of the creator's critical powers or imagination but also in response to "messages" emanating from the masses themselves as they attempt to break free of the constraints placed on the exercise of their own creativity by the repressive institutionalization of everyday life. For example, the music of the Beatles, the Rolling Stones, and the Kinks cannot be understood simply as a further development of tendencies internal to rock as it took shape during the late fifties and early sixties. Rather, as Richard Merton pointed out in his *New Left Review* article, "*John Went for a Rock Aesthetic*," these particular expressions of individual creativity by artists such as Jagger, Lennon, or Davies, are only comprehensible in relation to the expressions of social creativity unleashed in England at that time by "the deep spontaneous revolt of working class youth against British bourgeois society which it articulated" and which, while economically rooted, took predominantly cultural, even sexual, forms. In addition to constituting what Merton termed "in the first instance a violent inner reversal of a whole complex of traditional working class values in Britain—the puritanism and utilitarianism of the national proletariat [which constitute] the deadly assimilation by the working class of the culture of its oppressors," the cultural products of this revolt also constituted a simultaneous assault on the cultural hegemony of the bourgeoisie in a number of senses. For example, just as Black music in the America of the 1960s asserted the legitimacy of "Black English" and sought to enrich its symbolic vocabulary against the linguistic colonialism of the white media and schools, English rock during this period directly assaulted the linguistic hegemony of standard "U" English with such striking success that one may even find impeccably educated upper-class English youth affecting a Liverpool accent. In a sense, Shaw's Henry Higgins has become not the teacher but the student of Liza Doolittle. Indeed, the power that British rock derived from this collective drive has enabled it to counter-colonize much vanguard American music so as to assume a position in the later 1960s of international dominance.

If white American rock lacks the social dynamism derived by British rock from its origins in the revolt of working class youth or by Black music from its connection with the struggle for Black emancipation, it does articulate, despite (or because of) its "middle class" basis, with even greater clarity than British rock or Black music, certain themes suggestive of the utopian possibilities contained in the contemporary development of productive forces tending to burst the confines of capitalist social relations. Perhaps it is precisely because these white "middle class" youths have most profoundly experienced the new forms of compulsive consumption that they are also the first to experience the shallowness of the actual satisfaction involved and, discovering this, to first demand that the promises of the media (which imply a world free of want and of brutalizing labor) be literally made good. These demands, moreover, find expression not only in the content of the products of the American youth culture, which reveals the emergence of a new sensibility—the search for new forms of human interaction, sexuality, and community, for a new attitude toward the natural environment, etc.—but also express themselves much more significantly in the search for a new aesthetic which is not limited to the sphere of the "artistic." In particular, it may be said that what is really unique and unprecedented in the new popular music and the cultural tendencies associated with it is that it creates an avenue of expression in which there is little separation of those who produce art from those who own and "consume" it. It is therefore in this sense, rather than as regards its internal characteristics as a moment in the development of musical forms, that rock can be understood as prefiguring, regardless of all its ambiguities and confusions, the structure of a future art appropriate to a postrevolutionary social formation.

As we have already suggested, these eruptions of creativity and of utopian themes such as characterized rock and Black culture in the 1960s are by no means immune to cooptation and recuperation by the capitalist culture industry. Particularly as the spontaneous currents of contestation at the base of society which gave rise to them have subsided, they have become increasingly integrated within the system of repressive consumption as a means of inducing youth or Blacks to consume the material and spiritual products of this economy and as a constant source of the new styles and products needed to reinvigorate the mass consumer culture of the "adult," white, "middle class" society in general. In a sense, we may say that these dissident cultures are *created* by youth or by Blacks, but are *produced* by the system. Indeed, the very forms taken by such subcultures reflect the success of the system in fragmenting the proletariat and isolating its components within exclusive categories such as youth, Blacks, and women. These forms, while allowing a certain positive affirmation of collective identities, also tend to preclude any unification of these strata into a revolutionary subject. Once this reductive fragmentation is effected, moreover, the new identities simply become new objects of consumption within the broader system of pseudo-satisfactions constituting contemporary mass culture.

At the same time, however, it would be incorrect to over-emphasize the system's capacity to recuperate these partial currents of opposition within culture, as is suggested, for example, by the Marcusean theory of repressive desublimation. For far from being simply a new form of the old repressive swindle, the new life styles and modes of consumption, along with their reflections in the capitalist cultural industry, also contain the anticipation of something new, something which transcends the existing system. More specifically, the seemingly superficial pseudo-satisfactions offered by mass culture signify also forms of satisfaction which attempt to escape from the realm of mere appearance and become reality. In this second sense, they represent an impulse that cannot be completely stabilized as is suggested by the continual and general increase in frustration characterizing American society, even at times of political quiescence. Inasmuch as this mounting level of frustration is leading to new eruptions of spontaneity, most notably in the emerging revolt of young workers in America, and to new expressions of mass social creativity on the part of a new generation of workers, it becomes possible at least to speculate about the possible forms of artistic or intellectual creativity which may be emerging as a basis for a popular revolutionary art and culture. The first task of such an emerging cultural revolutionary project is necessarily the critical transcendence of the limitations placed by the earlier oppositional subcultural currents of the 1960s on the further development of a proletarian subject. In particular, in place of the prevailing fragmentation of the proletariat into exclusive cultures of opposition, such as "youth culture," and "Black culture," each of whose partial character corresponds to its partial integration, it is necessary to effect a new synthesis. The struggles for liberation from racial and sexual oppression, for example, must be reunited within a project recognizing their inseparability from the emancipation of the proletariat as a whole. In addition it is necessary to encourage the formation of a language and a revolutionary symbolism capable of bridging the former barriers of noncommunication dividing the proletariat along racial, sexual, or generational lines. In effect, the project of such a revolutionary art and culture would be first of all the creation of a new proletarian "public" in place of the present mass public of atomized consumers and fragmented identities.

Such a proletarian public would be characterized not only by the universalism of the themes and symbols addressed to it, but, above all, by a new relationship between this public and the production and dissemination of culture generally. In particular, in contrast to the organization of the existing capitalist public as a mass to which "culture" is disseminated from above through a pyramidically structured communications apparatus (for example, through the one-way transmission of messages from central transmitters to atomized receivers), a proletarian public would have as its basis a new horizontal organization of communications within which all "receivers" would also be "transmitters." With the crystallization of such a proletarian public in connection with the general coming-to-consciousness of the working masses in their struggle to reappropriate society's productive apparatus and means of decision-making, culture would at last be liberated from the ghetto to which the bourgeoisie consigns it. Instead of a sphere of pseudo-gratification produced by elites and dispensed to the masses as compensation for the real poverty of their everyday lives, culture would be reintegrated into everyday life—it would be created instead of consumed by the masses in the process of their general production of their own modes of existence.

— 7 —

Over the past half-century—particularly during the last fifteen years—young people raised in the United States have developed modes of social interaction and institutions that resist to some extent the hierarchically organized authoritarian institutions of family, school, and mass culture. Whatever possibility exists for the rise of autonomous political and social perspectives among the recent generations of workers must be ascribed to these pockets of resistance against the prevailing forms of society, rather than to the latent, liberatory content of the instinctual structure. The latter explanation neither locates the emergence of the forms of resistance within a specific historical context nor does it describe the ways that young people develop beliefs and desires for social action that counter those that have been handed down from above.

The struggle between childhood and maturity is the conflict between the relatively unsocialized individual and the constraints placed on each of us to become productive laborers within industrial society. On the one hand, the rapid rise in the productivity of labor has created the conditions for the prolongation of childhood, where the "permissiveness" of modern parents is a reflection of the release of the younger generation from the world of work. On the other hand, all the institutions of daily life have been organized to make sure that childhood remains constricted and controlled by adults.

The ideologies of mobility have been joined by the development of consumerism as an ideology to win the adherence of young people to the canons of labor, even as the older religious belief in the work ethic that served to rationalize the compulsions of labor entered into its period of decline. The family, school, and mass culture have not advocated the sanctity of production for its own sake. Instead, labor has been offered as a purely instrumental activity—as a means rather than an end of human action.

To be sure, the concept of labor as instrumental to personal ends is historically rooted in the religious belief that work is activity that makes a place for you in heaven. The transformation from the concept of work as intrinsically satisfying to the acceptance of it as a necessary evil corresponds to the passing of handicraft production in which the artisan, like the artist, experienced real enjoyment in work since the product could be perceived both as the outcome of his skills and as his possession. Mass production with its minute division of labor has transformed the character of work. One gives up one's labor power to the employer, but experiences this act as giving oneself up to the machine.

Presumably, the school has prepared the young workers for the structure of alienated labor. The classroom has generated a tolerance for boredom. The external imposition of authority—exemplified in the grading system, the domination of teacher over student and the administration over both, and the discipline of departmental learning where time is divided into segments and "subjects" contained in them—is expected to provide the student with standards of conduct that will be followed in the adult life in which supervisors replace teachers and the laws replace parents.

The rewards offered for disciplined behavior constitute the ideology of late capitalism: in return for following the rules, students are promised the *opportunity,* if not the actuality, of social advancement, and the symbolic, alienated power represented by mass consumption. Beneath the inducements lies the coercive power of constituted authority to deny these privileges. Young people enter the adult world as much out of the terror of isolation and nonsurvival, in the social meaning as well as the material meaning of the term, as they enter work for its positive rewards. To have a job in America is to be a citizen. Even if unemployment no longer results in starvation, the stigma attached to idleness remains. The bourgeoisie is obliged to maintain a massive welfare system to disguise the extent to which people have been rendered technologically redundant within our social system. Higher education is a more acceptable form of unemployment, but it still derives its rationale from the idea of training for jobs rather than from learning for its own sake or as a system of welfare. Similarly, the massive standing army that has evolved from the Second World War is justified on the basis of military needs rather than its economic function. The message conveyed to youth remains: to have a job is the condition of first-class citizenship—yet another ideology of a system that produces both a huge supply of idle labor and an ever-expanding work force.

Despite the interventions of public and social institutions to thwart the development of the autonomous individual in the wake of the need to postpone the entrance of youth into the labor force, the results remain problematic. Youth enters labor with mixed feelings. On one hand, having a job is a sign of the end of childhood. The young person is proud to have his own money—not to be dependent on parents, or on the meager income of a part-time low-paying after-school job. The factory or office job may be the way to get a car, decent clothes, entertainments that have become expensive such as rock concerts, skiing, X- and R-rated movies, and drugs. But there is another side to the contract. These returns for giving up "free" time to the employer, enduring the monotony of repetitive tasks, and suffering indignities at the hands of arbitrary authority, are insufficient. The young person finds that the conditions of his labor are only partially ameliorated by the rewards of status and consumption. Thus "bounded time" becomes less endurable.

Jules Henry has pointed out how many workers tend to structure their leisure time along the lines imposed by the labor situation.[29] The structure of unbounded time reflects the conditions of bounded time. People join clubs that are organized as workplaces are organized, and participate in do-it-yourself projects that resemble labor. Many workers of the generation that grew up in America in the 1920s and 1930s lead their leisure-time lives as if on a busman's holiday because the patterns of their earlier lives did not permit of an imaginary world that defied the dominant culture. Thus the question of whether young workers will rebel against the authority relations of the workplace depends largely on the question of whether they have developed the modes of social life that counter the prevailing culture.

Prior generations accepted the routine character of their labor as an inevitable price that must be paid for steady wages. They regarded the division of labor according to which skills were degraded and quantity replaced quality as the object of production as a part of the natural order of things. Drawing on the experience of equality encountered in play and friendship during an extended childhood, youth today enter labor with the rudiments of that alternate conception that makes traditional industrial discipline anathema.

Marx's view of the significance of social production has frequently been narrowly construed to mean only that labor is required to produce for humans their essential means of subsistence: Production for sake of production. There are few among us who would agree with Peter Berger that "work is among the fundamental human categories."[30] The idea that production "is a definite form of activity of individuals, a definite form of expressing their life, a definite mode of life"[31] seems strangely archaic in a society that glorifies those who work least and encourages us to view our labor as a means to something else rather than as a way to provide us with existential meaning in life. Indeed even the mythic "Protestant work ethic" asserts not that as persons work so they achieve authenticity, but that work is the means to prevent damnation. Work in capitalist society remains instrumental for everyone, even those who believe in its virtues for religious, much less pecuniary, reasons.

Marx is among the few social theorists who held to the idea of labor as expressive of human life itself. Production, he argued, is not only carried on in order to meet basic material needs, but "the nature of individuals . . . depends on the material conditions determining production."[32] Modern pseudo-psychoanalytic ideologies that proclaim the essential identity of the individual apart from what he "does" would be taken as sheer fantasy by Marx. The statement "I am who I am" or "love me for myself" is tautological according to the Marxian perspective because it asserts no more than the sheer indeterminate existence of the person stripped of qualities that are derived from practical activity. The conceptions of the essence of the human individual as a "whole" person and of the essential character of humanity as distinct from other members of the animal kingdom have their foundation in man's continuing attempt to transform nature, according to Marx. The object of human cognition, reified as external to consciousness, is actually humanized nature, just as Man is naturalized humanity.

In holding to the view of humanity that becomes itself through social production, Marx was only following the themes developed by Hegel. The very heart of Hegel's early philosophy is the notion that man is transformed from a being of sheer existence (man without qualities) into a self-conscious subject of history through labor.[33] Labor therefore is not only a process whereby the object, nature, is subordinated to human needs, but is in itself the means of self-realization. Accordingly, it is also a mediation through which humans relate to one another and achieve mutual recognition. For Hegel the achievement of self-consciousness through the abolition of the split between subject and object—that is, thought and feeling, man and nature, I and Thou—could only be the outcome of a process during which consciousness explored a variety of alternatives.

In a remarkable way Hegel anticipated not only the later development of Marxian theory, but forms of consciousness currently extant. In his view the relations of man are those of lordship and bondage, in which the lord possesses apparent power over the bondsman by virtue of the recognition by the bondsman of that power. At first, the bondsman cannot admit that his autonomy is restricted by the domination of the lord; like all humans, he seeks freedom but can only achieve it, at first, by denying the object, that is, by withdrawing into a private world where consciousness is free of the external constraints placed upon it. Consciousness knows itself, but not its actual relations. What Hegel calls "stoicism" is the mental outlook that cannot attain freedom because it has no understanding of the social relations that restrict the achievement of that freedom.

The modern attitude of individualism that denies the real relations of domination between employer and worker in the labor process but asserts isolated and abstract freedom "in the head" achieves nothing but "the notion of independent consciousness."

Hegel's second stage along the journey to self-consciousness, is skepticism, or the "negative attitude towards otherness, to desire and labor." Here the consciousness is aware of its dominated status and acknowledges the opposition of its interests to those of the lord. In a word, this second consciousness proclaims its independence by assuming certain obligations and codes in relation to the lord without attempting to alter its own position. The hostility of the British working class to the bosses is an excellent instance of this mode of consciousness. No working class in the capitalist world is more aware of itself as a class and yet so culturally dominated by its class enemy. British workers have formed a class party, constituted themselves in powerful labor organizations, developed their own autonomous social and cultural institutions including specifically working class pubs, sports activities, music, and language. But the pride of class is mingled with reverence for the monarchy, a fierce sense of national as well as class interest. Skepticism retains the split between subject and object even as it acknowledges its relationship.

In the skeptical attitude, the split between lord and bondsman is resolved falsely by the introjection of the lord's domination within the bondsman. This introjection "abolishes" the lord by incorporating him within the collective self. But the "abolition" means that the lord now resides within the bondsman and, just as modern workers become patriotic in behalf of the capitalist state even as they oppose the employers in the plants, the contradiction remains unresolved. Thus, the religious attitude, or the unhappy consciousness, results from the negation of the "bad" side of the bondsman, that is, the side that represents the alienated self, or the lord. The negation produces an unchangeable, that is alienated, spirit or being. For Hegel, God is created by man in the attempt to cancel consciousness that is unable to be at home with itself. God is the return to self as alienated spirit—and demands the subordination of consciousness. Yet the guilt associated with the existence of the bad self creates ascetic attitudes that regard work as punishment and call forth the repression of enjoyment and desire.

Marx drew out the implications of the contradictions by asserting that the resolution to the lordship/bondsman relationship can be found neither in religion nor in class-consciousness nor in personal liberation that denies rather than deals with the world. For Marx, the abolition of both lordship and bondage was the fundamental condition of freedom. Just as Hegel pointed out that the position of the lord, even if it appeared dominant, was actually subordinate to that of the bondsman because only the bondsman could appropriate the object, nature, into self, Marx argued that the modern proletariat was the only class capable of achieving freedom because it alone transformed nature through social production. While lordship desired the recognition of the bondsman as a condition of its existence, the bondsman was truly autonomous since its labor constituted true freedom. Marx demanded that the bondsman throw off the ties that chain him to the system of production in which the lord remains the controlling force. But the self, in the Marxian paradigm, cannot be autonomous unless the relation itself is overthrown, not just the lord.

The condition of capitalist survival, then, is the trivialization of labor in terms of the psychic self while its significance in relation to physical needs is retained. Under modern conditions, the self is only realized in the world of leisure, which now becomes the location for autonomy rather than work. The important question of the *purpose* of production is removed in consciousness from its historical context, and the notion of self-transformation and expression of humanity through work is obscured by the instrumental character of labor. It is important that labor retain its completely alien purpose if workers are to accept it as a form of life activity. For if workers become imbued with the notion of production for its own sake, that is, if they expect to measure themselves as well as others by what they produce rather than by its material reward, then the critique of capitalist society becomes devastating.

That is why, with few exceptions, workers expect nothing instrinsically meaningful in their labor, and satisfy their desires for craftsmanship in the so-called "private realm." For example, tens of thousands of young people have become "car freaks." The automobile is invested with much more than reified status or power. It has become a vital means for the realization of the frustrated need to make a direct link with the totality of material production for youth who are condemned to either the fragmented labor of the factory or the office or the truncated learning of the school. Similarly, the widespread playing of musical instruments reflects the impulse toward the transformation of "work" into "play."

But the consignment of these activities to leisure perpetuates the split between labor and private life. Under present conditions this split is absolutely necessary because youth cannot find pleasure in their jobs. Thus the "unhappy consciousness" relegates creativity to the fantasy life and enables the person to accept more easily the inevitability of alienated labor. Under conditions where the work situation appears irrational in relation to private activities, the split becomes increasingly difficult to maintain. Occasionally, the desire for fusing work and play is manifested right on the assembly line in water fights or in the invention of fantasy games that each worker uses to get through the day. Production becomes a mathematics game or a game of speed, and is converted to something other than itself in the imagination. These devices to inject the pleasurable into the performance of the most monotonous operations are fairly common.

On a more sophisticated level, workers survive their jobs by attempting to create forms of social intercourse with one another. One important form is the collective organization of self-help on the production line where workers perform identical work. In Lordstown, for example, workers have switched jobs with one another against the wishes of management, or spelled each other to relieve the fatigue and tedium. Often, workers use these occasions to talk to one another rather than enduring the isolation engendered by the deafening noise of the factory. While one person does the work of two, the other helps make the job easier by placing tools in their most convenient places, and carries on a conversation at the same time. These highly "illegal" arrangements are opposed by management because they occur in defiance of its authority and attempt to overcome the fragmentation that is a critical precondition for the maintenance of management's power to direct the work force. But such efforts are, at best, partial because they do not confront the nature of the work itself. They do not challenge the fact that no worker can comprehend the production process as a whole, that the choice of commodity is still the decision of the employer. While the new illegal work arrangements imply criticism of the kind of tasks workers are obliged to perform, this criticism is rarely made explicit.

The suppressed desire for work that is satisfying, that expresses the creativity of the person, that is not a denigration of human intelligence, has become more acute in the age of automatic production, where the worker is reduced to a watcher, almost an observer of the labor process. In the oil industry, in paper mills, in food processing, even the narrow range of decisions available to the machine operator has been removed from his control. The opportunity for a fragment of autonomy is reserved for a few technicians and maintenance mechanics who are responsible for keeping the machine going. Thus, the crisis of work has become exacerbated by modern production. No effort to reintegrate the individual with himself that ignores this phenomenon can hope to do more than scratch the surface of the problems associated with human alienation unless the issue of production is addressed directly. Neither the "human potential" movement that has emerged out of the anomie of middle class existence nor other attempts at the reunification of the human personality with its divided self have been willing to confront the possibility that the soul cannot be healed unless divided labor is reintegrated, unless the lost "instinct of workmanship" is found within the sphere of ordinary labor rather than becoming an "avocation."

One of the most interesting reflections of the attempt to deal with alienated labor is the tendency among some young people to return to the land, or, alternatively, become mechanics, artisans, and small proprietors. These are the people who refuse to remain atomized or to find symbolic power within the sphere of consumption. Their aspirations are usually framed within the ideology of autonomy ("I want to be my own boss"). Although these alternative conceptions of work are ultimately an avoidance of the larger issue of the separation of the person from commitment to work within the mainstream of industrial society, they are signs of a recognition that the problem exists and demands practical solutions. Yet, the artisanship that can be found on the economic margins of society remains the solution of the few, while the many are condemned to stay enslaved to the machine. Moreover, such efforts cannot be successful even for those who choose proprietorship. In the first place, small farming has become economically unfeasible, even for communes. Since agriculture is now big business requiring substantial capital investment in order to be competitive, many communal arrangements relying on the income derived from the land have collapsed beneath the economic weight of inadequate mechanization even when they have been able to withstand the interpersonal strains. Secondly, thousands of small businesses fail every year, even though there are always a great number of new attempts to make a living by starting small retail shops or artisan services. The standardization and interchangeability of parts, the proliferation of mechanical means of diagnosis of car and appliance defects, and the growing centralization of repair services in chains and dealerships have robbed the old repair mechanic of considerable skill and economic viability. Some handicraft specialties survive by charging exorbitant prices in order to compete with machine-made shoes, pottery, and jewelry. But these are the exceptions rather than a serious alternative to mass production.

Modern society has systematically denied the desire for instrinsic work satisfaction for the overwhelming majority of people. Moreover, the ideologies of instrumental labor and consumption have been generated in order to purge such desire from consciousness. On the other hand, the Calvinist work ethic is promulgated, albeit in a deformed way, for the purpose of making sure that a labor force is reproduced that willingly accepts the necessity of deferred gratification through labor. The double bind contained in these conflicting ethical precepts cannot be resolved within the framework of the imperatives of rationalized industrial production. Spontaneous revolts at the workplace, sabotage, and dropping out are only the most visible responses to the refusal of workers to accept the fact that they must live with the contradiction.

NOTES

1. Herbert Marcuse, *One-Dimensional Man*, Boston, Mass., Beacon Press, 1964.

2. V. I. Lenin, *Imperialism: The Highest Stage of Capitalism* in *Selected Works*, Vol. V, New York, International Publishers, 1943.

3. Wilhelm Reich, *The Mass Psychology of Fascism*, New York, Orgone Institute Press, 1946.

4. Wilhelm Reich, "What is Class Consciousness" in *Sex-Pol*, edited by Lee Baxandall, New York, Random House, 1972, pp. 277–358.

5. Herbert Marcuse, *Eros and Civilization*, Boston, Mass., Beacon Press, 1955.

6. Sigmund Freud, *Civilization and Its Discontents*, London, Hogarth Press, 1949.

7. Anthony Wilden, "Marcuse and the Freudian Model: Energy, Information and Phantasie" in *Salgamundi* Nos. 10–11, Fall 1969, Winter 1970, pp. 196–245.

8. Talcott Parsons, *The Social System*, New York, Free Press Paperback Edition, 1964.

9. See especially Talcott Parsons, "Social Classes and Class Conflict" in *Essays in Sociological Theory*, New York, Free Press Paperback Edition, 1964, pp. 329–35.

10. Talcott Parsons, *The Social System, op. cit.*

11. Jean Piaget, *Play, Dreams and Imitation in Childhood*, New York, Norton & Co., 1962.

12. Brian Sutton-Smith, "Piaget on Play: A Critique" in *Child's Play*, edited by R. E. Herron and Brian Sutton-Smith, New York, John Wiley & Sons, 1971, pp. 326–36, and "A Reply to Piaget: A Play Theory of Copy," *Ibid.*, pp. 340–42.

13. Stanley Aronowitz, "The Trap Environmentalism" in *Social Policy*, Sept.–Oct., 1972.

14. Herbert Marcuse, *Eros and Civilization, op. cit.*, pp. 170–74.

15. Hugh Duncan, *Communications and Social Order*, New York, Oxford University Press Paperback, 1968, p. 329.

16. I am indebted to Ernest Marraccini of Teachers' College, Columbia University, for letting me read his ethnographic descriptions of children's play in New York City playgrounds, Unpublished paper.

17. Philippe Aries, *Centuries of Childhood: A Social History of Family Life*, New York, Vintage Books, 1962, p. 411.

18. E. P. Thompson, "Time, Work Discipline and Industrial Capitalism" in *Past and Present* No. 38, Dec. 1967, pp. 56–97.

19. Michael Katz, *The Irony of Early School Reform*, Boston, Mass., Beacon Press, 1968.

20. *Ibid.*, p. 88.

21. Colin Greer, *The Great School Legend*, New York, Basic Books, 1972.

22. Joseph C. Grannis, "The School as a Model of Society" in *The Learning of Political Behavior*, edited by Norman Adler and Charles Harrington, Glenview, Ill., Scott Foresman & Co., 1970, pp. 139–48.

23. *Ibid.*

24. Noam Chomsky, *Aspects of the Theory of Syntax*, Cambridge, Mass., The M.I.T. Press, 1965, second paperback printing, 1969, p. 57.

25. Aaron Victor Cicourel and John I. Kituse, *The Educational Decision Makers*, Indianapolis, Indiana, Bobbs-Merrill, 1963.

26. Siegfried Kracauer, *From Caligari to Hitler*, Princeton, N.J., Princeton University Press, 1947.

27. Antonio Gramsci, *Selections From the Prison Notebooks*, New York, International Publishers, 1971, pp. 3–23.

28. Henri Lefebvre, *Everyday Life in the Modern World*, New York, Harper Torchbooks, 1971.

29. Jules Henry, *Pathways to Madness*, New York, Basic Books, 1972.

30. Peter Berger, *Some General Observations on the Problem of Work*, New York, The Macmillan Co., n.d., p. 211.

31. Karl Marx and Frederick Engels, *The German Ideology*, Moscow, Progress Publishers, 1964, pp. 31–32.

32. *Ibid.*

33. Georg Wilhelm Frederich Hegel, *The Phenomenology of Mind*, second edition, London, George Allen and Unwin, fourth impression, 1955.

PART TWO

The Formation of the American Working Class

3

The Formation
of the Industrial
Working Class

— 1 —

In 1894, Frederick Jackson Turner published his celebrated essay on *The Significance of the Frontier in American History*. The importance of the essay consisted in its attempt to distinguish social and economic development in America from that of all other Western countries. Turner was writing in a period when world capitalism was being severely tried. Indeed, in the last two decades of the nineteenth century, it appeared that the social breakdown Marx had predicted a generation earlier in the *Communist Manifesto* was in the process of being fulfilled. On the one hand, economic crisis had already become a routine feature of expansion. In the great cities of Western Europe and the United States, the lower classes were faced with the prospect of periodic unemployment. Economic growth was spasmodic, rather than smooth, and even some groups among the ruling classes were becoming concerned with the squalor characteristic of the industrial towns. On the other hand, the workers were not silent: in Western Europe Marxists and anarchists were successfully establishing their leadership within the working class, and there was a dramatic growth of socialist and trade union movements in all Western capitalist countries.

Although the United States was no exception to the general rule, Turner recognized certain unique features in both the pattern of American capitalist development and the rise of the working class movement. His thesis had the virtue of synthesizing ideology with history. His main object was to show why the American working class did not choose to affiliate itself with the revolutionary doctrines that had been infused into the European working class. In addition, he was interested in explaining the rapid success of American capitalist development after the Civil War. The gist of Turner's contribution was that, in the absence of a feudal tradition that would constrain economic development and class mobility, the distinctive feature of the American nation was its vast internal expanse, much of it still uninhabited, that constituted an effective safety valve for discontents among the underlying population.

In contrast, Germany, the one European country embarking on the high road of economic development, was mired in feudal conditions typical of Western Europe. Even as European capitalism destroyed the old mode of production by force and violence, it had been obliged to accommodate itself to the old hierarchies and aristocracies. In fact, members of the old nobility in many European countries transformed themselves into new capitalists rather than give way to elements of the subordinate social classes of the old regime. In this sense, there was very little social mobility for the peasants in the transition from feudalism to capitalism.

Turner did not attempt to deny historical reality: American economic growth had had its characteristic turbulence. Indeed, the frequency of panic and depression was no less than in other capitalist countries. But there had been no need for the American worker to seek revolutionary solutions to the problems of poverty and unemployment. The availability of cheap land that was open to settlement by workers in times of depression prevented socialists and anarchists from spreading their doctrines of class war among the working class of the larger cities.

Turner found that by 1890 the internal frontier had closed, with the expansion of railroads into the west resulting in the spread of industrial concentrations and the creation of large cities. In addition, agricultural production was becoming increasingly centralized in large units utilizing mechanized technologies that were simply not available to the small farmer. But in his view the closing of the frontier would not necessarily usher in a new period of class struggle: as Marcus Lee Hansen has pointed out, "The frontier theory had ceased to be merely a theory: it has become the basis of a program of action."[1]

Turner himself offered the answer of technological development to the dilemma faced by American capitalism in the wake of the closing of the internal frontier. Others were offering another way out. Admiral Mahan, John Fiske, Woodrow Wilson, Theodore Roosevelt, and others, argued that the frontier should not stop at the Pacific borders of the United States. Fiske's doctrine of Manifest Destiny made legitimate the expansion of United States interests throughout the world. Roosevelt's Secretary of State, John Hay, transformed doctrine into policy when he declared that the new basis of American foreign relations was the guarantee of an "open door" for American goods and capital in China, and, by extension, in the entire world.

In a major strain of radical thought, exemplified particularly by the work of William Appleman Williams and Paul Sweezy, the expansionist character of United States capitalism in the twentieth century is seen as the critical deterrent to the formation of revolutionary or even class consciousness among American workers.[2] To be sure, these theorists reject Turner's idea that a rigid system of social stratification is absent in America. Yet Sweezy, particularly, relies heavily on a reinterpretation of Turner's frontier thesis for his explanation of the failure of the working class in the United States and other advanced capitalist countries to fulfill its "destiny" as the historical revolutionary subject.

Similarly, according to Marxists who follow Lenin's discussion of imperialism, the success of capitalism in finding solutions for its structural tendency to crisis is attributable chiefly to its capacity to subjugate the less developed world. The fruits of conquest, manifested in the superprofits derived from the exploitation of raw materials and the superexploitation of labor through the export of capital are shared with a narrow stratum of the working class in the metropolitan countries. To be sure, according to Lenin, the mass of workers in advanced countries remained imprisoned by unrelieved exploitation of their own labor. In his view, the nonrevolutionary character of the Western working class as a whole had its roots in the domination by skilled workers and the reformist trade union and Socialist leaders over the entire labor movement. In turn, the success of imperialism provided the material underpinning for the development of reformism both as ideology and political practice.

There can be no quarrel with the characterization of the working class in the United States as nonrevolutionary; But the attribution of reformism to the ability of advanced capitalism to generate a social surplus sufficiently large to buy off the decisive sectors of working class leadership ignores the structure of the working class itself within advanced capitalism as a factor limiting political working class consciousness. Moreover, even if Lenin's thesis is correct, it fails to explain the apparent acquiescence of the unskilled and semiskilled workers to the perfidy of the leadership of the labor movement. Clearly, the most exploited workers could have resisted the direction of the labor aristocracy. A final objection must be offered: Both Turner and the radical theorists who offer economic expansion and contraction as explanations for the development of class consciousness or its failure, ignore the power of the cultural apparatus and the influence of the hierarchical organization of labor within the working class in generating ideologies and interests that vitiate the emergence of solidarity. The effectiveness of external expansion in overcoming the chronic tendency of American capitalism toward economic crises that result in large-scale unemployment, lowered production, and sharply declining rates of profit, is only a partial explanation for the configuration of working class consciousness. It is one-sided because it assumes that this consciousness is a function of the expansion of capital but forgets that capital is produced in specific circumstances. American capitalism developed within a social structure that was essentially hierarchical, despite the ideologies of infinite expansion that promised to level the distinctions between social classes to the extent that growth provided room for mobility. The scarcity of labor at the dawn of the American industrial revolution just prior to the Civil War was certainly a strong factor underlying the relatively high wage rates offered American workers, but these benefits did not ameliorate the fact that the overwhelming majority of both immigrant and native-born workers were confined to working class occupations. It was the divisions within the working class that constituted the critical deterrent to the development of a unified working class social and political movement. These divisions were embedded in the preimperialist period of American capitalism and were sustained, in part, by American overseas expansion, but were not created by it.

The essential questions raised in this chapter concern the historical roots of the division within the working class. They are the same questions as those raised by Turner and Sweezy. However, the focus of our investigation differs from that of those who seek answers in the concentration and centralization of capital in fewer hands, its international expansion and integration, although these have been important factors in the suppression of the capitalist contradictions that remain beneath the surface. Instead, we shall concentrate on some issues having to do with the development of the working class itself, particularly its formation out of immigrant and native-born people, the social structure that emerged from the division of social and technical labor, and the ideologies and practice that were generated from these divisions.

The consensus of liberal historians following Turner has been that America came near to the fulfillment of the classical bourgeois dream of democracy and social equality. According to the leading historians of immigration, Oscar Handlin and Marcus Lee Hansen, the conservatism of the immigrant worker is partially attributable to America's fluid social structure and the opportunities available within it for geographical and social mobility. In Handlin's opinion, the immigrant was not so much interested in social change as in social justice: American society in the immigrants' eyes was a promise of deliverance from the subservience demanded by the countries of their origin. Even if America had not freed itself of social ills, the immigrant knew that here there was a chance to make a decent living (that is, more than in the old country). For his children, the immigrant believed that the sky was the limit. Handlin argues that radicalism had no chance among the immigrants: First, its doctrines were imported from Europe and were not appropriate to the American experience; in particular, the doctrine of class struggle simply did not apply to a society offering class mobility. Second, despite the large number of immigrants who affiliated with the socialist and anarchist movements in the last decades of the nineteenth century, the major trend in the labor and radical movements was with a strong anti-immigrant bias. We may find corroboration of Handlin's thesis in the fact that even Samuel Gompers, an immigrant from England, led the fight for legislation to restrict immigration in the early years of the twentieth century. Native-born socialists such as John Spargo, a leading Socialist Party theoretician, as well as social trade unionists like Max Hayes, who had opposed

Gompers for the presidency of the AFL in 1908, were also strong advocates of the exclusion of the foreign-born on the ground that as cheap labor they threatened the hard-won conditions of skilled American workers.

There is much evidence to show that despite the myth that the socialist and communist movements were essentially importations from Europe (or, more recently, Asia), the overwhelming majority of members of the Socialist Party in the United States in the early twentieth century were native-born Americans—71 percent in 1908, according to Charles Leinenweber.[3] Leinenweber has persuasively demonstrated that the anti-immigrant bias of the Socialist Party and the radical movement is among the reasons why these groups generally never made significant inroads among immigrant workers. Indeed, both the leadership of the AFL and many leaders of the left as well as the right wings of the Socialist Party believed strongly that the "new" immigrant from Eastern and Southern Europe was unorganizable, if not completely undesirable. Since Eastern and Southern Europeans constituted the preponderance of the unskilled and semiskilled workers in large-scale American industry by 1910, the failure, or rather, refusal, to organize them was quite decisive in alienating the immigrants from the Socialists.

Up to the First World War, both the Socialists and the trade union movement found much of their support among skilled workers and professionals who were either native-born or part of the Northern European immigration. The large segment of Eastern European immigrants who affiliated with the left wing of the Socialist Party became much more influential only after the split in the party following differences regarding the question of affiliation to the new Communist International in 1919.

The fledgling Communist Party relied heavily for support on the foreign language federations, groups deeply influenced by the success of the Russian Revolution. Their membership was largely working class in composition, and provided many leading cadres of Communist Party leadership in the 1920s. Contrary to the Socialist Party experience, the Communist Party found comparative difficulty in establishing roots among native-born, English-speaking workers, even though its national leadership was graced by members who had been long-time trade union and radical organizers among these very workers—particularly William Foster, Elizabeth Gurley Flynn, Earl Browder, James Cannon, Charles Reuthenberg and others.

In 1917 Morris Hillquit, one of the best-known leaders of the Socialist Party, was the party's candidate for Mayor in New York City. The central issue of his campaign was the Socialist opposition to the World War, and Hillquit allied on most issues with the party's ideological left wing. But on the question of immigration, he had this to say:

> The Socialist Party of the United States favors all legislative measures tending to prevent the immigration of strike-breakers and contract laborers, and the mass importation of workers from foreign countries brought about by the employing classes for the purpose of weakening the organization of American labor and lowering the standard of life of American workers.[4]

On the surface, Hillquit's opposition to immigration appeared to be a function of a prolabor class struggle philosophy. His belief was that the only justified immigration was that based on a policy that attracted the highly skilled and professional strata among Europeans:

> The majority of American Socialists side with the trade unions in their demand for the exclusion of working men of such races and nations as have not yet been drawn into the sphere of modern production, and who are incapable of assimilation with the working men of the country of their adoption and of joining the organization and struggles of their class.[5]

Reflecting a majority within the Socialist Party, Hillquit in effect opposed the immigration of peasants, making the judgment that since they were unorganizable owing to the pre-capitalist character of their labor they were undesirable from a labor and Socialist point of view.

The Socialist and trade union hostility to immigration was rooted in the deteriorating economic position of skilled workers after the Civil War. The rise of modern industry, contrary to popular belief, did not result in the elevation of skills, but their degradation.

The effect of the rise of machine technology was to allow unskilled and semiskilled workers to occupy crucial positions within the production process. Until the last decades of the nineteenth century, technological change in the period of industrialization was not mainly the product of the work of independent inventors, trained as scientists and engineers; it was the product of the work of artisans and semiskilled workers. The later development of science and engineering as professions represented a stage in the evolution of the social, not the technical, division of labor. Such men as Thomas Edison and Henry Ford, who have made the Horatio Alger myths an effective ideology, were mechanics first and inventors only as a concomitant of their labor. Engineers, such as Frederick W. Taylor, were engaged not in the invention of machinery, but in finding alternate means of organizing production in order to increase output. Artisans, on the other hand, engaged themselves in ways that lightened their work load by finding means of transferring tasks to the machine.

While, on the one hand, the Socialists and other groups opposed the importation of immigrants of peasant origins because they were "unorganizable," employers, on the other hand, gradually became resistant to the mass immigration of skilled, Northern European groups. Prior to the 1880s, the fledgling iron and steel industry had welcomed the importation of skilled workers from England and Scotland who had long experience as artisans in British manufacturing establishments; these workers were inventive of new methods designed to lighten their tasks, which of course had the anomalous effect of setting the stage for their own future redundancy. Increasingly the mechanization of the production process was welcomed by employers not only because it meant that more low-paid, unskilled labor could operate the simplified machine-based factories, but because this labor force was more manageable. Skilled workers, both those who were native-born and immigrants from Northern Europe, brought with them strong trade union and working class political traditions. English workers had fought employers in the factory and in the legislature since the eighteenth century. French workers had constituted a political force of sorts as early as the French Revolution. German artisans came to the United States following the defeat of the 1848 revolution and promptly formed Marxist study circles, published German-language workers' newspapers, and organized trade unions of skilled workers. In the United States trade union and political struggle among the native-born working class could be traced back to the Revolutionary War and continued into the nineteenth century, particularly in New York, Philadelphia, and Boston, where workingmen's parties made their appearance in 1828.

Traditionally, historians have explained the rise of American capitalism as a product of the availability of free land, natural resources, and favorable trade conditions. Consequently, the industrial revolution is seen as a natural outgrowth of the internal expansion of the American nation, and the viability of its mercantile class and ideology. And there can be little doubt that these factors constituted a tremendous impetus for the transformation of cottage industry and the putting-out system to the factory system in the 1850s. But the influence of another factor upon the unique character of the American industrial revolution is too often ignored—the importance of capitalist agriculture, particularly in the South, in stimulating capital formation. The Black slave labor that produced cotton and tobacco, accounted for nearly 30 percent of the U.S. labor force in most of the years prior to the Civil War, and was about 40 percent of the farm labor force in 1860. Moreover, in comparison to textiles, rails, and other industries generally believed to have spurred the development of the crucial iron and steel industry, recent evidence shows that it was the agricultural sector that consumed the lion's share of prewar iron production, especially in the form of farm implements.

Even after the Civil War, American agriculture remained a crucial element contributing to industrial growth. The significance of agriculture in the process of capital formation can hardly be underestimated. According to Stanley Lebergott, agriculture continued to account for over half the labor force until some time between 1880 and 1890.[8] The cash crops of tobacco and cotton and the tremendous wheat production of the central plains region constituted the base of the industrialization process. The Northern financial interests that controlled the tobacco and cotton crops contributed heavily to capital investments in manufacturing industries, while wheat became an important export crop as well as a source of relatively cheap and plentiful food for the burgeoning industrial labor force (thus permitting relatively lower wages).

The efficiency of agricultural output in the United States became a powerful pressure on the development of European agriculture and industry. American agriculture was among the crucial factors influencing both the pace of industrial growth at home and the acceleration of capitalist farming in Europe that often led to a mass population exodus from the least efficient lands of peasants. Thus it helped set those forces in motion at home and abroad that brought millions of immigrants from European lands to America's factories and farms, and to the growing European cities as well.

Brinley Thomas has pointed out that a major fraction of total capital formation was spurred by the increasingly large number of immigrants arriving on America's shores who not only were important sources of labor power to assist the transformation of American industry, but generated investments in construction industries, particularly residential construction and transportation. These industries, in turn, created demands for capital goods, particularly iron and steel.

The American industrial working class then, was formed on the base of the highly successful agricultural industry and its offshoot, the construction industry, that arose largely to create the infrastructure of canals, roads, and rails that made the United States an important exporter of agricultural commodities; this industry, in turn, formed the base of an accumulation of industrial capital at an extremely rapid rate compared to Europe.

The basic elements that constituted the substance of the industrial working class in the years after 1850 were the following: (1) native-born artisans who had occupied crucial positions within handicraft industries dating back to the years prior to the American Revolution; (2) a relatively small number of farmers, principally from New York State and New England, who came to the cities and towns in the 1830s and 1840s instead of going west, an alternative that was fraught with uncertainty. On the other hand, the cities of the northeast were beckoning displaced farmers with jobs; (3) German, French, Scotch-Irish, English, and Welsh immigrants who came to the United States possessing definite industrial skills, particularly in textiles, iron, and mining; (4) Irish peasants who emigrated from Southern Ireland in the wake of the well-known potato famine, and Chinese. The Irish and Chinese constituted the first genuine American proletariat. They were propertyless in the historical sense of possessing neither capital nor land, as well as in the modern sense of possessing no skills that would give them status within the industrial system. They were employed principally in railroad construction, where large numbers of unskilled laborers were required.

The Southern and Eastern European migration to the United States did not begin in earnest until the 1880s. It is important to realize that Southern and Eastern Europeans were brought to this country to occupy job categories in precisely the same industries that had prompted the migration of the earlier groups of immigrants. As mass production of iron, textiles, and minerals replaced artisan methods, the demand increased for unskilled workers in these industries. In the Schuylkill field in Eastern Pennsylvania, an important mining area where foreign-born workers constituted the great majority of laborers, only 4 percent of the immigrants were from Eastern and Southern Europe in 1880. By 1890 their ratio had increased to 25 percent, and, by 1900, they constituted more than half the foreign-born workers in the field—their increase corresponding to the mechanization of mining.

Similarly, in textiles, as the old crafts of the mule spinner and weaver were replaced by power-driven looms, the proportion of workers from England, Scotland, and Wales decreased as these workers were replaced in the production process by Italians, Irish, and later by Portuguese. In the iron industry, the ratio of Northern Europeans to the total number of foreign-born decreased in direct proportion to the modernization of this industry, that is, the relative decline in the numerical and technical significance of skilled labor. In 1870 the Northern European immigrants constituted 75 percent of the foreign born, among these the Irish constituted almost one half the total number—a reflection of the growing significance of unskilled labor. A decade later, this proportion dropped as the Slavs and Hungarians rose among the ranks of the unskilled, and by 1890 the significant change in the ethnic composition of the labor force was the decline of the proportion of unskilled Irish workers.

Within two decades, in the steel industry that had rapidly replaced iron, the Eastern Europeans were well on the way to occupying the preponderance of unskilled categories. As a result of the introduction of the open-hearth process, the need for unskilled labor expanded dramatically and employers chose to recruit from among the Slavs and Central Europeans rather than the Irish. The Italian immigration in the early years of the twentieth century was a product of the full flowering of the steel industry, the further expansion of unskilled rail construction labor, the rise of the clothing industry in the same period, and the growing importance of building construction concomitant with the growth of the cities.[7]

The replacement of skilled by unskilled and semiskilled labor in the industries that constituted the economic matrix of the country transformed the social position of skilled workers. They were no longer the core of productive labor. According to Leon

Wolff, "Charles Schwab [the head of the United States Steel Corporation at the turn of the century] claimed . . . that he could make an efficient melter out of an intelligent farmhand in as little as six weeks."[8] In the wake of mechanization, the highly organized skilled workers were increasingly threatened. Their union scale, once respected by employers eager to use their invaluable skills, now became an anachronism. Steel barons like Schwab and Andrew Carnegie resolved to break the economic power of the artisans in proportion to the already evident decline of their technical power.

Skilled workers were replaced, on the one hand, by semiskilled workers and unskilled laborers. On the other hand, skills were bureaucratized with the rise of engineers and technicians. These new professional groups were no longer characterized by their independent crafts or trade unions. Instead they were incorporated into management as adjuncts to supervision. Their central task was to find means to enlarge profit. This was accomplished by three devices in the 1880s and 1890s. First, by the introduction of machinery that was a direct replacement of human labor of all kinds. Second, by the rationalization of the labor process through simplification of tasks. Third, by the speedup of production and lengthening of the working day.

At first, skilled workers hailed mechanization because it promised to make labor easier and to permit the shortening of the working day. But employers were not inclined to share the benefits of technological change with them. Instead, they demanded that craftsmen agree to pay cuts and ultimately to reductions in the protections afforded by trade union agreements. Moreover, employers claimed that the new machine processes demanded continuous production in order to be economically viable. The twelve-hour day became standard in the most mechanized industries, replacing the ten- and eight-hour days that had been established through the efforts of trade unions.

The 1892 Homestead Strike became a symbol of the economic and social changes experienced by American industry. Although supported by many of the Eastern European immigrants occupying the least skilled jobs, the strike was essentially a protest by the skilled workers against the employers' assault upon their privileged position in the mills. Carnegie and his cohorts demanded nothing less than the proletarianization of the crafts. But as we shall see, despite his victory, neither industry nor the skilled workers were prepared to surrender the hierarchical division of labor within the factory. What was desired by the employers was a greater dependency by the skilled workers on the corporations. The capitalists still required technological change to achieve their goal of maximum profits. But they were equally interested in the division of the working class. The solution to these apparently contrary requirements was found in the promotion of the artisan to a supervisor or a technician, and his consequent dependence on the corporation rather than on his own strength. Those who resisted the simultaneous erosion of their skills and elevation of their status were dismissed and blacklisted from the industry. In many cases, the militant Northern European immigrant returned to Europe rather than submit to the humiliation demanded of him by employers, just as, years later, following World War I, Eastern and Southern European working class militants were forcibly evicted from the country, or in a few cases, murdered.

Skilled workers occupied economic niches within the remaining sectors of American industry less susceptible to mechanization. German craftsmen dominated the printing industry and the still-undeveloped machine tool industry where machines were as yet unable to displace the requirement for hand precision. The English and the Welsh became weighers, foremen, and technicians in the mining industry, gang bosses on the railroads (together with the Irish who moved up as the Slavs, Italians, and Blacks replaced them in common labor), and loom fixers in textiles. In the iron industry, Germans were heavily represented among the machinists; the Scotch-Irish and English remained skilled workers in the steel fabricating section of the industry that manufactured byproducts of basic steel and were employed as maintenance mechanics in the basic steel industry. Typically, the Irish and English were the foremen of labor gangs in this industry. According to David Brody, by 1910 13 percent of the recent immigrants had achieved skilled jobs and another 42 percent were holding semiskilled jobs.[9] Although he represents this development as evidence that the Southern and Eastern immigrants actually had attained social mobility, and that this accounts for their presumed docility and lack of class consciousness, the fact remains that in 1910 75 percent of the unskilled labor force in the steel industry were Southern and Eastern European immigrants. Moreover, mobility within the lowest rungs of the working class did not signify real movement between classes or a large rise in the number of skilled workers.

In 1910, even though the Northern European immigration (exclusive of Scandinavia) accounted for about 40 percent of the total male, white immigrants in the labor force, they comprised more than 62 percent of the skilled immigrant workers.[10] Workers from Great Britain and Germany were to be found in greater proportion than all foreign-born in the crucial occupational categories of the skilled, the professionals, and small proprietors. The Irish rose rapidly within the hierarchy of occupations, except among proprietors. As for the Eastern and Southern Europeans, they occupied significant proportions of the unskilled and semi-skilled ranks well into the twentieth century. Brinley Thomas has commented:

> Evidence has been presented... to show that by the end of the century, the sons of immigrants who had come from Britain and northwestern Europe were consolidating their hold on the better class jobs in a society that was gradually becoming more stratified.[11]

In contrast, among the Slav, Italian, and Hungarian immigrants, more than 70 percent were unskilled. In 1907, in the Homestead steel mill fifteen years after the strike was lost, Slavs earned $12 a week, English-speaking immigrants were in occupations earning $16, native-born whites were making $22, and Blacks, who had been brought into the mill together with Eastern Europeans to help break the Homestead strike, were earning $17. It is important to note that Blacks were more heavily represented among skilled categories than Eastern and Southern European whites at this time.

These differential wage rates corresponded to the stratification of labor based, in part, on the ethnic distribution within the hierarchies of occupations. Nearly the entire middle and upper management stratum within the steel industry, mining, textiles, and railroads were native-born or descendant from earlier Northern European migrations, particularly from England, Scotland, and, to a much lesser extent, Germany. "Native-born," referred to two distinct groups: those whose parents had been born in the United States and those whose parents arrived in the United States prior to 1850. Managers in basic industries were clearly members of the first group. In 1910 few of them were Irish or German, although later on some of these people found their way into echelons of middle management. American industry was organized, therefore, not only on a highly stratified basis with respect to skill levels or educational credentials, but on the basis of unequal access by different ethnic groups with respect to both industry and job category. For example, during the twentieth century in the clothing and textile industries, the Italians occupied a large proportion of the lowest economic niches and were joined soon after by the Portuguese. Within the New England textile industry, almost all Northern European workers remained in the skilled ranks or moved up to low and middle management. A similar division was reflected in the clothing industry, with the exception that Jews found their way into the cutting craft and became small manufacturers as the century wore on, with the unskilled and semiskilled jobs increasingly taken by Puerto Ricans in New York, wives of unemployed white miners in Pennsylvania, and unemployed textile workers in New England.

The consolidation of labor stratification meant that most Southern and Eastern European immigrants remained at the unskilled and semiskilled levels. In most cases, their "native-born" children did not become skilled workers, professionals, or proprietors. Instead, first-generation workers from these nationality groups reentered the mills as unskilled or semiskilled labor or became workers in service industries and in the public sector. As we shall see, entrance into skilled occupations was restricted as trade unions established mechanisms, such as separate seniority lists, that distinguished between crafts and the rest of the labor force: unskilled and semiskilled workers were to remain barred from skilled jobs even when they accumulated seniority. This separation was reinforced in the early part of the twentieth century by the employers as well as the skilled trades that were unionized in industries where the unskilled remained without representation. But even the rise of industrial unions in the 1930s did not radically alter this situation. Instead, skilled workers maintained their differential wage levels and seniority lists and forced even the most progressive industrial unions to accommodate to this early pattern.

The overt exclusion of the unskilled immigrant workers from the trade unions and their covert exclusion from the bulk of the radical movement did not mean that these workers failed to organize themselves or that no efforts were made by certain radical groups to organize them. They did not remain "unorganized" in the social meaning of the term, even if they could not affiliate themselves with traditional working class institutions. Instead, they formed thousands of social and fraternal groups for the purpose of mutual aid and protection against the vicissitudes of urban and industrial life. Nationwide organizations such as the Sons of Italy, the Polish National Home, the Workmen's Circle, and the German Workmen's Benefit Fund served a two-fold purpose, providing a place where persons who spoke the same language and shared the same woes could congregate as well as important services such as health benefits, burial sites, pensions, and college scholarships. Among some immigrants these benefits were provided by hometown associations, a form of small organization still popular among newer immigrants, particularly Puerto Ricans. For example, my grandmother was the leader of the Smagoner Society, an association of persons who came to the United States from a town in Lithuania. Although this organization never established a physical hall equipped with facilities for social activities—a feature of organizations like the Polish Falcons —its members were able to receive health and death benefits, similar to the benefits furnished later by industrial unions with large memberships among immigrant groups. In a few instances, particularly among Irish-born coal miners in Pennsylvania, the fraternal organization became a center for industrial struggle. The Ancient Order of Hibernians, for example, established itself with the dual purpose of serving the "welfare" needs of the large Irish immigrant population and dealing with their industrial needs as well; its members, the "Molly McGuires," led bitter miners' struggles against the coal operators in the 1870s. But, in the main, the fraternal groups were benefits-oriented, and gradually came under bureaucratic control.

There were also efforts to organize among unskilled immigrants at the workplace. The Industrial Workers of the World (IWW), a revolutionary labor union that attempted to organize workers regardless of skill, nationality, or race, made special efforts among this group because it understood that the unskilled, as well as being the most exploited group of workers, were rapidly becoming the center of capitalist industry and constituted the source of its power. "Negroes, immigrants, and migratories always served as the major objects of the IWW's efforts and (such as they were) the sources of its strengths," wrote Melvin Dubofsky.[12]

Some of the most important mass strikes in twentieth-century America were conducted among immigrants under IWW auspices. These included the Pressed Steel Car Company strike at McKees Rocks in 1909, the famous 1912 Lawrence textile strike, and the Paterson silk strike during the following year. There can be no question that the suppression of the IWW during the First World

War was due, in no small measure, to its increasing success among industrial workers between 1912 and 1914. Similarly, the hostility of the AFL and the main body of the Socialist Party to the IWW after 1912 was closely related to its assertion that the "One Big Union" was to be the center of revolutionary activity rather than the narrow craft unions or the parliamentary-minded majority of Socialists.

During World War I Bill Haywood and the other leaders of the IWW chose to concentrate on day-to-day organizing at the shop level and consciously decided to soft-pedal their opposition to the U.S. entrance into the war. In contrast, the majority of Socialists were not only opposed to U.S. involvement, but conducted vigorous efforts to prevent it. Yet, ironically, notwithstanding the imprisonment of Eugene Debs, the perennial Socialist spokesman, for speaking out against the war in 1918, the main thrust of the government wartime repression was against the IWW and those immigrants affiliated with radical movements. Indictments and convictions of IWW leaders for criminal syndicalism, deportations of immigrants, and raids on IWW offices were taking place at the same time as the Wilson administration was seeking the cooperation of the AFL in prosecuting the war and trying to persuade large corporations to recognize unions in order to preserve labor peace. The obsession of government and politically reactionary groups with the IWW was connected to the general movement against immigration that became powerful following 1910 and culminated in congressional legislation that cut back the flow of Eastern and Southern European immigrants after 1920, when, owing to the slower rate of economic growth, their labor was no longer needed.

It must be admitted that the IWW at no time came close to initiating a national movement among unskilled workers in any industry. On the contrary, it was the AFL itself that spurred the organization of the mass of packinghouse workers in 1917 and steel workers in 1919. But there can be no doubt that the IWW's impetus at Lawrence, Paterson, and in many smaller strikes generated constant pressure on the craft unions to abandon or modify their craft union philosophy and their anti-immigrant bias. The IWW had demonstrated the possibility of militant activity among immigrant workers as had the Socialist-led needle-trades unions. Samuel Gompers, the nativist and virulently antiradical president of the AFL, was never so committed to his prejudices that he could not see the handwriting on the wall. His employment of the erstwhile syndicalist and IWW member William Z. Foster in 1917 to lead the packinghouse campaign and, subsequently, the 1919 steel organizing campaign, showed that he could face reality and use it for his own ends. Gompers used radicals to bring the immigrant, unskilled workers into the House of Labor without sacrificing his control, thus pointing the way for similar techniques employed by the leaders of the CIO fifteen years later.

— 2 —

Some commentators such as Oscar Handlin have explained the relative lack of social mobility among the Eastern and Southern Europeans in this period by the theory of historical succession. According to this theory, the differences in the technical and social division of labor among immigrant groups can be traced to the periods in which they arrived in the country. Thus, one would expect "natives" to be higher-status, higher-paid citizens occupying the best jobs and enjoying the best chance for social mobility. Consequently, in this view, as successive waves of immigration occurred, the previous groups were pushed up and the new immigrants occupied the bottom niches of the occupational and social scale. According to the prevailing historical explanations, the ideal of equality was kept alive by the reality of *occupational mobility* within the working class, even if the most sophisticated among these theorists are critical of Turner's social mobility claims. Undoubtedly, only a few of the English and Scotch-Irish (from Northern Ireland and Scotland) and some Germans were able to become big capitalists, or even acquire the legendary free lands. In both cases, the crucial deterrent to mobility was the lack of capital possessed by the immigrants. At most, claims Marcus Lee Hansen, "new" immigrants, that is those from Eastern and Southern Europe, could hope to occupy better-paid skilled jobs created by the expansion of industry.

For the Eastern and Southern European immigrants, however, there was actually very little occupational mobility within the working class because industrial expansion did not create as many skilled jobs as unskilled jobs. In fact, American expansion was preeminently technological both in the sense that machines replaced human labor and in the sense of the division of manual labor into simplified tasks such as are to be found on the assembly line, in section work, in highly rationalized piecework, and in construction.

Steven Marglin, of Harvard University, has advanced a most interesting argument to explain the emergence of technologies that relied on the minute division of labor for accelerating output. Contrary to most opinion, he denies the determining role of either efficiency or the drive to maximize profit in the choice of production methods. Instead, specialization of tasks is seen as a product of the recognition by capitalists of the importance of devising technologies that maintain the crucial role of management in organizing production. With the reduction of artisan skills to relatively simple tasks, no individual worker or group of workers is able to master the intricacies of either the production process or the market, and the capitalist's centrality to the process of production and distribution of commodities, which consists in his ability to coordinate the relationship between the producers and the market, remains secure.

Marglin's attempt to demonstrate that the organization of production according to this premise historically precedes the appearance of complex machinery and was transferred to the machines socially is convincing. Less convincing is his proposition that alternate technologies would have been equally efficient in terms of physical output for profit maximization. Here the evidence is quite fragmentary, although suggestive for further investigation. In any case, it appears incontrovertible that the influence of social relations on technological methods is substantial. Moreover, contrary to Marx, who claimed that capitalist social relations constituted an historical brake on the further development of the forces of production (machinery, human skills, labor), Marglin's thesis suggests that the concept of "forces of production" as an independent variable is open to question. His assertion that these productive forces are shaped, not only advanced or retarded, by social relations casts an entirely different light on developments generally considered external to the exigencies of social struggle.[13] Just as the occupations of "scientist" and "engineer," formed out of the creative aspect of artisan labor, have been reified by professional credentials, specialization of functions and of language, and greater access to prestige, pay, and power within the capitalist social order, so technology has been separated from social relations except as an exterior force upon them. The reification of technology as an independent variable reinforces the domination of labor by capital by establishing the indispensability of the latter.

As we have noted, the substance of the professional engineer's job at the turn of the century was to organize the labor process in a way that yielded the highest possible profit. In many cases, his efforts were directed at finding ways to break down traditional skills into their components and to describe the limits of these discrete components as new jobs.[14] For example, the worker who is able to produce the whole garment must know designing, cutting, the sewing operations of darts, seams, and buttonholes, and pressing. The manufacturing process not only introduced new machines to replace hand labor, such as the electric-powered knife, sewing and pressing machines, but divided the various tasks involved into separate jobs. Further rationalization occurred when the sewing machine operator became a specialist in darts or in seams, or in buttonhole making. At each level of rationalization the versatility of skills was reduced as well as their number.

However, in clothing as well as other industries, the minute division of labor did not result in the erosion of the social category "skilled worker" even as the technical content of each job was made less demanding. Instead, workers were promoted to "skilled" jobs that bore little correspondence to the older skills in their actual operation. The formation of an aristocracy of labor in the midst of the degradation of artisan skills is one of the critical features of the history of American workers. The aristocracy was formed out of specific ethnic groups whose traditional skills had become rationalized, but whose social role was necessary for the domination of all labor within the industrial system. Skilled labor became more important as an ideological concept than its actual role in the production process warranted. The new technologies resulted in the narrowing of technical differences between "unskilled," "semiskilled," and "skilled workers." These became conceptual or labeling categories that were increasingly less rooted within the production process itself.

One way of providing justification for the position of the skilled worker or that of the industrial "professional" (who was nothing more than a skilled worker who had lost his independence either as a small proprietor or an artisan, or both) was the formalization of training. The informal methods of apprenticeship gave way gradually to formal schools that granted credentials. Even such mechanical and hand skills as are to be found in the construction trades were elevated in this manner by union and industry. A specific period was provided for training, after which the worker was certified as a craftsman. Similarly, professional training became more common as an aspect of higher education institutions in the later years of the nineteenth century. Such training became the material substratum of the ideology of skill, and disguised its ephemeral character at the point of production.[15]

The argument typically offered for this development is the alleged rise in the need for qualifications dictated by the advances in technology. Yet, the rise of the unskilled immigrant worker from peasant origins was prompted by, but did not generate, technological change. On the contrary. In the steel industry, for example, after the introduction of the Bessemer and subsequent open-hearth processes and the mechanization of the rolling mills in the years just prior to the turn of the century, there was little basic technological advance until the 1950s. The availability of cheap immigrant labor combined with the relative cheapening of the wages of all labor that was a byproduct of the smashing of unionism in steel, offered few incentives to employers for further mechanization until the rise of the United Steelworkers of America in the 1930s and 1940s; this was to have as great an impact on the technological development of the steel industry as artisan labor did after the Civil War.

Similar constraints have prevented the textile industry from advancing beyond the development of the power loom and automatic carding machine. The weakness of textile unionism corresponds to the decline in the employment of skilled labor, the increasingly peripatetic propensities of this labor-intensive industry, and the severity of international competition. Even the plentiful supply of low-paid immigrant labor could not induce the industry to remain in New England and the Middle Atlantic states in the wake of the depression in textiles that prefigured the Great Depression of the 1930s by almost a decade. Instead, the industry which had prospered when the crisis of European society in the nineteenth century sent hundreds of thousands of immigrants into the mills attempted to recover its position by preying on the crisis of American agriculture. In the period between the world wars, millions of native white and Black American farmworkers were displaced. The textile and the clothing industries moved south and found a large, unskilled labor force ready and available, even if initially hesitant about leaving the land. Lacking the skills needed for genuine geographic, much less social, mobility, Southern whites were forced to accept low wages, thus enabling the textile industry to survive. It was not until the post–World War II period that technological improvements were introduced into the mills in response to the threats of foreign competition that made even the low wage levels in this depressed industry noncompetitive in terms of the rate of profit of the industry on an international level.

In the mining industry the skills of the old Welsh craftsman were substantially eroded by the first mechanization of production in the late 1890s, but did not finally disappear until 1950, when technological advances were brought in by the companies in response to the union's success in raising wages and controlling working conditions. In the intervening years, the mines had been largely populated by immigrants from Eastern and, to a lesser extent Southern, Europe. The Northern Europeans became the aristocracy—aboveground workers or supervisors who earned higher pay and were increasingly integrated into the middle and upper echelons of the companies or left the industry for better, less-hazardous employment.

After the turn of the century, the notion of the self-made man applied accurately to those English-speaking workers of native or Northern European origins who graduated from the ranks of the skilled workers to proprietorship of taverns, or ran small shops that produced parts on contract with larger corporations, or were enticed into supervision, or remained "skilled" only in the sense that in the social division of labor within the plant they were assigned the less arduous tasks of maintaining equipment or working in such departments as the rolling mill, inspection, or administration.

Those ethnic groups found little opportunity for movement upward within the industrial structure, with a few notable exceptions—the Irish, the Jews, and to some extent the Germans and the Greeks—and most of these had been artisans and proprietors and not of peasant classes in their native lands. Irish immigrants came here in two phases. The early immigration that began in the 1840's was completed in 1860. After the 1880s a second wave arrived. Those who came in the first group were swiftly recruited for common labor in railroad construction and personal services. These jobs were plainly assigned to the bottom of the occupational structure. In the mining industry the Irish were somewhat less important until the later part of the century. By the time of the second immigration, however, the Irish were moving up the occupational scale within the working class, although they were not moving out of it as fast as other Northern Europeans. In comparison to the foreign-born as a whole, only 66 percent as many Irish became proprietors, and 81 percent as many became professionals. Yet, partially because of their familiarity with political and organizational skills, the Irish participation in clerical trades exceeded that of all other foreign-born, including other Northern Europeans.

The four hundred years of Irish struggle against Great Britain had created a broadly disseminated political culture that reached deeply into the peasantry as well as the urban poor. The rise of the Irish in city government was in part a consequence of this tradition. The large number of Irish immigrants and first- and second-generation Irish who entered city government became central to the various bureaucracies within it. In the major cities of New York, Chicago, Boston, and Philadelphia, they became the substance of the police power that was often used to break strikes and to repress dissident movements. They also had major spheres of power within fire departments, school systems, and the clerical trades that required administrative skills. There were the opportunities offered the Irish to find a way out of common labor and a place in the great American sun. To the extent that they were able to manipulate the political process to facilitate their own advancement, they became more integrated than other immigrants of peasant origin into the capitalist system and lost their native culture at a much faster pace than other immigrants who were constantly reminded of their ethnicity by occupational segregation in American industry.

It must be remembered however, that the Irish were not only important as guardians of private property, they were among its staunch opponents as well. Many of the most talented and militant working class and radical leaders were either immigrant Irish or their descendants. These included: William Z. Foster, the leading tactician of industrial unionism before John L. Lewis; his long-time collaborator, John Fitzpatrick, the leader of labor movement activities in Chicago during the years in which Foster was organizing packinghouse and steel workers on a large scale; James Larkin, the transport worker who was a leader of the Irish rebellion and, in exile, a founder of the American Communist Party; Elizabeth Gurley Flynn, IWW orator, American

Civil Liberties Union activist and Communist leader; Bill Haywood, the dynamo of the IWW. One of the most quixotic figures in the history of the American working class was Michael Quill, president of the Transport Workers Union. On the one hand, Quill's political and oratorical style owed a heavy debt to the Socialist as well as the Irish revolutionary tradition. On the other, he ran the union he headed in a way reminiscent of an Irish ward politician, with loyalty rather than talent being a main qualification for promotion of members of the union's staff. Quill would enter an alliance with anyone to advance a specific interest and would dissolve such alliances when they became obstacles to the maintenance of his political power. In 1955, he was virtually alone on the CIO side in opposition to its merger with the conservative AFL, and his argument was a model radical critique of the business unionism he so often practiced himself: the AFL had fully capitulated to the two capitalist parties; it was racist; its president, a fellow Irishman, George Meany, had once boasted that he never walked a picket line and this statement defined the deep-seated conservatism of the Federation.

Yet Quill himself was well-known for his colorful, but ultimately conservative bargaining tactics. Despite earlier years of labor party politics, Quill had supported Democratic candidates on the municipal and national level long before 1955. In fact, his leadership in the TWU was often criticized by rank-and-file opponents for its close relationship with city politicians in New York and other large cities where the union represented subway, airline, and street transport workers. Despite the declining position of the Irish within the industry and the rise of Black workers, nearly all TWU locals were dominated by the skilled workers of Irish descent.

But other Irish union leaders also maintained a certain political double standard. Until he split with the Communist Party shortly after the war, Joseph Curran of the National Maritime Union followed the CP industrial union line even as he established one of the most celebrated dictatorships within the labor movement. Tyrannical in his methods, Curran rarely hesitated to use physical force to quell his opposition within the union or, after his break with the party, to work closely with the federal government to screen his adversaries off the waterfront on the basis of their alleged Communist affiliations.

Of course, not all trade unionists of Irish background had close links with the revolutionary traditions of their homeland.

Dan Tobin of the Teamsters was the arch-opponent of industrial unionism; George Meany, whose political stance is often somewhat to the right of Richard Nixon, scrambled his way to the top of the labor movement from the plumbing trade, and was distinguished by his notorious anti-Communism while head of the New York State Federation of Labor. Joseph Bierne of the Communications Workers represents the epitome of the labor aristocrat in his ideology and practice.

Like the Irish, the Germans possessed skills in the political arena. Many craftsmen who emigrated in the 1850s had participated in the democratic revolution of 1848. They brought with them a tradition of radical activity, political sophistication, and sufficient independence as a result of their considerable industrial skills to play an important role in the formation of early labor unions and radical groups here. All over the country, while the Irish were capturing Democratic Party municipal organizations, Germans were making either the Republican Party, or, in some cases, the Socialist Party, an effective political machine to serve as another means of consolidating their positions within the mass of labor. As often as not, the emergent leaders of the urban political machines were political refugees. Carl Shurz, a powerful figure within the Republican Party, was an exile of the 1848 revolution. Many of the German Socialists who succeeded in gaining political control of Milwaukee by 1910 had been active in the growing socialist movement in their native land. Led by skilled brewery workers, machinists, and other crafts workers, the Socialist Party in Wisconsin comported itself like any political party interested in municipal power. It was undoubtedly more honest than its Democratic counterparts in the industrial Northeast, but it served the same interests: it became the keeper of the immigrant working class, dispensing benefits to the poor by cushioning the shock of the panics and depressions of the nineteenth and twentieth centuries, and providing some mobility to a selected number of immigrants of all nationalities by making possible their entrance into jobs in city government.

The Jewish immigrant experience unlike that of other groups, seems to validate the ideologies of mobility both within the working class and between classes. Proportionally more immigrant and first-generation Jews advanced to professions and white collar occupations than other groups and retained control of the trade union bureaucracies in the industries into which they had originally flowed. Of course, there were differences among Jews themselves; the German Jews who arrived here with some capital and industrial skills were able to enter business, a few rising to large business ownership. But the Eastern European Jews were not in the same position. Lacking capital, they remained part of the working class or at best rose to petty-bourgeois status as proprietors of small businesses or professionals. Yet the relative mobility of Jews in the past one hundred years has been ubiquitous beyond its social implications. Compared to other ethnic groups that comprise the critical sectors of the industrial working class, their rise in American society has been unique.

The fate of the majority of immigrants of peasant and lower class origins was sealed by the completion of industrial stratification. They remained at the bottom and achieved some degree of economic benefit from the general rise of the labor movement that increased their wages (but not as much as the skilled workers), and the expansion of American capitalism internally and abroad. Within the working class, only a few of them attained a minimum of occupational mobility, except in industries such as construction, where groups like the Italians were able to dominate the entire labor force (with the exception of the mechanical trades such as plumbing, steamfitting, ironwork, and electrical work that remain to this day the "job property rights" of the Northern European immigrants and their first- and second-generation sons). For the most part, ethnic heterogeneity of the labor force within a specific industry meant that material and status rewards were distributed differentially on the basis of broad definitions of skill. In turn, skilled and technical workers were most characteristically recruited from among those who had been urban artisans in their countries of origin. For the most part—with the exceptions noted—peasants, particularly those of Eastern and Southern European origins and the first native-born generations of these nationality groups remained unskilled and semiskilled workers.

Since the turn of the twentieth century a dominant theme in the ideology of American mobility has been the idea that the United States constitutes a melting pot in which the social and ethnic differences inherited from the European experience are destined for oblivion. The homogeneity of the melting pot was the dream of American social reformers and some immigrants. It was the cultural side of the American egalitarian ideal and was presented as the antithesis of the hierarchical organization of European society. An undercurrent of the claim that America could achieve unity within diversity was the widely held belief that only by adapting to American customs and ideals could the immigrant achieve integration into American life. The early settlement house movement, with its educational and social work among new arrivals, was quintessentially a movement for integration. It asked the immigrants to divest themselves of old country attitudes in order to find a place in the American sun. At the same time, the early settlement workers were fervent social reformers. They constantly reminded the captains of industry that their indifference to the squalor of the working class districts would lower the faith of workers in the democratic ideal and produce political disruption and labor unrest.

But even as social reformers worked tirelessly for the integration of the immigrant, neither employers nor workers were prepared to abandon the European differences of status and consciousness. In the main, immigrants brought their experience with them and held on to it rather tenaciously, despite the powerful appeals for "Americanization." In the first place, large portions of industry were ethnically divided. For example, coal operators actually built towns on the basis of ethnic identities. Some Pennsylvania mining towns were populated exclusively by Slavs, and others were largely Italian in composition. Textile and shoe manufacturing became the source of the employment of Italians in Maine, Rhode Island, and many towns in Massachusetts such as Fall River and New Bedford. Similarly, the heavy, hot labor required in the steel industry became almost exclusively the province of Poles and other Eastern Europeans. Consequently, the western Pennsylvania towns of Homestead, Braddock, McKees Rocks, and others were largely Eastern European, and large sections of Chicago's and Gary's working class districts were heavily populated by these groups. The reality that industrial labor was divided by ethnicity reinforced the old country culture. "Little Italy," "Little Poland" became euphemisms for the working class districts in many cities and towns. Until the Depression when plant closings and the precipitous decline of production forced millions of Americans to take to the road in search of work, the old country still played a major role shaping both daily life and social consciousness.

Just as the Irish and Germans brought with them their political traditions, the Eastern and Southern Europeans saw America through the prism of their peasant origins. It is important that relatively few northern Italians migrated to the United States after the turn of the century. The north became the industrial heartland of Italy and was preferable to the arduous and uncertain future offered by immigration. The most socially and politically conscious Italians remained in Italy. These were the artisans, the city proletariat, and the agricultural workers of the northern Italian regions. In contrast, most of the immigrants from Italy were recruited from the central and southern regions, particularly Sicily, an impoverished agricultural area where feudal social relations had survived well into the twentieth century. The southern regions were largely devoid of industrialization and mechanization. Lacking the means to compete with more advanced agricultural areas, Sicily became an area much like the U.S. south. Its main export was its youth and their destination was the least advanced industries of the more highly developed industrial countries of Europe and the United States.

Italian and Polish peasants provided a perfect labor force for an industrial system that demanded complete subordination of the worker to his rationalized preordained tasks and to supervision. The awe of established authority was carried over from Europe by these immigrants. Equally important, there was no room for them in their relatively overpopulated and economically underdeveloped native lands. Although the New World held nothing for them but long hours and hard work, they believed that their children would be provided for. These workers were imbued with the inevitability of social domination. They had absolutely no basis for any other beliefs. The great Italian and Polish democratic movements of the nineteenth century had barely touched the peasantry. They were movements of the urban middle classes supported at the periphery by the feeble city working classes who had barely entered manufacturing employment. Besides, these movements had failed to supplant the old monarchies that were controlled by the traditional landlord classes. Moreover, the peasants remained devoutly Catholic. Their religion was the spiritual expression of the subordination to which they were subjected in the closed world of feudal agriculture. It reinforced their concept that they had a place in the world that allowed them to predict the future on the basis of the present. Their position in society was part of the natural order of things.

The peasants brought these attitudes and the institutions that supported them to the United States. The demands of employers for absolute discipline and hard work were not difficult for them to accept. But it was difficult for them to assimilate the lack of a code of justice in the new industrial system that granted certain rights to the subordinates. The absolute power of the employer to organize and run production enforced by the early capitalists had the status of natural law for immigrants who had never participated in social rule. But even the old European agricultural commune had had a specific set of rights accorded the peasants as well as duties for which they were held responsible. The new order provided none of these benefits. Thus, the rise of unions among the unskilled in America was replete with appeals for justice in behalf of immigrant labor, that is, for a system that set limits on the power of capital just as the old feudal codes had established limits on the power of the landlord.

Capitalist resistance to unionism was both a moral and an economic issue. Employers objected to the concept of limits on their authority as much as they objected to the effect of these limits on profits. In fact the issues were connected. The old trade union contracts in which skilled workers placed a ceiling on production had been undermined by the technological improvements that transformed the individual efforts of the craftsman into the collective relationship of labor to the machine. The demand of unskilled workers for some code that would regulate relationships between the employer and worker was regarded as inimical to capital accumulation. To the extent that accumulation itself replaced the ethical code of mutual obligations of lord and serfs, trade unions were rejected by the employers. It was precisely the attempt to reestablish the old code of obligation that attracted Eastern and Southern European immigrants to the unions. At the same time, when companies learned to maintain paternal relations with employees—even to the extent of encouraging "employee representation" committees possessing merely advisory status to management—it was possible to thwart the efforts of industrial unions for many years. "Paternalism," that is, the employer practice of assuming obligations to individual workers, was widespread among coal mining and steel corporations. These obligations grew largely out of the concept of "noblesse oblige," that is, they were not contractual. Instead, notwithstanding the recognition by employers of their responsibility to the individual worker's welfare, they were based on the mutual recognition of the existing relationship of employer domination. But they granted workers no grievance machinery that would effectively constrain the arbitrary actions of the employer. The historic function of the unions was to introduce a contractual basis for mutual obligations based on recognition by the employer of the workers' power and right to withhold their labor. Yet the structure of the old aristocratic relationship is preserved in the labor contract. The power of capital over the work process is merely maintained within some limits set by negotiations.

The fact that Southern and Eastern European workers were not strongly attracted to independent labor unionism in the early years of immigration attests to the force of the old consciousness, and the awareness by employers of the importance of ethnic consciousness in keeping the workers from any form of self-organization. In the steel mills, Eastern Europeans speaking different languages were deliberately placed next to one another in the labor gangs to prevent communication and to provide a basis for enforcing one-way communications between foreman and laborer.

In the early years many immigrants regarded work in America as a temporary choice. As soon as a man earned enough money he would return to Europe and open up a small business. In fact, large numbers of immigrants returned to Europe. These were the most aggressive workers, for whom the alienating environment of this country represented nothing but a provisional defeat for their aspirations. Many of these workers were the most militant and resistant to the rapacious features of the American industrial system. After they returned, or were deported, those who remained were the ones most adaptive to the new industrial system.

— 3 —

Richard Hofstadter's apt characterization of Catholicism as "the religion of the immigrant" in American life is particularly important for understanding the consciousness of an enormous segment of the working class. For even though the Catholic Church represents only about one-fourth of the American population, its significance among industrial workers is much greater than this proportion would indicate, particularly in the great concentrations of the Northeast and Middle West.

The political influence of the church has been most evident recently in relation to such issues as abortion and education. But even more consequential has been its cultural influence. The secularization of the church in modern times has been of extreme importance in relation to its daily activities and its role in industrial society. But the process of secularization has been much slower than in other religious denominations of comparable membership. More than any other religious institution, the Catholic Church has retained its ideological ties with its feudal heritage. Predictably, it has failed to develop a coherent intellectual tradition in the United States that is generally supportive of modernity. Instead, it has become a bulwark of the theological doctrines that resist what Peter Berger has called the "ethical rationalization" of the world and its doctrinal secularization. The Catholic Church's stress on obedience, even as it provides the safety hatch of intermediate as well as ultimate absolution, and its promise of cosmic deliverance from this-world suffering, has provided a powerful counterbalance to socialist and liberal religious doctrines that argue that salvation lies in worldly achievement. Hostility to intellectual dissent within the church has meant that the sources of opposition to its hierarchy have been forced out of the fold in order to register their protest.[16]

It is impossible to stress the influence of Catholicism on working class consciousness too strongly. Its early role as an acculturation institution for its huge immigrant membership was made possible by the fact that it represented continuity with the deepest traditions of the peasantry. The church provided the opportunity for working class families who felt stranded in large cities to overcome the isolation of urban living. It was preeminent as a social center for women and children. Its educational institutions were superb training grounds for a disciplined labor force, yet provided bonds of solidarity that could not be found in the public schools. Together with the family, the Catholic Church was a shield for the worker against an alien world. Thus its cultural importance outweighs its direct political influence on American life.

In the late nineteenth century and the first decades of the twentieth the church recognized its responsibility to deal with the growing unrest emanating from among the members of its own constituency, a large segment of whom were the industrial workers whose support radicals, Socialists, and industrial unionists were seeking.

Marc Karson has demonstrated[17] that the Catholic Church's hierarchy was at once sensitive and conservative with respect to the problems raised by the struggles of industrial workers for social justice. In order to respond to the felt needs of its constituency, the church was persuaded that it had to intervene in labor struggles and labor politics. However, this intervention often took an explicitly antiradical stance. The church worked among trade unionists of the Catholic faith to prevent the formation of socialist and labor parties, arguing that such organizations as the IWW were godless and unworthy of worker affiliation; it fought to win the adherence of trade unionists to the Catholic doctrines on labor enunciated at the beginning of the century by Pope Leo XIII. According to these papal encyclicals, which were rigidly followed by the leadership of the American church, it recognized the dignity of common labor and the rightness of its struggle for justice and at the same time, it preached reconciliation between classes, eschewing the revolutionary and militant doctrines of class war, and the use of strikes and violence to achieve the demands of labor.

The Irish have been, and remain to this day, the dominant force within the hierarchy of the American Catholic church. Not one single cardinal is of Eastern or Southern European descent; only one cardinal, from St. Louis, has been German.* All others are of Irish background, including the most powerful prelates of the New York archdiocese, Francis Spellman and his successor Cardinal Cooke. Many priests and nuns are of Italian or Polish background, but rarely move beyond the rank of Monsignor or Mother Superior. Among parishioners, however, the Irish constitute a distinct minority, especially if one takes account of the Chicano population and remigration to the mainland of millions of Puerto Rican people.

It was not only the corporations and unions that reinforced ethnic divisions; the Catholic Church also was powerfully committed to this approach. It was careful to provide its immigrant laity with priests and nuns of the corresponding nationalities; in some cases it went so far as to conduct church services in the language of homogeneous immigrant parishioners. It was as sympathetic to ethnic culture as it was hostile to ideologies of class solidarity.

Church doctrine also interpreted "the dignity of labor" to

---

* Many diocesan bishops were of German descent and a few of Slavic and Italian backgrounds. But the pinnacle of the hierarchy remains Irish-dominated.

mean that the worker should be satisfied with his station in life and not attempt to reach beyond his class, especially since such movement would inevitably put him in contact with adherents of Protestantism, plainly a middle-class religion both in form and content. Insofar as the hierarchical organization of religion corresponded to the hierarchical organization of social labor, Catholicism as ideology was more relevant to the preservation of the status quo than the more egalitarian middle-class Protestant ideologies that often glorified the individual. Its doctrines relied more heavily on the feudal concept of station or estate than the modern notion of class.

The similarities between Catholicism, Baptist sects, and the pentecostal religions of lower-class Protestants must here be noted. All lack the Calvinistic notion that "by their fruits you shall know them." Instead, each demands the adherence of the person to the mystical deity. Such adherence is exemplified in the rituals of worship that depend on the recognition by the worshipper of the authority of the priest or minister to mediate the relationship between God and the individual, even though some groups, notably the Jehovah's Witnesses, overwhelmingly lower class, regard each Witness as "minister." Salvation in both the Catholic and the lower-class Protestant religions is found in investing all faith in the healing powers of Jesus and in emulating his sufferings—thus valuing humility more than success. Thus these religions eschew mobility in contrast to the middle-class Protestant faiths which celebrate it.

In recent years, especially after the Second World War, Catholic churchmen have become ubiquitous in their involvement in the trade unions. The significant part played by Catholic priests in combatting the so-called "left-wing" unions in the CIO was a major feature of the ideological split within the labor movement that preceded the advent of McCarthyism as a major national political force. In fact, as Paul Blanshard has documented, the senator from Wisconsin had no support stronger than that which he received from the Wisconsin diocese.[18] The Catholic hierarchy's support for the senator's virulent anti-Communism was consistent with church doctrines.

But anti-Communism has not circumscribed the extent of Catholic involvement with labor. "In general American priests tend to be sincerely prolabor," writes Blanshard.[19] He attributes this sentiment to their own humble beginnings, and undoubtedly there is truth in the statement that the Catholic church is interested in workers' problems because its own low-level hierarchy was recruited from the workers and represents a kind of upward movement from the working class.

In the 1950s, the church even became vitally interested in the problem of corruption and gangsterism in labor unions. The Association of Catholic Trade Unionists (ACTU) and a number of so-called "labor priests" on the waterfronts of New York, New Orleans, and other major ports worked closely with government officials concerned with reform and with rank-and-file workers who resented the fact that their jobs depended on the arbitrary control of hiring bosses, more often than not closely linked to corrupt union officials and alleged gangland operatives.

In this situation, the close ties of the church to government agencies placed it in an ambivalent position with respect to rank-and-file interests. There was little doubt that government intervention into waterfront affairs could materially benefit longshoremen in the vital area of job security, yet while the church was pressing for honest democratic unionism it was also supporting measures designed to limit the autonomy of the unions and the rank and file to deal effectively with the employers.

In the 1960s the earlier concerns of the church with anti-Communism and corruption among the workers gave way to activities in behalf of minority group workers victimized by unions, general economic deprivation, greedy employers, and the government. In a burst of ecumenical fervor the Catholic Church was responding to several internal developments as well as developments among its constituents.

The original impetus for the church's entry into social action was closely tied to its perception that its old constituency in the cities was diminishing in proportion to the migration of industry to outlying areas. The new Catholic mission among the very poor was not unmindful that a large segment of the new city proletariat had Latin origins, particularly Puerto Ricans and Chicanos who were traditionally Catholic. Puerto Ricans in particular have been notoriously ambivalent toward their religion. The Catholic Church in Latin America was among the most reactionary forces in that region and has been viewed by Puerto Ricans as part of the ruling structure of the island. However, most Puerto Ricans remain nominally Catholic. The church encouraged its younger officials to enter ghetto and slum communities to reestablish contact with the Latin segment of its constituency with whom it had tenuous relationships. There can be no doubt that it has also sought the affiliation of Blacks, and has been sensitive to the issues that concern them. The paradox here consists in the fact that the church has presented itself to Blacks as a vehicle for achieving upward movement within American society by providing social services, such as its system of schools, that compete admirably with similar public functions. Blacks become Catholics as both a symbol of their reaching beyond the ghetto and an opportunity to separate themselves from other Black people.

The church has consistently been an instrument of the socialization of the working class into the industrial system in conformity to the prevailing occupational hierarchies. Traditionally, to be sure, the church hierarchy has used its schools to select those immigrants most fit to join its lower rungs and become priests and nuns within ethnic neighborhoods and organizations. The Catholic educational system has always helped reinforce the myth of mobility by making priests of some children who would ordinarily join the working class. But this aspect of its work has been subordinate to its main job of providing continuous ideologies that link the feudal traditions of the old country with the specific forms of capitalist domination. It is only among Blacks that this role is clearly subordinate to the task of selecting whole congregations for mobility.

Today the church has, in the main, retreated to its early role as a keeper of the faith and a political power broker. It has refused to confront its white working class followers with the imperatives of social action except in instances where it perceived that the result of urban redevelopment would be a loss of membership and organizational coherence. When the Catholic hierarchy of Chicago supported the efforts of Saul Alinsky to thwart the slum clearance policies of the municipal administration in the "back of the yards" district where large numbers of Polish and other Eastern European workers lived, it acted out of sheer self-interest. Here Alinsky promised nothing more than success in a limited objective.

Just as no political or economic bureaucracy will stand by and watch its power decomposed, the church has never really tolerated any broad opposition to its policies, such as was represented by the Catholic left in the 1960s. It has shown infinite flexibility in absorbing segmented discontent among important elements of its constituency, but has consistently refused to abdicate power over the church itself. Successfully weathering its splits, frequent crises and disaffections since the 1860s, it has remained an effective instrument for integrating its laity within the framework of American social relations.

— 4 —

One important indication of the relative status of immigrant groups was their position within the trade union hierarchies. Nearly all major trade unions established after the Civil War have been dominated by skilled workers of Northern European origins. The leadership of the Mine Workers Union has followed a typical pattern. Here, despite the decline in the numerical importance of Irish, English, and Welsh miners after 1890 and the simultaneous rise of the Slavs and Italians, no significant national leaders of the union or challengers to leadership were of Eastern or Southern European origin until the late 1960s. John Mitchell, John L. Lewis, Tony Boyle, and opponents John Brophy, Powers Hapgood, and others were of Northern European backgrounds. The one exception Joseph Jablonsky, the leader of a rank-and-file opposition movement that finally captured power in 1972, was killed before the victory of his caucus. His successor was a native American of Northern European derivation.

The leaders of the rail unions, even of those unions such as the American Railway Union that attempted to organize workers on the basis of industry rather than craft, were recruited from among the most skilled categories of workers—again usually of Northern European extraction. Eugene Debs, the founder of the ARU, was a skilled worker, having been a member of the Fireman's Union before attempting the amalgamation of all groups.

Textile unionism in its early years was characterized by leadership drawn from among loomfixers, weavers, and other skilled workers. Despite the recent recruitment of Italians and some Jews to top positions, native-born and Northern European workers have been dominant in union leadership for the past half-century. Emil Rieve, a skilled hosiery worker and leader of the Textile Union during the rise of the CIO, was succeeded by William Pollock, a Philadelphia weaver of Scottish parentage.

One notable exception to this pattern was in the needle-trades unions, but here Jewish hegemony was possible only after the Irish-led United Garment Workers, an AFL affiliate composed largely of cutters, were successfully ousted. Even after overthrowing the old regime, both the International Ladies Garment Workers and the Amalgamated Clothing Workers remained in the hands of the cutters and highly paid sewing machine operators. Both David Dubinsky and Sidney Hillman, as well as those who have succeeded them as union leaders, were from the "craft" categories in an industry where the overwhelming majority of operatives are employed as section workers.

The CIO was organized principally by leaders of the mining and clothing workers unions that had successfully established themselves as industrial organizations in the first decades of the century. However, it relied heavily on the support of the unskilled workers in the key mass production industries, and criticized the old AFL craft unions for the racism, nativism, and elitism that dominated new workers and made them incapable of organizing the great mass of unskilled and semiskilled workers in such industries as auto, steel, packinghouse and rubber. Indeed, the ideology of the CIO was its adherence to industrial democracy. The new union federation was to be of, by, and for the assembly line and low-skilled workers generally.

Yet a closer examination of the ethnic, racial, and skill composition of its principal leadership on the national level as well as in the shops reveals an enormous disparity between ideology and practice, as borne out by the following table of the principal leaders of important CIO unions in 1950.

Phillip Murray, Steelworkers	Irish miner
Walter Reuther, UAW	1st generation German toolmaker
Homer Martin, UAW	Minister, 1st UAW President, English origin
L. S. Buckmaster, Rubber	English skilled worker
S. Dalrymple	Skilled tire worker, Scotch-English descent
O. A. Knight, Oil	Scotch-Irish skilled worker
John L. Lewis, Miners	Welsh miner
Jacob Potofsky, Amalgamated	Jewish cutter

Joseph Curran, Maritime	Irish seaman
Harry Bridges, Longshore-men	Australian
James Carey, Electrical	Irish, worked briefly in industry
Michael Quill, Transport	Irish

The ethnic composition of the leadership of the AFL unions that organized large numbers of industrial workers in the 1940s and 1950s is much the same.

Pat Gorman, Meatcutters	Irish, skilled
Al Hayes, Machinists	Scotch-Irish, skilled
David Dubinsky, Garment workers	Jewish cutter
Dan Tobin, Teamsters	Irish

Currently, the ethnic and skill composition of the leadership of these unions has not changed radically in the face of the large influx of Black workers, the relative stability in number and proportion of skilled workers in each industry, and the decline in the proportion of workers of Northern European origins. The machinists, teamsters, autoworkers, steelworkers, oilworkers, electrical workers, and miners are still led by men of Northern European origins, although the nationality of the top officers has changed in some cases. In the Textile Workers the top offices are now occupied by a first-generation Jew and an Italian respectively, one a former dyehouse worker who built his actual career in the union hierarchy rather than in the plants, and a skilled carpet weaver who became a full-time official in his twenties. The top leadership of the Rubber Workers has finally passed to an Italian, reflecting the strength of this nationality group in three important districts of the union: Ohio, the Middle Atlantic States, and New England.

The CIO and AFL organizing drives of the 1930s and 1940s were organized and led by skilled workers. At the plant level, these workers occupied key positions in a great majority of locals. In the New Jersey steel plants that I worked in during the 1950s, the leader of one local was a machinist named McHale and the other local leader, Walsh, was a maintenance mechanic. A large proportion of the managers of textile workers, joint boards, presidents of steel locals, auto locals, and other industrial local unions also reflect the supremacy of skilled, Northern European workers.

The central role of this group within the industrial union movement despite their minority status both in terms of skills and nationality in many industries has had profound implications for the configuration of trade unions in American society. First, unskilled and semiskilled workers were deliberately excluded from AFL craft unions until the pressure emanating from the earlier Industrial Workers of the World, the Communist-led trade unions of the early 1930s, and the later CIO—all concentrating on unskilled workers—forced the leaders of the craft unions to recruit the workers in less skilled categories into their organizations. Even after acknowledging the role of unskilled Eastern and Southern Europeans in the labor movement, the craft unions succeeded in maintaining the separation of the skilled from the less skilled within industrial plants. This strategy not only affected the shape of craft unionism, but ultimately determined the way in which the industrial unions were to conduct themselves in the factories.

To all appearances the CIO carried out the "One Big Union" concept of the early twentieth-century radicals who had formed the IWW, incorporating whole the left-wing ideology of industrial unionism. The unskilled or semiskilled worker was viewed as neither unorganizable nor inherently inferior. On the contrary. Like the syndicalist left, the CIO placed heavy reliance on workers in mass production industries. Their vision, however, did not extend as far as that of the IWW, which had seen these workers as potential catalytic agents in the transformation of society, since capitalism depended for its strength on the technologies of mass production with its minute division of labor and emphasis on the machine. Craft unionism in this view was a relic of the artisan phase of production long since surpassed by the factory system, mechanical and electrical power, and the assembly line. No movement hoping to change the social relations of production to benefit the masses could hope to base itself on skilled craftsmen.

Although neither Sidney Hillman nor John L. Lewis, the CIO architects, was revolutionary in his aims, they had hoped that the industrial unions they built in their own domains would play an important role in creating the conditions for a just society. The genius of Lewis and Hillman consisted, in part, in their recognition that the workers in mass production industries would never be attracted to the new organizations unless the CIO presented itself as the champion of the most oppressed and exploited workers in the factories. The traditional craft union practice of establishing separate groups euphemistically called "B" locals to accommodate the less skilled were strictly eschewed by the CIO leaders. Like the IWW, the CIO sought to organize all workers within a shop regardless of craft. The radicals who helped the CIO recruit mass production workers may have been somewhat disturbed by its failure to adopt the radical ideological stance of the IWW, or of the incipient left-wing unions of the Depression period, but they were willing to defer raising political issues until the industrial unions had achieved strength and stability, as long as the new unions were committed to eliminating the distinctions based on craft, nationality, and race and welcomed persons of differing political persuasions to their ranks.

The optimism that marked the formation of the CIO seemed justified by its early practice. In the first five years (1936–41), the new federation of unions was not only brilliantly successful in organizing the great majority of auto, steel, nonferrous metal, electrical, packinghouse, and rubber workers and establishing significant beachheads in textile, shoe, oil, longshore, transport, retail, and among public workers, but was the cutting edge of all unionism. Even the recalcitrant AFL was forced to expand its jurisdiction in order to compete successfully with the upstart.

Moreover, the CIO appeared to be faithful to its promise to abolish, as far as possible, distinctions based on skill, race, and nationality. Unskilled and skilled workers each had one vote in the election of officers, approval of the contract, and the general operation of the union regardless of former status. But it did not take long for the skilled workers to recognize that, despite their adherence to the new unionism, their interests were not served by its egalitarian ideology. The battle to reestablish skilled worker supremacy in the unions began in earnest before World War II and was continued after the war.

A major defeat for the industrial union concept was the right won by skilled workers, professional and technical workers, and white-collar categories to hold separate elections under the National Labor Relations Act of 1935. Naturally, employers were strong proponents of the separation of units, both for the purpose of determining representation as well as for the purpose of collective bargaining. Under the old arrangements, employers had been able to divide the workers on the basis of skill and ethnicity. This advantage had helped to break more than one strike before the 1930s. The Homestead Strike of 1892, the miners' strike a decade later, the great steel strike of 1919 were only a few of the more noteworthy cases where Black and Eastern European workers had been brought in as scabs to replace native-born or Northern European workers. It was out of the long experience of ethnic and craft division that the CIO decided to organize workers based on industry alone. The establishment of the Labor Board combined with court decisions (e.g., *Globe Machine and Stamping Co.* 3 NLRB 294 [1937]) that permitted the separation of craft from unskilled workers were significant blows to the industrial unionists, but they were to prove merely the first round in a series of measures that resulted in the collapse of industrial unionism in the succeeding decades and its replacement by de facto craft arrangements even as the form and ideology of egalitarianism was partially preserved within the CIO.

Within the union hierarchies skilled industrial workers almost invariably captured key positions. Their mobility within the plant was an important factor in their rise to leadership. Usually, in mass production industries, their tasks consisted in plant and machine maintenance, installation, and repair, which required them to constantly move about the plant in connection with the performance of their duties. Unskilled and semiskilled workers, on the other hand, were chained to their work stations. Given the technical division of labor, operatives and laborers had little opportunity to grasp the problems of either the production process as a whole or issues affecting the entire work force. In contrast the technical position of skilled workers within the production process enabled them to enhance their social position and manipulate the union to serve their particular needs.

The second major factor influencing the rise of the skilled workers within industrial union hierarchies was their achievement of a greater degree of craft solidarity, based on the frequency of interaction among them during the day. Mechanics have far more time during the workday to talk to one another and to the machine operators and laborers. They quickly establish their own relationships among themselves as well as their hegemony over the operatives. Characteristically, skilled workers within industrial plants recognize their privileged objective position and wish to maintain it. They are far more trade union conscious than the rest of the work force because they are aware of the degree to which they can influence production if they act in concert. Unskilled workers lack this confidence in their indispensability. Consequently, only by overwhelming numbers can they make their power felt and their demands heard by the employers. Achieving these numbers on any given issue was made immeasurably difficult in the 1940s and 1950s by the division of large plants into discrete departments separated by relatively large distances, the fragmentation of functions engendered by the division of industrial labor, and by the awareness by unskilled workers that they could be replaced at any time by other persons willing to perform their simple work tasks. The standardization of parts and functions within the production process was matched by the interchangeability of labor.

In the late nineteenth and early twentieth centuries, the peasant origins of the Southern and Eastern European workers served to reinforce the occupational and trade union hierarchies. Compounding their unskilled status was the lack of political experience of these groups within the agricultural areas from which they had migrated to the United States. (Later, Southern white and Black workers entered such industries as the auto industry and found themselves in an analogous position.)

The fundamental basis of the immigrations and migrations during this period was the uneven development of capitalism within Europe, between sections of Europe and the United States, and within regions of the United States itself. As capital migrates from industry to industry or from country to country in accordance with the expectation of higher profit rates, so labor migrates in the expectation of job opportunities. Those who have nothing to sell but their labor power are assigned to the least favorable position in terms of its sale. On the other hand, the skilled workers who were recruited from among the artisans in small handicraft production in Northern Europe, or from the English factory system that preceded our own by nearly a century, or the Scottish and Welsh mines, had long trade union and political traditions behind them. They did not arrive on the shores of this country in any way grateful for the opportunities afforded them by American capital. They came here fully expecting to fight for what they received. And they did become the driving force of trade unionism during the period of the expansion of American capitalism. But they monopolized the benefits of the union growth. They made sure that the crafts remained a self-perpetuating hierarchy within the framework of industrial plants as well as in the construction trades.

There were three mechanisms for achieving this patrilineal arrangement: first, these workers demanded that separate seniority lists, job classifications, and wage differentials be codified in the union contract. For example, in the typical steel or auto plant there is movement between unskilled and semiskilled jobs because there is *one* seniority list among these groups for the purposes of upgrading on a plant-wide basis. In steel, auto, and electrical manufacture, labor grades up to the skilled categories are ostensibly open to all workers. Beyond these designated unskilled and semiskilled jobs, however, a seniority list is maintained only for those designated as qualified for crafts, and this list is not open for application by those in the lower job classifications. Entrance to jobs labeled "crafts" or "skilled trades" is limited to those who have completed an approved apprenticeship program that in turn typically admits only those who are strongly recommended by the skilled workers themselves. Additional protection for individual crafts is afforded by the separation of seniority lists among them. Thus, an electrician can only move laterally within the electricians' craft and the rigger has similar restrictions.

The range of discretion available to management to restrict movement among the lower labor grades is equally assured by many union contracts. Increasingly, upgrading requires the worker to possess ability and/or qualifications in addition to the highest seniority in order to be promoted. Even though the union can appeal the management decision, its position is often weakened by its own complicity: even the semiskilled workers hold their jobs as a "property right" in industrial plants.

It is important to remember that it was partially against the concept of job property rights that industrial unions arose. The reintroduction of the concept in recent years is a reflection of the persistence of occupational hierarchies, even when established by the simple device of labeling certain jobs as "skilled" that were formerly not considered to be in this category. The typical provision of the industrial union contract that perpetuates divisions based on craft within the plant is job classifications. Job classifications are relatively arbitrary gradations of work tasks based on presumed differential skill levels. Typically, they carry pay scales that are hierarchically arranged according to labor grades that are groups of jobs determined to be of proximate skill. Thus, within industrial plants there are three broad categories of job classifications: the crafts, that is, jobs whose prerequisite is an approved apprenticeship program or its equivalent; semiskilled jobs, which are achieved by promotion from unskilled ranks, the attainment of certain educational levels, or aptitude tests (increasingly the latter two qualifications are replacing simple seniority); and unskilled labor, which requires little or no prior educational background or experience.

The trade unions have acted to perpetuate divisions based on skill and ethnicity even in industrial plants by their cooperation with management in maintaining separate seniority lists for crafts and their insistence on job classification, as a mechanism for legitimating wage increases and wage differentials within the noncraft categories of labor. At first, the distinctions among the jobs considered less skilled were justified by union leaders on the ground that such job classifications opened the chance to win wage increases for workers without the need for a general rise that could only be achieved at the termination of the contract. From the point of view of the industrial unions, this innovation was self-defeating with respect to the original purpose of the organization. It served to reestablish the hated divisions among the workers. Typically Blacks, Southern and Eastern European immigrants, and "hillbillies" occupied the lower rungs of the occupational ladder, rarely to rise even to the ranks of the semiskilled. The first generation native-born workers of Eastern and Southern European descent were recruited into the semiskilled occupations and rapidly established these jobs as their own property to be protected against the Blacks and the Southern white migrants, who constituted a third wave of new workers into industrial plants after the two world wars had wiped out the viability of non-mechanized Southern agriculture by reducing cotton and tobacco prices so that only corporate farms could survive.

The further divisions of industrial labor engendered by job classifications reinforced the myth of mobility among immigrant white workers, even though most of them were unable to rise to other social classes or even to the most privileged sectors of the working class. At the same time, these hierarchies within the ranks of the less skilled created the conditions for racism, both among immigrant groups and between the white immigrants and their offspring, and the new migrants from the South.

Job classifications were negotiated between management and union committees upon which sat representatives of craft and semiskilled workers. Their arbitrary character is revealed by the fact that they were negotiated. Determination of classification not only depended on such factors as educational requirements and manual dexterity, but took into consideration health and safety hazards, the range of operations in a particular job however simple each one was, the closeness of tolerance where quantitative measurement of the product was required. In the last analysis, there were no exact methods of determining classification. Decisions were made on the basis of the relative power of any given group within a plant and union, the willingness of management to agree to the union's demands, and the biases of the local union committees that negotiated the classification system.

The all-male committees frequently operated on a crude notion of the sexual division of labor. The idea of "equal pay for equal work" that ostensibly is a reasonable way of insuring the equality of labor regardless of sex, ran aground in the face of interpretations of job classifications that discovered women's work to be unequal to that of men. It was not uncommon to find separate seniority and job classification systems in industrial plants that distinguished women's jobs from those of men and did not permit movement between the systems. But even where there was an effort to integrate all jobs on the basis of skill rather than sex, women's jobs were assigned the lowest labor grades on the basis of allegedly "objective" valuations. Just as nurses are classified inferior to doctors in the occupational hierarchy of the health industry, so women assemblers of instruments or electrical parts for small aircraft were regarded as being of lower skill than men performing similar tasks and were awarded lower wage scales. In fact, in some plants, notwithstanding the Equal Rights Ideology, the highest work performed by women is paid a lower wage than the lowest labor grade of "male" jobs, regardless of comparable skill.

The devices of union-enforced seniority and job classifications justified the hierarchies within the labor force. They were invented to protect the interests of those who had already achieved power within the industrial hierarchy: the employers and managers who were afraid of solidarity based on class rather than on skill, ethnicity, and race; and the skilled workers who had consolidated their hold on the crafts in the earlier years of the American industrial revolution. But the democrats within the working class had yet another rallying point around which to create unity: the progressive narrowing of wage differentials between skilled and unskilled, mental and physical labor, men and women.

In the early days of the CIO strong elements within the organization had argued for a frontal assault on wage differences based on skill. One way to achieve this objective was to demand cents-per-hour wage increases rather than increases based on percentage. Until 1950 this approach was widely applied in some industries, particularly auto and electrical. Then a turning point came just when the differentials were approaching disappearance. Craft unionists in the CIO—the UAW, the electrical unions, and elsewhere—began to demand that differentials be maintained by two bargaining devices: the uniform conversion to percentage wage increases and an additional increase based on "inequities" of job classification. At first, the leadership of the UAW resisted the craft unionists' demands. The Skilled Trades Department within the UAW threatened to withdraw from the union and establish a separate organization unless they were granted their chief demand, that no contract could be approved without the agreement of the separate groups of skilled and unskilled. This demand accorded parity to the skilled groups despite their numerical minority. Clearly, the skilled workers were militantly interested in maintaining separate seniority lists, wage differentials, and separate bargaining. The leaders of most industrial unions capitulated to all these demands, because the skilled workers had already become the substance of the union itself at all levels of the union structure. Democratic ideology was no match for the political power of the trades. Moreover, given the job classification system that had been established among the less skilled, the percentage basis of wage determination corresponded to the immediate interests of a relatively large proportion of the older, higher seniority workers. By the mid-1950s the stranglehold of the skilled workers on the industrial unions was complete and so was the dominance of the Northern European workers over the skilled trades within industrial plants and in the construction industry. First- and second-generation workers of Italian and Eastern European origins were effectively excluded from all but semiskilled jobs that had been accorded the status of craft by union contract. When the Blacks and women entered the plants, a new seniority system was negotiated to protect the tenuous status of the semiskilled. In many factories, a plant-wide seniority procedure that allowed upgrading from unskilled to semiskilled labor gave way to departmental seniority, a measure used to exclude new workers from semiskilled jobs. The social divisions within the factories based on ethnicity, race, and sex were even more rigidly enforced than previously by the unions, and thus the solidarity achieved during the CIO drive two decades earlier was destroyed. Access by children of immigrants to types of industrial jobs different from those held by previous generations was denied. The burgeoning white-collar, technical, and sales occupations became the new basis for egalitarianism insofar as no historic interests had established their hegemony in these strata as yet.

— 5 —

It is often difficult to recall the fact that the industrial working class in America is barely a century old. Unlike the British working class, which developed its political and class consciousness as a result of centuries of common experience and struggle, the industrial working class in the United States was formed mainly out of disparate migrants from both feudal and early industrial societies in Europe and within America who spoke different tongues and shared no common culture. The ability of the corporations that dominated American society after 1890 to control the working class depended upon its diverse composition, the complicity of the trade unions and the bulk of Socialists, in maintaining the social and occupational hierarchies, and, most important, the recent agrarian origins of the largest group of unskilled and semi-skilled migrants and immigrants. Moreover, the occupational structure of American industry reflected the hierarchical character of European society. Italians, East Europeans, Black and white Southerners arrived on the scene with an inheritance of feudal and semifeudal social relations. As peasant or agrarian classes, they had been assigned to underdevelopment from an industrial standpoint, even during the steep ascent of Northern European and North American capitalism. Contrary to the commonly held belief that the success of our economic development has been due, in a large measure, to the absence of a feudal past, it is evident that the genius of American capital consisted in its ability to incorporate the institutions of rank and obligation, the separation of mental and physical labor, the distinction between town and country, and the authority relations that marked feudalism. Feudalism was not denied, but transformed and used by employers in the development of capitalism.

For the most part, there was always a labor surplus during the expansion of capitalism, despite frequent labor shortages. This surplus generated conflict among those groups of unskilled workers sharing the same or similar social positions. Racism and nativism became powerful forces splitting the working class and allowing for the development of mobility ideologies, that, notwithstanding meager results, held sway over large sections of immigrants. Instead of opposing this trend, the early radicals supported the nationalist bias of the employer class.

It is not surprising that neither Blacks nor immigrants from Southern and Eastern Europe perceived the Socialists as representing their interests. As John Laslett has shown, the Socialist appeal was largely to workers of Northern European origins who were attracted to the socialist movement as a result of their own protest against the erosion of traditional crafts by industrial capitalism.[20] On the other hand, the Socialist Party of the 1900–12 period inherited an important segment of the old populist tradition that had not been integrated into the Democratic Party by Bryan's antimonopoly appeal. The large Socialist vote in Texas and Oklahoma reflected farmer interest in "the cooperative commonwealth" program and elected many Socialist mayors and other officeholders. In fact, the great centers of popular Socialist strength were not found in the large cities, where, with the exceptions of German, Jewish, and some Irish workers, the party had only scattered appeal among recent immigrants. Laslett's argument that among trade unionists in the machinist and mining unions Socialist influence derived from the populist demand for democracy as much as from the demand for a revolutionary reconstruction of society must be taken seriously.[21] Socialism in its heyday was largely a rural movement with its real influence of any importance among skilled workers, small farmers and laborers, and miners.

The Communist Party in the 1920s, unlike the Socialist Party, had the ability to perceive the specific position of Eastern European immigrants and Black migrants and the capacity to fight for the immediate demands of these groups in periods of economic decline. To some extent this sensitivity derived from its Leninist politics, that paid particular attention to those who constituted the "weak link" of imperialism—the workers and peasants in the colonial and semicolonial countries and regions who were the most oppressed owing to the fact that their labor was the source of capitalist superprofit. Yet there is no doubt that relatively few Blacks were attracted to the Communist movement even though they were willing to work with Communists to redress immediate grievances. Similarly, most immigrant workers were as disdainful of the Communists as they had been of Socialists and trade unions earlier in the century.

To a large degree, according to C. Vann Woodward, Southern Blacks had preferred an alliance with the old planter aristocracy after the Civil War rather than placing their faith in white populists or Socialists. This preference was somewhat attenuated in the 1920s and 1930s as a result of the Black migration to Northern industrial centers in the midst of economic crisis. But the New Deal restored the substance, if not the form, of the older alliance. Neither ideological radicalism nor liberal trade unionism could offer as many concrete results as the government and the corporate ruling class. Despite the militancy of the civil rights movement, the Black working class remained somewhat submerged until the 1960s. It has emerged recently as a power within major sectors of American industry—but it is no longer led by the Black bourgeoisie nor does it seek an alliance with the white liberal bourgeoisie as previous generations have done. The new Black worker is young, independent, and relatively distant from the Southern roots. This generation of Black workers no longer accepts the leadership of the churches, the NAACP, and the Black middle class. Although most of the revolutionary Black workers' organizations that sprang up in the late 1960s no longer exist or have been seriously depleted, their development is symbolic of a generation that no longer looks toward the old left or liberal solutions to deal with the problems unique to its social position. Many Black workers have achieved a degree of class awareness unknown before. This awareness is not expressed in articulate ideologies as much as in modes of action that are antibureaucratic and are undertaken on the basis of class as well as racial politics.

— 6 —

Much discussion about the Negro's civil rights, his political significance, his social status, and his aspirations can be shortened and simplified by a clear understanding of the economic status assigned to him in the New Order. Emancipation and Reconstruction had done little to change that picture. The lives of an overwhelming majority of Negroes were still circumscribed by the farm and the plantation.[22]

C. Vann Woodward has written about the position of Blacks in the period immediately following Reconstruction. There is no need for another essay describing the gross discrimination suffered by Blacks in American history. Throughout the enormous quantity of material devoted to demonstrating how Black Americans are victims of racism, explanations for this phenomenon almost always rely on the perfidy of whites. Blacks are discriminated against, in this view, because they are Black. This statement has validity to the degree that any group that can be successfully stigmatized within a hierarchical occupational and social structure is likely to suffer economically and socially in greater measure than others in the system. Black Americans are stigmatized by race; the racial difference sets them apart from all other groups and has certainly been an important determinant of their selection for discrimination among sectors of the working class. In other industrial countries, however, the position of the most despised, discriminated against group has been occupied by migrants of no particular racial difference from that of the dominant group. In Germany, Slav, Italian, and other immigrants have been assigned to unskilled, low-paid, hot and dirty labor. "Great Russian chauvinism" against other Slavs became the basis for a division of labor among Eastern Europeans. In this case, those nationalities in the least-developed regions of the Russian Empire were assigned the task of feeding the Russian cities that became the seat of manufacturing industries, and this division continued after the Revolution.

The stigma attached to any peasantry within a developing industrial society does not require racial stigma based on skin color. The non-Russian nationalities were labeled stupid, animalistic, and inherently unfit for civilized society even when they were blond and blue-eyed. When the peasants come to the city in response to the demand for industrial labor, they are assigned to the lowest rungs of the occupational ladder. "Native" Germans, Russians, or Americans who occupied the higher positions within the occupational hierarchy of their respective countries have regarded any newcomers as potential threats to their hard-won economic and social position. Racist ideology arises on the soil of competition among laborers, especially in the wake of technological change and uncertainty about economic stability.

As we have already noted, the preeminence of cotton and tobacco in the United States export trade prior to 1890, as well as the critical significance of agriculture as a market for the nascent iron and steel industry before the turn of the century, was an important element in the formation of American industrial capital. Black people were at the center of the agricultural work force that underlay the primitive accumulation of capital both before and after the Civil War. The betrayal of Emancipation and Reconstruction by Northern capitalists and politicians has been explained by reference to their need to consolidate their hold on the national government by making an alliance with the former Southern ruling class, or by the Republican Party's treachery regarding Southern Black interests. These explanations are undoubtedly necessary fragments of the story behind the so-called Hayes-Tilden compromise that capped the swift dismantling of Reconstruction and constituted nothing less than a counterrevolution against the only serious attempt to change social relations in American history. But the sufficient explanation must be found in the centrality of Black workers to Southern agriculture, and, by extension, to the vitality of the American economy. By 1890 the cotton crop had doubled in comparison to 1860. Cotton prices "hovered around 11 cents"[23] and had remained stable. The importance of Southern production to the railroad, steamship, textile manufacturing industries can hardly be underestimated. In these circumstances, Black migration remained restricted. This fact can also account for the terror perpetrated against Blacks who attempted to leave the plantations. The most fertile land was occupied by Black sharecroppers and Black labor prevailed in the production of cotton until well into the 1880s, even though white owner-farmers occupying poorer lands were, according to Woodward, "rapidly gaining on the black in the proportion of cotton produced."[24]

International competition and overproduction were important factors determining a fall in cotton prices after 1890. That decline forced cutbacks in the size and distribution of the labor force. Mechanization of agriculture, only intermittently applied in the years following the Civil War, was greatly accelerated between 1890 and 1910. Black tenants and sharecroppers were thrown off the land in increasing numbers during these years and began the long migration to the cities of the North and South.

Among the most important events illustrating the relations between Black and white labor after 1860 were the New York "draft riots" of 1863 and the use of Black workers as strikebreakers during the Homestead Steel Strike of 1892. The "draft riots," so named for the refusal of Irish workers to enter the military service of the Union government, were suffused with an undercurrent of racial conflict. The Irish were not only unwilling to join the Union army; they were equally fearful that Black labor would be recruited to take their jobs after they had been drafted. As the least-skilled among all workers in New York, the Irish felt they had more to lose than to gain from the Civil War. This event illustrates an important basis for racial sentiment among all white workers facing the vicissitudes of industrialism. As new technologies eroded traditional skills and the workers could no longer rely on their command of the production process to secure their position within society, intraclass competition became more common. Similarly, the reputation of Blacks as strikebreakers was enhanced by their employment in the Homestead Steel Strike when employers found their skills to be acceptable replacements for both craft and unskilled workers who had downed their tools.

Prior to 1890, Black labor had been kept on Southern lands as a landless proletariat by force, if necessary, but often by persuasion as well. Black workers were not eager to join the city working class that had already experienced the impact of depressions and wars. Rural life was certainly not idyllic, but compared with the slums and ghettoes of the cities, the long hours of factory labor, and the low wages offered by service industries, it had its compensations. Moreover, there is considerable evidence to show that, at first, large segments of the Southern white population were willing to enter political alliances with Blacks around their mutual interests. The populist movement in the South, which grew in the 1880s and 1890s, became powerful, in part, because of the alliance of white and Black agrarianism against the growing Northern industrial penetration of the South.

Among white populist political leaders, no more articulate spokesman for the incipient alliance could be found than Tom Watson. Although he later became one of the most virulent of the racist spokesmen for the resurgent Old South, in the early 1890s Watson framed his appeal to Black farmers in terms of the theory of self-interest. As the nineteenth century reached its conclusion, attempts by white populists to seek political support from Blacks resulted in a short-lived alliance. These attempts always had elements of manipulation and cynicism in them, but even so the populist alliance with Blacks was a position far superior to the "white only" policy of a large number of Northern labor unions. For most trade unionists of the period, the Black worker was a scab, an employers' tool, an inferior element that threatened their economic gains. Like the Chinese and the Eastern European immigrants, Black migrants to Northern industrial centers were regarded with both hostility and contempt by the craftsmen of native-born and Northern European origins.

By 1910, the volume of Black migrants to the cities had grown enormously. The land no longer offered the chance to make even the meager living of former years. Banks were demanding payment for loans extended against future crops and were taking possession of lands by default or by purchase. Capitalism in Southern agriculture was no longer confined to mercantile interests that controlled only the disposition of the crops. Financial institutions took over the land itself from both Black and white farmers. The marginal white farmers and small plantation owners were foreclosed.

The white Southern tenant farmer and sharecropper driven off the land had few options. The growing Southern textile manufacturing industry was trying to attract him and, in the main, was eventually successful. Poor whites entered Southern cotton mills that were perched on old farming lands. Like the mining towns of Pennsylvania, cotton mill towns were marked by company housing, company stores, company-owned amusements, and company-controlled churches. Similarly, cotton mill workers constituted a rural proletariat and never became urbanized like immigrant steelworkers, shoe workers, or Northern textile workers. The genius of the entrepreneurs of Southern industry was to perceive that the rural South could be transformed *in place* from agriculture to industry both from the point of view of proximity to raw materials and from the point of view of social and economic control.

The new rural industrial centers did not welcome Black migrants. They were kept in reserve as a threat to Southern whites, who were the lowest paid of American factory workers, possessed even fewer rights than they had enjoyed as independent farmers, and were living under the constant shadow of the company. To this day Black workers have never become an important part of the textile or rural industrial labor force. They have remained sweepers and have filled other categories of nonproduction jobs in the cotton mills. In the main, they work in sawmills, lumber camps, cordage factories, and other relatively marginal industries in the rural South.

The prevalent image of white Southern labor is that of docility. To some extent this image is borne out by the record. Unionism never sank deep roots in the South except among miners, building trades workers, and, later on, among steelworkers and teamsters. The textile and clothing industry employers have been notoriously antiunion. Yet it would be a mistake to ascribe the failure of unionism to "docility" or "paternalism." The record of struggle of Southern workers, for the most part native-born, compares favorably with other groups of unskilled and semiskilled workers entering industry for the first time. Their failure to establish substantial labor unions may be laid to several influences that were largely beyond their control. First, the craft union bias of the AFL during the first thirty years of the twentieth century prevented it from undertaking a serious drive to organize Southern workers at the most favorable time. The rise of the cotton textile industry took place on the backs of the agrarians who had been displaced by the crisis that beset American agriculture, especially in the South, after the turn of the century. Going into the factory was neither pleasant nor rewarding economically. The low wages and long hours of cotton mill workers combined with the alienated life of mill towns were not attractive to Southern whites. In fact, labor shortages were severe in Southern mills in the first decades of the century and provoked sharp struggles there, forcing employers to grant wage increases in order to attract workers.

A second barrier to union organization was the problem of plant location. The deliberate decision of manufacturers to locate mills in rural areas separated by miles of agricultural land militated against labor organization to the extent that it reinforced the sense of isolation of workers from one another. Unlike industry in large cities with high industrial concentration, rural industry afforded little opportunity for contact among workers. Even though by 1927 there were nearly 300,000 workers in Southern cotton textile mills, these were scattered over seven states; most of the plants had fewer than 200 employees. North Carolina, the leading textile producer, had only 95,000 workers dotting the countryside. Thus the physical impediments to solidarity were an important obstacle to Southern unionism.

Third, Southern mill towns were organized along lines that were consonant with the life and culture of the plantation South. Feudal social relations were superimposed on capitalist production, that is, the obligations of paternal employers to the workers were seen as contractually returned by loyal labor. The concept of *noblesse oblige* established in the antebellum South was a substantial belief of the mill-owners just as it had been an article of faith of plantation aristocrats. Often they were the same people. Plantation owners adjusted to the new industrial growth of the South by becoming employers. There is no question that the paternalism of the mill-owners had functional relevance to the exploitation of labor. But it would be an error to relegate it merely to a reflection of cynical class interest. Southern employers believed that the worker in the company town would not experience the anomie of life in big cities; the sense of community that had been lost in the transition from agricultural to industrial production would be preserved. Of course, the worst evils of industrialism were not overcome. The Southern employers were rampantly devoted to child labor and argued that unless the whole family was employed in the mill they would be forced to recruit immigrants or Blacks to fill jobs. From the point of view of the workers, child labor was more than an economic necessity; they, too, feared the invasion of the immigrants as much as they abhorred the specter of Black labor.

Labor struggles before 1929 were conducted largely without outside leadership. Workers in a given mill rose up to protest a wage cut, or to demand better conditions in the mill. Whether they achieved their goal or lost the strike there were only rare cases of union recognition. Spontaneous outbreaks were far more in evidence than well-financed, organized efforts to establish recognized trade unions.

From 1898 to 1929 there were two main periods of overt labor unrest in the Southern mills. The first strike wave occurred during and immediately following the First World War. Thirty thousand members were recruited to the United Textile Workers Union, an AFL affiliate. According to Broadus and George Mitchell, the uprising of 1919 petered out because of depressed conditions in the industry after 1921.[25] But the revolt flared up again in 1929. Famous strikes of the period, now almost forgotten, were conducted in Elizabethton, Gastonia, and Marion. In all cases union organizers entered the situation after the workers themselves had walked out, giving pause to contemporary charges that Socialists and Communists had initiated the strikes. Nevertheless, Socialist and Communist direction of the strikes was established. The bitterness, endurance, and solidarity displayed by the workers surprised not only the manufacturers, but the union officials, who had all but abandoned Southern textile workers, and the left-wingers who jumped in after the fire started.

These relatively scattered events prepared the way for the

great national textile strike of 1934, the largest walkout of industrial workers until that time. More than 400,000 millhands walked out in response to a relatively feeble strike call by the phlegmatic United Textile Workers. The shock of militancy buoyed up the union leaders, but once again they were unable to do more than prevent employers from transferring the burden of the Depression entirely to the workers' shoulders.

The Depression ushered in a new era in the textile industry. Falling prices, international competition, and mechanization contributed to the movement toward corporate mergers. By the end of the Depression, cotton textiles were well on the way toward domination by a few large corporations, controlled from the North. More than any other single factor, the rise of textile unionism in the late 1920s and 1930s is attributable to the breakup of the old system of industrial organization and the increasing incidence of absentee ownership. The significant remnants of paternalism that remained became mixed with racism, which figured more largely as ideology and culture than in actual everyday relations between employers and workers.

The decision to enforce Black exclusion in Southern industry, except in mining where Blacks constitute to this day an important proportion of the labor force, determined the major pattern of Black migration to Northern cities. If in the first period of our history Black agricultural labor constituted a central ingredient in the drive for economic development, Black urban labor was to play an entirely different though no less important role in the twentieth century.

The main Black migration took place during the interwar period. Swiftly, the thirty years between 1910 and 1940 witnessed the shift of the major portion of the Black population from Southern rural areas to the Northern cities. But the pace of economic growth had slowed considerably. Black labor only found space within the industrial labor force of the North during periods of labor shortages, or, as in the 1919 steel strike, as replacements for striking immigrant workers. In short, Black workers closely corresponded to Marx's concept of an industrial reserve army to be employed as a ready source of cheap labor during expansion periods and to become the first sector of the labor force to be laid off during times of depression or stagnation.

During the 1919 steel strike 30,000 Black workers were recruited to work in the mills. After the strike was over, most of them were dismissed. But they could no longer return to the South (unlike the Chinese, who had been shipped back to China after the railroads were built). They occupied the residential sections of the central cities that had been reserved for other immigrants just two decades earlier. Few could find employment within the factories. Almost always, in the 1920s, they were assigned the most menial jobs as laborers, were used as casual workers on the docks and in the warehouses of port cities such as New York, Philadelphia, and Baltimore, or, in the case of women, gradually replaced the Irish in domestic services. The less fortunate became part of the emerging number of permanently unemployed people for whom the economy had simply no room.

During the First World War, many Blacks found berths in packinghouses, laundries, and steel mills, where hot and dirty labor was performed. These industries provided the exceptions to the general rule of Black exclusion from industrial labor. In addition, some Blacks became construction workers, having transported their skills from the South and the Caribbean islands, where they had constituted the most important elements of artisan labor. But in these trades few Blacks could enter the unionized crafts; they were confined to branches of the industry that remained low-paid and nonunion, such as residential construction, rehabilitation, and highway construction.

It was not until the years just prior to the Second World War that the situation was somewhat altered. Once again, it was the outbreak of war in Europe and the rearmament of the United States in preparation for entry that helped change the pattern of exclusion—rather than the activities of the trade union leaders or radicals. In point of fact, the rise of Black workers within industry took place *despite* the trade unions. After 1934, A. Philip Randolph, the president of the all-Black Brotherhood of Sleeping Car Porters and a devout Socialist and trade unionist, consistently introduced resolutions at AFL conventions to bar unions that discriminated against Negroes from Federation membership. Consistently his eloquent pleas were denied. Instead, according to Ray Marshall, the AFL relaxed its total exclusionist policy to permit international unions to establish segregated Black locals or chartered these locals directly.[26]

Nor was the CIO free of segregation and discrimination, despite its image as a champion of racial equality. Widespread separation of Black from white workers in Southern locals was condoned by CIO officials, even as they proclaimed their devotion to integration and equality. The sentiments of Woodworkers, Textile workers, Packinghouse workers and Steelworkers unions in Southern states were more allied to traditional Southern practice than the resolutions of their own international union conventions proclaiming equality.

The one union and the one industry that has often been cited as an exception to this general rule is auto, whose workers belong to the overtly militant United Automobile Workers. But even though the UAW has had a more consistent legislative record in support of national civil rights issues than other unions, its performance in the plants has been considerably less distinguished. By the 1950s, many Black workers were no longer willing to believe the brave words of union officials about their devotion to equal rights. Black caucuses within the union began to appear in reaction to the slow pace of upgrading within auto plants and the absence of high-level Black officials within the UAW leadership. The war boom of the 1940s had brought large numbers of Black workers into auto and aircraft plants. They constituted as much as 30 percent of the labor force in some plants, but were concentrated in the body shops, foundries, wet-sanding, and other jobs requiring much physical effort and little skill. Although a significant number of Black workers became tool and die makers during the war, a general increase in the number of all skilled workers during this period left the number of Blacks in the same proportion.

The first serious Black caucus movement in the auto industry was formed in 1949 by Black left-wingers in such plants as Ford's River Rouge complex, which employed nearly 60,000 workers, of whom at least a quarter were Black. The National Negro Labor Council that developed from the caucus had substantial backing in its early years, but fell victim to the rash of red-baiting that infected the labor movement in the early fifties. Some of its leaders were driven from the plants and others became integrated into the union hierarchy. The thrust of the movement was dissipated, although there was some success in making small gains and raising the question of Black representation sharply within the UAW.

Later in the decade, the Trade Union Leadership Council (TULC) was organized explicitly to deal with discriminatory hiring practices within auto and other big city plants to combat the lily-white character of the union leadership, and to fight for upgrading within the occupational hierarchy. Its first efforts were devoted to pressuring the union leadership and the companies for equal opportunity. Despite the record auto production of the mid-fifties and the resurgence of Black employment in the shops, neither the proportion of Black skilled workers nor the composition of the top UAW leadership had changed. Black anger increased in proportion to the recalcitrance of the liberal unionists.

By this time, because of the seniority accumulated from the war years, many Black workers were able to achieve permanent status and thus withstand the frequent layoffs. Because the Black auto workers were now in a more powerful position, the TULC constituted an important challenge to the union bureaucracy in its early years of existence. Yet it failed to conduct a sustained battle against the leadership. Instead, the UAW recognized its demands for berths within the hierarchies of the Detroit city government and the union and quietly decimated its ranks by proffering jobs to its cadres. A Black vice president was elected to the UAW executive board and the TULC became an adjunct of the UAW leadership rather than remaining in opposition.

But the struggle in the shops was irrepressible. Despite promotion of a few Black militants to union staff jobs, the Black worker remained consigned to the bottom. By the mid-1960s many plants in Detroit and other auto centers had as many as 60 percent Blacks on the assembly lines and in parts plants. In 1969, petitions, resolutions at union conventions, rank-and-file movements to replace local union leaders, and attempts to use the grievance machinery under the union contract gave way to direct action.

In Detroit and Mahwah, New Jersey, Black auto workers employed by the three large automobile manufacturers organized independent movements that were not caucuses seeking power within the existing union. Particularly at the Ford plant in Mahwah, where Blacks constituted one-third of the work force, the Elton Avenue plant of the Chrysler Corporation, the Ford plant at River Rouge and others in the area, Black workers founded organizations that were neither tied to the ancestral left nor to the union leadership. In Detroit, the League of Revolutionary Black Workers, defining its goals beyond unionism and its mode of action outside the union structure, closed the Elton Avenue plant in the face of company and union opposition, demanding equal job assignments and more Black supervisors. At Mahwah, almost simultaneously, Black workers succeeded in establishing their power to close the plant over similar grievances. The United Black Brothers had emerged from persons who had worked in the 6000-worker plant there for some time. Some of its leading figures had participated in the civil rights struggles in the early sixties as members of the NAACP or CORE. Some had been close to the local leadership of the union and had worked for years to reform the union to make it more responsive to their needs.

At both locations the plant shutdowns were indications that a new generation of Black workers had arisen. The migrants that came from the Southern farms to work in the Northern mills and live in the city ghettoes in the 1920s had been convinced that, through education and political organization, Black people could achieve social and economic equality. They were aware that the North was worse in some ways than the South, but they had some faith that the "progressive" trade unions and the middle-class liberals were capable of reversing the long experience of racism. For a time the CIO and the Roosevelt coalition within the Democratic Party promised a New Deal for Black workers. A. Phillip Randolph became a symbol of the promise within the labor and Socialist movement. But by the beginning of the Second World War, it had become necessary for Randolph—even in opposition to Socialist and Communist allies—to threaten that Blacks would march on Washington before the Roosevelt administration would issue a Fair Employment Practices order. No doubt the prospect of masses of Blacks declaring their unwillingness to fight the war in behalf of a Jim Crow system contributed to the reform that, together with the 11 million-man military draft, brought the first large wave of Blacks into basic American industries since the First World War. It was also true that the prewar race riots in Detroit, Philadelphia, and elsewhere were reminiscent of the earlier draft riots. White Southern migrants and East European immigrants were simply too insecure within the prevailing social division of labor to welcome Black workers into the steel mills and auto plants.

The Black migrants, like the earlier European immigrants, were impressed by the minority among them who rose to skilled worker status, or in fewer cases to professional and other middle class occupations during and immediately after the war. But it is remarkable that by 1960, after nearly seventy years of migration, only 14.1 percent of nonwhite male workers had attained the status of skilled workers and professionals combined. This figure corresponds roughly to the position of Eastern European immigrants in 1910. In 1960 only 2.3 percent of employed Black men, compared with 11.5 percent of white men, were considered members of managerial strata. In contrast, more than 50 percent of employed nonwhite males were unskilled and semiskilled workers and farm workers, compared to 25 percent in these categories for white males.

However, the influence of the "talented tenth" among American Blacks in forming mobility ideologies and social aspirations among the Black proletariat was far more important than the meager gains Black people as a whole had achieved. From 1948 to 1962 there was virtually no change in the proportion of Black managers to the employed Black population, although their number increased slightly. The proportion of skilled workers rose by 1 percent as the proportion of private household workers declined —by 1 percent. In this fourteen-year period—highlighted by the brave civil rights declarations of the Truman administration, the Supreme Court decision ending segregation, the sit-ins and the freedom rides, the rise of the Southern civil rights movement to unprecedented heights—the actual social position of Blacks changed little. Yet this fact was obscured by the capacity of the Black church leadership, the emerging civil rights leadership drawn from the narrow black professional stratum of ministers, doctors, and lawyers, and the growing numbers of active Black political figures in large Northern cities agitating for political power, much as the Irish had done in the late nineteenth century, to persuade the Black workers that the pot could melt for them as much as it allegedly had for other migrants. The role models for Black youth provided by W. E. B. Du Bois and Thurgood Marshall were powerful tools of the mobility ideology. Yet at the base, almost nothing had happened except the decline in the number of farm workers in the countryside and the rise of the number of unskilled and semiskilled industrial laborers, a trend that hardly can be described as corresponding to the American dream.

Writing in 1967 Peter Blau and Otis Duncan were surprised to find that "nonwhites are more likely to be downwardly and less likely to be upwardly mobile than whites"[27] despite their lower socioeconomic origins which suggested the only place to go was up. Among whites they found that lower-class Southerners are more disadvantaged than lower-class Northerners and that their status is comparable to the status of Blacks because, in their view, both have been poorly prepared to compete for occupational advancement in comparison to white Northern workers. Although race is a significant factor determining the relative chances for occupational mobility between Southern whites and nonwhites, the differences between the two groups are not as significant as their similarities. The internal twentieth-century migration occurred as American expansion was displaced to the international sphere. After the turn of the century, only in times of war was it possible for new entrants into the labor force to achieve places within the basic industries. In the main, Black and white Southern workers were assigned to light consumer-goods industry, services, domestic work, and other low-paying jobs.

Just as ethnic and racial divisions had been established within industries, the division of labor between industries corresponded to migration patterns. To the extent that similar labor was paid differently depending on the position of the given industry within the economic structure, the entrance of Southerners into Northern and Southern manufacturing reflected their subordinate status within the working class as a whole.

Blacks and whites from the South came too late. Their late entrance into industry was a symptom of the uneven development of American capitalism, particularly the semicolonial position of the South in the economy. It was precisely this uneven internal development combined with the uneven development of the international economy that made possible the rapid growth of the American industrial system. Concomitant with this pattern, the persistence of racist ideology and of nativism is explicable. These ideas were articulated by the Founding Fathers of the American nation and during the colonial period became a clear justification for the institution of slavery. The genetic inferiority of Black people was given as a justification for their inferior position in society and in the labor process. Racist ideology became even more obvious during the aftermath of Reconstruction. But it was when Black labor was placed in direct competition with white labor that it became a popular creed and established deep roots among the working class as a whole. It expresses, in ideal form, the genuine fears of people in the throes of spatial as well as social transition.

— 7 —

In all precapitalist societies women's work was inextricably linked with that of men. Even though agricultural production was based, in part, on a sexual division of labor, to the extent that women were charged with the rearing of children, housekeeping, and domestic production of goods immediately consumed by the family, women also participated in the basic work of planting, cultivating and harvesting crops, and caring for domestic animals.

Even within American agriculture at the middle of the nineteenth century, the sexual division of labor was less important than the relative equality between women and men in the performance of necessary production tasks. Since the whole family was the basic unit of production, women and children were expected to participate fully in heavy and light labor in the fields as well as in the household. Some women were also engaged in cottage industries, where such products as textiles, canned goods, and wearing apparel were transformed into commodities and offered for sale, rather than being produced for the immediate consumption of the family alone. As a matter of fact, it was the women rather than the men who acquired the skills of weaving, garment-making, and shoemaking that presumably made them more desirable for the factories that were established in the early nineteenth century to produce these commodities.

At the dawn of the factory system female and child workers constituted the heart of the burgeoning textile industry's labor force, and majorities in the shoe and clothing industries. According to Edward Kirkland, "in 1831 it was estimated that 68 percent of all the employees in the [cotton] industry were women and girls; two decades later the percentage was 62. Proportionately women played a much greater part in the cotton industry than in that of Great Britain."[28] By 1850, women constituted about twenty-four percent of all employees in manufacturing establishments, including heavier industry.

Women entered the factories precisely at the time when agriculture still constituted the major laboring activity of the American nation. Often they, as well as children, were sent to do factory work to supplement the meager income of the farm family, but returned to the farm during planting and harvesting seasons to assist in these tasks.

The entrance of women into cotton mills and shoe factories was assisted by the relative sparseness of New England crops and presumably by the invention of semiautomatic machinery in these industries that simplified tasks and lightened the physical workload.* Employers were able to justify the low wages paid to women and children on the grounds that they could only perform light factory work because of their limited physical capacity; these workers were credited, however, with being ideally suited to their jobs because of their superior manual dexterity and their greater degree of patience. Another justification of the low wages paid to women was that they were secondary wage earners, that is, not primarily responsible for the support of the family. Yet, typically, the early factory women were single farm women or Irish immigrants arrived in this country without their families. A majority of them actually were responsible for their own livelihood or were vitally important to the income of fairly small farming homesteads.

Few native-born women in the mid-nineteenth century viewed factory work as a permanent vocation. As well as providing a supplementary income for their families, it offered them an opportunity for social contact that might lead to marriage and family life. The factory was, in fact, regarded as a kind of "finishing school" for those young single women who either had no desire to remain on the farm or no real prospects for doing so. It was an institution that provided boardinghouses, social activities, and some educational services in addition to a livelihood.

As long as manufacturing was an incipient economic mode of production in the agricultural era, women had a relatively secure place in such important industries as textiles and apparel. In the latter third of the nineteenth century, when heavy capital goods manufacturing occupied the center stage of the American economy, the sexual division of labor was to assert itself in full force, and women would be assigned to paid domestic services that corresponded to only a peripheral aspect of the economy. A small number would still be employed in the consumer goods sectors. Later in the early 1900s, most women would only be able to find jobs in nonproductive white collar work.

* Contrary to the popular notion that women are physically unsuited to perform heavy labor and have been excluded from it throughout history, there is considerable evidence that in Great Britian, as just one example, they performed heavy work both in agriculture and in such industries as mining.

Despite the centrality of women to early manufacturing, by the last decades of the nineteenth century it was apparent that they were not to be permitted entrance into the basic capital goods sector of industry. Iron and steel, machine tool production, mining, and oil and heavy chemical production became largely closed to them and have remained so down to our own time.

The transition from agricultural to industrial society had radically altered the position of women. No longer could they be spared for the factory. In the first place, as large portions of the agrarian populations streamed into the cities, mass unemployment among men became among the vital concerns of the rising capitalist class. The presence of women in the factories was regarded as disruptive to social order because many jobless men were roaming the streets and becoming increasingly angry that society had provided no place for them in the new environment.

But there was an even more important reason for removing women from industrial labor, or at least restricting them to light manufacturing and domestic service. Industrialization required of the worker a clear break from the old habits of farming. No longer could the family be viewed as the center of production. The worker had to be prepared to accept the fact that he had to present himself individually at the plant gates, rather than as a member of a communal unit. He had to withstand the backbreaking conditions of work but, even more important, accept the essential alienation both from the ownership of the product of his labor and the methods of work. The fragmentation of factory labor was a traumatic experience for people who had enjoyed a sense of totality on the land.

In the new division of labor only the nuclear family could preserve the sense of wholeness even if the actuality was that no totality could be achieved. The family became the heart of the heartless world. It ameliorated the pain associated with the degradation of industrial labor to the extent that it provided sanctuary for the repair of body and soul. Within the family the male worker would exercise the power denied him in the ever more authoritarian factory. Women were needed to create homes that made tolerable the misery of the workplace, to provide the primary socialization experiences for children, and to create an everyday life that shut out the alien reality. Women created the neighborhood out of their role as producers of the household. In turn, the neighborhood became the locus of social interaction, the force for resisting isolation against the assault of urbanism upon the old concepts of rural community. Capitalism required the nuclear family to re-create labor every day and women became the center not only of the physical reproduction of the new generation of workers but the social reproduction of these workers as well. However crucial their work—the maintaining of the household and the rearing of children—it was never accorded the status of productive labor. In commodity producing societies that status can only be achieved when labor is exchanged for money wages.

The women who entered factories and remained there during the twentieth century were primarily heads of households or married women whose income was the most sustaining economic source for their families. It is no accident that light industry migrated from large cities of the North to rural agricultural areas in the South and decimated industrial areas in Pennsylvania and New England. Here, women who could be recruited for low pay constituted the lifeblood of rural economies where massive unemployment among men had reached epidemic proportions. In the South, where the tradition of labor struggle was relatively weak, women's fear of losing their jobs deterred unionism. In the North, however, there was widespread organization among women industrial workers, and women became active within the unions—typically serving as organizers rather than officials. The talents of women organizers such as Rose Pesotta and Fania Cohn of the Ladies Garment Workers and Julia Maietta, Eula McGill, and Bessie Hillman of the Amalgamated Clothing Workers were essential to the founding of these organizations in the first decades of the twentieth century, and their subsequent revival during the Great Depression. In the 1920s and 1930s a handful of women became members of the General Executive Boards of these unions, as directors of the Southern regions, where there was an overwhelming proportion of women workers even in "skilled" classifications and a relatively low level of organization among them; these regions, however, never represented sufficient power within the union hierarchies to influence crucial decisions. Genuine authority remained in the hands of male leaders of the established locals and boards.

The agitation for "protective legislation" to safeguard the health of working women and children emerged precisely during the years when labor agitation and other forms of industrial unrest suffused the economic landscape as skilled workers faced the assault against their relatively elevated position in the social division of labor by employers who had found that once-proud crafts could be decimated by machines. These workers were quick to perceive that their unemployment and deteriorating economic position were due to women, children, and "slaves" who were willing to work longer hours for lower wages. A new ideology that declared women congenitally inferior in certain areas of work was invented.

The exclusion of women from certain types of factory employment in the late nineteenth century must be compared to the movement to exclude children. In both cases the original impetus for exclusion came from two key sources: the middle-class reformers, who fought child labor and such practices as homework, long hours, and heavy labor for women on the grounds that they were inhuman, and the labor unions who were pressing for restrictive legislation as a means of protecting the income and employment of adult male workers and who also argued against the employment of women and children on "humanitarian" grounds.

It is interesting to note that Samuel Gompers, the president of the AFL during the years when restrictive labor legislation was being pressed by reformers and unions, argued against the use of law for the protection of male workers, since such government protection would discourage union organization. At the same time, he was an ardent supporter of restrictions on immigration, of the abolition of child labor, and of severe limitations on the freedom of employers to hire women in certain industries and trades.

The Women's Trade Union League, an organization devoted to recruiting women into trade unions and an instrumental force in the formation of the International Ladies Garment Workers Union in the first two decades of the twentieth century, was an effective champion of the AFL position with respect to restrictive labor legislation. Rose Schneiderman, vice president of the League, argued in 1924 before a legislative hearing in New York State that women cannot do "the same work as a man" and that "equal rights cannot keep them in work for which they are not fit." Moreover, she argued for the economic interest of male workers: "And the women who are strong enough to work beside men, and who want to work in the same hours of day or night and receive the same pay, might be putting their own brothers, sweethearts, or future husbands out of a job."[29]

But the unions and such groups as the Settlement House

movement, the National Consumers League, and the liberal press were opposed not only by those employers who used women as low-wage laborers, but by groups of women who were practicing skilled trades, particularly printing. On February 27, 1918, women printers, members of the New York Typographical Union, Local 6, submitted a brief against proposed legislation that would prohibit women from working nights. They argued that such legislation would effectively eliminate women from the printing trades since most newspapers were printed during the late evening and nighttime hours. Groups such as the Equal Rights Association and the Women's League for Equal Opportunity branded legislation to restrict the right of women to work in certain industries as discriminatory. Ella M. Sherwin, Brooklyn printer, argued against "welfare legislation" aimed at protecting women:

> Welfare legislation, if persisted in, will protect women to the vanishing point. Whatever its intent, it can have but one outcome. It will drain women out of all highly paid and highly organized trades, because the law will prevent them from doing the same work that men do and the unions will prohibit them from working for a lower wage than the men.[30]

Another group of women, the National Women's Party, was equally adamant against protective legislation. Its president, Mrs. Oliver H. P. Belmont, and its director, Alice Paul, agitated against all protective legislation and for a federal equal rights amendment. The social base of the National Woman's Party was clearly upper class and its opposition to protective legislation was interpreted as a feminist concomitant to the position taken by the Associated Industries, an employers' organization, whose members had a clear economic interest in exploiting women. The weakness of the Woman's Party on this count forced its eventual neutrality on questions of industrial restriction since many state branches of the party supported welfare legislation.

It was evident that proponents of exclusionary legislation were motivated similarly with respect to women and children. But it was equally plain that while total exclusion was sought for children, restriction was the strategy employed with respect to legislation regarding women. Militating against total exclusion of women was their persistence as a major source of light manufacturing labor and their importance in the growing clerical occupations, for which they were actively recruited as the corporations rapidly replaced individual enterprises toward the end of the nineteenth century and generated the demand for a huge bureaucracy of workers to assist in the enlarging administrative functions of industrial as well as financial institutions.

It is interesting to note that the legislation excluding children from the factories coincided with two other developments: the agitation for mass compulsory public schooling and the development of the ideologies that glorified the nuclear family as the bedrock of civilization. The history of restrictive labor legislation with respect to women and children is replete with testimony purporting to show that delinquency and infant mortality rose among families with working mothers. According to contemporary reformers, the schools and the family were needed to insure the moral and physical health of the young. Factory labor, although necessary for social progress, also contained evils that required amelioration. As long as children were not in school and women were not returned to the home, the moral fiber of the whole society was in danger, not to mention the requirements of industry for a trained, disciplined work force.

Throughout American social history these ideologies have been resurrected during times of substantial labor surplus and suppressed during times of expansion when it became important to find new sources of labor. The two world wars, for example, witnessed a dramatic reversal of previous popular images. During the First World War, employers and the government actively enticed women to enter or return to work, even though compulsory school attendance had not yet been effectively enforced for their children. Similarly, "Rosie the Riveter" of World War Two vintage replaced the demure, hardworking housewife of the Depression era.

Within the few years between 1940 and 1945, the so-called natural biological constraints placed on women in heavy industry were forgotten: women could perform heavy lifting, work the midnight shift, spend many hours of overtime, and learn trades for which they had been presumed to be intellectually and physically inferior. But the end of the Second World War generated the return of 11 million men to civilian life in the midst of economic uncertainty and women were swiftly removed from shipyard, metalworking, and transportation industries. Some returned to the home only to reemerge during the 1950s and 1960s to meet the growing demand for labor in government, retailing, and proliferating corporate bureaucracies. Some women were leaving the home in order to help support their families, whose income was stretched to the breaking point by inflation and the diffusion of the urban core to the suburbs. Others were entering the labor force because divorce had made them primary wage earners.

Still, the economy failed to provide jobs for all who sought them. Millions of women were left behind during the industrial upsurge generated by the Second World War, particularly Black and white Southerners and those from mining regions who came to the cities in flight from the depleted rural areas. Once more, the ideologues of social order came forth to proclaim the sanctity of the nuclear family, the deleterious effects of its breakup as a result of migrations and economic pressure, and the consequent impact on moral norms and social mobility. In 1969 Daniel Patrick Moynihan, in a curious juxtaposition of Catholic doctrine and sociogenetic cant, set out to show that the inferior status of Blacks and other minorities was not the result of racial discrimination in employment, education, and other public accommodations as much as it was caused by the structural deficiency of their social institutions. The Black family did not conform to the structure required by an urban industrial society, but was formed under agricultural conditions. This matriarchal pattern and the extended kinship arising from it produced confusion and low performance among its children. Thus did Moynihan end up by blaming the victims rather than the society. In 1971 President Nixon's opposition to legislation that would have resulted in the expansion of federal support for day-care centers was accompanied by his attack against attempts to destroy the nuclear family as the bedrock of American civilization. Implied in this position was the familiar doctrine that women's place was in the home, that social ills such as drug abuse, crime in the streets, and widespread instances of indiscipline in the schools, were a direct consequence of the breakdown of the family resulting from the entrance of women into the work-world.

The segregation of both Black and white women within American manufacturing industry has been even more severe than that of Black males. Even though Black men were ultimately able to occupy more than one-third of the production jobs in the auto and steel industry, women have only recently been able to find jobs on the assembly lines and are still represented to a lesser degree than they were during the Second World War. Although they have continued to be important in the low-paid, low-status industries such as textiles and light electrical engineering, their situation in the steel industry, in heavy chemicals, machine tools, and in the mines remains as it has been for nearly a century. There are virtually no women employed in production and the likelihood of an early breakthrough is barred by substantial unemployment in all these industries, except chemicals, which includes the female labor-intensive pharmaceutical and cosmetics industries. In fact, the women on manufacturing payrolls, as reported by the U.S. Department of Labor in 1968, were nearly all in clerical categories.

Like its predecessors, the women's movement of today is split on issues affecting women in industry. During the recent debate on the Equal Rights Amendment, many women from trade union and working class backgrounds or sympathetic to these points of view argued in favor of the need for special laws protecting women workers in matters affecting their working conditions. Their objection to the Equal Rights Amendment consisted in the possibility that the blanket removal of protective legislation on the grounds of its discriminatory character would be discriminatory in the reverse. According to some, the protection of the safety and health of women afforded by restrictive legislation should be extended to all workers rather than removed. Proponents of the Equal Rights Amendment were more concerned with the discrimination against women in the professions rather than within factories and manual occupations. Despite the middle-class origins and aspirations of these feminists, the arguments that women could perform all jobs equally with men have the weight of historical evidence.

It is clear that, however well motivated, the objective effect of protective legislation for women has been to reinforce ideologies already at work that proclaimed the physical and intellectual inferiority of women on the one hand, and the importance of women's role in the physical and social reproduction of a disciplined, morally trained labor force on the other. With the exclusion of children from the factories, the dangers to the social order were immediately perceived by ruling elites. With the help of the progressives, they created the legal and ideological conditions for containing children. At the same time, they redefined women as a reserve labor force. The trade unions, having regarded women and children as threats rather than allies, were happy to receive the new ideologies if they removed yet another depressant on wages and trade union organization.

— 8 —

By the first decade of the twentieth century industrial capitalism had pushed both Blacks and women to the periphery of the American economy. Although the majority of Black people were still on the land, agriculture was no longer the center of the economic system. The Black worker was transformed from a vital link in the whole economy to a surplus labor force. Similarly, women were being held in reserve for future expansion of production and services. Meanwhile their role was to be confined to the production of the labor force rather than goods.

The emergence of the two groups as a reserve labor force, invited to participate in production during times of war or other spurs to economic growth, and forced to perform the lowest paying, least secure jobs at other times, did not take place in the same way. In the preindustrial phase of American economic development, women were actually crucial for the few manufacturing industries that existed in this country. Their participation in the goods producing sector was made possible by the fact that the "real" labor of men was still farming, mercantile activities, or small-scale artisan production. With the rise of heavy industry after 1850, made possible by the commerical use of steam power, women were gradually replaced as the most important segment of the industrial labor force. Apart from protective legislation, the major device used to exclude them from production was the promulgation of the ideology of "women's place." This ideology was to permeate the American consciousness in proportion to the urbanization of the farming population.

Since the family was no longer the goods producing core of society as it had been in agriculture, its main role now became the social reproduction of the labor force, and women became responsible for the household. The sexual division of labor became visible in industrial society as never before, and the consciousness of women themselves as the heart of household production was accentuated. The entrance of a woman into the wage-earning working class was almost invariably viewed as a temporary measure designed to meet a few household luxury needs that could not be provided by the husband's wage, or alternatively an emergency measure to meet some patriotic requirement. This attitude was given the status of a statute by the Department of Labor's designation of married women as "secondary wage earners." Thus, married women supplement their husband's social security benefits, but are not accorded equal status. If women enter the factory or become part of the office force after marriage, it is naturally assumed that their labor deserves less compensation than comparable "male" jobs. Despite the fact that nearly two out of every five married women living with husbands are employed, the myth of the temporary status of women workers persists.

The path by which Blacks were transformed from the crucial capital producing laborers to surplus labor is exactly the obverse of that of women. In 1850, cotton and tobacco were this country's entrée to the international market. Until 1890 no more important cash crops were grown in the United States. In a real sense, the Black worker, both as slave and "free" laborer was simply too valuable to expend on manufacturing or rail construction. Nor was it desirable, from an economic standpoint, to assign him to activities appropriate for women and children or "unskilled" and unproductive Irish or Chinese immigrants.

For most of the nineteenth century, agriculture provided a certain destiny for Black people in the United States. Even much of the struggle for freedom was shaped in terms of agrarian reforms that would transfer ownership of the land from the old plantation bourbons to the Black workers. Reconstruction was an attempt to implement a new system of land tenure as much as an effort to grant full civil rights to Black people. The breakup of the slave system did not immediately signal the move toward industrialization as far as Black workers were concerned. Industrialism, a doctrine promulgated by former bourbon intellectuals actually became the program of a segment of the old white ruling class. A central mission of Booker T. Washington at the turn of the century was to bring Black people into the cities of the New South as productive laborers in the manufacturing and construction industries that had grown up on the ruins of the fallen King Cotton.

But Southern Blacks were quick to understand that, with few exceptions, urbanism held small rewards for them. The experience of Black Northern workers was not happy. When not employed at the most menial service occupations, they were consigned to marginal industrial jobs in sawmills and construction. The skills acquired by Black building tradesworkers in the South were only employed in Northern cities in periods of labor shortages. At other times, especially during the frequent economic convulsions between the early 1870s and the First World War, organized white labor viewed the Blacks as serious threats to their economic security. Employers were well aware of the importance of maintaining Black workers as a reserve labor force as a means of continuing to exert power over the working class as a whole: the conspicuous use of Black workers as strikebreakers was widespread at the turn of the century.

But there was no way to effect the exclusion of women from new industries without the cooperation of large corporations that controlled many state legislatures during the "gilded age" of capitalist expansion, 1865–1910. It was the ruling class itself that finally agreed to the sexual division of the working class just as it had perpetuated racial and ethnic divisions. It was their influence in the legislatures, particularly in New York where the large manufacturing and financial interests always dominated the state senate, their importance in Congress, and most significantly their control over the factories themselves, that swung the weight to restrict women's labor. After the Civil War, women were able to enter only the lowest-paying, least mechanized industries, such as the manufacture of collars for shirtwaists, shoes, textiles, and clothing. Meanwhile, with the help of trade unions and middle-class reformers, employer-dominated legislatures were placing restrictions on the type of work women could perform. Although 4 million women were employed in 1890 and about ¾ million were in factories, only a bare fraction of these were in the skilled trades, chiefly in printing. More than three million were in domestic services and extensions of housework such as hotel and restaurant work, and laundries and dry cleaning. Although women had been essential to agricultural production in the era when family farming was predominant in this sector, they were quickly relegated to the services during industrialization or remained in the least modern industries.

It is important to remember that during the decade 1880–90 the number of women entering the labor force increased by one-third or 1.3 million. In the same period 5 million immigrants came into this country. Although the male immigrants got the heavy factory jobs, entered the construction trades, and, to a lesser extent, went into farming, women were never out of the labor force during the industrialization period; on the other hand, Blacks had been specifically excluded. In the decades just before the end of the nineteenth century, woman's role in goods production was ideologically defined in terms of her role as a houseworker. It became inevitable that women should be tapped for white collar work after the turn of the century when secretarial workers were labeled "office wives," corporate housekeepers, or servants.

Yet capitalism needed Blacks and women as much as other groups. They were to become the chief sources of new cheap labor after the supply of immigrants was exhausted. With the rise of the "service occupations" women became permanently excluded from basic goods production as the doctrine of women's congenital inability to perform such work permeated the popular mind. Eventually, Blacks were permitted entrance into some heavy industries, especially those requiring sheer physical effort, because immigrants were no longer available to occupy these niches. They became the labor force most relied upon for real capital expansion in comparison to women, who were always to remain central to the service and light manufacturing sectors. Despite these differences, however, there is one characteristic that ties Blacks and women to the same fate as generations of the Eastern and Southern European immigrant. As unskilled workers they are the most vulnerable to technological change. To the extent that mechanization eventually penetrates all industry, whether in goods, producting, or services, the least skilled are the first to be displaced. Just as the replacement of agriculture by industry irreversibly changed the role of immigrant women of peasant origins and Blacks in the economy, so automation is destined to effect another decisive transformation.

NOTES

1. Marcus Lee Hansen, *The Immigrant in American History*, New York, Harper Torchbooks Edition, Harper & Row Publishers, 1964, p. 56.

2. See especially Paul Sweezy, "Marx and the Proletariat" in *Modern Capitalism and other Essays*, New York Monthly Review Press, 1972, pp. 147–65.

3. Charles Leinenweber, "The Socialist Party and the New Immigrant," *Science and Society*, Winter 1968, XXXII, 1, pp. 1–25.

4. Proceedings National Congress of Socialist Party, 1910, p. 99, quoted in Leinenweber, *ibid.*

5. Morris Hillquit, "Immigration in the United States," *International Socialist Journal*, July 1907, p. 71, quoted in Leinenweber, p. 11.

6. Stanley Lebergott, "Labor Force and Employment, 1800–1960" in *Output, Employment and Productivity in the United States After 1800*, New York, National Bureau of Economic Research, 1966, p. 127.

7. For a discussion of the significance of immigration in the growth of the steel industry see especially David Brody, *Steelworkers in America, The Non-Union Era*, Cambridge, Mass., Harvard University Press, 1960, Chapter V, pp. 96–111, and Leon Wolff, *Lockout: The Story of the Homestead Strike of 1892*, London, Longman's, 1965, pp. 241–43.

8. Leon Wolff, *Lockout: The Story of the Homestead Strike of 1892*, London, Longman's, 1965, p. 229.

9. David Brody, *op. cit.*, pp. 107–08.

10. Brinley Thomas, *Migration and Economic Growth: A Study of Great Britain and the Atlantic Economy*, London, Cambridge University Press, 1954, p. 153.

11. Brinley Thomas, *op. cit.*

12. Melvin Dubofsky, *We Shall Be All*, Chicago, Ill., Quadrangle Books, 1969, p. 9.

13. Stephen A. Marglin, *What the Bosses Do: The Origins and Functions of Hierarchy in Capitalist Production*, Cambridge, Mass., Harvard University Research Paper, May 1971.

14. For an excellent discussion of this point see Siegfried Giedion, *Mechanization Takes Command*, New York, W. W. Norton Library Edition, 1969, pp. 96ff.

15. On this development see the interesting account by Berenice M. Fisher, *Industrial Education: American Ideals and Institutions*, Madison, Wisc., University of Wisconsin Press, 1967, pp. 52–71.

16. For a good discussion of the intellectual role of Catholicism in American life, see Peter Berger, *The Sacred Canopy*, New York, Doubleday & Co., 1967.

17. Marc Karson, *American Labor Unions and Politics 1900–1918*, Carbondale, Ill., Southern Illinois University Press, 1958.

18. Paul Blanshard, *American Freedom and Catholic Power*, Boston, Mass., Beacon Press, 2nd edition revised and enlarged, 1958.

19. *Ibid.*, p. 299.

20. John H. Laslett, *Labor and the Left: A Study of Socialist and Radical Influences in the American Labor Movement, 1881–1924*, New York, Basic Books, Inc., 1970, especially Chapter VIII.

21. *Ibid.*, Chapters V and VI.

22. C. Vann Woodward, *The Origins of the New South*, Louisiana University Press, 1951, p. 205.

23. Albert D. Kirwan, *Revolt of the Rednecks: Mississippi Politics, 1876–1925*, New York, Harper Torchbooks, 1965, p. 93.

24. Woodward, *op. cit.*, p. 208.

25. Broadus and George Mitchell, *The Industrial Revolution in the South*, New York, New American Library, 1970, pp. 207–08.

26. Ray Marshall, *The Negro and Organized Labor,* New York, John Wiley & Sons, 1965, p. 31.

27. Peter M. Blau and Otis Dudley Duncan, *The American Occupational Structure,* New York, John Wiley & Sons, 1967, p. 209.

28. Edward C. Kirkland, *A History of American Economic Life,* New York, F. S. Crofts & Co., 1939, p. 337.

29. Elizabeth Faulkner Baker, *Protective Labor Legislation with Special Reference to Women in the State of New York,* New York, AMS Press, 1969, pp. 201–02.

30. Anne O'Hagen's article in *Touchstone Magazine,* August 1919, quoted in Baker, *op. cit.,* p. 190.

4

Trade Unionism:
Illusion and Reality

— 1 —

The configuration of strikes since 1967 is unprecedented in the history of American workers. The number of strikes as a whole, as well as rank-and-file rejections of proposed union settlements with employers, and wildcat actions has exceeded that in any similar period in the modern era.

The most notable feature of the present situation is that the unions are no longer in a position of leadership in workers' struggles; they are running desperately to catch up to their own membership. There are few instances in which the union heads have actually given militant voice to rank-and-file sentiment. In many cases, union sanctions for walkouts have followed the workers' own action. In others, the leadership has attempted to thwart membership initiative and, having failed, has supported a strike publicly while sabotaging it behind the scenes. For the most part, the national bureaucracies of the unions have sided with employers in trying to impose labor peace upon a rebellious membership. What is remarkable is that the rebellion has been largely successful despite enormous odds.

The unions are afraid to oppose the rank and file directly. Their opposition has taken the form of attempting to channel the broad range of rank-and-file grievances into bargaining demands which center, in the main, on wages and benefits, while the huge backlog of grievances on issues having to do with working conditions remains unsolved. Rank-and-file militancy has occurred precisely because of the refusal of the unions to address themselves to the issues of speedup, health and safety, plant removal, increased workloads, technological change, and arbitrary discharges of union militants.

Wages have, of course, also been an enormously important factor in accounting for the rash of strikes. Since 1967, workers have suffered a pronounced deterioration in living standards. Despite substantial increases in many current settlements, real wages for the whole working class have declined annually, for there are few contracts which provide for cost-of-living increases in addition to the negotiated settlements. Even where C-o-L clauses have been incorporated into the contracts, there is usually a ceiling on the amount of increase to which the company is obligated. In many contracts, the first-year increase is equal to the cost of living increase as tabulated by the Bureau of Labor Statistics for the previous year. But the second- and third-year increases are usually not as great and during these years workers' real wages are diminished significantly.

Long-term contracts, which have become standard in American industry, have robbed the rank and file of considerable power to deal with their problems within the framework of collective bargaining. Workers have been forced to act outside of approved procedures because instinctively they know that the union has become an inadequate tool to conduct struggles, even where they have not yet perceived the union as an outright opponent to their interests.

For most workers, the trade union still remains the elementary organ of defense of their immediate economic interests. Despite the despicable performance of labor movement leadership during the past thirty years, and especially in the last two decades, blue- and white-collar workers regard their unions as their only weapons against the deterioration of working conditions and the rampant inflation responsible for recent declines in real wages.

In part, trade unions retain their legitimacy because no alternative to them exists. In part, workers join unions because the unions give the appearance of advancing workers' interests, since they must do so to some extent to gain their support. A national union bureaucracy can betray the workers' elementary demands for a considerable period of time without generating open opposition among the rank and file. Even when workers are aware of the close ties that exist between the union leaders and the employers, rebellion remains a difficult task for several crucial reasons.

First, in many cases, the union bureaucracy is far removed from the shop floor because membership is scattered over many plants or even industries. In unions like the United Steelworkers, only half the 1.2 million members are employed in the basic steel sector of the industry. The rest of the membership spans the nonferrous metals industry, steel fabricating plants, stone-working, can companies, and even a few coal mines. Most of the membership is in large multiplant corporations that have successfully decentralized their operations so that no single plant or cluster of factories in a single geographic region is capable of affecting production decisively. The problem of diffusion is complicated by the recent trend of U.S. corporations to expand their manufacturing operations abroad rather than within this country. In these circumstances, many workers, unable to communicate with workers in other plants of the same corporation since the union has centralized communications channels, feel powerless to improve their own conditions.

Second, the structure of collective bargaining enables the national union to transfer responsibility to the local leadership for failures of the union contract on working conditions issues, while claiming credit for substantial improvements in wages and benefits. This practice has been notable in the Auto Workers, the Rubber Workers, and others that have national contracts with large corporations.

Although the last decade has been studded with examples of rank-and-file uprisings against the least responsible of the labor bureaucrats, in nearly all cases, the new group of elected leaders has merely reproduced the conditions of the old regime. In the steel, rubber, electrical, government workers and other important unions one can observe some differences in sensitivity to the rank and file among the newer leaders. They are more willing to conduct strike struggles and their political sophistication is greater. But these unions can hardly be called radical nor have they made sharp breaks from the predominant policies of the labor movement in the contemporary era.

Some radicals explain this phenomenon in a purely idealistic way. According to them, the weakness of the factional struggles within the unions over the past decade has been that they have been conducted without an ideological perspective that differs from the procapitalist bias of the prevailing leadership. The left has been largely irrelevant to them. Therefore, if the new leadership merely recapitulates "the same old crap" (Marx's words), radicals should blame their own failure to concentrate their political work within the working class. Presumably, a strong left could have altered the kind of leadership and the program of the rank-and-file movements.

There is undoubtedly some truth in these assertions. Yet the disturbing fact is that the Communist left was very much a part of the trade union leadership for several decades prior to 1950; in some unions there are remnants of the left still in power. There is a tendency to explain the failure of the old Communist left by reference to its "revisionist" policies. Such superficial explanations assume that if only the politics of radical labor organizers had been better, the whole picture would have been qualitatively different. This will be shown not to be the case.

If the trade union remains an elementary organ of struggle, it has also evolved into a force for integrating the workers into the corporate capitalist system. Inherent in the modern labor contract is the means both to insure some benefit to the workers and to provide a stable, disciplined labor force to the employer. The union assumes obligations as well as wins rights in the collective bargaining agreement.

Under contemporary monopolistic capitalism, these obligations include: (1) the promise not to strike, except under specific conditions, or at the termination of the contract, (2) a bureaucratic and hierarchical grievance procedure consisting of many steps during which the control over the grievance is systematically removed from the shop floor and from workers' control, (3) a system of management prerogatives wherein the union agrees to cede to the employer "the operation of the employer's facilities and the direction of the working forces, including the right to hire, suspend, or discharge for good cause and ... to relieve employees from duties due to lack of work,"[1] and (4) a "checkoff" of union dues as an automatic deduction from the workers' paychecks.

The last provision, incorporated into 98 percent of union contracts, treats union dues as another tax on workers' wages. It is a major barrier to close relations between union leaders and the rank and file. Workers have come to regard the checkoff as another insurance premium. Since they enjoy little participation in union affairs, except when they have an individual grievance or around contract time, the paying of dues in this manner—designed originally to protect the union's financial resources—has removed a major point of contact between workers and their full-time representatives. This procedure is in sharp contrast to former times when the shop steward or business agent was obliged to collect dues by hand. In that period, the dues collection process, however cumbersome for the officials, provided an opportunity for workers to voice their complaints as well as a block against the encroachment of bureaucracy.

The modern labor agreement is the principal instrument of the class collaboration between the trade unions and the corporations. It mirrors the bureaucratic and hierarchical structure of modern industry and the state. Its provisions are enforced not merely by law, but by the joint efforts of corporate and trade union bureaucracies. Even the most enlightened trade union leader cannot fail to play his part as an element in the mechanisms of domination over workers' rights to spontaneously struggle against speedup or *de facto* wage cuts, either in the form of a shift in the work process or by inflationary price increases.

The role of collective bargaining today is to provide a rigid institutional framework for the conduct of the class struggle. This struggle at the point of production has become regulated in the same way as have electric and telephone rates, prices of basic commodities, and foreign trade. The regulatory procedure in labor relations includes government intervention into collective bargaining, the routinization of all conflict between labor and the employer on the shop floor, and the placing of equal responsibility for observing plant rules upon management and the union.

The objective of this procedure is to control labor costs as a stable factor of production in order to permit rational investment decisions by the large corporations. The long-term contract insures that labor costs will be a known factor. It guarantees labor peace for a specified period of time. The agreement enables employers to avoid the disruption characteristic of stormier periods of labor history when workers' struggles were much more spontaneous, albeit more difficult.

An important element in the labor contract is that most of the day-to-day issues expressing the conflict between worker and employer over the basic question of the division of profit are not subject to strikes. In the automobile and electrical agreements as well as a few others, the union has the right to strike over speedup, safety issues, or a few other major questions. In the main, however, most complaints about working conditions and work assignments are adjusted in the final step of the grievance procedure by an "impartial" arbitrator selected by both the union and management. Even in industries where the strike weapon is a permitted option, the union leaders usually put severe pressure on the rank and file to choose the arbitration route since strikes disrupt the good relations between the union bureaucracy and management—good relations which are valued highly by liberal corporate officials and union leaders alike.

With few exceptions, particularly in textile and electrical corporations, employers regard labor leaders as their allies against the ignorant and undisciplined rank and file. This confidence has been built up over the past thirty-five years of industrial collective bargaining.

The trade unions have become an appendage of the corporations because they have taken their place as a vital institution in the corporate capitalist complex. If union leaders are compelled to sanction and often give at least verbal support to worker demands, it is most often because the union is a political institution whose membership selects officials. However, almost universally the democratic foundations of the trade unions have been undermined.

The left understood that the old craft unions were essentially purveyors of labor power, controlling both the supply of skilled labor and its price. The most extreme expression of their monopoly was the terror and violence practiced by craft union leadership against the rank and file. Since the old unions were defined narrowly by their economic functions and by their conservative ideology, the assumption of the Socialists and Communists who helped build industrial unions which included the huge mass of unskilled and semiskilled workers was that these organizations would express broader political and social interests, if not radical ideologies.

On the whole, despite corruption and bureaucratic resistance to the exercise of membership control, many unions in the United States have retained the forms but not the content of democracy. It is possible to remove union leaders and replace them, but it is not possible to transcend the institutional constraints of trade unionism itself.

Trade unions have fallen victim to the same disease as the broader electoral and legislative system. Just as the major power over the state has shifted from the legislative to the executive branch of government, power over union affairs has shifted from the rank and file to the corporate leaders, the trade union officials, and the government. Trade unions are regulated by the state both in their relations with employers and in their internal operations. Moreover, the problems of union leadership have been transformed from political and social issues to the routines of contract administration and internal bureaucratic procedures, such as union finances. The union leader is a business executive. His accountability is not limited to the membership—it is extended to government agencies, arbitrators, courts of law, and other institutions which play a large role in regulating the union's operations.

The contradictory role of trade unions is played out at every contract negotiation in major industries. Over the past several years the chasm between the leadership and membership has never been more exposed. During this period, a rising number of contract settlements have been rejected by the rank and file; in 1968, the proportion of rejection was nearly 30 percent. In contract bargaining the rank and file has veto power, but no means of initiative. In the first place, many major industries have agreements which are negotiated at the national level. There is room for local bargaining over specific shop issues, but the main lines of economic settlements are determined by full-time officials of the company and the union. One reason for this concentration of power is the alleged technical nature of collective bargaining in the modern era. Not only leaders and representatives of the local membership sit on the union's side of the bargaining table, but lawyers, insurance and pension experts, and sometimes even management consultants as well; the rank-and-file committees tend to be relegated to advisory or window-dressing functions or simply play the role of bystander. The product of the charade that is characteristic of much of collective bargaining today is a mammoth document which reads more like a corporate contract or a mortgage agreement than anything else. In fact, it is a bill of sale.

The needs of the membership only partially justify the specialization of functions within the trade unions. Insurance and pension plans do require a certain expertise, but the overall guidance of the direction of worker-employer relationships has been centralized as a means of preventing the direct intervention of the rank and file. More, the domination of specialists within the collective bargaining process signals the removal of this process from the day-to-day concerns of the workers. The special language of the contract, its bulk and its purely administrative character put its interpretation beyond the grasp of the rank and file and help perpetuate the centrality of the professional expert in the union hierarchy.

In this connection, it is no accident that the elected union official has only limited power within the collective bargaining ritual (and, in a special sense, within the union itself). Few national union leaders make decisions either in direct consultation with the membership or with fellow elected officials. It is the hired expert who holds increased power in union affairs and who acts as a buffer for the union official between the corporate hierarchy and the restive rank and file. As in other institutions, experts have been used to rationalize the conservatism of the leadership in technical and legal terms, leaving officials free to remain politically viable by supporting the sentiments expressed by the membership while, at the same time, rejecting their proposed actions. The importance of the experts has grown with the legalization of collective bargaining, especially the management of labor conflict by the courts and the legislatures, with legislation, and restraining orders limiting strikes, picketing, and other traditional working class weapons. In industries considered public utilities, such as the railroads, a strike is almost always countered by a court order enjoining the workers from taking direct action on the grounds that such action constitutes a violation of the national interest. The lawyer has become a key power broker between the workers, their unions, and the government. He is considered an indispensable operative in contemporary labor relations.

Some unions have promoted their house counsels from staff to officers. The secretary-treasurer of the Amalgamated Clothing Workers of America was formerly general counsel; its president began his career as counsel for the Detroit Joint Board of the union. The president of the United Packinghouse Workers was also its counsel for many years. But even without holding executive office the labor lawyer is placed in a position of both influence and ultimately of power within the organization by the increasing volume of government regulation of all types of trade union affairs. The same tendency can be observed within corporations where, together with financial experts, attorneys are replacing production men as the new men of power.

During the past decade in the auto, steel, rubber and other basic manufacturing industries, the critical issues of working class struggle have been those related to control over the workplace. The tremendous shifts in plant location, work methods, job definitions and other problems associated with investment in new equipment, expansion, and the changing requirements of skills to operate new means of production, have found the union bureaucracies unprepared. The reasons for trade union impotence at the workplace go beyond ideology. They are built into the sinews of the collective bargaining process.

Many important industries have national contracts covering most monetary issues, including wages. In the electrical, auto, and steel industries, negotiations are conducted with individual companies, but in reality there is "pattern" bargaining. A single major producer is chosen by the union and corporations to determine wage and fringe benefit settlement for the rest of the industry. All other negotiations stall until the central settlement is reached.

National union leadership always poses wage demands as the most important negotiating issues. Problems such as technological changes, work assignments, job classifications, and pace of work are usually negotiated at the local level after the economic package has been settled. And by the time the local negotiations begin —often conducted between rank-and-file leaders and middle managers—the national union has lost interest in the contract. Its entire orientation is toward the narrowly defined "economic" side of the bargaining. Although many agreements stipulate that resumption of work will not take place before the resolution of local issues, the international representatives and top leaders of the union put enormous pressure on the membership to settle these issues as quickly as possible. It is at the plant level that most sellouts take place. The local feels abandoned, but resentment is diverted to the failure of the shop leadership rather than that of the top bureaucracy, because the national union has "delivered the goods" on wages and benefits.

For example, after every national auto settlement, a myriad of local walkouts are called over workplace issues. These strikes are short-lived and usually unsuccessful. In the main, in struggles against speedup, young workers and Blacks are the spearhead.

The impatience of the bureaucracy with this undisciplined action is usually expressed in long harangues to local leaders and the rank and file by international representatives who are employees of the national union. When persuasion fails, the rebellious local is sometimes put into receivership and an administrator is sent from the head office to take it over until order is restored.

Among radicals the conventional wisdom of today is to admit the conservative character of trade unions in the era of monopoly capitalism—their integration and subordination to the large corporations. At the same time, many radicals stress the important defensive role trade unions perform during the periods when growing capitalist instability forces employers to launch an offensive against workers' living standards and working conditions. Despite the conservative ideology of labor leaders and legal constraints upon them, rank-and-file pressure today is occasionally able to force unions to lead the fight against employer efforts to transfer to the working class the burdens of recessions or the dislocations of the labor force that occur during periods of technological change.

A recent illustration was provided by the 1969 national General Electric strike. The conjuncture of inflation, deteriorating working conditions, and the arrogant bargaining posture of the company produced the first unified strike in the electrical industry in twenty-three years. It does not matter that the leaders of the AFL-CIO unions representing most of the workers wanted neither the strike nor unity with the independent United Electrical Workers. Rank-and-file pressure within the largest AFL-CIO union in the industry, the International Union of Electrical Workers, was sufficient to threaten the hegemony of the leadership and reverse the timid collective bargaining strategies of past contract negotiations. Repeatedly rejecting offers by the unions for arbitration of outstanding issues, GE attempted to win a clear-cut victory in order to break the emerging solidarity of the workers and set a pattern for other industries. Its objective was a return to the old divide-and-conquer practice of a separate agreement with each union, but for a time it had little success in encouraging back-to-work movements.

Yet it would be a mistake to infer from the GE experience that temporary trade union militancy in response to employer opposition signals an end to class collaboration or the institutional constraints of collective bargaining on workers' autonomy. In fact, the GE strike points sharply to the persistence and dominance of these constraints. The call by the unions for arbitration and acceptance of the intervention of "neutral" political figures such as Senator Javits in a fact-finding investigation was an indication that the leadership lacked confidence in the ability of the workers to win their own struggle and sought to end the strike as soon as possible. The trade union movement, particularly the AFL-CIO with its tremendous financial resources and 13 million members, could not effectively mobilize support for the boycott that had been called by AFL-CIO President George Meany to supplement the electrical workers' own efforts.

The weakness of the strike was not a lack of willingness to fight on the part of workers. Despite the past sellouts, and the paternalism and anti-Communism used for years to split their ranks, GE workers exhibited tremendous courage and a capacity for organized struggle in defending their living standards. But, locked within the apparatus of bureaucratic unionism, the workers were unable to broaden the struggle beyond the quantitative economic terms framed by the leadership. The strike was settled on the basis of agreement on wages and the cost-of-living clause —with all other demands referred to arbitration and discussion.

In 1971, top union leaders reacted with militant rhetoric to President Nixon's announced wage freeze; in this case, they could not simply give outright support to government and corporate efforts to discipline the work force. Officials from all wings of organized labor attacked the freeze, declaring that it amounted to a windfall for big business. George Meany led the barrage of invective against the administration, threatening a rash of strikes if the freeze was maintained. Leonard Woodcock, the head of the million-and-a-half member United Auto Workers, declared that the union would cancel its contracts with auto-makers unless the freeze was rescinded or the government took steps to place severe enforceable restrictions on prices at the same time. Harry Bridges of the West Coast Longshoremen, the grand old man of labor's decimated independent "left-wing" unions, refused to end the coastwide strike currently in progress.

Behind the threats of mass strikes and scorn for the wage freeze demand, however, were factors more indicative of the real positions of the unions. In the first place, the unions would have risked another blow to their declining prestige among the rank and file if they had refused to protest the blatant inequality contained in the President's order. Second, Meany himself had been proposing a wage-price freeze since 1969. Union leaders were willing to suspend the strike weapon and demands for wage increases if the administration was prepared to impose similarly stringent controls over prices. In effect, they were prepared to accept another step in the direction of government regulation of labor relations if the corporations would agree to the principle of "equality of sacrifices." Third, unions had warmly cooperated with two previous freezes imposed by Democratic administrations during the Second World War and again during the Korean War. There was much suspicion that the unions would not have reacted so vocally to the order of a Democratic President. In the end, after much vacillation, top union leaders, even the "liberal" Woodcock, rejoined the Board set up by President Nixon to implement the freeze.

Even during the 1950s union leaders were often forthright in their criticism of the big-business orientation of the Republican Eisenhower administration, particularly with respect to economic policies. But one must recall the feeble union response to the enactment of the Landrum-Griffin Act in 1959 to keep the infrequent evidence of rhetorical militancy in perspective. Although the bill to extend controls over labor's financial affairs was introduced by a Republican and a Southern Democrat, it had genuine bipartisan support, including the active backing of then Senator John F. Kennedy. Union lobbyists welcomed Kennedy's participation in the formation of the legislation because they appreciated his efforts to moderate the extent of controls. Only the Teamsters Union and the handful of other independent unions really opposed the bill. For the most part, union leaders were unwilling to fight the legislation because they felt that it was inevitable. Moreover, they had been convinced by many of their loyal congressional supporters that outright rejection of the idea of reporting and disclosing union finances would merely provoke a movement for stronger requirements. The unions offered tepid opposition because they would not risk hurting Democratic chances in the 1960 elections.

Until the strike wave which began in 1967 in response to the decline of real wages, economic issues have not been sufficient to spur workers to undertake protracted strikes. For example, the 116-day steel strike in 1959 was fought over the right of the company to change work rules and institute technological changes without consulting the union. The two-year-long oil strikes that began in 1963 were conducted over the question of layoffs and job security in the wake of technological innovations. Most auto walk-outs in recent years have been over speedup and other working conditions issues. Even the lengthy GE strike was fought against the arbitrariness of the company; its attack was against working conditions as much as wages.

But the trade union structure has become less able to solve elementary defensive problems. Higher wages for organized workers since the end of World War II have been purchased at a high price. One result of the close ties between unions and corporations has been the enormous freedom enjoyed by capital in transferring the wage increases granted to workers in the shop to the shoulders of workers as consumers. Wage increases have been granted with relative ease under these circumstances in the largest corporations and the most monopolized industrial sectors.

Equally significant has been the gradual increase of constraints in the collective bargaining agreement on the workers' freedom to oppose management's imposition of higher production norms, labor-saving technologies, and policies of plant dispersal. (The last left millions of textile, steel, auto, shoe, and other workers stranded in the forties and fifties.) The bureaucratization of grievance procedures has robbed shop stewards of their power to deal with management on the shop floor. The inability of workers to change their working conditions through the union has had two results: workers limit their union loyalty to the narrow context of wage struggles, and they go outside the union to solve their basic problems in the plant. Thus the wildcat strike has become a protest not only against the brutality of industrial management, but also against the limits imposed by unionism. The conditions pertaining to the role of trade unions during the rise of industrial capitalism in the United States no longer apply in the monopoly epoch.

— 2 —

A little more than fifty years ago, in 1919, the first national strike among unskilled workers in a mass production industry ended in defeat. Judge Elbert Gary, the last of the old barons of the steel industry, defeated the efforts of the 350,000 workers by the tenacity born of the immense resources of the U. S. Steel Corporation, combined with the use of divisive propaganda to sever the fragile unity of skilled and unskilled workers, plain scabherding, and other more blatant forms of strikebreaking. Some old-timers and trade union historians claim that the real cause of the defeat lay in the old AFL style of organization by craft which dominated the strike even though the organizers of the strike were strong advocates of industrial unionism.

Although the strike was not successful, it was remarkable for the fact that workers stayed out for over three months to gain union recognition. Their chief demand was the right to bargain collectively with the giants of the steel industry. The employers agreed that they would unilaterally meet many of the other demands of the strikers, including a cut in the number of work hours—U.S. Steel actually reduced the twelve-hour day to eight hours, with an accompanying 25 percent increase the following year—but they would never deal with outside representatives of their employees. The open shop was a sacred principle of Judge Gary and his fellow steelmen. After the strike the union withered until the great industrial union movement fifteen years later.

However, the corporation heads of the steel industry and other mass production industries were by no means unified on the question of collective bargaining. The older production men heading the large corporations were haunted by memories of the great Homestead Steel Strike of 1892, the national strikes in mining and in railroads at the turn of the century, and the development of the Socialist Party into an important force in American politics. They were in genuine fear that a unionized work force would lead to radical social change.

The kernel of their objections to unionization was not that unions would elect more representatives to public office or even that they would provide organized pressure for wage increases and more social benefits. Gary himself was one of the leading proponents of corporation-sponsored "welfare capitalism," a phrase denoting the recognition by the corporations of their obligation to make provisions for the nonwage needs of the workers. The near monopoly position of the giant industries in the American economy was already making them more receptive to economic demands.

The old robber barons who headed the major corporations were afraid that unions would intrude on the prerogatives of management and would represent a threat to corporate control of production and the direction of the labor forces. But a newer group of corporation directors had made their appearance in American industry about 1910. They were not cut from the mold of the self-made man or the production manager. They were sales experts and financial wizards. Charles Schwab, Gary's successor, was a professional fund raiser and administrative expert who had reorganized several faltering corporations prior to his assumption of the position of chief executive officer of U.S. Steel. Similarly, Gerard Swope, the head of General Electric, had not been a production manager before assuming leadership of the giant electrical corporation. These men were interested in lower production costs and uninterrupted production. They were keenly aware of the costs of the long steel strike to industry.

As early as 1915, Swope was prepared to entertain the possibility of dealing with labor organizations. He even went so far as to suggest to Sam Gompers, the president of the AFL, that GE could be organized. Swope, undoubtedly influenced by the mass strikes in mining and textiles and the garment trades during the previous five years, was looking for ways to stabilize labor relations—to make labor a known cost factor as well as to delimit the influence of unions in determining the pace of work and the direction of the work force. He was also impressed by the role of unions in disciplining the work force. In the same year, a member of the Employers' Association of the Chicago Men's Clothing Industry praised the leader of the Amalgamated Clothing Workers' Union, Sidney Hillman, who later would become a major force in the CIO. "We regard Sidney Hillman very highly," he said. "We believe him honest, high-minded and capable.... With Hillman dead or dethroned we would be in the hands of the old grafting pirates who would not enforce an agreement, who would foment shop strikes . . ."[2]

To be sure, most corporation leaders did not look to the AFL as the solution to the labor problem, even though Gompers had become a junior crony in the National Civic Federation—an early attempt to find a meeting ground between labor, management, and the public in the interest of advancing American capitalism. Instead, the main direction of their efforts was to establish employee representation plans.

Despite the reluctance of some sectors of industry (notably, the recalcitrant Judge Gary), the "works councils" or employee associations strengthened the belief of many corporate liberals that collective bargaining provided the best hope of retaining control over the labor force and dissipating the more radical elements in the unions.

During the First World War, hundreds of company unions were ordered formed by government edict prompted by employers who were frightened by the chance that genuine unionism would challenge their power. In many cases, including the steel and packing industries, the union militants succeeded in taking over these organizations and the companies were forced into primitive collective bargaining under pressure of the government's resolve to insure continuous production of war materiel.

With the ranks of labor, however, the idea of collective bargaining itself was not a universally accepted strategic goal. Around the turn of the century, revolutionary syndicalism, a doctrine whose origins were to be found among workers in under-industrialized countries such as Spain and Italy, had begun to take root in America, even though the idea had been espoused by the Socialist Labor Party as early as the 1880s.

The spread of syndicalist ideas was remarkable among the native-born American miners as well as Italian shoe and textile workers and Jewish garment workers. Unlike the Socialists, who believed that the struggle for liberation from capitalist oppression must be preceded by a prolonged period of reformist struggles, especially through collective bargaining and peaceful parliamentary activity, the syndicalists advocated the formation of revolutionary unions whose object was to capture power in the factories, smash the state since it attempted to protect property, and establish a society controlled directly by the producers.

In contrast the demands of AFL leaders, Socialist and non-Socialist, were by definition reformist, since they attempted to wrest concessions from employers without fundamentally changing power within the factory or in society. For the craft-minded AFL, the ability to win depended on the skill of the workers as much as on their degree of organization or their economic conditions. Where unskilled or semiskilled workers had flocked to the unions, as in the garment and mining industries, it was explained as aberration. The AFL leaders held that the skilled craftsmen in these industries, such as cutters and weighers, were the soul of the struggle. Without their support, union organization was out of the question. By themselves, unskilled workers could not carry through a successful battle, even if they could be organized—a doubtful prospect in any case.

Between 1905, the year of the formation of the Industrial Workers of the World (IWW), and the Depression of the 1930s, the syndicalist spirit continued to be an influence among American workers, even when the fortunes of the IWW were low. The IWW never succeeded in generating a national strike. Its most dramatic activities were confined to individual strikes in mass production industries. But it showed that unskilled workers were indeed capable of sustaining long strikes and were potentially, at least, a force to be reckoned with by both employers and reformist-minded unions.

The IWW abhorred collective bargaining. It believed that the uprising of a group of workers within a particular industry was produced by their grievances and could only end when the grievances were totally redressed. The employers could restore a wage cut, slow the pace of work, or grant other concessions, but the workers should decide independently whether to return to work or spread the struggle to other industries. The IWW hoped for the general strike which would bring down the system of industrial slavery and capitalist governments. In any case, they refused to sign contracts guaranteeing labor peace. If the workers returned to their jobs, they reserved their right to strike at any time.

The IWW was more of a movement than an organization. Its bureaucracy was fairly loose, its organizers undisciplined. In many industries, such as the garment trades, IWW sympathizers belonged to the established union but agitated consistently for no compromises with employers, for the general strike, and for flash strikes over grievances.

The revolutionary ideology of the IWW infused its organizing tactics: it was prepared to employ any means necessary to achieve the goals of the class war. Yet even though in its propaganda it had contempt for legality, one of its most important achievements was its remarkable defense of civil liberties in Seattle, Paterson, and other places where local public officials attempted to limit its right to operate. For most of its colorful career, the staid guardians of the traditional craft unions remained adamantly opposed to its attempt to organize "dual unions," that is, organizations that competed actively with AFL affiliates in particular trades and industries. The IWW's lumber workers affiliate was in competition with the AFL carpenters union; its efforts among textile and metal workers were regarded as direct affronts to established crafts. The old union leaders regarded the IWW as "hoboes," "riffraff," and "vagabonds" who gave the legitimate labor movement a bad name. Even many trade unionists who were members of the Socialist Party held this view, although, it must be remembered, some Socialists such as Eugene Debs were present at the founding convention of the IWW. Others, like members of the Brewery Workers and the Western Federation of Miners, which were led by confirmed Socialists, who at least believed in the radical reorganization of society, were unable to affiliate with the IWW over the long run, because they perceived that trade unionism was incompatible with political sectarianism. In the main the Socialists remained part of the traditional labor movement even if they were sympathetic to IWW strikes and gave material support in such instances as the Lawrence and Paterson textile struggles.

Sidney Hillman of the Amalgamated Clothing Workers (ACWA) and the leaders of the International Ladies Garment Workers Union (ILGWU) ruthlessly opposed the efforts of anarchists and syndicalists within their unions. The Amalgamated was particularly hostile to the idea of revolutionary unionism. By 1914 it had embarked on a course from which it was never to depart, when it proclaimed the era of permanent labor-management cooperation in the men's clothing industry as a result of its victory in the Hart Schaffner and Marx strike the same year. Industry-wide boards regulating piecework rates, establishing welfare programs, and consulting on industrial conditions were established on a bipartite basis.

However, the Amalgamated remained militant with respect to the unorganized sector of the industry. Indeed, the subsequent twenty years were marked by strikes and energetic organizing campaigns to consolidate union power. But the Socialist leaders of the union were clear about the separation of politics from economics. Socialism was a doctrine to be preached in the union publications and in educational programs; it had no place around the bargaining table. Although the Socialists who were active in the union disagreed with Gompers on many ideological issues, including the necessity for unions to get involved in the mainstream of American politics (the ACWA supported Socialist candidates until 1936), their disagreements with the AFL president on trade union matters were limited to tactics. The Amalgamated was one of the first unions to become a sophisticated purveyor of business interests as the best insurance of its own members' welfare.

It is interesting to compare the role of Gompers during the First World War with that of Hillman during the Second. Each became the labor spokesman within the government as well as the government spokesman within the ranks of labor. The presumed antagonism between industrial unionists and Socialists within the AFL on the one hand and the business-minded leadership of Sam Gompers and his successors on the other revolved around the methods rather than goals. The AFL had sponsored the steel strike of 1919 and given it direction. Its goals were fully consistent with AFL philosophy. The fact that the strike was lost may be a function of the incompetence and venality of the old type of craft organization which spent more energy jockeying for jurisdictional positions than working to win the strike. But its object, collective bargaining for unskilled as well as skilled workers, prefigured essentially the program of the CIO.

In 1919, employers had not yet accepted unions as an essential element of the industrial structure; it was not until the 1930s that they were willing to listen carefully to those who claimed that unions would be important allies in the quest for labor peace. The 1920s witnessed the near destruction of the most powerful of the industrial and craft unions and the end of the growth of unionism in some basic industries, such as steel and packing, where beachheads had been established during the war. The ten-year period following World War I brought a return to the prewar conditions of wage cuts, arbitrary firing of working class militants, and attempts by conservative trade union leaders to make bargains with employers in order to insure the survival of the union and their own leadership within it. The prosperity of the 1920s had its reflection in rising wages, but it cannot be said that the trade union was instrumental in determining the wage level.

After the 1929 crash, most of the corporation leaders and their government allies were in confusion and disarray. Big business had no program to deal with the economic and social crisis beyond measures to transfer the burdens of shrinking employment, profits, and production to the workers, farmers, small businessmen, and other countries. Only a minority of those with power sought to prepare a broader program for economic revival.

The remnants of the AFL leadership were caught in the interstices of the big-business offensive and their own desire for institutional survival. They held tenaciously to a keyhole vision of the crisis. With their organizations reduced in numbers and their political influence at a low ebb, the stolid guardians of the "House of Labor" whined their litany of complaint but firmly rejected mass struggle. Only the ex-Socialist Sidney Hillman of the ACWA and the United Mine Workers' president, John L. Lewis, leaders of the two most important industrial unions in the Federation, were able to seize the opportunity presented by the rebellious mood of the workers.

The Amalgamated, the International Ladies Garment Workers Union, and the Miners were able to recover somewhat from the dismal union decline of the 1920s and to organize thousands of new members. But most craft unions shrank to skeletal size as building construction ground to a near-halt, industrial production declined nearly 50 percent, and millions of skilled workers joined the ranks of the unemployed.

John L. Lewis and Sidney Hillman were old AFL men. Both believed in the strike only as an ultimate weapon to force employers to deal with unions over the bargaining table. Both opposed the radicals within their ranks until the radicals came over to their way of thinking. When the radicals proved loyal to trade union objectives, they were permitted to join the effort to organize workers in mass production industries into the CIO. In some cases, they were even permitted to lead unions, provided they represented no sharp departures *in practice* from the policies of the central organization. Autonomy was permitted to international unions on all matters not specifically covered by CIO policy. During the organizing upsurge of the early 1940s left-wingers who veered from CIO doctrine of support for Franklin Roosevelt's foreign policy were slapped on the wrist but not opposed frontally. Later, after the upsurge was spent, the left was unceremoniously removed.

In the 1930s, shorn of the genuine radical wing, which had been represented by the now-defunct IWW, the trade unions had moved rapidly to cement their alliance with both employers and the government. The union drive against General Motors in 1936–37 was militant because the company, still ensconced in the old ways, refused to recognize the union. A week after the sit-down strike at GM resulted in union recognition, Myron Taylor of U.S. Steel concluded an agreement with John L. Lewis recognizing the Steelworkers Organizing Committee as bargaining agent for its employees. Between 1933 and 1937 the bulk of workers in basic industries were organized by the CIO or its rival AFL.

Perhaps it was indicative of the future direction of labor-management relations in the steel industry that U.S. Steel's recognition of SWOC took place across a dinner table rather than across the picket line. From that time on the Steelworkers' organizing drive was to be conducted in a relatively mild way, compared to the battles of earlier years. There was only one major battle ahead—the strike of 1937, which was conducted against the so-called "Little Steel" corporations. They were to prove more resistant to union organization. According to a leading historian of the CIO upsurge Walter Galenson, the Republic, Bethlehem and smaller steel companies refused to follow the example of U.S. Steel for two main reasons: at the time of the union organizing campaign among the Little Steel producers, the "second depression" was already under way and steel, normally extremely sensitive to economic vicissitudes, was among the first to record the downward movement of the economy. Apart from economic conditions, the figure of Tom Girdler, the recalcitrant president of Republic Steel and a veteran union opponent, loomed large in the determination of other corporations to resist the SWOC organizing drive. Girdler had been plant manager of the Alaquippa works of the Jones & Laughlin Company before coming to Republic and, by all accounts, had greeted with terror the attempts to organize the huge works in 1934. Conditions had changed by 1937. Instead of a relatively isolated drive by a weak union, the steel industry was being challenged by a well-organized, coordinated effort aimed at all holdouts. Yet once again the use of terror through firings, shootings, and blacklisting succeeded in stemming the union tide.

There is no doubt that the steel companies were holding the whip hand in the 1937 strike. Despite the ability of the union to shut down a large number of mills, the economic conditions and the united front of employers slowed the organizing campaign seriously. It was not until 1941 that the first breakthrough was achieved among Little Steel companies, but this time it was through a representation election conducted by the National Labor Relations Board rather than through strike activity. By then the demand of the Roosevelt administration for uninterrupted war production, combined with an increasingly buoyant economy, helped turn the tables for the union. According to Galenson, "An important factor in the growth of the SWOC...was the assistance rendered by the National Labor Relations Board in a number of important decisions."[3] These included reinstatement of "a considerable number of strikers with back pay" after the ill-fated 1937 events, upholding the union's claim that some companies had engaged in unfair labor practices under the law by refusing to bargain in good faith with the union, and declaring that the "Bethlehem plan,"[4] an employee representation scheme to stave off union organization, was company dominated, another violation of the Labor Relations Act.

The SWOC leadership had learned an important lesson from the 1937 defeat: "the methods used in the early SWOC campaigns had become stale.... Early in 1940 there were no signs of anything like the hysterical enthusiasm of 1937. Consequently the organizing campaign against Bethlehem was settling down to a long-run educational program"[5] rather than mass strikes, which in the eyes of the SWOC leaders were ineffective against determined employer resistance. The Steelworkers and other CIO affiliates became more and more dependent on government assistance and peaceful methods. The remainder of the Little Steel companies were organized by representation elections rather than strikes and the use of legal means became a critical factor in determining victory or defeat in the overwhelming preponderance of unionization drives. For five years after the formation of SWOC, it was difficult for the membership to achieve a real voice in the affairs of the union, since most of the funds for the organizing drives came from the CIO. The leadership resisted forming an international union with a formal constitution and elected officers. Decisions regarding the disposition of dues, collective bargaining objectives, and political issues were made by the interim officers who had been appointed by John L. Lewis. As one delegate to a Wage and Policy convention ironically mused: "The Steelworkers Organizing Committee is a democracy. It is a democracy of steel workers and for steel workers but not by steel workers."[6]

The Steelworkers were to become almost unique among the CIO unions in the absolutism of its bureaucratic methods of operation, its lack of social vision, and its fervent anxiety to please the corporate heads of the industry. But, business unionism, which seemed so anachronistic in the early years of the CIO, became more common in the postwar era. The patterns of internal bureaucracy and close collaboration with the employers prefigured a unionism that was to become dominant later on.

Popular explanations for the rapid victory of industrial union-ism rely heavily on the influence of the economic crisis. But this explanation is not good enough. The wave of union organization actually occurred during an economic upswing, not in the depth of the Depression. Between 1929, when there were two important textile strikes in the South, and 1933, the year of the mass strike among miners and the general strike in the garment trades, both union organization and strike struggles were at their ebb.

Beginning in 1933, the companies started to hire again. Most of the new work force were young. Able to stand the swift as-sembly line pace, they were eminently employable and had been able to find work even in the depths of the Depression. For the entire period, even during the upswing, the hardest hit sections of the work force were the older workers, recently displaced agricultural workers, and minority group workers.

The new organizing upsurge began in 1933. By all accounts the spearheads of the drive in the shops were the young work-ers, and it was they who made the victories, helped to some extent by older veteran unionists who had spent much of the previous decades in small, often secret, union groups that rarely enjoyed company recognition. The younger workers were more militant because they had not experienced the dismal defeats suffered by the entire working class after the First World War and were thus more optimistic about the chances of winning. They were not cowed by the employers to the same extent as older workers, for whom steady work had become a blessing after the lean years between 1929 and 1933, and they resented the attempts of corporations to exploit them by demanding more work for less pay and forcing them to endure speedup, stretchout, and other measures designed to increase profits.

Almost all of the most important plant leaders of the CIO organizing drive and a fair number of national CIO figures were under thirty-five. These were the workers for whom the Depression had not meant soup kitchens and breadlines. The preponderance of youth was particularly evident among the leadership of the auto and electrical workers. Few of the most important militants of the auto sitdown strikes of 1936–37 in Detroit, Cleveland and Flint were over thirty. Organizers Richard Frankenstein, the Reuther brothers, Robert Travis and most of the key rank and file activists were in their twenties or early thirties. In the electrical industry the picture was similar. James Carey was twenty-four years old when he assumed presidency of the United Electrical, Radio, and Machine Workers of America. As a worker in the Philco plant in Philadelphia, Carey had been twenty-one when in 1933, he signed the first contract recognizing the in-plant union as collective bargaining agent for the company's workers. Julius Empspak, a union leader at the Schenectady plant of GE, and James Matles, the leader of a few locals of an independent machinists union that affiliated with UE, were equally youthful.

Strikes in the mid-thirties occurred as much because of speedup and the authoritarianism of management as they did because of declines in real wages, whether caused by wage cuts or price increases engendered by the government's policies of providing investment incentives. Between 1933 and 1935 industry-wide strikes broke out in the mines and in the garment and textile industries; general strikes paralyzing San Francisco and Minneapolis arose from walkouts of workers in important transportation industries. Flash strikes broke out in auto, steel, electrical, and rubber plants, but these were local struggles and failed to encompass the whole industry until several years later.

In this recovery period of 1933–36, corporations and smaller employers felt particularly bold in putting pressure on workers, both because of the persistence of large-scale unemployment in the midst of the upturn and because of the protection afforded business by the government's policy of assuring high rates of profit through artificially stimulated prices.

The general strike in San Francisco, the Minneapolis teamsters' strike, and the national textile strike of more than 300,000 workers, took place in 1934, a full year before the passage of the Wagner Act. The organization of these struggles occurred mainly outside the framework of the AFL or other branches of organized labor. Led by young workers, some of whom were Communists, the strikes took place in part as a revolt against the conservative policies of the AFL unions who held formal jurisdiction in these industries. The unions—both the AFL and the short-lived Communist variety—actually sought to thwart or channel these struggles. In most of the labor struggles of the thirties, the militants were defeated in the end. Suffused with uncompromising spirit, if not syndicalist ideology, they opposed settlements, refused to sign no-strike agreements, and became oppositionists even in the so-called left-wing unions.

If the necessary condition for the success of industrial union-ism in the thirties was the revolt of young workers, this did not prove sufficient to determine the character of the labor movement or labor relations. There was a stronger force that was to be far more influential—the historical tendency within both employer and trade union ranks to formalize and regulate labor relations, which was to find fertile soil in the development of state capitalist forms during the New Deal period.

The economic expansion of modern capitalism depends upon the close integration of the state and the corporations. The same policies responsible for attempting to synchronize the activities of the government and of private corporations to guarantee re-covery and sustain economic growth were responsible for develop-ing the means to make labor a stable factor of production, that is, to make it possible to predict its price with a degree of accu-racy sufficient to enable the undertaking of corporate and state planning. When corporate and government leaders understood the critical importance of coordinating their efforts in order to prevent disaster in the economic crisis of the early 1930s, they immediately recognized the importance of bringing unions into partnership. For if workers were to continue to struggle around their needs without regulation, the whole enterprise of state capi-talist planning could be disrupted. From the point of view of the national economic and political leadership, the economic crisis was an emergency akin to war.

The first New Deal measures after the corporatists (whose national coordinator was Roosevelt) had ascended to power were not addressed to problems of hunger or disease. Rather, Congress was asked to delegate to the executive branch of government powers to restore the banks, stimulate investment, regulate wages, and increase prices. The National Recovery Act was the agency charged with the task of dealing with trade, of which labor rela-tions were regarded as a dependent variable.

The first attempts at government regulation of labor relations were somewhat crude. Union representation on the industry boards responsible for setting wages and prices was too weak to influence the decisions of these bodies except in scattered in-stances, such as the clothing industry, where they had managed to preserve some of their pre-Depression strength. For the most part, the union leaders cooperated with Roosevelt's program of massive state intervention to save the tottering social and eco-nomic system, hoping for some crumbs from the corporate table.

The reward for their cooperation was Section 7A of the National Recovery Act, which guaranteed the right of workers to join unions of their own choosing; in practice, this guarantee was neither legally enforced by the government nor capable of practical implementation by the unions, whose financial resources remained meager and whose moral stature among workers had been damaged by the degrading company unionism of the 1920s. In a few instances, the NRA provisions helped viable labor organizations to recruit new members. In the main, the workers in the mass production and transportation industries remained outside the traditional trade unions during the early years of the New Deal. It was no easy task to impose a partnership on the rank and file even if the discredited labor leadership was eager to be absorbed in the emerging state capitalist Roosevelt coalition.

In the first two years of the New Deal, prior to the 1935 Wagner Labor Relations Act (which established government machinery for regulating trade unions and was the first serious attempt to bring the class struggle under the aegis of government supervision), there had been the unprecedented outbreak of mass strikes in many important industries. In most cases the strikes had a spontaneous quality of reaction to immediate causes, although they were preceded by considerable agitation, partial walkouts, and organizational activity conducted by radical and labor organizers. Where unions captured leadership of these strikes and were able to direct them into acceptable collective bargaining channels, this was often accomplished after the strikes had already begun.

The Communist Party, the left wing of the Socialist Party, and other left-wing groups—viewed the early New Deal with open hostility. In the radical view, the New Deal was created to achieve economic, social, and political stability in the interests of the continued domination of the country by the giant corporations, rather than in the interests of workers, Black people, and farmers. The left denounced the NRA as an attack on workers' living standards. They described Section 7A as a chimera designed to lull the working class into false security.

Historically, there had been disagreements on the left over the application of the rule of law to trade unionism. The traditional IWW position, shared by many other radicals, was that workers should not seek union contracts, since they limited or prohibited the right to strike and narrowed the possibility of militant struggle against onerous working conditions. The CP, which dominated most of the radical movement after 1931, never took a clear-cut position on these questions of trade union practice. In 1936, when the party supported the Wagner Act and other state capitalist measures affecting workers, it did so without explaining or justifying its position.

In the period from the onset of the Depression in 1929 to 1935, the CP labor policy in this country had pursued two paths. The main thrust was to form independent, dual unions. But it also urged its members to "penetrate the fascist mass organizations like the AFL."[7] In cases where the leadership of established AFL unions was both powerful and so repressive that militants were barred from effective functioning as in the United Mine Workers, the CP formed dual "revolutionary unions." In other cases, as in the auto industry, CP militants were no weaker than their AFL counterparts. In these instances, the party leadership was often forced to acquiesce in the wishes of its own rank and file and countenance the formation of independent unions. In fields such as the electrical, food, and maritime industries, where there was barely the shell of an AFL affiliate, the CP helped form independent unions, sometimes under its own domination but sometimes in coalition with other independents.

Prior to 1935, the party wielded its two tactics in a flexible manner. Many of its leading trade union cadres were AFL stalwarts, especially those in the building trades. Even though the party policy was officially inclined toward dual unionism for much of the 1929–35 period, it allowed deviations from this line when the realities of the situation did not permit dual organization.

In the early days of the New Deal prior to the Wagner Act, industrial unionism was viewed by the AFL as a radical product, which it largely was, since most of the effective unionism during this period had taken place outside the AFL. It was John L. Lewis and Sidney Hillman who recognized that the New Deal, combined with the persistence of the economic crisis, presented a new opportunity for the rise of union organization among unskilled and semiskilled workers. They were acutely aware of unrest among these workers and vainly attempted to convince Gompers's successors of the necessity of establishing leadership over the new industrial union movement.

Both men were close to the Roosevelt administration and did not hesitate to use the prestige of the administration to assist recruiting drives within their own industrial jurisdictions. Hillman saw a rejuvenated labor movement as an important ally to Roosevelt's coalition. The evidence of his activity points to the distinctly political character of the Amalgamated's interest in helping to form a Committee for Industrial Organization within the AFL.

It was plain to Lewis and Hillman that unless the AFL acted decisively to control the developing mass upsurge among industrial workers, the left could pose a serious threat to conservative and liberal leaders of the unions and upset the emerging Roosevelt coalition. An ardent supporter of NRA section 7A, Lewis was convinced that workers would never join unions as long as they appeared to be radical and subversive. But, according to Saul Alinsky, Lewis's best biographer, the miners' president "could read the revolutionary handwriting on the walls of American industry" in the 1934 strikes.[8] After several years of futile appeals, Lewis finally convinced the AFL to set up the Committee to thwart the threat from the left, and insure that workers would be firmly ensconced within the AFL House of Labor.

The year 1935, however, brought a sharp reversal in CP policies. Instead of attempting to form independent, dual unions under their own leadership, the Communists were now committed to collaborate with the Socialists and trade union leaders within the mainstream of political and trade union organizations. The Seventh World Congress of the Communist International of 1935 heard its General Secretary, Georgi Dimitrov, proclaim the end of the period when Communists would attack Socialists and the bourgeoisie with merciless equanimity. Now the crucial task of the working class was to oppose fascism. The defense of liberal capitalism and civil liberties was the basic precondition of revolutionary action in the future. The Communist policy of branding Socialist and liberal forces as "social fascists" had backfired severely in Germany and Italy. Now fascism was about to overthrow the Spanish Republic, was threatening to capture power in France, and was even bidding for a mass constituency in the United States. According to the new policy of the world Communist movement, the time had come to put aside sectarianism and join forces with all democratic organizations to prevent Hitler's drive for world domination. The Soviet regime made proposals at the League of Nations for collective security against Hitler. The new policy meant that the Communists were no longer to be found in the opposition to the liberal state and the social-democratic labor leaders.

Within the United States, Communists were obliged to abandon their virulent attacks on the Roosevelt administration and on the liberal wing of the AFL. The Trade Union Unity League, the CP instrument in the labor movement, was dissolved, and militants were urged to merge with AFL unions in their industries. In many basic industries, the CP and TUUL organizations were transformed into nuclei for the CIO organizing drive. In his report to the 1936 convention of the party, CP General Secretary Earl Browder declared:

> The Committee for Industrial Organization has taken up the task of organizing all mass production industries in America in industrial unions. The success of this effort is a basic necessity upon which depends the future of the American labor movement in all other respects. The CP unconditionally pledges its full resources, moral and material, to the complete execution of this great project.[9]

The CP remained somewhat critical of Roosevelt, but supported his reelection in 1936. They also supported the state capitalist measures of his administration, including the National Labor Relations Act, which simultaneously widened government intervention into the collective bargaining process and protected the right of workers to join unions. The CP and most radicals never perceived the dangers inherent in greater government regulation of labor relations. They were dedicated and tireless organizers within the "center-left" coalitions led by Lewis that welcomed the enlarged government role in collective bargaining.

In 1935–36 CP trade unionists in New York, Michigan, Wisconsin, and elsewhere worked for the formation of local labor parties, patterning themselves after the Minnesota Farmer-Labor Party, which had succeeded in electing its candidate for governor, Floyd Olson, in 1934. The strategy underlying CP support of the Farmer-Labor Party movement was twofold: on the one hand, it would provide a mass base for the defeat of the ultra-right in American politics and mitigate its influence over liberal capitalists such as Roosevelt. On the other hand, it would represent the political expression of the developing trade union and farmers movement, providing at the same time a wider political base for Communist influence. The CP also attempted to influence the leaders of the newly emerging CIO, which was then regarded as the main force for worker organization.

Although CP leadership urged its rank and file to build the Communist Party as the mass party of the American working class, these appeals were subordinated to the main task of building "the people's front against fascism" and its core organization, the CIO. In effect, the party became a pressure group on the Democratic Party and the CIO. The Farmer-Labor parties, particularly the American Labor Party in New York State, which represented the political left-center coalition, were little more than another line on the voting machine to harness labor's support for the Democrats. In the tradition of the British Labor Party, the ALP had a dual structure. On the top were the leaders of the key industrial unions, particularly of the garment trades and transport workers. In the neighborhoods, the left-wing activists, members of the CP or on its periphery, or active rank-and-file trade unionists, performed social services for constituents, organized rent strikes, consumer protests, and election campaigns.

After 1937, the modest criticisms of Roosevelt and the CIO leaders still evident at the 8th CP Convention during the previous year all but disappeared. In the July 1937 issue of *The Communist,* the party's chief theoretical organ, its editor, Alexander Bittleman, vehemently defended both Roosevelt and Lewis. Against the charge that Lewis had become a "labor dictator with great power," Bittleman replied: "The crime of the CIO is not that it is a dictatorship but on the contrary that it is a progressive labor movement seeking to build itself up on the basis of inner union democracy as well as a force for democracy in the country."[10] He went on to say, "The CIO is already one of the chief fortresses of democracy, its brightest hope and promise of realization. That is the message Communists must spread widely among the masses."[11]

Roosevelt was defended by the Communists against those who criticized his proposal to enlarge the Supreme Court from its traditional nine members in order to give his program more support. The CP was also critical of those left-wingers who blamed the administration for the shootings of steelworkers by Chicago police in May 1937 during a demonstration demanding union recognition from the Little Steel companies.

By 1939 Communists had become entrenched in the top echelons of several important CIO and, to a lesser extent, AFL organizations. At one point it was estimated that a third of the CIO membership belonged to unions euphemistically called "left-wing." In practice, they were mostly not under direct CP control but had top leaders and secondary officials who were close to or in the party. The "left-wing" unions included those of electrical workers, auto workers, West Coast longshoremen, maritime workers, transport workers, metal miners, packinghouse workers, furni-

ture workers, distributive and department store workers, fur workers, office and professional workers, food and tobacco workers, and
public workers.

Among AFL unions, Communists did not play leadership roles
on national levels, but were important in local and district organizations of painters, carpenters, hotel and restaurant workers,
railroad brotherhoods, and some others. In a remarkable article
written for *The Communist* in November 1939, William Foster,
twenty years earlier the secretary of the AFL committee directing
the 1919 steel strike and now a leading American Communist,
wrote an article on CP trade union policy of the preceding two
decades. The article represented the perspective of a man who
had long since renounced dual unionism. Foster's two key points
were that Communists must now work for AFL-CIO unity, basing
themselves on the tactic of pressuring the decent elements in
both the Federation and the government, and that the CP should
no longer maintain factions within the CIO. On the first point,
Foster wrote:

> Roosevelt in his unity efforts reflects the desires of the great
> majority of New Dealers. Lewis speaks for the solid unity
> sentiment of the entire CIO. . . . Tobin expresses the unity will
> of a big majority of AFL members, and Whitney undoubtedly
> does the same for the bulk of railroad unionists."[12]

And on the second, he stated:

> The organizational forms of Communist trade union work
> have changed radically to correspond to the present period
> (of center left unity). Party members do not now participate
> in groupings or other organized activities within the unions.
> The party also discountenances the formation of progressive
> groups, blocs, and caucuses in unions; it has liquidated its
> Communist factions, discontinued its shop papers, and is now
> modifying its system of industrial branches. Communists are
> policy making and administrating on an unknown scale . . .
> building the highest type of trade union leadership based on
> efficient service and democratic responsibility to the rank and
> file.[13]

Not only did the CP abandon dual unionism and subordinate
its organizing thrust to the CIO under Lewis, it abandoned its
own political identity. Important trade union cadres became trade

union bureaucrats for whom an independent rank and file was anathema.

However, even as early as 1940, well before the so-called McCarthy attacks, the left was used as a scapegoat by labor leaders. When some delegates to the 1940 Wage Policy convention held by the SWOC distributed a leaflet calling for immediate action to draw up a constitution and hold a convention to establish an international union, Philip Murray of the CIO declared: "Now I am wondering, I am just wondering, if it is the business of the Fascists or the Nazis or the Democrats or the Republicans or the Communists to tell us what we are supposed to do in these conventions. . . . Anyone else outside who wants to help us that's all right as long as it's constructive help . . . and cooperation—I welcome that, but I do not welcome and I do not want and I am not going to tolerate undue interference with the work of this organization."[14] As president of the CIO, Murray had learned to live in peace with Communists as long as they did not interfere with the affairs of "his" union. But now his attitude had changed. The use of the words "Fascist" and "Nazi" and the mention of the other two political parties before the CP were evidently a veil for the real attack against what Murray and his associates believed was a CP campaign to push for a formal union structure. Ironically, in contrast to many other CIO unions where Communists had been prominent in the top leadership or influential among the middle levels of power, the CP had never gained a foothold in the Steelworkers' hierarchy. The left-wing activists that were elected to office were mainly to be found in large local unions in the Chicago area, and in a number of Little Steel locals around the country, particularly in Bethlehem's Baltimore and Buffalo plants.

During World War II Communist trade unionists became indistinguishable from their liberal colleagues. Left-wing leaders of the new mass industrial unions in auto, electrical, and other basic industries put the objective of winning the war ahead of the workers' immediate interests and voluntarily gave up the right to strike. Communists joined their liberal allies and urged workers to abandon their traditional hostility to piecework schemes and incentive pay. In some industries where company efforts to introduce these methods of speedup had been the catalyst for union organization—packing, steel, and the electrical industries, for example—day-work systems gave way to incentive pay geared to productivity or even to outright piecework. In the auto industry, the assembly line was simply speeded up, while workers were asked to maintain their no-strike pledge and wage freeze.

Wildcat strikes were frequent in the auto industry, shipbuilding, and other areas of mass production during the war. In many cases, the deep resentment of the workers was corralled by opportunistic leaders like Walter Reuther, who used the occasion to attack the "center-left coalition" which led the UAW. After the war, Reuther easily defeated the Thomas-Addes leadership of the union which was supported by the CP.

When the U.S.S.R.–U.S. alliance was erased by the Cold War, the combination of rank-and-file resentment against "red company unionism," open red-baiting, and repression by the corporations and the government, and the sectarian policies of the Communists themselves sealed the isolation of the left from the mass of industrial workers. In the steel industry, many older workers became openly hostile to "Communism" after the Soviet takeover of the countries of their birth or ancestry. The Steelworkers leadership was particularly close to the Catholic Church, which conducted active propaganda against the repression of organized religion in Hungary, Poland, and elsewhere. Many Steelworkers local leaders were among those who most frequented Communion breakfasts that often served as thinly veiled occasions for anti-Communist discourses. In those years the Catholic Church, particularly its Jesuit wing, became extremely influential in such sections of the labor movement as steelworkers, electrical workers, New England textile workers, and the building trades. These industries were centered in the Northeastern region of the country, and in several large cities of the Midwest where the bulk of American Catholic workers lived. Of course, the church was concerned that Communist influence, built up in the labor movement during the Depression years, would constitute a serious challenge to its constituency. There was a close connection between the fierce anti-Communism of the steelworkers, CIO electrical workers, textile workers unions with the importance of Eastern and Southern European Catholics among their membership, and in the ranks of the officialdom.

Some radicals in the unions survived the Cold War. They were trade unionists who functioned as open Socialists, who vigorously fought with workers against the deterioration of working conditions, and who refused to become part of the trade union bureaucracy. They included members of all radical tendencies. Their distinguishing feature was not their political affiliation. It was their radical sensibility.

In the auto industry workers distinguished for shop floor militancy, who had been members of Trotskyist groups or even of the CP, remained in the plants throughout the darkest days of the Cold War. Elsewhere, known radicals remained active shop leaders among metal miners, fur workers, electrical workers, and in the railroad and trucking industries. These workers were by no means immune from company or union discrimination because of their political views. Many were fired from their jobs with the implicit approval of the union. But in many cases their fellow workers rose to the defense of the left-wingers because of their honest political views as much as their ability to fight effectively over day-to-day grievances.

Yet there is no doubt about the effectiveness of the Cold War campaign against the political left among the working class. By the mid-1950s left-wing influence was all but erased from the plants, the mining industry, and transportation sectors. The fragments of radical influence that remained were never of sufficient weight to influence the outcome of major trade union policies or struggles. In the cases where left-wingers threw their limited resources into factional fights against the conservative trade union leaders, their influence was almost always separate from their political position. In the steelworkers' fight against the McDonald leadership in the late 1950s, a few radicals participated both on the insurgents' staff and among rank-and-file workers, but, just as in the 1930s, they played no independent role as *radicals*. Instead, in the farmworkers, hospital workers, and public employees unionization efforts, they were merely good labor organizers. Most of them felt, with some justice, that their ideas had no currency among workers, therefore the best they could do was to aid the most progressive sections of the labor movement as technicians rather than political influences.

In 1950, following a period of rhetorical militancy, the articulate former Socialist, Walter Reuther, engineered a five-year contract with the auto industry. The contract signaled the end of an era in industrial unionism. Saddled with a no-strike provision which permitted the company to speed up the assembly line without effective counteraction within the framework of collective bargaining, the rank and file was forced to act outside the union structure. The wildcat movement in the auto industry during

1953–55 embraced all major companies and sections of the country. Thousands of workers participated in flash walkouts as the companies tried to increase production from 48 to 50 cars per hour to more than 60. Often the walkouts were initiated by the body-shop workers, who do the heaviest and dirtiest jobs in the plant, or by the workers in wet-sanding departments, most of whom were Black.

The extent and frequency of the walkouts forced the union to restore the right to strike in the next contract and to cut down the contract duration. But strikes were permitted only when management changed the pace of work or for safety reasons. Even then, workers were not permitted to walk out at the point of the change. They could elect to strike only after enduring a long period of aggrievement through the procedure established by the contract. In one stroke, Reuther bowed to the realities of the situation and tried to cool workers' militancy by placing conditions on the strike weapon.

In 1955 the UAW and other industrial unions became concerned with automation and other forms of major technological change that would create joblessness among the workers. During the year, a large conference on the shorter work week was sponsored by the UAW to coincide with the opening of negotiations of a new contract. However, the new contract, when it was finalized, merely contained an agreement that companies would provide supplementary unemployment benefits to laid-off workers. Shortly thereafter, steel followed suit with a similar agreement and the shorter work week was dead.

Although the wildcat strikes of the early 1950s were smashed, the challenge to the unions did not abate. The next phase of the rank-and-file attempt to capture control over their own conditions was the mushrooming of movements to replace the old leadership. Beginning in the late fifties and early sixties, there was a parade of electoral challenges to the leaders of many key industrial unions. Although most of the pretenders to the thrones were middle-rank, full-time paid leaders, they rode to power on the strength of membership discontent. Such contests took place in the Steelworkers Union, in the Rubber Workers, Textile Workers, Oil and Chemical Workers, Teachers, State, County and Municipal Employees, the Electrical Workers, and in many locals of the Auto Workers where each collective bargaining defeat was followed by the defeat of a raft of local union incumbents.

The outcome of the movement for internal reform was surely

disappointing to union members who hoped for the reawakening of the aggressive brand of trade unionism that was characteristic of the CIO prior to the Second World War. At best, the new leaders who emerged from the factional struggles in the 1960s offered more collective bargaining militancy and a determination to conduct active organizing drives among open-shop employers. The promise of internal democracy was almost never fulfilled. I. W. Abel, who had defeated McDonald, carried on the tradition of centralization of union command. And more ironically, he began a concerted campaign in 1970 to persuade union members to cooperate with employers to raise productivity and prevent foreign competition from eating away at their jobs. This plea corresponded to a period of high capital investment within the industry that resulted in substantial layoffs because of the introduction of labor-saving equipment. As tonnage increased, steel employment was dropping steadily. The Steelworkers Union was becoming an instrument of modernization, speedup, and labor discipline for the steel industry.

Another manifestation of the emergence of rank-and-file discontent in the sixties was the rise of the Teamsters Union as a major challenger to traditional union jurisdictions. The apparent militancy of this "outlawed" union meshed neatly with rank-and-file disgust with the softness of the now middle-aged CIO labor statesmen. The merger of the AFL and the CIO had prevented workers from seeking alternative representation when their unions revealed company union practices. The expulsion of the Teamsters from the House of Labor in 1957 provided disgruntled workers with a powerful alternative to the old labor unions.

But by the late sixties the initial enthusiasm of the workers for competitive unionism and internal union reform had ebbed. Real wages had declined each year since 1967 and, after a period of economic growth as a result of the Vietnam War, the economy began to slow down. The first effects of the slowdown were reflected in rising layoffs and the elimination of overtime, which took the gloss from pay envelopes. But the slowdown in production and employment did not have a counterpart in the movement of prices, which kept rising.

The last two years of the sixties and the opening of the 1970s were marked by the reawakening of rank-and-file militancy. This militancy took different forms in different sectors of the work force. Among public workers and workers in voluntary institutions such as hospitals, a wave of union organizing and strike movements took place. This wave was led by teachers and hospital workers. The impact of public employee organizing was peculiar because every strike of this group of workers is, perforce, a strike against the state. In many places, the pent-up frustration of these workers, who had borne the worst effects of the inflation and the fiscal crisis of the public sector, caused widespread disrespect for laws prohibiting strikes of public employees and court injunctions aimed at enforcing the law. In many cities, particularly on the eastern seaboard, the leaders riding the crest of the wave of militancy became important political figures and were ultimately absorbed by the municipal governments as warm allies and important sources of political power. But the chronic shortage of funds available to local governments prevents a secure alliance of the workers with government authority.

Another manifestation of militancy has been the reappearance of the wildcat strike. The vaunted authority of the Teamsters over the membership, its reputation for militancy and toughness at the bargaining table, its myth of invincibility, collapsed beneath the insurgent rank and file, which acted independent of the bureaucracy for the first time. The wildcat strike of postal workers in 1970 took place over the heads of the union leadership and became a national strike without central coordination or direction. The strike was preceded by the twenty-year efforts of the national postal union leadership to operate within approved legislative channels through lobbying methods and political pressure on the administrative directorate. Even more dramatic than the postal rebellion was the extraordinary 1969–70 wildcat strike by 100,000 teamsters in the Middle West and the West Coast in rejection of the contract negotiated by their national leaders.

Unionism in the public sector is still somewhat raucous and unpredictable from management's standpoint. Even when labor leaders fervently desire close relations with public officials and are prepared to cooperate in confining membership action to approved channels, the workers in hospitals, schools, post offices, and city agencies often succeed in changing the script.

Among the most important reasons for the rise of public employee unionism is the entrance of large numbers of young workers and Blacks into this branch of employment. The privileged status accorded veterans in civil service examinations, the sharp rise of public sector jobs during the fifties and sixties compared to manufacturing, and the relatively high pay of these jobs made public service an attractive option for Black people and women.

The changing attitudes of young people toward their labor, particularly their relative indifference to the old values that motivated civil servants (job security and a moderate commitment to useful work) made them less subordinate to supervisors and more impatient with the infinitesimal steps of the job leaders in civil services. They were not content to wait a full year for a $200 raise, or study for the civil service examination providing an opportunity for promotion. Many came to public employment with the understanding that they were workers like anybody else and were there for the money. The old appeals that suggested white-collar work as a privilege reserved for the best of the working class had clearly lost their force. Postal workers, for example, could not mistake their jobs for anything but industrial labor.

— 3 —

The bureaucratization of the trade unions, their integrative role within production, their conservative political ideology and their dependence on the Democratic Party are not primarily the result of the consciousness of the leading actors in the rise of industrial unionism. To the extent that the left participated in redefining the trade unions as part of the corporate system, it must now undertake a merciless critique of its own role before a new working class strategy can be developed.

It is not enough to admit bureaucratic tendencies in the unions or in their left leadership, however. The strategy flowing from this focus is to reform the unions from within in order to perfect their fighting ability and rank-and-file class consciousness. This line of thinking categorically denies that the unions can remain a dependent variable within the political economy dominated by corporate capitalism.

One of the important concepts of Marxist orthodoxy is that economic crisis is an inevitable feature of capitalist development, and that the tendency of employers will be to attack and reduce the power of trade unions during periods of declining production. Accordingly, it is believed that the government-employer attempts to circumscribe workers' power by restricting trade union functions will produce rank-and-file pressure confronting the leadership with the choice of struggle against capital or their own displacement. Thus the unions become objectively radical in their view despite their conservative consciousness.

However, strategies for rank-and-file reform ignore the bureaucracy and conservatism inherent in the present union structure and function, as well as the role of the unions in the division of labor. The growth of bureaucracy and the decline of rank-and-file initiative is built into the theory and practice of collective bargaining.

During periods of crisis or stagnation, the union bureaucracy seeks an accommodation with management on the basis of the parochial interests of its immediate constituency. This practice can be observed in the settlement of the 1969 GE strike, where the unions agreed to a long-term contract which partially protected workers from inflationary pressures, but made no substantive advances. The forty-month contract provision of the agreement was a sign that the leadership was prepared to settle for consolidating its gains in the wake of the recession in the economy. Long-term agreements have been viewed traditionally as a management tool to stabilize production and labor costs. Militant unionism has always fought for one-year contracts based on its view of contracts as per se a limitation on workers' power to deal effectively with problems on the job.

GE workers were forced to strike against inflation and the attempt by the company to make gains against wages and working conditions. The company's attack was repulsed. But the struggle to prevent GE from making up for wage increases by other devices was not won. In this area, top leadership of the unions permitted the company to raise prices and increase productivity without protest and resistance. Local struggles to deal with the problems of women workers, production norms, and new machinery were fragmented. All unions, except the independent United Electrical Workers (UE) agreed to drop their demands for an end to discriminatory wages for women and for workers in the South. Since the International Union of Electrical Workers AFL-CIO (IUE), the largest union in the coalition, provides for contract ratification by its top committees, this meant the rank and file had no genuine voice in accepting or rejecting the settlement except through elected representatives.

But there is a more structural difficulty confronting trade unions in dealing effectively with the day-to-day issues on the shop floor. An increasing tendency can be observed in many unions toward the elimination, or the severe modification, of the shop steward system. One of the most progressive features of the CIO at its inception was the insistence of many of the new unions such as the Auto Workers and Electrical Workers that the members' basic grievances should be resolved at the workplace, since it was at the point of production that workers came face to face with problems of working conditions. Shop stewards were elected in each department, or even in each section of a department, on the basis of one steward for every twenty-five to thirty workers. The steward was not paid for union business either by the company or by the union and only left his/her work station when there was a grievance. In the early days of industrial management, foremen were still accorded more than marginal authority over the work forces. Foremen often performed the hiring and firing functions as well as distributing work and overtime to employees. Even as late as the early 1950s line supervisors and stewards fought out "beefs" right on the shop floor; failing a settlement, workers sometimes took "job actions," that is, refused to work or slowed down until the grievance was settled.

The centralization of management in the 1950s relieved the foremen of a great deal of their decision-making power. Nearly all decisions affecting production, including discipline, were now defined as policy issues reserved for professional personnel, directors or middle supervisors. Now nothing could be settled on the shop floor without direct independent action by the workers. Such action was opposed by union hierarchies.

In some instances, this opposition was not the result of venality or class betrayal by the union officials. For one thing, the Taft-Hartley Labor Relations Act imposed severe penalties for walkouts in violation of the terms of the labor agreement. Even when the walkout is not authorized by the union officials, the union is held responsible for penalties that may be ordered by a court. Some unions that have refused to order members to return to their jobs during wildcat strikes have been subjected to heavy fines and imprisonment of union officials by courts. Most union leaders have rejected the job action or the "quickie" as a self-defeating measure that can solve nothing and, on the contrary, make more problems.

Labor leaders attempted to adjust the grievance machinery to the realities of corporate power that removed decision-making from the work station. The rank-and-file steward was replaced by the "committeeman" in the United Auto Workers agreement with the "Big Three" manufacturers of the industry in 1946. The committeeman is employed virtually full time on union business and is paid by the company to deal with grievances. Instead of representing a small group of workers who do the same or similar labor in a relatively small area, the typical committeeman represents several hundred workers scattered over many different jobs and even geographic locations in the shop. He becomes the organizing force in the shop instead of the workers themselves. The argument for this system relies on the perception that the company will not deal with a steward because it has robbed its own line supervisor of real power.

The early version of the committeeman or business agent, the "walking delegate," was a post originally invented by craft unions whose membership was scattered over a large number of small shops. The commonly held belief among these workers in the latter half of the last century was that they must have a representative who was not paid by the company and was not required to work all day at the bench. But the introduction of the committee system into industrial plants can only have bureaucratic justifications. In large workplaces, this system has produced a union structure that is as alien to the line worker as to the company. The committeeman is perceived as a "man in the middle," having interests that are neither those of the rank and file nor those of management. His structural position is untenable from any point of view other than the performance of his main task: to police the union contract as well as possible and prevent both the rank and file and the management from going outside of it to solve problems. Many committeemen are sincerely interested in the welfare of union members and are frequently able to thwart the most arbitrary of management's actions against individuals. But they are powerless to deal with the issues that have produced the unauthorized job actions and wildcat strikes: the speedup of production, introduction of labor-saving machinery, plant removal, and disciplinary layoffs that do not result in immediate discharge.

The last thirty-five years of industrial unionism have failed to effect any substantive change in the distribution of income. Trade unionism under conditions of partial unionization of the labor force can do no more than redistribute income *within* the working class. Workers in heavily organized industries such as auto, rubber, and steel have relatively high wages compared to workers in consumer goods industries such as garments and shoes (which have migrated to the South), retail and wholesale workers, and most categories of government and agricultural workers.

The high wages of certain categories of industrial workers depend as much on the high proportion of capital to living labor and the monopoly character of basic industries as they do on trade union struggle. The tendency for employers in heavy industry to give in to union wage demands presupposes their ability to raise prices and productivity. In competitive industries such as light manufacturing, the unions have been transformed into stabilizers of industrial conflict in order to permit high rates of profits where no technological changes can be introduced. The result has been low wages for large numbers of Blacks, Puerto Ricans, and poor whites locked into these jobs.

Since advanced capitalism requires consumerism both as ideology and as practice to preserve commodity production, its payment of high wages to large segments of the working class—and minimum income to those excluded from the labor markets—is not objectively in the workers' interest. It is a means to take care of the market or demand side of production.

The ability of workers to purchase a relatively large quantity of consumer goods is dependent on the forces of production, which include the productivity and skill of the labor force and the scale and complexity of technology. Technological development, in turn, is dependent on the availability of raw materials and the degree of scientific and technical knowledge in society.

The most important issue to be addressed in defining the tasks ahead is not the question of inflation, wages, or general economic conditions. No matter how inequitable the distribution of income, no matter how deep the crisis, these conditions will never, by themselves, be the soil for revolutionary consciousness.

Revolutionary consciousness arises out of the conditions of alienated labor, which include economic conditions but are not limited to them. Its starting point is in the production process. It is at the point of mental and manual production, where the world of commodities is produced, that the worker experiences his exploitation. Consumption of waste production, trade union objectives in the direction of enlarging wages and social benefits, and the division of labor into industries and sections are all mediations which stand between the workers' existential exploitation at the workplace and their ability to comprehend alienated labor as class exploitation.

Radicals of most persuasions have tended to address the problem of consciousness from the wrong end. Some believe that racism, trade unionism, conservatism, will be dissolved by discussion and exhortation alone, while other believe that "objective" conditions will force new understandings among workers. The notion that ideologies can be changed through ideological means or that capitalist contradictions will change consciousness with an assist from ideologically correct lines or propaganda is a nonrevolutionary position: in both cases, the role of practice is ignored. Nor will workers' struggles against economic hardship necessarily raise political consciousness.

In this connection one must reevaluate the rise of industrial unionism in the 1930s. Many radicals and labor historians have interpreted the failure of the CIO to emerge as an important force for social change as a function of the misleadership of its officials and the opportunism of the Communist Party and other radical parties that participated in its formation.[15] According to a recent work on the development of the CIO by Art Preis, a contemporary labor reporter writing from a Trotskyist position, the 1930s were a prerevolutionary period. Preis writes: "The first stage of awakening class consciousness was achieved, in fact, with the rise and consolidation of the CIO. The second stage will be marked by a further giant step, the formation of a new class party based on the unions.[16]

No important left-wing critique exists of unionism itself. Left-wing evaluations of the 1930s find the economic crisis a necessary condition for the development of class consciousness, but blame the Communist and Socialist policies for the fact that no significant radical force developed among the mass of workers.

I would dispute this theory since there is no genuine evidence that the CIO could ever have become an organized expression of a new class politics in America, or that trade unionism in the era of state capitalism and imperialism can be other than a force for integrating workers. After the disappearance of the IWW from the labor scene, there was no radical alternative offered within the working class. The trade union activists who belonged to Marxist parties functioned, in the main, as instruments for liberal union leaders. Their political thrust was dissipated by two factors. First, they were unwilling to become pariahs by opposing the rise of industrial unionism within the liberal consensus. Instead, they hoped to gain an operational foothold in the mass industrial unions from which to develop radical politics later on. Second, radical politics gradually became more rhetorical than practical for the left-wingers who entered the CIO. And it did not matter whether the left-winger was in the CP or anti-CP; the central thread was the same. Most radicals were all too willing to follow John L. Lewis. To them, he was performing the necessary preparatory work for socialism, later—despite his procapitalist bias, now.

Most non-Communist radicals within the labor movement refused to follow the CIO leadership into the New Deal coalition. It was the one distinguishing feature separating their politics from those of the CP. But insofar as they supported the CIO itself and subordinated themselves to its program, they could not but aid the despised Democratic Party.

In sum, radical ideologies and organizations played virtually no independent role in the trade unions after 1935. The few dissenters were swiftly cast aside in the triumphant march of industrial unionism.

One hundred years ago workers fought desperately for their right to form unions and to strike for economic and social demands. Unions arose out of the needs of workers. In the period of the expansion of American capitalism they were important means for restraining the bestiality of capital. Even into the twentieth century, long after the labor movement as a whole stopped reflecting their interests, workers fought for unions. But their hope was not to become new agents of social transformation. Industrial workers joined unions in the twentieth century seeking a share in the expansion of American capitalism, not its downfall.

Since the 1920s, the ideology of expansion has permeated working class consciousness. On the one hand, many workers have no faith that the corporations will provide for their needs unless forced to do so by powerful organizations. On the other, American expansion abroad and the intervention of the government into the operation of the economy have convinced workers that the frontier of economic opportunity is not closed to them. The persistence of the idea of individual mobility amidst recognition of the necessity for collective action is partially attributable to the immigrant base of a large portion of the industrial working class in the first half of the twentieth century. As previously noted, the comparative advantages of American capitalism over the semifeudal agrarian societies of Europe in the early part of this century remained vital influences on workers' consciousness despite the Great Depression. For the minority of radical immigrant workers who didn't accept the expansionist ideology, corporations and the government reacted with constant deportation, and jail terms.

Thus the violence of American labor struggles has had a contradictory influence upon the development of working class consciousness. Although it indicates the militancy with which workers have been prepared to conduct their struggles, the readiness of employers and the government to use methods of severe repression to break strikes and purge the working class of its most militant elements has become a powerful object lesson. Working class consciousness is suffused with a sense of the awesome power of the corporations over American life. Workers have sought and helped create unions which mirror the hierarchical structure of corporations and can compete with them in marshaling resources to bargain effectively with them. To many, James Hoffa was a hero not because he represented a challenge to the robber baron but because he was the labor equivalent of him; as the quintessential business union, the Teamsters was seen as a formidable opponent of the corporations.

Strikes in the United States are of longer duration than in any other advanced capitalist country. Workers know that large corporations cannot be immediately crippled by walkouts and that corporate resources are usually ample to withstand months of labor struggle. Moreover, in some industries employers have created strike insurance plans to protect themselves. Similarly, unions have developed institutional forms of strike insurance. The largest unions boast of huge strike funds. Although the threat of starvation is no longer an immediate deterrent to militancy, the legitimacy of labor unions among workers is reinforced by their ability to raise money and to render concrete assistance to strikers' families. During the 1970 auto strike, however, the multimillions in the United Auto Workers strike chest were exhausted within a few months, even though benefits never exceeded $25 a week for the several hundred thousand GM workers. At the same time, thousands of workers lost their savings. The companies had driven home another lesson to the workers; despite unions, strikes are expensive.

In 1946, the workers in most large American industries conducted a mass strike for substantial wage increases. The strike was largely successful since workers had been forced to endure a wage freeze for the entire period of the Second World War.

Neither union leaders nor corporate opposition could thwart the resolve of industrial workers to walk out, and neither union leaders nor the corporations were anxious for the strike. Its resolution, however, did have an important influence on the course of the postwar economy. The companies finally acceded to the workers' demands, but exacted a major concession from the unions. The immediate consequence of the wage settlement was the announcement by the steel companies of a significant price increase. Union leaders remained mute, thus giving tacit support to the companies. Together, unions and corporations imposed the pattern of the wage-price spiral on the whole society. Organized workers learned that their power was sufficient to make gains in real wages, provided they did not make social demands; that is, challenge the profits of the companies or the commodities they produced. Further, they were convinced that the growing international role of the United States, particularly in rebuilding Europe, was necessary for their economic well-being. The 1946 mass strikes ended in reinforcing the ideology of expansion among workers. Consciousness was fragmented, since the workers could separate their role as producers from their role as citizens and consumers.

When the Communists, following the lead of the Soviet Union and the world Communist movement, opposed the extension of U.S. hegemony abroad, they were not supported by the workers. Of course, it was true that the CP had lost much prestige by its wartime support of repressive labor policies. But, more important, it was also true that workers perceived the opposition to U.S. foreign policy as a threat to their own welfare; they watched in silence while the government, aided by liberal union leaders, put Communists in jail for violating the non-Communist affidavit required by the Taft-Hartley Act.

It cannot be denied that working class militancy has generally been ambivalent in the United States. Workers are no less anti-employer than any other working class in the world. Strikes are bloodier, conducted for longer periods, and often manifest a degree of solidarity unmatched by any other group of workers. But working class consciousness is industry-oriented, if not always job-oriented. Workers will fight their unions and the companies through wildcat strikes and other means outside the established framework of collective bargaining. But they are ideologically and culturally tied to the prevailing system of power, because until now it has shown the capacity to share its expansion with a large segment of the working class.

These ideological ties, however, are much weaker among those segments of the working class that have historically been excluded from these shares—Black workers, women, and youth. But since 1919 it has not been accurate to claim that Black workers are not integrated at all into the industrial work force. Although they are excluded from unions representing skilled construction workers and underrepresented within the top echelons of union leadership, Blacks constitute between ⅓ and ⅖ of the work force in the auto and steel industries, and smaller but significant proportions of other mass production industries. Most union response to the large number of Black workers has been characterized at best by tokenism.

Union discrimination against Blacks and, to a lesser extent, young white workers, has led to the formation of caucus movements, particularly inside the auto and steel unions, based on the specific sectoral demands of these groups. Some Black caucuses seek more union power and, at the same time, demand upgrading to better-paying skilled jobs. Youth caucuses have been organized within the UAW making similar demands, but have gone further to suggest that the rigidity of industrial labor be relaxed. Some caucuses have asked that the uniform starting time of most workplaces be rescinded, that supervision be less severe, and that ways be found to enlarge job responsibility so that the monotony and meaninglessness of most assembly line tasks be mitigated. Young workers are groping for ways to control their own work, even though they are making piecemeal demands. Black workers are demanding liberation from the least satisfying of industrial tasks and more control over union decision-making processes.

But these are only tentative movements toward a different kind of working class consciousness. Workers are still oriented toward making demands on companies and unions, and do not aim at taking autonomous control over their own lives. Within the American working class, no significant movement or section of workers defines itself as a class and sees its mission to be the same as the liberation of society from corporate capitalist social relations.

Such consciousness will never arise in America from abject material deprivation. The position of the United States in the world has become more precarious since the end of World War

II, but workers know that American capitalism has not reached a dead end. However, the consciousness that most work in our society is deadening and much of it unnecessary has permeated the minds of young people, including the new entrants into the factories and offices. The growing awareness of the need for new forms of labor manifests itself in spontaneous ways. Corporations are becoming more concerned that young workers are not sufficiently disciplined to come to work on time or even every day. The new ideas for fewer workdays, even if the 40-hour work week is retained, are not likely to catch fire in the near future. But they indicate that corporations are searching for new methods of coping with the manifest breakdown of industrial discipline among the millions of workers who have entered the labor force in the past decade and have not experienced the conservatizing influence of the Depression. After all, if poverty is really not a threat for large numbers within our society, how can they be expected to endure the specialization of work functions and their repetitive character? The specter that haunts American industry is not yet the specter of Communism, as Marx claimed. It is the specter of social breakdown leading to a new conscious synthesis among workers.

It is the practice of trade unions and their position within production that determines their role in the social process. The transformation of the working class from one among many competing interests groups to capitalism's revolutionary gravedigger depends on whether working class practice can be freed from the institutions which direct its power into bargaining and participation within the corporate structure and can move instead toward workers' control.

The trade unions are likely to remain both a deterrent to the workers' initiative and a "third party" force at the workplace, objectively serving corporate interests both ideologically and in the daily life of the shop, and remaining a diminishing instrument of workers' struggles to be employed selectively by them. But the impulse to dual forms of struggle—shop committees, wildcat strikes, steward movements—may become important in the labor movements of the future.

The rise of new instruments of workers' struggle would have to reject the institutionalization represented by the legally sanctioned labor agreement administered by trade union bureaucracies. Workers would have to make conscious their rejection of limitations on their freedom to take direct action to meet their elementary needs at the workplace. Although many wildcat strikes are implicitly caused by issues which go beyond wage demands, these remain hidden beneath the more gross economic issues. Labor unions are not likely to become formally committed to the ideas of workers' control over working conditions, investment decisions, and the objects of labor. On the contrary, they will remain "benefits"-oriented, fighting incessantly to improve the economic position of their own membership in relation to other sections of the work force rather than in relation to the employers. They will oppose workers' efforts to take direct action beyond the scope of the union agreement and to make agreements with the boss on the informal basis of power relations on the shop floor.

The forms of consciousness that transcend trade unionism within the working class are still undeveloped and have not caught up with practice. Moreover, the perception that unions have become less useful institutions in the defensive as well as offensive struggles of workers, is confined to long-organized sections of the working class that have experienced the deterioration of the labor bureaucracies into instruments for the suppression of independent workers action. But barely 25 percent of the work force are members of trade unions. Workers in service industries and government employment who have been without union representation often regard trade unionism as a social mission.

For example, trade unionism still appears as a progressive force among the mass of working poor, such as farm and hospital workers, who labor under conditions of severe degradation. At first, unionization seems to be a kind of deliverance from bondage. But after the initial upsurge has been spent, most unions fall back into patterns of class collaboration and repression. At the point when grinding poverty has been overcome and unions have settled into their conservative groove, their bureaucratic character becomes manifest to workers.

We are now in the midst of a massive reevaluation by organized industrial workers of the viability of the unions. However, it is an action critique, rather than an ideological criticism of the union's role and the legal implications of it. It is still too early to predict its precise configuration in the United States. In the end, the spontaneous revolt will have to develop its own alternative forms of collective struggle and demands.

NOTES

1. Collective Agreement between Oil, Chemical, and Atomic Workers International Union and Gulf Oil Co., Port Arthur, Texas, 1966–69.

2. Mathew Josephson, *Sidney Hillman: Statesman of American Labor*, New York, Doubleday & Company, 1952, pp. 124–25.

3. Walter Galenson, *The CIO Challenge to the AFL*, Cambridge, Mass., Harvard University Press, 1960, p. 112.

4. *Ibid.*, p. 112.

5. Robert R. R. Brooks, *As Steel Goes*, New Haven, Conn., 1940, p. 147, as quoted in Galenson, *ibid.*

6. Steel Workers Organizing Committee Proceedings of the Second International Wage and Policy Convention (1940), p. 132.

7. Earl Browder, Speech at Extraordinary Conference, July 1933, Communist Party of the United States in *The Communist*, Summer 1933.

8. Saul Alinsky, *John L. Lewis: An Unauthorized Biography*, New York, G. P. Putnam & Sons, 1949, p. 72.

9. Earl Browder, *The People's Front*, New York, International Publishers, 1938, p. 40.

10. Alexander Bittleman's Review of the Month in *The Communist*, July 1937, p. 583.

11. *Ibid.*, p. 584.

12. William Z. Foster, "Twenty Years of Communist Trade Union Policy" in *The Communist*, November 1939.

13. *Ibid.*

14. Steelworker's Organizing Committee, Proceedings of the Second International Wage and Policy Convention (1940), p. 137, quoted in Galenson, *op. cit.*, p. 114.

15. For a recent example see Staughton Lynd, "The Possibility of Radicalism in the early 1930's: The Case of Steel" in *Radical America*, VI, 6, Nov.–Dec., 1972. In this article, Lynd ascribed the failure of union democracy in the Steelworkers Union to the ambivalent position of the Communist Party in pursuing its trade union policy.

16. Art Preis, *Labor's Giant Step*, New York, Pioneer Publishers, 1964, p. xvi.

5

The Formation
of the Professional
Servant Class

The organizing role of the state in behalf of the whole economy
has become the most characteristic feature of modern American
capitalism. Contrary to myth, the American industrial revolution
was not made by independent entrepreneurs, who, as self-made
men, clawed their way to the top of a highly competitive free
enterprise system. Since the Civil War, the rise of large-scale industry has always relied heavily on the support of the federal
government.

The myth of free enterprise is no more plainly controverted
than in the example of the circumstances surrounding the extension of the United States border from the Atlantic to the Pacific
ocean in the nineteenth century. Not only did the government
play a crucial role in purchasing lands and territories from which
raw materials could be extracted for the use of business, employing military forces to seize these lands when necessary, but public
funds were allocated for the building of railroads and canals and
the establishment of highways and other communications and
transportation routes. In the nineteenth century, the government

became an instrument of large financial and industrial interests and was used to assist them in securing the conditions of economic growth. The enlarging role of the state has been continuous ever since.

The significance of the development of the large corporation as the characteristic institution of American economic life can hardly be underestimated. Not only did it result in a tremendous concentration of economic and political power in relatively few hands, but it had lasting impact upon the social and occupational structure of the United States, striking a blow at the two great sectors of the old middle class—the small businessman and the independent farmer, and calling into being a multitude of occupations and some entirely new strata of workers whose work was no longer divided according to the classical divisions of nineteenth-century capitalism.

The old middle class had been fiercely independent. Possessed of both social and economic weight, and ably represented by Jefferson and Jackson, it had imposed its ideology upon American politics and culture during the first half of the nineteenth century. Its long decline began after the Civil War, with the rise of manufacture occurring increasingly on the basis of the large corporations. The small manufacturer or artisan began to find it more and more difficult to compete successfully with those corporations able to amass huge aggregates of capital, raise worker productivity, and reduce prices. Even in sectors such as retailing, the large chain department store was straining the existence of the small shopkeeper, forcing him onto the margins of distribution. Thus corporate influence and power extended beyond the factory to all corners of American economic life.

The new middle class arose with the division of the entrepreneurial function within large-scale industry and commerce. No longer did a single man raise capital, plan and organize production, supervise the workers who executed it, and keep the records of production and distribution of the product so that future planning could take place. Now, the capital-raising role within the corporate enterprise was most often taken by those whose ownership of shares was sufficient to place them in effective control of the corporation, or by a surrogate manager. The planning and organization of production became another segment of the managerial function that was performed under the direction of owners who continued to set objectives, make overall policy for the firm, and raise the funds needed to meet these policies and goals. The new managers were recruited from the supervisory staff of production crews, from among successful small entrepreneurs not previously connected to the corporation, or from the growing "professions" of engineering and business administration. Regardless of the source from which they came, by the turn of the century they signaled the transformation of the old "self-made man" into a salaried employee of the corporation. Notwithstanding high salaries, pension benefits, stock options, and liberal expense accounts, the new middle class was essentially no longer in control of the basic direction of the corporation, but became a professionally trained servant of it.

Capitalist progress depends a good deal on the capacity of the corporation to generate innovative methods of producing, distributing, and marketing goods. As late as the 1880s, many of the inventors, and organizers of such activities were mechanics, artisans, and salesmen who drew from their experience in the workshop or in the marketplace. Within a few years, these industrial and commercial geniuses soon found themselves salaried employees of the new entrepreneurs, those capable of combining the capital of many small producers with the additional financial resources supplied by banks.

Decision-makers within industry are those capable of mobilizing capital and coordinating it with the process of production and distribution of goods. Such men as Andrew Carnegie, John D. Rockefeller, Andrew Mellon and J. P. Morgan were important examples of this type. In the twentieth century the large corporation has separated this role from the actual processes of production and distribution, which are now directed by professional managers. The new corporate capitalists may or may not have an intimate knowledge of the techniques of production or marketing; their essential task is to direct the labor of those who do possess knowledge. Their specific métier is the manipulation of people, the raising and management of capital, and the making of ultimate corporate policy with the advice of important lower managers and key stockholders.

But most managers, except those involved in the highest councils of the company, make decisions only in their own realm. Even if they are highly paid, and own a small portion of corporate property in the form of stock, they are often unable to comprehend the whole of the corporation's activities, since their own work is confined to a fragment of it and represents only a part of the labor of the old entrepreneur. The Marketing Director, the

Vice President in charge of production, the Director of Research and Development, the Directors of staff functions such as Corporate Finance, Personnel, Industrial Relations, Public Relations, and Advertising, are persons who have risen from the ranks of the company bureaucracy or have been recruited from organizations with parallel structures, such as the government, the military, or other corporations. These are men whose function is to direct the work of others within the broad framework of the overall company goal of profit maximization. Few ever truly become top managers, that is, those who will coordinate all these functions in conformity with the overall political and economic objectives of the corporation. More often than not, they become victims of shifts in top management or changes in ownership of the corporation. Thus their fate is often determined by other than technical factors such as competence; they are, like high appointees of government administrations, eminently political in their structural position within the corporation.

The changing patterns of recruitment in recent years reflect the close and often interlocking relations between the government, the corporations, and the military. These ties in turn have been generated by the increasing reliance of the whole corporate economy on government coordination and government purchases of goods produced by the private sector. As is well known, these purchases are largely in the "defense" sector, but what is important here is the fact of the government as consumer, not the particular area of government purchase.

This dependence of business on government assistance actually was evident prior to the advent of the permanent war economy. As early as the latter half of the nineteenth century, government subsidies to rail construction and other industrial endeavors were acknowledged to be an essential element in the successful development of U.S. industry. At the turn of the century, subsidies in the form of cheap land and capital were supplemented by the establishment of government regulatory agencies in public utilities whose effect was to coordinate and finally restrict competition among the producers of electric power and other energy resources, transportation services, and communications—industries that constituted the infrastructure of American capitalism without which industrial expansion would have been severely limited. The New Deal, as Edward Kirkland has argued, was an extension of this long-term trend toward private sector reliance on government support and regulation.[1] Indeed, it carried the process of integration a step further. Responding to the economic crisis, the emphasis of New Deal legislation, particularly the National Industrial Recovery Act, the Agricultural Adjustment Act, and the Reconstruction Finance Corporation, was on the attempt to regulate prices, the size and direction of capital investment, and the volume of production. These measures were supplemented by expanded government activity in capital-generating (and employment-producing) activities such as road building, housing, and electric power construction, which benefited not only those directly engaged in public works, but the industries producing steel, cement, building materials, and machinery.

It was not until the federal government became a massive purchaser of goods and services, in 1937–39, that these evolving relationships became solidified. By the end of the Second World War it was clear that business recovery and survival depended on government-generated activities. Even the high concentration of wealth and ownership in the hands of a relatively few corporations and their ability to control sectors of the market had proven insufficient to insure continuous expansion and prevent disastrous economic crises. Nor had the growth of government regulation and the initiation of state planning in agriculture and in some areas of industry been adequate to maintain sufficiently high levels of investment, profits, and employment. Nothing less than a permanent government commitment to purchase more than one fifth of the total goods and services produced in the United States was sufficient to stimulate levels of economic activity consistent with the goals of profit maximization and political stability.

In 1968 the basic industries of steel, electronics, machine tool manufacture, aircraft, instruments, did more than 10 percent of their business with the Department of Defense. Some of these, like ordnance and aircraft, were almost totally dependent on government purchases. Each of them sold in excess of 70 percent of its total product to government agencies. More than one-third of the product of the radio, TV, and electronic components industries and one-fourth of the transportation equipment and machine shop industries were devoted to defense work. One sixth of scientific instruments and primary nonferrous metals business was done with the Defense Department. More than a dozen other basic industries, such as steel, transport, chemical, rubber, and engines and turbines sold between 8 and 10 percent of their total product to the Defense Department. Given the fact that profits on sales rarely exceed 10 percent after taxes, these statistics reveal the degree to which modern corporations depend on the political apparatus to create a market for their goods and thus help them realize the prevailing volume and rate of profit.

The remarkable feature of the defense business is that it has to a large extent eliminated the marketplace as the regulator of economic activity. The two-fold character of commodities, exchange value and use value, postulated by Marx as their central feature, is controverted by the fact that these products lose their use value in the old sense. The basis of their value in exchange is quite arbitrary. In government contracts, the profit rate is the fulcrum upon which the price at which goods are exchanged swings. The price is not negotiated on the basis of its "free market" value. Instead, it becomes a subject of calculation whose central determinants are political rather than economic. Moreover, the outcome of the transaction is the production of goods whose price has no stable relationship to its value calculated on the basis of any of the classical determinants. Neither the amount of labor necessary for the production of defense goods nor the "marginal utility" to the mythic consumer becomes the basis of its value in exchange. The substance of technological innovation within defense industries has rarely had impact on the other sectors of the economy. Defense expenditures are socially unproductive even though they often result in a material product. Yet, in this "best of all possible worlds" for the benefiting corporations, such allocations of social resources become the key to relative economic stability, to the extent that they provide a market for the investment of capital, sources of employment for millions of workers, and the focus for the labors of vast armies of scientific and technical workers.

Moreover, since much of government activity has increasingly been involved in the buying of goods and in the administration of huge organizations, the skills acquired through these functions make high government officials logical candidates for high posts in corporate management. Military leaders have found lateral mobility as well. The appointment of General Lucius Clay to head the Board of Directors of Continental Can, of General Alexander Haig to assist top foreign policy adviser Henry Kissinger, or of countless Pentagon military officials to top posts in the aircraft and ordnance manufacturing industries is more than a reflection of their ability to influence government policy: it reflects the growing convergence of the private and the public, the closing of the gap between the state and civil society, between politics and economics. The reverse has become true as well. Corporate officials such as Robert McNamara of Ford; Douglas Dillon of the Dillon-Reed investment banking firm; Luther Hodges of the textile industry; John Volpe, a construction executive; John Foster Dulles of the corporate law firm of Sullivan, Cromwell; George Romney of American Motors, are just a few who have moved from corporations to government service.

The corporations, having colonized and subordinated the public sector to their needs, come to accept the operational supremacy of the political elite. In the political elite's hands are placed the tasks of overall planning and coordination of vital investment decisions such as are determined by rates of interest and the level of the national, state, and local budgets (much of which is distributed to the corporations in the form of defense and civilian contracts for goods and services).

Critics of the close relationship between the government and the corporations have focused most often on the defense sector. The implication of their critique has been that sharp cutbacks in war-related expenditures would loosen the ties between business and government and help pave the way for the revival of grassroots democracy. Although war-related expenditures and activities accounted directly for more than 3 million jobs in both the public and the private sector in 1968, and, indirectly, in the employment of a much larger number of workers in private industry and the government, those who would substantially reduce the defense budget are confident that social expenditures and, in Seymour Melman's opinion, capital investments to modernize sectors of U.S. industry that have literally gone to seed in the wake of shifting national priorities, would more than fill the gap left by defense cutbacks.

The arguments that have been advanced by such economists as Emil Benoit, Melman, and others for a shift of public priorities rest on two central assumptions: (1) that the corporations would benefit as much from emphasis on social expenditures as they have from defense-related work, and (2) that the government has not been closely connected with large corporations in determining social as well as military priorities.

As for the first assumption, the real issue is not the type of expenditure but its payoff in terms of profit maximization and the long-term guaranteed market. Prior to the arms buildup after 1937–38, the new feature introduced by the New Deal was the permanent use of the state as a consumer of the goods and services of private industry. Since 1932 government spending has provided a direct stimulus to investment and has accounted for nearly half of all investment capital. The impact of government spending in defense and other areas as well, combined with manipulation of the interest rates, the employment of a large bureaucracy to administer state affairs and social welfare benefits, has been decisive in preventing the "normal operation" of the business cycle that historically threw millions out of work and caused havoc not only among the working classes but within the capitalist class as well. The question that must be answered when attempting to discover an alternative to defense spending as a mechanism for the stimulation and regulation of economic activity is what other commodities or services can provide steady sources of corporate income that will not be limited by the fact that the projects will eventually be completed. The virtue of war matériel and defense services is that they can easily be destroyed in actual combat or by being declared technologically obsolete, and these noneconomic factors regenerate demand. On the other hand, a baseball stadium, a new school or a new hospital, once built must remain in use for a long period of time. A further advantage of defense spending is that it requires a huge standing army of military personnel and an equally large force of civilian administrative and technical employees to maintain it. The jobs and services generated by war spending do not encounter the constraints of limited population growth as does education; there is no time horizon for the completion of the task short of world peace and disarmament, a goal that rests entirely on political determination rather than technical criteria; there need be no end to the source of profits provided that ideologies and politics can be maintained that justify military expenditure as a national "need." Even though the maintenance of depolluting activities and educational and health services would always require employees, the relatively fixed initial capital investment in these areas would be amortized over a fairly long period of time. In contrast, defense expenditures and space exploration permit huge reinvestment opportunities at rapid turnover rates, according to political determinants.

It is possible to interpret the survival of the entire aircraft and electronics industry in these terms. Many corporations have risen to international importance as a result of the defense business and are relatively immune from changes in the party in power. A corporation such as General Electric, now the fourth largest industrial corporation in the country, has been able to increase its size tremendously as a result of its continuous claims on public funds. GE is a leader in the production of engines and turbines, electrical and industrial apparatus, radio, television, and communications and electronic components. Its share of the defense "market" in these sectors exceeds the industry average. GE owes at least one-third of its sales to the defense business. The International Business Machines Corporation, the fifth largest industrial corporation, is among the Defense Department's largest contractors. RCA, the eighteenth largest industrial corporation, in 1971 also did a large part of its business with the government, as do Litton Industries, Lockheed, Eastman Kodak, Ling-Temco-Voight, Boeing, United Aircraft, McDonnell Douglas, and North American Rockwell, all of which are listed among the top fifty corporations. Thus, one fifth of the elite corporations in the United States owe the majority of their growth or near it to the political-economic decisions of government managers. It would not be rash to suggest that the high number of government officials originally employees of these firms have been placed in government for reasons that go beyond a sense of public duty and patriotism. Nor would the fact that the metals production and fabricating industries rely heavily on defense account for the persistence of this sector as an important link between government and industry.

In making a shift from defense to social expenditures of the type suggested by many liberals the problem would become how to find a way to insure capital turnover at the same rate, and to obviate the political and economic weight of those giant corporations who benefit directly from such expenditure as well as the many others more indirectly involved. Compounding the difficulty is the relationship between the prime defense contractors and the largest financial corporations, such as Chase Manhattan, First National City, and the Bank of America—the three largest banking institutions—that are crucially involved in the ownership and control of many of the defense contractors.

But it would be entirely one-sided to claim that the government has not been involved in the privately owned "civilian" sector as well. The nature and extent of this involvement goes beyond general "macroeconomic" policies such as regulating interest rates on loan capital, establishing controls over prices and wages to stem inflationary pressures, or undertaking initiatives in foreign relations that facilitate U.S. spending and investment abroad and open up external markets for U.S. goods. These activities have become a routine feature of all governments and cannot be ascribed to recent developments in the relations between government and business; nor can the enormous support given by the government in assisting industry to bring its goods to market by creating the preconditions for the expansion of enterprise be regarded as unusual. These functions inhere in all modern economies.

Just as the government had been instrumental in promoting rail transportation rather than other forms of overland travel in the nineteenth century, it wielded its power to insure the transition from rails to trucks and airplanes in the post–Second World War era. Robert Fogel has shown that there was no technological or economic inevitability in the choice of rails over waterways and other means to transport goods in the nineteenth century—rails were no more economically viable than canals.[2] It was the combined political weight of banks, rail corporations, and metals manufacturers, owing to their economic power, that turned the tide of state support. Similarly, the archaic rail stock that had deteriorated in the decades after the First World War owing to the standstill in rail construction, and the low level of investment in repairs during the late 1920s and the Depression, was never replaced adequately after World War II because of political pressure from the oil and automobile industries. The government instead transfered its support to highways and aircraft as the emerging means for the transportation of goods and people. The $100 billion highway program and the airport construction programs, approved by Congress in the early years of the Eisenhower administration, represented the key "social welfare" achievement of that administration. The enormous injection of federal funds for highways and airports not only meant the end of the railroads as a prime source of passenger transportation, it accelerated the transformation of the face of the entire nation.

These programs enlarged the options available for the expansion of American industry to rural areas. Technologies were no longer limited by scarce land. Gradually, most basic industries moved from the center cities to the suburbs and old agricultural lands. As I have noted in the previous section, the automobile became elevated to a daily necessity for millions of workers. Finally, highways and dispersed industrial growth signaled the dramatic shift of working class residential patterns.

In 1949 the Federal Housing Act spelled the end of the New Deal commitment to public housing. For the first time workers could obtain federal guarantees on loans for private, one-family homes—although the one-family home was no more "necessary" in preference to apartment houses than the emergence of the automobile in preference to the railroad. Federal action had again been decisive in determining the configuration of private investment. It was the convergence of a series of corporate and government policies, arrived at through joint planning by high officials of each constellation of institutions, that played the decisive role in determining whether mass transit or the automobile, whether the railroad or the truck, whether public housing or private housing, would dominate the canvas of American life.

In this group of high official planners we have a startling example of the emergence of the new professional servant stratum as a subordinate, although crucial, link binding politics and economics. This service class has been aptly characterized by Ralf Dahrendorf as being "committed to the ruling norms which it administers without having made them; more than others the members of this class tend to be conformist to the prevailing norms."[3]

— 2 —

Operating within a general framework of assuring high levels of capital accumulation for those corporations most directly involved in what John Kenneth Galbraith and others call the New Industrial State, the professional servant stratum contains within it several groups that function at different levels of the corporate hierarchy and have different degrees of delegated power. Only a small minority of the professional servants are in the top echelon managerial positions in corporations or the institutions that serve it. Most members of this group occupy "middle managerial" niches in the bureaucracy. These are district sales managers, managers of service facilities of manufacturing corporations, production superintendents, department heads of large universities, or directors of research programs.

The middle stratum possesses only the authority delegated to it by the technocratic stratum of professional servants. Typically, middle managers adhere to technocratic ideologies without generating them. In the past, they were recruited from among the technicians and represented the reality of mobility for the technical and scientific strata of the working class. The transformation of middle management from an art that extends from the position of the technician in the division of labor into a profession that has its own legitimations, has meant that entrance into this stratum is increasingly restricted to those who have endured the rituals of schooling that produce a specific management credential. The role of education as a specific prerequisite for middle management buttresses the subjective as well as the objective perception of the managerial stratum as a distinct class.

Just as top echelon managers represent the corporate interests at the national level in political and civic life, middle managers reproduce this function at the state and local levels. IBM, General Electric, oil companies, and other large corporations encourage their local officials to become members of school boards, leaders of community philanthropic activities, and even to run for public office. In areas where a single large corporation constitutes the only industry or the dominant source of employment, its participation in community institutions is eagerly solicited by members of the old middle class of small shopkeepers or farmers in the area. With few exceptions, the pockets of resistance to the invasion of the corporation into small town life are swiftly overcome since the stark reality of the situation is that without the corporation's economic strength the town or county would be reduced to rural poverty.

Thus, their role in the matrix of social and political life as much as in the workplace itself makes the middle managers a stratum without character. Middle managers are persons whose lives have little or no private dimension. Their friendships, recreational activities, social connections within the community, are intimately bound up with their position as the full-time representatives of the corporation. Their ideologies and political behavior conform to corporate needs and strictly preclude dissent on operational and policy decisions, except those carefully delineated for them from above.

The boundaries of autonomy are internalized by the managers both implicitly and explicitly. Organizational flow charts specify the range of operations permitted to managers and their responsibility within their assigned terrain. Where the job description does not specify areas of authority or jurisdiction, managers are trained to consult with superiors before making decisions. Thus both the object of cognition and its manipulation are severely restricted. Just as the production worker is limited to his specialized operations, the manager knows the limits of his job and internalizes those limits as personal traits.

In the past thirty-five years, technological and organizational innovations have been largely confined to corporations involved in "defense" because public funds have remained the chief source of scientific and engineering research and development. Frequently public funds have been channeled into those institutions that agree to work on projects and in areas most directly relevant to the priorities established by the ruling elites. The university, its research institutes, and the corporate foundations have become knowledge factories that are charged with the responsibility of developing the management and scientific technologies needed by the technocrats. Here we can observe the transformation of the university into a mirror image of the large corporation. Even though remnants of the "pursuit of truth" ideology that characterized the medieval university remain (and some scholars are retained to give life to this image in every large university), the typical university dean or officer functions as a corporate executive. Just as "going to Washington" is an important part of the job of many executives of large companies, so the university bureaucrat makes his trek to the nation's capital or the state capital for research contracts for defense purposes, grants from the offices of Education for general college purposes such as construction of new facilities and establishment of new scientific and technical departments. The government decision-making apparatus, having been fully integrated with larger public and corporate needs, has been mobilized to deal with hundreds of thousands of requests for assistance from educational institutions in terms consistent with current policies. In turn, the university that seeks increased influence on national decision-making as well as public assistance to maintain its existing programs learns to frame its proposals in the language and objectives of the changing priorities of the state and national governments.

The university has become the quintessential professional servant of the corporations. Often its top officials share in planning responsibilities with other elites because its apparatus has become so fully integrated with corporate needs. To the degree that "technical intelligence" operates, in changed form, as an

aspect of the entrepreneurial function of the old individual capitalist, it is delegated to members of the university hierarchy, who
occupy the same social position as the corporate and government
professional servants. Within the university, technical intelligence
is organized along the lines of the rationalized division of labor
characteristic of all other spheres of modern economic life.

Directors of research, and those employed on consulting or
training projects under contract to government agencies at state
and national levels, are usually tenured full or associate professors
whose academic role is less significant in the actual performance
of their duties than their administrative expertise in the manipulation of people within the project through the assignment of tasks
and approval of their results, the assumption of responsibility for
discipline, and the resolution of personnel issues such as salaries
and promotion, and of conflicts within the working staff.

The power of the administrator derives from his ability to
perpetuate the organization created for the specific function even
after the job has been completed. For example, the director of a
project to evaluate a particular government-sponsored job-train-
ing program will attempt to get another contract in a related field
(or even an unrelated field) well before the initial contract that
created his organization has been completed. Thus, the research
organization becomes the mirror image of the conglomerate that
follows the "profit picture" rather than a specific industrial emphasis. In order to be successful it cannot be mired in specialization but must move rapidly from one endeavor to another without regard to its appropriate content. Therefore, a second aspect
of administrative work within the university is the business of
grantsmanship, that is, the flexible manipulation of symbols and
rhetoric in accordance with the previous norms established by
technocratic elites in order to get money.

In the context of the modern university, teaching serves two
distinct functions: first, to maintain academic ideologies about
the role of the university in society; second, to actually train, that
is reproduce, various levels of technical managers for all institutions of corporate society, and to train technicians for subordinate
roles within the bureaucracies.

The division of labor within the universities is matched by
divisions between them. Certain universities train the ruling class
and technocratic elites (Harvard, Yale, Columbia, Stanford, and
the most prestigious state universities, e.g., the University of

Michigan, Wisconsin, certain branches of the University of California, and Cornell, a school that is a joint effort of the private and public sector). These are the institutions that are recipients of huge defense contracts, foundation funds, and other forms of outside subsistence for research and development activities. In addition to generating "knowledge" for technical applications in industry, they are responsible for generating ideologies and techniques for the increasingly critical task of managing people.

During earlier periods of industrial capitalism, philosophy, political economy, and even sociology—during its infancy—were pursued as critical disciplines even by those who supported the prevailing social order. Today, critical theory has been debased to the level of technical intelligence, subordinate to meeting operational problems. Thus, sociologists are interested in such issues as the causes and cures of juvenile delinquency, "criminal" behavior of all kinds, and deviance from established social norms. Contracts are obtained from government agencies and foundations for the explicit purpose of providing guides for policy-making, chiefly in areas of institutional management and administration. Under these circumstances, "reform" is defined as changes in the patterns of care and treatment of acknowledged social deviants who, in turn, are defined and categorized by social science. Social theorists become institutional managers in their own realm.

The contemplative and critical character of reason has given way to instrumental reason. The social scientist as activist is a professional servant of the corporate apparatus. He has taken his place in the hierarchy of power and become an important element in the modern division of labor. The product of his labor is no longer assessed qualitatively, but by the cost-benefit criteria that measure the viability of any commodity.

During the Kennedy and Johnson administrations, the technical intelligentsia was impressed into government service to a degree unknown in the history of our country. Not since the Second World War, when natural scientists, philosophers, and social scientists such as Einstein and Herbert Marcuse were employed in government work ranging from the diciphering of ideologies—that is, "intelligence" work—to the development of scientific principles in the service of the war, had the government utilized the intellectuals to such a degree. Scientists and other intellectuals justified their wartime service on political grounds, even if their political sensibilities were somewhat offended by the practical uses into which their talents were channeled.

Under the rubrics of the necessity to wage an unrelenting war on poverty, to achieve world peace, and to secure a more just social order, intellectuals became part of the middle level technocratic elites in the postwar era as well. Daniel Bell of Harvard and Columbia and Daniel Patrick Moynihan of Harvard and MIT were among the quintessential examples of intellectuals turned technocrats. Their specific function was the transformation of theory, even ideas that had roots in an oppositionist intellectual culture, into instruments of policy for the social control and management of masses of people. The policy directions indicated in their formulations of social problems became government directives for research and development activities in universities, where college curricula were tailored to conform more closely to the requirements of the emerging technocratic order.

In the nineteenth century the colleges and universities served several narrowly defined functions. The most important task of schools such as Harvard and Yale was, and remains to a lesser degree today, the preparation of political and economic elites for social rule. Higher education consisted in assisting the student to become aware of the broad dimensions of historical knowledge. Among those of inherited wealth and power, technical and professional training for such occupations as the law or medicine was an option reserved for a minority who possessed either intellectual curiousity or a sense of personal and social mission. But the chief object of the schools of higher learning was to provide a means for members of the emerging ruling class to make contact with one another and to internalize the values and needs of their own class as personal goals. It was common knowledge that the university was a kind of finishing school that made the student a "cultured man" or served to give him social graces appropriate to his class.

The second important role of the top schools was to train professional elites in the fields of law and medicine and those destined to occupy positions of political and corporate importance, but not necessarily decisive power within these institutions.

With the rise in the twentieth century of the corporation as the characteristic business institution, the need for a large number of technically trained professionals, especially in the fields of law and technology, proliferated beyond the capacity of the offspring of the ruling class to fill these roles. To the traditional professions were added the new fields of engineering and management, professions geared specifically to the tasks of profit maximization. Both of these professions represented the bureaucratization of what had formerly been the responsibility of the capitalist entrepreneur or of the old middle class professional such as the general civil engineering contractor.

The elite university now became the training ground of teachers and scholars for the university itself. Such scholars could be recruited from among members of the corporate elite, but it was equally important to find worthy sons of members of the old middle class who had grown up possessed of the bourgeois ideologies of individualism and free enterprise, but were inclined toward critical thinking. Such men as the historian John Fiske, the philosopher John Dewey, sociologists Lester Frank Ward and Charles Horton Cooley became important intellectuals of the new order. With the exception of Fiske, who was an outright celebrant of the expansionist tendency of corporate capitalism, each was a critic of the changing order without challenging the underlying premises of nineteenth-century American capitalism. Essentially, the progressives who had themselves been trained within the elite universities became "house" critics of monopoly capitalism. But they criticized its most blatant injustices without challenging the underlying assumptions of capitalism. They failed to discover the roots of the vices of the new order in the philosophy of classical liberalism which had been the foundation of their own education. Instead they viewed these vices as aberrations from an essentially healthy American democracy and saw themselves as instruments of reform to restore the new order to the values of the old.

These were the intellectuals who became the tutors of the new ruling class and provided them with the political rather than technical intelligence needed to balance the more mundane aspects of everyday life in the corporate world. Men like Robert Hutchins and Robert Park of the University of Chicago, John Herman Randall and the progressive educators at Columbia, upheld the best of the bourgeois tradition within the framework of the objectives of preparing the corporate rich for their tasks, on the one hand, and providing the leadership for emerging institutions of social control such as schools and welfare institutions on the other.

The welfare institutions that became the salve for the wounds inflicted by a rapacious capitalist order were the creation, in part, of the liberal intellectuals who collaborated with enlightened members of the corporate bourgeoisie to convince the state that such reforms were necessary if the social order was to survive. As James Weinstein has shown, the provision of social welfare, contrary to popular myth, was not the product simply of the demands of the working class for the amelioration of the worst ills of society.[4] Among the most prominent social reformers were members of the ruling class and the intellectuals who constituted the loyal opposition. These farsighted people were persuaded that the preservation of the essential configuration of social relations in the wake of economic dislocations and political turbulence depended on the ability of the new order to discover the idea of social responsibility.

At first, the corporate mind resisted involvement with any activities that diverted it from the business of making profit. At best, corporate leaders were prepared to continue the *noblesse oblige* traditions of the old aristocracy by philanthropic means. But the challenge of laborism and socialism proved too strong in the first years of the twentieth century to maintain this rather limited social horizon.

Even though it was not until the Great Depression that the last resistance of the bourgeoisie finally gave way, the trend toward corporate support of social welfare at the turn of the century was clear, even though the corporations decided to place this burden on the state rather than assuming direct responsibility for it. The first form of support came when large industry backed reforms in industrial legislation that ostensibly protected the health and safety of women and children, and established universal compulsory public education to replace the factory and the workplace as the prime institution of socialization to the imperatives of industrial labor.

Intellectuals such as Dewey were active in the movements for educational reform and helped organize teacher training colleges and experimental schools within the colleges for the purpose of providing a laboratory for the teachers who would become the leaders of the new public education institutions. Dewey hoped that his philosophy of "progressive" education would become the dominant methodology for the burgeoning public schools. Even though his most central ideas were never adopted fully by the public school systems, many were incorporated piecemeal in them and soon became part of the new traditions.

Columbia and Chicago became centers for the training of high bureaucrats and intellectuals in the expanding social welfare institutions. A school of social work was established at Columbia to train the new professionals in the field who were needed to replace the early reformers who had set up settlement houses to simultaneously incorporate and counter the socialist traditions among the newly arrived immigrants. Just as the experimental school was the training ground for educational leaders, the universities founded hospitals or developed close relations with existing institutions to provide training for the expanding bureaucratized profession of medicine. The large elite universities were rapidly becoming academies for planners and policy-makers destined to lead a large array of social welfare institutions that were being established by the state to attenuate the effects of industrialization.

Since the corporate institutions were making enormous demands on the elite schools for more trained scientific and technical managers than had been provided by the relatively small programs that previously were oriented to the pursuit of "pure" research, it became necessary to create additional educational institutions —state universities, land-grant colleges, teachers colleges, and technical institutes—formed specifically for the purpose of providing credentials for technicians. Most of the programs established by these lower colleges were initially of two years' duration, since the knowledge gained by training was highly specialized, designed for specific tasks within the factory, the school, or the social welfare agency. Two- and four-year colleges are teaching institutions. Characteristically, they lack the laboratories of hospitals and elementary schools, as well as elaborate equipment. In general, they impart less theory and concentrate instead on technique.

In the past half century, these schools have assisted industry and the state in the formation of a new stratum of technicians that is currently the fastest-growing sector of the labor force.

— 3 —

One of the truly remarkable features of late American capitalism is that it has reached the point where only two workers in five are engaged directly in the production and distribution of goods. When this figure is refined, the observations are even more startling. In 1880 half of all producers were working the land; today, ninety years later, less than 5 percent of all who are employed in the goods producing sector are in agriculture, and some of these produce commodities other than food. The family farmer has all but disappeared and has been replaced by the corporate farm; many "farmers" are now full or part-time wage earners.

It is important to understand that the mechanization of agriculture is now almost complete. In fact, together with the oil industry and a few other highly technological branches of manufacturing, agriculture is among the few "continuous flow" operations. On the corporate farm automatic production has almost completely replaced both hand work and individual operations of machinery. The development toward continuous flow methods is most advanced in dairy and livestock production but is also a growing tendency in the production of grains. The relative backwardness of fruit and vegetable production may be attributable to the availability of large quantities of cheap, imported migrant labor who still constitute the basic work force in these sectors. There is no doubt that if historical trends in agriculture are followed unionization will result in a dramatic impetus toward technological change just as labor scarcity became the major cost factor in the nineteenth century that spurred initial agricultural mechanization.[*]

Somewhat less than another 3 million, or less than 5 percent of the employed population, are employed by the crucial industries of mining, steel, auto, oil, and chemicals, which produce the basic raw materials and the most important manufactured commodities. The enormous productivity of American workers in the basic goods producing sector has been among the most significant

[*] For a fuller treatment of this point, the work of Habakkuk on the relationship between labor scarcity and technological development in nineteenth-century America is very interesting. See H. J. Habakkuk, *American and British Technology in the Nineteenth Century*, Cambridge University Press, 1962.

social changes of our era. Its impact has been felt not only in our economic life, but in social, political, and cultural spheres as well.

Since 1947 goods production has multiplied more than two and a half times, while the number of workers engaged in these sectors has only increased by slightly more than 40 percent. The reasons for this substantial advance in productivity are not difficult to find. Since the Second World War, knowledge has become the critical productive force, especially in those industries that produce basic commodities. The replacement of physical by mental labor has not been so dramatic in the highly competitive industries such as garments, shoes, and textiles, but there is no question that scientific and technical developments in both war-related and heavy industries have increased the productivity of labor in a dramatic fashion.

The second reason is not nearly as obvious, and seems to run counter to prevailing ideologies that claim most Americans have had it better than ever. Industrial workers in America simply work harder, faster, and for a longer duration than in any other advanced industrial nation in the world.* I have spoken to a great many foreign labor delegations that have visited American automobile plants and steel mills. They are almost universally amazed at the brutal pace of work that they observed while here. Mass production techniques are not as advanced in European nations, even though some of them are far ahead in machine-technologies. Speedup, increased work loads, and other labor-intensive factors determining production have been important in the annual production increase of more than 5 percent in manufacturing, even though overall economic growth has averaged less than 3 percent per year.

The high rate of productivity has had a multitude of consequences. First, it has been the fundamental source, at least in the twentieth century, of high wages in mass production industries. Indeed, without these high wages, the great volume of consumer goods produced by American workers could never be consumed. This fact has led some economists to claim that high wages are less a function of the militancy of trade unions than the mechanization of American industry and have been granted as a subsidy to consumption.

* The official work week in the United States, 40 hours, is shorter than that in several European nations. But, there is a considerable amount of overtime in many industrial plants, and a large number of workers hold more than one job.

The second implication of the tremendous volume of goods produced by American workers is the need to constantly create markets for these goods. A huge army of sales and advertising personnel has been created by the goods-producing sector. The economic role of the sales effort is to help reproduce capital by guaranteeing the effective consumption of goods. Culturally, the sales effort has as its objective the generation of new needs that facilitate consumption, needs which become an internal necessity for the underlying population. The main point of advertising is to evoke images which have nothing to do with traditional concepts of economic necessity. Mass communication calls forth the repressed sexual needs that are only partially fulfilled by the consumption of the infinite variety of goods created by American industry.

Without the sales effort capital could not be reproduced in our society at the rate necessary to perpetuate and expand current levels of economic activity. But the sales effort has a second function: in 1970 it provided employment for 11 million Americans, or about 12.5 percent of the labor force, who themselves constituted an important market for the large volume of goods.

All nonproductive labor (in the sense that I have used it) has a two-fold character: (1) it is an indirect way to close the chronic gap between high volume of production and the restrictive character of consumption of those in the goods-producing sector, and (2) it generates ideologies of mobility and of privilege. These ideologies are reinforced by the fact that 60 percent of employed Americans wear a white collar, stand behind a counter, or work in a government agency. What is obscured by the social position of this proliferating newly created work force is that its existence rests on the productivity of American labor.

Some social scientists and philosophers of different and opposed political persuasions have argued that we have reached a kind of postindustrial society in which there has been a replacement of large quantities of physical labor by mental labor and machines. The object of economic activity, no longer contained by the drive for capital accumulation, instead finds its rationale in the maintenance of power by those who control the apparatuses of economic, political, and cultural institutions, and it is the enlargement of the apparatuses of control that accounts for much of the growth of white-collar work in the contemporary economy. Although in their view profit remains an important motive of economic activity, those who insist that Western capitalism has evolved into postindustrial conditions are convinced that the drive for maximum profits as an end in itself no longer controls key economic decisions.

In the new society, according to such writers as Daniel Bell, the replacement of physical by mental labor, and the primacy of control over accumulation have changed irreversibly the prospects for the development of a revolutionary working class movement. The key operatives have become the technocrats and technicians (those possessing scientific, technological, or organizational skills) and the intellectuals—not the owners and manual workers who were the significant actors of nineteenth-century capitalism. According to postindustrial theory it is on this new class, made powerful by the new forces of production and the close relation of government and the corporate sector, that the future of society rests.

Other social theorists, particularly the French sociologist Serge Mallet, have argued that the social power generated by the new forces of production has been captured by technocrats, or the stratum of professional servants, but it is the scientists and technicians (that is, mental workers possessing no power over their labor) who have become the new revolutionary class. With this analysis as the basis of his "now" working class theory, Mallet argued that the new, advanced forces of production, that is the high technological levels of key industries and the emergence of knowledge as the critical productive force in advanced industrial socieites, had superseded the old issues of deprivation upon which revolutionaries had based their strategy of political action. Instead, Mallet and others offered a strategy that relied on the contradiction between the requirment of a high general level of knowledge in the entire working class, particularly its technical stratum, and the inability of capitalism to grant control over the work process to those whose expectations and abilities permit aspirations to power. Contrary to the mass of unskilled operatives created by the old productive forces, the new capitalism has brought into being the first class in history fully capable of managing production without relying on the services of the old managers. It is precisely the arbitrary character of technocratic authority in relation to the new labor force that constitutes the principal conflict in contemporary societies.[5]

Andre Gorz, a French journalist and editor of the intellectual journal *Temps Modern,* sought to heighten this contradiction by a strategy that called upon technicians to demand a series of reforms that would challenge the rationale of that authority. In his book, *Strategy for Labor,* he argued that the struggle of the proletarianized technicians was to be for reforms that could not be granted by a corporate system committed to its own domination over both the workplace and the supporting institutions of society. Beyond the demand for workers' control, Gorz raised the cultural issues of the deterioration of the quality of urban life, the concentration of social power and cultural goods in the metropolises and the deliberate perpetuation of backwardness in agricultural and rural industrial areas within the advanced industrial countries, which he linked to the priorities of the technocratic elites.[6] Alain Touraine has shown that the impulse behind the May 1968 student revolts in France was not at all material deprivation, but rather the gap between the growing technical skill and social knowledge of the college students, destined to be the most important technical and administrative cadre of French capitalism, and their subordination inside an overcentralized bureaucratically organized and authoritarian university.[7] More to the point, as I will show in Section 7, the strike of General Motors workers in Lordstown and Norwood, Ohio, was impelled by the resentment among young workers against working conditions that robbed them of their autonomy and control more than by issues of speedup or pay. In both cases, we see illustrations of the fact that the economic issues that propelled nineteenth-century capitalism, that is, the struggle of the mass of humanity for bare survival, have been superseded by the new contradictions of industrial society. These contradictions are primarily cultural in character. They are about the quality of life, and not its quantitative aspects.

Martin J. Sklar, writing from a Marxist perspective, has argued that if capitalism can be defined as the production of commodities by means of the basic commodity, labor, then United States capitalism can no longer be described in terms of the old categories of accumulation. Instead, investment both replaces labor and is capital saving at the same time. Each unit of new investment accumulates capital, but increasingly can only be invested within the present structure of corporate capitalism in wasteful "disaccumulation" that adds little, if any, real wealth to society. The most important example of this process is the defense industry. The goods produced are not commodities in the ordinary sense. They are produced neither for the satisfaction of human wants nor as an addition to the stock of capital used for the production of new commodities. They are characteristically destroyed or declared obsolete. Similarly, the hidden waste embodied in consumer goods such as automobiles that are engineered to break down in a few years represents such disaccumulation. Less obvious but equally relevant is the proliferation of commodities that find a market only through the bludgeoning of the public by mass communications—the most blatant examples of which are the seemingly infinite variety of cosmetic hair sprays and deodorants that litter the market place.

Sklar's theory argues that the accumulation criteria for material production is becoming increasingly irrational and wasteful, but recognizes that the criterion of profit maximization as the motive of capitalist economic activity remains.[8] Touraine, Bell, and others have noticed an extremely important tendency inherent in the development of large-scale corporate organizations toward the creation of a new technically trained stratum that makes important decisions for the corporation, but, as Touraine tries to show, is deprived of control over the whole production process. But their "postindustrial" conclusions are unwarranted. Rather, the significance of the new forces of production that are displacing larger quantities of manual labor is that new contradictions have been created between the postindustrial potentialities of technology and the tenaciously perpetuated authority relations, expressed in the social division of labor and the organizational hierarchies characteristic of industrial societies.

Our productive apparatus has created the objective possibility of satisfying essential material needs, even at the present historical level, without impelling the underlying population to devote most of its waking hours to alienated labor, and thus the essential structures of work and discipline and authority have lost their material basis. In the past, the repressions imposed by less developed societies were objectively necessary because of the relative backwardness of the productive forces. In advanced industrial societies, we find the phenomenon of surplus repression, which consists of those constraints on human activity dictated by authority per se, with no causal relation to necessary production. Herbert Marcuse concludes that technology, contrary to its historical mission to relieve humankind of eternal subordination and backbreaking labor, is now a system of domination itself. It has been turned into its opposite by the failure of the underlying population to transcend in the cultural and political spheres the deprivations that have been made obsolete by the new historical forces of production.

In order to preserve itself, modern capitalism literally requires that scarcity be artificially created. In constantly generating new needs, mass culture plays a part in maintaining work discipline that finds its major justification in consumption. From the point of view of the employer, logic of accumulation dictates its cultural concomitant: the sales effort merely insures the rapid turnover rate of inventory and opens new outlets for capital investment. There can be no real post-scarcity if the present social structure is to maintain its hierarchical configuration.

The claims of theorists who have accurately observed trends in advanced capitalism but have concluded that these transformations constitute its essential transformation are premature. Modern U.S. capitalism remains dominated by the ethos and the mechanisms of capital accumulation. To the degree that such accumulation increasingly fails to add to the actual socially useful stock of capital and to fulfill genuine human wants, the perceptions of Sklar and Marcuse contribute much to the understanding of the emerging order. But it is precisely the disparity between the new developments and the persistence of the presuppositions and structure of industrial capitalism that constitutes one of the central contradictions of mature capitalism.

The proliferation of occupations and industries that serve to decoagulate the sclerotic bloodstream of the economy attest to the crisis character of U.S. capitalism. But these sectors are organized in the very same manner as large-scale industry. Their conformity to the structure of authority, the profit criteria for business activity, and the corporate form of organization has made them preeminently *industrial* institutions and has imprisoned the consciousness and practice of white-collar workers in the same framework as that of manual workers.

The heavy yoke of industrial organization that weighs upon the "postindustrial" work force has produced strains among the ever-larger proportion of workers whose expectations have been generated by educational ideologies that proclaimed their deliverance from factory work. The weapons possessed by corporations to maintain the coherence of the workplace among the most technically advanced sectors of the working class and those who perform clerical and sales tasks but are divorced from the centers of corporate decision-making must go beyond the provision of economic benefits and become chiefly cultural. In postindustrial society the ideologies of professionalism and privilege on the one hand and consumerism on the other uphold a social division of labor no less hierarchical and a structure of authority no less repressive than those among factory workers.

We now turn to an examination of how the white-collar labor force has been industrialized by modern corporate capitalism.

NOTES

1. Edward Kirkland, *A History of American Economic Life,* New York, F. S. Crofts Co., 1939.

2. Robert W. Fogel, *Railroads and American Economic Growth,* Chicago, University of Chicago Press, 1964.

3. Ralf Dahrendorf, "Recent Changes in the Class Structure of European Societies" in *A New Europe: A Timely Appraisal,* edited by Stephen Graubard, Boston, Mass., Beacon Press, 1967, p. 315.

4. James Weinstein, *The Corporate Ideal and the Liberal States, 1900–1918,* Boston, Mass., Beacon Press, 1968.

5. Serge Mallet, *La Nouvelle Classe Ouvrière,* Paris, Editions du Seuil, 1963.

6. Andre Gorz, *Strategy for Labor,* Boston, Mass., Beacon Press, 1967.

7. Alain Touraine, *The May Movement,* New York, Random House, 1971.

8. Martin J. Sklar, "On the Proletarian Revolution and the End of Political-economic Society" in *Radical America,* III, 3, May–June, 1969.

6

The White-Collar Proletarians

— 1 —

"White-collar" is a residual category that has come to designate anyone not engaged in the production of material goods. It has become the most ubiquitous and confusing of all designations of American occupations. C. Wright Mills defined the members of this stratum as those who manipulate symbols and persons rather than things.[1] Surely the large number of service workers who manipulate things—gas station attendants, television repairmen, laundry and dry-cleaning workers, "porters" and transit workers are not "white-collar." But such a broad designation, which combines a multitude of occupations and industries, says very little except that an increasing number of Americans have become separated from the production or distribution of material commodities.

The labor force is ordinarily divided according to the categories established by the United States Department of Labor, which distinguish manufacturing, mining, construction and transportation workers, generally designated "blue-collar" workers, from those in agricultural production on the one hand, and "services" on the other. The trouble with this separation is that it obscures more than it illuminates. It divides the work force according to criteria having to do with qualities such as type of work or type of industry rather than class or authority relations. This leads to the widely held view that the manager of an insurance company and the clerical staff of the same company have more in common with one another than each has with others whose social position is similar even if the particular goods or services they produce are different. And this is precisely the foundation of the notion carefully promulgated by corporations, and shared by many who work in offices, of the community of interest between managers and employees. Thus "white-collar" is a label that presupposes an essential difference between the structure of labor in the factory and the office. It is a category of social ideology rather than of social science and has evoked the image of a system of social stratification that regards office work as a higher-status occupation than factory work, administration as more prestigious than manual labor, or, indeed, any occupation related directly to the production of goods. The bare fact is that "white-collar" is less a description of an actual group of workers than a conceptual tool for a specific perspective on social class.

It is evident that C. Wright Mills accepted the essential homogeneity of those working within non–goods-producing occupations and industries. This reservation does not obviate the pathbreaking significance of his work. In *White Collar*, Mills described for the first time the proletarianization of most of those who are grouped under this rubric. His evocations of the concepts of alienation to classify most office and sales work, his meticulous and detailed descriptions of the boredom and unrelieved subordination of those performing the endless volume of paper work required by modern corporations, his recognition of the political and social impotence shared by all who occupy the lower economic niches of the "white-collar world," went a long way toward lifting the veil from the romance of clerical and administrative labor. But Mills failed to deal with the proliferation of clerical, administrative, and sales jobs in terms of the overall historical development of the economy. He tacitly accepted the community of interests of those who are condemned to the atomization endemic to nonproductive labor, rather than tracing the relations of authority and domination that permeate all labor in our country, regardless of the particular sector. However, he did provide a useful scheme of industrial classification: his categories delineating different kinds of "white-collar" work—sales, corporate administration, and government employment—still constitute the chief conceptual divisions applied to the nonproductive sector.

The term "white-collar" has traditionally been employed to designate those engaged in office work. Implicit in this definition is a demarcation between those who work with machines and those who work in offices. But this distinction does not embrace the most recent developments in the economy. More Americans than ever before are employed by industries that have no direct connection with the administration of corporate organization. Education and health are among the largest and fastest-growing of all American industries. These workers do not work in offices, but in schools, hospitals, or welfare institutions; they neither produce goods nor administer their distribution. They are engaged in the production of "services." Their work may be manipulating things, that is they may be called "blue-collar workers," or they may be engaged in manipulating symbols, commonly identified with white-collar labor, but they are employed within institutions that deal directly with people rather than goods.

In the area of goods production, the nature of labor has also changed significantly. Here we find an increasing proportion of mental rather than manual workers who are no less production workers than the semiskilled and craft laborers who operate machines or repair them, although they wear white and gray collars and their instruments of labor are pencil and paper. They work on the production line or in the testing laboratory where the product is verified and make up the growing stratum of technicians whose labor has more in common with that of factory workers than of clerks.

The mechanization of the office is the most important development among the traditional white-collar sectors of the economy. Many who are called "bookkeepers," for example, actually spend most of their time operating machines that perform most of the calculations once reserved for pencil and paper. In fact, the whole bookkeeping skill, an important occupation of officeworkers, is becoming rapidly mechanized. The old "full charge" bookkeeper is still important in smaller businesses. But large corporate offices have already replaced this semiartisan worker by dividing the job into several parts: At the bottom, the key-punch, accounting, and tabulating machine operator; at the top, the accountant; and in the middle, the computer operator and programmer. The mechanization of bookkeeping has resulted in the creation of a new hierarchy of occupations that barely resemble the old skill. Instead, the accountant possesses delegated authority over those whose education and skills do not warrant the label of "profession."

At the bottom of office occupations, the question of "white-" versus "blue-collar" labor becomes a purely ideological issue. The deafening noise of a key-punch room, the repetitive character of the work, the factorylike discipline enforced by supervision, generate the atmosphere of industrial labor rather than the more genteel environment associated with old notions of white-collar work. The new conditions in the modern office evoke the images of industrial society—there is an increasingly minute division of labor, standardization of both product and of tasks, and denigration of skill to so many units of unskilled and semiskilled work, which can be mastered in a matter of weeks. But patterns of supervision and hierarchically arranged power remain that produce sharply distinct images among workers.

Most corporate offices are extremely sensitive to issues of rank and prestige. The configuration of the hierarchy is plainly evidenced by such symbolic differences as the size of offices at different levels of supervision, whether or not carpeting is on the floor, whether an executive has a private secretary, gets his work done by a typing pool, or must share the time of a secretary with another supervisor. And the social position of the "boss" is reflected in the differential status and prestige accorded his subordinates. The secretary to the president of the company is higher-paid and enjoys greater regard than the secretary to a lower official, despite the nearly identical character of their labor. Down the line, the steno-typists working in the general pool are accorded least pay and status. Social mobility for them consists in getting a job as secretary to a single company official or leaving the company to perform a higher function elsewhere. The social interaction within levels of corporate supervision is equally restricted. The democratic ethos may be widely disseminated in schools or in the mass media, but consciousness of rank and prestige is rigidly enforced at dinner parties and at the golf course. Since many corporations attempt to eliminate private life and instead seek to merge work and leisure by encouraging a series of formal and informal relations among their leading cadre, the person who serves in a supervisory capacity with a large corporation cannot fail to locate his position in the social hierarchy or his chances for advancement by the configuration of social contacts he is able to make.

The awareness of social divisions arises from the actual division of labor in the workplace. In the typical large office, tasks are rationalized much the same way as they are divided on the assembly line or in machine manufacture. But there is even more stratification between office occupations than in the factory. Each task is accorded a different rank, so that the labor of the file clerk is differentiated from that of the typist, not only in terms of job description but in relation to salary scale as well. The confusion introduced by concepts such as "white-collar" is compounded by the differential rewards accorded workers performing different tasks who occupy the same structural position of subordination in relation to managerial authority.

Neither the divisions based on presumed levels of skill between various types of low-level secretarial labor nor the hierarchy of supervision correspond to a necessary technical division of labor. I shall examine the implications of this statement later in this chapter. What is important here is to understand that in the white-collar world there are very few people who consider themselves workers. Instead, they are called, and call themselves, by the higher-status term "employees." Even though substantial authority is usually reserved for the very few managers who are perched at the top of the pyramid, the necessary work of the office is divided in such a way as to generate internalized ideological and class distinctions among the working people. These distinctions are reinforced not only by the differences in the actual work performed, but by the authority delegated to workers over one another. Thus, an administrative secretary in a large office may supervise the work of a number of typists and stenographers who perform exactly the same work she does except for the assigning of tasks to subordinates and acting as policeman. Nevertheless, despite the similarity of her job with those of her subordinates, the front-line supervisor believes that her interest is identical with others in the office who possess genuine authority over the operations of the department or the whole business.

The concept "white-collar" expresses an ideology of privilege based on type of work and relative status, rather than social power. It becomes ambiguous in relation to the large number of government employees who are actually manual workers—perhaps more than 25 percent. These people are employed in parks, transportation, building maintenance, sanitation, highway construction and repair, post offices, and other work that involves physical labor. Similarly, many "administrative workers" are machine operators, janitors, maintenance repairmen, elevator operators and other manual workers.

The majority of clerical workers in corporate offices and government bureaucracies are women. Just as they became the low-paid and low-status manufacturing operatives earlier in the nineteenth century when men remained on the farms, so women were assigned to clerical tasks when industrial capitalism came into its own. With the expansion of paperwork and the sales effort, women were the reserve labor force available for these occupations. In the main, the change from small, one-woman offices and retail counters to large organizations has meant a transformation not only of the character of the labor but of the status and compensation attached to it as well. Today, unlike earlier periods, clerical work is low paid in comparison to many branches of semi-skilled manufacturing and transportation labor that are predominantly performed by males. For example, in 1968 wages for all manufacturing workers averaged $122.51 a week—nearly ten dollars a week higher in heavier industries, and more than ten dollars a week lower in light industry. But in all manufacturing, women constituted only one-third of the work force and were concentrated in the light nondurable sector, where wages were an average of $109 a week. On the other hand, within industries such as wholesale and retail, where women constituted the majority of the nonsupervisory work force, weekly salaries averaged only $86.40; within financial and insurance offices, which employed a major segment of the corporate clerical labor force, the average weekly salary was $102.51.

There are more than 22 million clerical and sales workers in the United States, slightly more than 25 percent of the labor force. Women account for one-half of all government employees, but nearly two-thirds of the "white-collar" group. And they generally occupy the lowest labor grades. Nearly half of all retail employees are women, but the proportion of women working in low-salary sales positions in the retail sector is nearly three-fourths of all employees in this industry. These occupations of the retail industry, comprising the largest number of employees, are about 20 percent unionized, mostly in large metropolitan areas of the Northeastern states, the Middle West and California. Women comprise half the employees of financial and insurance companies, but are heavily concentrated in clerical occupations. These industries are practically nonunion.

Although women constitute more than one-third of the labor force, their distribution in occupational categories is lopsided. Fewer women than men are represented in all occupations in factories, in managerial occupations, among farm workers, and in construction and mining. They are overrepresented in clerical, service, and sales occupations, which are least unionized and expanding fastest of all sectors of the economy. The failure of the unions to recruit women is the main reason they have constituted a progressively decreasing proportion of the labor force. We have already discussed the factors inherent in the occupational structure and the ideologies of the "white-collar" world that inhibit collective action. But there are other reasons for this difficulty having to do with the attitudes of union leaders toward women that are inherited from both general social biases and from the historical experience of the trade union movement itself.

Women are believed by union leaders to be the group most resistant to labor organization. Their alleged temporary tenure on their jobs, the wide-spread beliefs that they are "secondary" wage earners who enter the labor market for extra money and can leave it at any time, that they tend to be more dependent upon and loyal to the company than men, and that internecine warfare constantly rages among them are some of the notions that make male-dominated unions reluctant to recruit women. Moreover, the experience of women within the unions is no more satisfactory than within their jobs. Unions within manufacturing industries such as garments and textiles that have employed a large proportion of women are controlled by skilled male workers and a growing stratum of lawyers and professional union officials who have recently occupied high elected offices. Although it was courage and persistence of women workers that sustained the early organizing drives of these unions, the efforts of these women are not reflected today in the leadership composition of any union where the majority of workers are female.

The tradition of male domination of unions within female-preponderant industries has been carried over in white-collar unionism. The leadership of the Office and Professional Workers International Union, of the State County and Municipal Employees, of the American Federation of Teachers, of the two largest unions among retail employees, and of the important service unions such as the Hotel and Restaurant Employees is predominantly male. In some of these groups, notably among government employees, teachers, and the Hotel and Restaurant

Union, there have been conscious efforts to recognize women and promote them to secondary leadership. But these have been acts of paternalism that are betrayed by the failure of the unions to wage an unremitting struggle for upgrading women to "male" jobs and to raise demands for elevating the wages of the lowest "female" categories to the wages of men in similar categories. In some cases, particularly at the local level, women have organized among themselves to capture important union posts. Such figures as Myra Wolfgang, a vice president of the Hotel and Restaurant Union from Detroit; Lillian Roberts of District Council 37 of New York's State, County, and Municipal Employees; Doris Turner of the New York Hospital Workers Union are representative of the still tiny number of women leaders among government and service employees.

Yet the sexism of male unionists and the hierarchical structure of offices and salesrooms cannot fully explain the fragmentation of the male white-collar workers and their reticence concerning collective action. There is another explanation for past failures that is often ignored by those who have examined this question.

The office and sales worker has been quintessentially a transient worker. Insurance corporations and financial institutions, corporate head offices and retail stores, consciously recruit younger women for low-level jobs. Although most working class women remain in the labor force for a good part of their lives, they leave their jobs after marriage to have children and typically return after four or five years of absence. During the Depression and subsequent periods of economic downturn this tendency was somewhat arrested, but has been resumed during periods of recovery and expansion. Although a larger number of women than ever before remain at work today, even after childbirth, the historical pattern still persists in consciousness. Eventually the rising rate of divorce may make women clerical and retail workers more stable within the individual workplace. Certainly, the rise of government employees' and teachers' unions, which are the fastest-growing of all U.S. labor organizations, is partially attributable to the fact that pay increases and the concomitant welfare benefits including maternity leave have made these jobs more attractive to women or at least more difficult to quit. In contrast, private-sector offices and stores welcome a rapid turnover rate among their low-level employees. Since the expenditure of time and money needed to train workers is relatively small, fast turnover saves them a lot of money in fringe benefits such as pensions and medical payments that increase with the age of the work force.

Even though many younger officeworkers find that they are employed for a much longer period than originally expected, there is a tendency among these women to maintain the myth that they are working temporarily. The persistence of this attitude undermines the prospects for labor organization. The office discipline, which often resembles the repressive rules of the high schools from which they have recently graduated, is tolerated as an ephemeral annoyance to be fought underground rather than openly confronted. The routine and boring operations of typing and filing are often performed absently since concentration on the substance of the work would be maddening.

For many, the real life in the office is not the work at all. It consists of the social contacts among women made at the coffee urn, the ladies' room, at lunch, and in informal after-work activities. For many people, the workplace is the main place to form friendships and overcome the isolation of the city. But such friendships are often of limited duration because of the short-term employment tenure of low-level white-collar workers in most large corporate offices. The longevity of government work often creates the possibilities among employees for forming enduring relationships, but the private-sector office offers social life of a peculiarly transitory character. Some young women are introduced to men through contacts made at work and gradually move away from the old basis of social life in the high school or the neighborhood. For them, there are compensations at work that they cannot find elsewhere. The conviviality of large offices, lunchtime shopping trips, and coffee breaks are important means by which workers reduce the boredom and meaninglessness of their banal tasks.

The corporations tolerate social interaction because they are aware that to repress it would generate resentments about the mindless and routine labor tasks that might lead to manifest discontent. Many large companies even attempt to take over the natural intercourse among their employees by incorporating social, cultural, and sports activities as a regular part of their personnel services and fringe benefits. In corporations such as IBM and Eastman Kodak such paternal efforts are a vital component of industrial relations policies and are almost overtly ideological in their presentation to the workers. Employees learn that the company wishes to create a "family" of employees, just

as Ford creates a "family" of fine cars. Employees are encouraged
to view their jobs as only one aspect of the participation in the life
of the corporative family; at all occupational levels these corporations fight for the loyalty and dependence of their workers by
trying to create a total corporate world. The symbolic evocation
of the family is a direct and conscious effort to reach down to the
anxiety many workers feel about the anomic character of their
lives and to offer a way out of isolation that eliminates the distinctions between private life and work. The failure of labor unions
to penetrate the private sector corporate office is in part attributable to this ingenious use of mass psychology. Reinforced by higher
wages and fringe benefits than those offered by smaller companies, the most sophisticated versions of corporate paternalism
fulfill some of the repressed needs of the mass worker and have
been more than a match for the crude, mechanistic economic
appeals of the unions. No longer representing the values of class
solidarity or human brotherhood, American unionism has little
psychological attraction for the alienated psyche.

It is among those workers employed by impersonal government bureaucracies and quasi-public institutions such as hospitals
that white-collar unionism has been successful. Within the context of the brutalized world of "public service," unions have offered these workers a way of fighting the Machine, particularly
in terms of gaining economic benefits.

In the 1930s social theorists first noticed that the white-collar
workers as a "new middle class" were particularly attracted to
European facism. The search for their significance was intimately
bound to the attempt to understand the attraction that authoritarian political ideologies and movements held for large segments of
the dependent classes in advanced industrial societies. C. Wright
Mills attributed their sense of impotence to the nondescript character of their labor and their dependent social position. As the
"men in the middle," white-collar workers were anchored neither
in production nor in administration of the essential goods of
society. Their negativity defined their situation; they could generate neither affirmative ideologies nor affirmative practice. Lacking sources of social and political power, this proletarianized
middle class was, for Mills, easy prey for corporatism and fascism
that promised to deliver meaning to their tawdry lives by tying
them even more closely to the state and to the ruling classes.
Fascism appealed to the authoritarian fantasies of this stratum so

totally deprived of autonomy and power in daily life. It was upon his observation that the white-collar stratum was growing numerically with no concomitant rise in social power that Mills asserted the inexorability of mass society and mass culture—the transformation of the "public" into a mass resulting from the concentration of corporate power over cultural as well as material production.

Yet the white-collar stratum of the working class is not fully identified with the corporation or with approved social values, despite its ambivalent position. The complaint of many white-collar managers is that the productivity of this stratum continues to lag behind that of industrial workers, notwithstanding the mechanization of many office tasks and the invention of the self-service retail store. Not even company paternalism and the provision of amenities within the office have prevented the notorious unproductivity of office and sales workers. In fact, as Victor Fuchs has shown, most of the growing service occupations are characteristically labor rather than capital intensive.[2] Nor have computers succeeded in transforming the office into an enormous automatic adding machine. The bare fact is that the proliferation of administrative tasks has outdistanced the ability of the computer or other mechanical, labor-saving technologies to integrate functions. Much to the chagrin of the managers, the office force continues to grow. Much of this growth is due to the expansion of supervisory positions at a more rapid rate than the clerical workers working under them in these last two decades. Often managerial status disguises work that was formerly part of the duties of the non-supervisory stratum. But the large number of supervisors in government and corporate bureaucracies (about one supervisor for every three-and-one-half workers) is evidence that considerable managerial energy must be spent to make the white-collar labor force productive. The effort to boost productivity by proliferating supervisory personnel is a tacit recognition that resistance to work routines among office and sales workers is as widespread as among the more militant groups of manual workers. Large corporations frequently promote officeworkers to the rank of supervisor without altering the fact that their jobs are still defined by their output. The working supervisor is merely a person who performs two jobs. She is responsible for actually producing the same amount of paper herself as the subordinate; in addition, she is held responsible for the production of the subordinate as well.

The industrialization of the office and the separation of the office worker from the old loyalties has produced all of the discipline nightmares for management that plague it in the factories. Absenteeism and lateness are no less rampant than in the factory. The large number of work errors reflects the distance that office workers have come from close identification with the corporation as well as from the ethic of work excellence.

Among some branches of large corporations management has taken steps to improve work discipline and productivity. At Metropolitan Life's computer centers in New York and eastern Pennsylvania, employees have been scheduled for a twelve-hour day—three days a week. From the company's viewpoint, the experiment has been proven a success. A few American companies are even considering emulating Fiat's experiment in flexible scheduling implemented among half of its white-collar labor force at its Turin facility. Workers are given the option of coming to work at any time, provided they agree to put in an eight-hour day. These efforts are a direct response to the partial breakdown of industrial discipline among the office force, especially among technicians and machine operators who resent the rationalized labor they are obliged to perform. The corporation has not offered to alter the character of the labor, but it has understood that the risks of low output and outright sabotage are increased in proportion to the arbitrary discipline workers are obliged to suffer on their repetitive and uninspiring jobs. Economic costs are not the great obstacle to implementation of policies permitting employees to work fewer days per week. The Metropolitan Life program neither reduces the hours of work substantially nor increases the pay. But this program has been undertaken successfully among the most skilled, male workers in their office force. Women cannot be persuaded to work twelve hours a day on a regular basis since they generally hold two jobs—one for pay in the office and one unpaid job in household labor as well. Flexible scheduling, however, does not even encounter this difficulty. Undoubtedly it would be welcomed by many women anxious to leave work early in order to get to their second jobs. The Fiat experience shows that most workers come to work earlier when permitted to do so.

In most cases management remains fearful of granting its employees autonomy in any area of decision-making regarding the work process. The Fiat innovations resulted from sharp struggles by large sections of the labor force for control over aspects of that process. The massive strikes of 1969–70 in the plant and offices ended with the attempt of management to incorporate the protest by granting concessions such as the flexible scheduling program.

It was the conscious struggle of the workers that created the pressure for change, not management's intentionality.

In the United States, most white-collar protest remains subterranean. Petty thievery, sabotage, and indiscipline are the individual methods employed by workers to fight back against the fact that there is always a supervisor looking over their shoulder in offices and stores, that the work is incredibly stultifying and intrinsically meaningless. The protest of the individual worker against onerous working conditions is contained by management's toleration of petty crime even as it attempts to solve the long-range problem by the computerization of the office, intensification of paternalism, and frequent crackdowns on lateness and absenteeism. Like James Thurber's character Walter Mitty, the white-collar worker lives a secret sexual fantasy life that permits the reproduction of his/her labor. Part of the fantasy consists of acting out a myriad of indiscretions that become substitutes for more direct forms of contestation. For male clerks there are also the dreams of power, promotion, and recognition. For millions of young women it is the promise that this job in this particular office will be short-lived that sustains them, even though most of them know that the return to work is inevitable after a relatively short period at home.

Many of the productions of mass culture are directed at the frustrated clerical worker, as well as the frustrated housewife. The images of airline stewardesses smiling their way around the world in the company of handsome, successful businessmen evoke the dream of escape to exotic places, the opportunity to meet an up-and-coming young male professional, and even the chance to perform a glamorous job in the bargain. The travel ads that clutter the television screen provide constant nourishment for the repressed desires of women and men who can look forward to little more than another day at the office.

The explosion of the leisure industry is rooted in the rising wages of the white-collar worker combined with more intense work frustrations. It has become the grand receptacle for the realization of the pleasures denied these workers in their jobs as well as the excitement denied in daily life. Skiing, traveling to "rustic" resorts, are no longer reserved for special times during the year. They have become routine weekend escapes for an increasing proportion of the white-collar labor force.

In the cities, secretaries, saleswomen, and the male professionals and supervisors need no longer spend evenings alone in front of a television set. The growth of "singles" bars, housing developments equipped with recreation facilities, social clubs, sports groups, and encounter groups directed specifically at the white-collar "market" resonates to the emotional starvation that is a product of the atomization of large portions of the American public. The need for community among this stratum supports the transformation of social life into a commodity. The desperation with which the search for human contact is pursued by those isolated in the commercial centers of our country has generated a flourishing industry that has stimulated the expansion of civilian airlines, the clothing industry, important consumer goods manufacturing, and a large share of the proliferation of service industries geared to creating and satisfying the demand for leisure.

— 2 —

In 1970 there were more than 11 million workers classified by the U.S. government Department of Census as "professional," "technical" employees, or about 12 percent of the labor force. More than 3 million of these were employed as nonsupervisory scientific, engineering, and technical workers in manufacturing and transportation industries or within universities and private organizations in industry-related research.

These technical workers constitute the most important group among those not engaged in manual labor who are, nevertheless, directly involved in the production process. These are the workers whose character and function grew out of the bureaucratization of artisan skills by the corporation, and who were made dependent professionals by the universities that trained them and provided credentials. They are engaged chiefly in industries characterized by a relatively high technological development; that is, where manual labor has been widely replaced by machinery. Industries such as oil, electronics, chemicals, and the advanced sectors of the paper, food-processing and machine-tool industries are marked by a high ratio of technical to manual labor.

In the oil refining industry, for example, where fewer than 150,000 workers are employed as production and maintance workers, technicians number more than half as many as blue-collar workers. This high ratio of technical to blue-collar labor reflects the high ratio of capital to human labor. In technological terms the oil industry is a vanguard industry. Relatively few workers produce huge quantities of goods because the production process is nearly fully automated; that is, machines are self-adjusting, the transfer of the product between work stations takes place mechanically, and the production process is automatically recycled. Continuous-flow operations, such as in the oil industry, require operatives for only a narrow range of tasks. The operator watches gauges, reports irregularities, and may institute minor adjustments to meet production standards. A few semiskilled workers in the oil refineries and chemical plants are responsible for mixing ingredients and pouring them into vats, but they have few actual manual operations to perform.

Most nontechnical workers in these industries are maintenance mechanics. Their skills consist in being able to repair equipment. But the operational control of the day-to-day process of production is invested in technically trained workers. They are typically responsible for the control of the quality of production in terms of the specifications. These specifications are checked by laboratory tests performed by a less-trained technician under the direction of a low-level chemist or engineer. The professionally trained workers, that is those with four years or more of college, have become the low-level supervisors in the technologically advanced industries. They direct operations and maintenance work within the limits set by managers and high-echelon scientists and engineers. They constitute an increasing proportion of workers within these industries because they are directly involved in production: in effect, they are simply more skilled operatives. Their position is determined by their technical knowledge. But like the production and maintenance workers, they neither control the production process, whose object, specifications, and methods are determined from above, nor their own work, which is defined rigidly within the occupational hierarchy.

The labor of the engineer or scientist who functions as a technician within advanced industry rarely corresponds to the extent of knowledge acquired in college. He has become the new front-line production worker. Typically his work is so rationalized that its routine character is preponderant, although fragments of creative judgment may be required from time to time. Among those professional workers engaged in the production of goods, the designations "chemist," "metallurgist," and "engineer" have become labels that describe not the old middle class artisan who was engaged in scientific invention and technical innovation, but a worker whose tasks are often as routine as a machine operator's, with one crucial difference: the professional now has responsibility for the day-to-day production process and a measure of control within hierarchically established norms. But he has no power over his own labor or within the corporate organization. His power is limited to supervision of the prefigured work of the manual workers.

The contradictions inherent in the position of the professional workers are between the expectations generated by their training and the boredom and rote of their work tasks, between the degree of responsibility they possess for the production process and the absence of power to control more than its quantitative and, within set limits, qualitative adjustment. As with the skilled craftsman, the distance between skill and performance has generated frustration and sometimes rebellion. There has been a mild tendency among technical workers toward union organization, particularly in industries where manual workers have been fully organized— as in steel, electrical manufacturing, and auto. But these professionals so far have been unable to bring to consciousness their increasingly proletarian status. This is partially due to the fact that corporations, especially in advanced industries, have had enough economic strength to maintain the wage differential between so-called blue-collar and "gray-collar" workers, despite the enormous proportionate growth of technicians in recent years. But economic benefits alone cannot explain the relative quiescence of this group. It must be examined in terms of issues having to do with their position within the occupational hierarchy.

As I have noted, the bureaucratization of the professions corresponds to the rise of corporations and the simultaneous decline in the position of artisans and the old middle class. The proletarianization of the professions has consisted in the transformation of technical labor from independence to dependence. The debasement of the professional within the corporation has given rise to considerable enlargement of the role of the outside consultant, either an individual or often itself a corporation of some magnitude. The consultant has become especially important in the business of goverment. Since professionals now perceive themselves as extensions of management rather than permutations of labor, their situation is reified and reinforced by their relative power over semi-skilled workers. Thus, their control of people is experienced in their daily work and constitutes the starting point of their identification with the company. Moreover, within the occupational hierarchy they have been able to aspire to the position of middle management. It was from among those who functioned as front-line supervisors or quality control and research technicians that industry formerly recruited its department heads, directors of research and production managers. However, this avenue of advancement for the technician is now narrowing considerably. The rapidity of technical change combined with the fact that management, even of technical personnel, is increasingly separated from the actual technical nature of the work makes professionally trained workers who remain in production or research less desirable for promotion than those with other types of training, particularly those trained in "management" as an occupation. On the path to mobility ordinary engineers and scientific workers may first move laterally out of production into marketing and sales; from there they may be recruited as middle managers, since corporations value marketing skills more than technical skills and have recently recruited some of their middle managers from those successful in the sales effort.

The obstacles to mobility are revealed by salary patterns for engineers and other professionals. Typically a graduate of a professional school with an engineering or scientific degree may earn a starting salary of about $12,000 a year—considerably higher than most teachers and social workers. But the top salaries after ten years of experience stabilize at about $18,000 a year, hardly more than the salaries of many skilled workers and a growing number of teachers and social workers as well. Only when the industrial professional has moved into sales and middle management do these maximum salaries increase. For the most part, those who stay in production or research for more than five years find their work repetitive, their responsibility narrowed rather than enlarged, and their salary scales relatively stable.

The ideologies that proclaim the bureaucratic professional as a new middle class confuse the technocrat with the technician. Technocratic power does not derive from professional training; it is a concomitant of the direction exerted by management over the whole life of the institution, particularly its ability to determine the allocation of resources, the assigment of the work force, and the manipulation of capital. The technician performs rationalized labor whose nature is disguised by its limited supervisory function and responsibility on the one hand, and the credentialing system that constitutes a prerequisite for entrance on the other.

When associations of technical workers have used professionalism as a means to justify the maintenance of privileged economic benefits and social prestige for their constituencies, large corporations and government have been very willing to go along with these demands and have even encouraged professionalization of other occupations not formerly considered more than semiskilled labor. Thus the ideology of professionalism has become more powerful in inverse proportion to the proletarianization of technical workers. The coalition between the professional associations and the corporations to maintain the label of "professional" in the wake of debased skills corresponds to the earlier efforts of artisans to maintain their position through the trade unions.

Where technical workers have become the organized the hierarchical organization of labor has been reinforced by unions and professional associations.

For the corporation the hierarchy of occupations performs a valuable role. At the most elementary plane, the high ratio of dependent professionals to blue-collar workers in industry and public bureaucracies constitutes an important source of strike insurance for employers. The 1965 strike of 3600 workers employed by the Gulf Oil Company in Port Arthur, Texas, around the issue of the progressive reduction in the number of production and maintenance workers resulted in a defeat for the workers that was partially due to the ability of 600 "supervisors" to operate the plant at two-thirds production capacity. Similarly, the 1971 strike of New York Bell Telephone repairmen was defeated by the ability of supervisors and technicians (employed at a ratio of one to four blue-collar and white-collar workers in Bell's maintenance, operating, and business departments) to perform vital service functions and prevent the breakdown of the system.

The hierarchy of social labor masked as technical necessity by concepts and techniques such as "scientific management" has assumed the status of ideology as well as an instrument of political and social power. It is generated from the recognition by corporations of the importance of maintaining differences within the underlying classes. Mobility ideologies are maintained by the minute division of labor and the labeling apparatus that assigns higher status, income, and responsibility to those possessing credentials, notwithstanding the routine character of their labor.

— 3 —

Among the most crucial differences between modern capitalism and the traditional ideological conceptions of competitive capitalism is that "industrialization to the twentieth century is invariably the result of vigorous and direct action by the state."[3] This statement by the German sociologist Ralf Dahrendorf refers to recent changes in European capitalism. As we have seen, it is no less germane to the United States. In fact, much of the nineteenth-century U.S. industrialization was the result of this relationship. The primacy of politics over economics constitutes a basic trend in the contemporary U.S. economy. The relationship is complicated by the interchangeability of corporate and state personnel, by the relative autonomy of the political administration in its day-to-day operations, and by the continuing importance of democratic ideology, which proclaims that social and political power is the outcome of the struggle of a multiplicity of interest groups rather than the result of the supreme influence of the large corporation on the state.

The works of C. Wright Mills, William Appleman Williams, Paul Sweezy and Paul Baran, C. William Domhoff, and others have convincingly described the political and economic hegemony of the large corporations over U.S. society, notwithstanding the fact that the state enjoys a degree of administrative independence, especially in the case of disputes among giant corporations. A giant government bureaucracy has arisen in American life precisely for the purpose of preventing the collapse of American capitalism. Government intervention into economic life is wholly intentional and necessary. The maintenance of a standing army of nearly 3 million men and women in "peacetime," and the provision of services ranging from public assistance to individuals and families to purchases of goods and services from private corporations, often obscure another important function of government in our society: the maintenance of relatively full employment. This function ranks just behind the role of government in the manufacturing sector and sales effort. In 1970, 13 million workers were employed at various levels of the public bureaucracy, representing one out of six workers in the country. This phenomenon is a stark illustration that much of the political and economic stability of the society rests on institutions of social control which themselves are parasitic on the labor of those directly engaged in production and distribution. This dependency is formed by taxes on the wages of workers in the private sector and the redistribution of this revenue to workers who would be otherwise unemployed, as well as to corporations that sell goods and services to the government. The usefulness of nearly all government work depends entirely on the presumption of the legitimacy of the existing social order. Most government services are ideologically partisan but are masked as "education," "welfare," "public safety," or "defense." Since all of these services are intimately bound to the survival and growth of the prevailing socioeconomic system, the question arises as to whose needs they actually serve. The ambiguity inherent in public services and public employment arises from their vital importance to the majority of citizens within the framework of the existing order at the same time that these services are means of perpetuating domination of the existing order over its citizens.

In this sense, the very term "public service" embodies an ideological conception. It expresses a value judgment on the work of the government bureaucracy that serves particular interests, even though the term purports to validate the claim of government to represent all the people as a constellation of institutions standing above the social structure rather than being an integral part of it. In this way, the government preserves its image as the mediator of conflict within society. Instead of viewing taxation as a means of redistributing income from one section of the population to another, most Americans believe that such funds are employed in public services that are of a neutral character, that is, devoid of ideological content. In practice the old image of the public servant has lost its luster. The worker employed by a typical government agency, performing rationalized and routine tasks that are no less alienated than industrial labor, can in no way be compared to the dedicated town clerk of early nineteenth-century America who was intimately acquainted with the "public" and could render actual services to it. The old public servant worked in a small town of independent shopkeepers and farmers with a fair number of artisans and small manufacturers as his constituents. For such a person, public employment was often more than a way to avoid joblessness or to achieve economic security. It was often a vocation pursued with fervor.

The horrific fantasies of Kafka and the underground novels of Dostoevski are no longer fictional treatments of the relation between the citizen and the government in modern life. Unlike employees of private corporations, few of those ranked low on the occupational scale in public service identify themselves with the bureaucracy. For many, public employment represents a mild descent from loftier aspirations and an indication of the loss of artisanship. One need only read any contemporary novel, or observe the bureaucracy in action, to comprehend the emotional separation of the public worker from the content and the objects of his labor. A recent novel *Post Office*, by Charles Bukowski, depicts in excruciating detail both the automatic and routine character of the work of a postal clerk or letter carrier in a big city post office and the arbitrariness of authority. Such description poses a powerful counterpoint to the service ideology of the public institutions and accounts in part for the recent upsurge of union organization and strike activity among public employees who have finally brought to awareness the similarities of their social position as well as the type of labor they perform to those of other industrial workers.

The new postal worker bears no correspondence to the rural carrier of the last century. Today he owes his job to the fact that he has a high school diploma and has passed a civil service test; typically, he is unable to find employment except in the public sector. Post-office work is commonly viewed as white-collar labor, but is characteristically perceived by the workers themselves as a variant of factory work. The discipline enforced on the job, the mechanical tasks that constitute the labor of both carrier and clerk, and the salary scale that resembles the wages of semiskilled industrial labor has made workers in the postal service impatient with the old myths derived from the era of rural America.

The 1970 postal walkout was remarkable both for its militancy and for the break with the old traditions of postal unionism that relied on legislative solutions for improving the lot of workers. Not only did the walkout flagrantly disregard the antistrike injunctions of both the law and the courts, but it marked a schism between the union leadership and the rank and file. Moreover, the strike revealed the magnitude of the economic and political threat posed by a disruption in this vital means of communication. After a few days, President Nixon ordered troops to move mail in the New York postal district as a symbolic show of force and a warning to the workers to return to work. The ploy was successful, but the nationwide extent of the wildcat strike that spread without the benefit of central leadership had enormous impact on public unionism, which could no longer pretend that the interests of its membership could be well served by lobbying and other forms of legislative pressure.

Government employees, those engaged in retail and wholesale trades, and workers in corporate bureaucracies performing manual operations on accounting machines or typewriters can hardly be considered radically different from industrial workers in general. The transformation of the office into a large-scale organization has been accompanied by the imposition of efficiency engineering or scientific management upon work relations. The typical officeworker is as little able to perform the whole process of administration as the assembly line worker is capable of performing the entire production process. The most characteristic feature of modern labor is the convergence of mental and manual labor. This convergence is not only the result of the mechanization of the office that converts a clerk into a machine operator, but also the factorylike method of symbolic production that reinforces the clerk's self-image of being eminently replaceable just like machine parts.

Even teachers, medical "professionals," and technicians in industrial plants have experienced their work as labor rather than vocation. To the degree that those on the lower rungs of the professional hierarchy in public service institutions have recognized that their self-image as proletarians in a factory setting is more than a metaphor but corresponds at least in a great measure to their actual position within the organization, the demands of unions and professional associations have increasingly concentrated on more pay for fewer hours and smaller work loads. The demands of teachers and doctors who have either walked off their jobs or threatened strikes over the past several years have not been confined to wages. Equally prominent among the issues propelling strike movement among these groups is the desire to cut the size of classes or the number of patients treated. At first sight, it appears that such demands are motivated by a desire to improve the quality of service. Upon closer examination these demands reflect concern for the old "professional" standards among only a minority of these workers. Underlying them the real intention proves to be the reduction of professional commitment to the institution both emotionally and in time and effort.

The withdrawal of professional cadres from institutional involvement flows from the accelerating pace of centralization of power within schools and health institutions. Although both teachers and medical professionals enjoy higher pay and prestige than manual workers and exercise surrogate power over lower rungs of the occupational hierarchy, they have begun to perceive their own individual position as one of powerlessness that can be overcome only through collective action. The sharp ideological reversal from previous beliefs has not resulted in greater social consciousness among these technicians. On the contrary, their newly acquired awareness of self-interest has been analogous to the attitudes of craft unionists and has represented for some a deterioration of social consciousness and much of their pride of workmanship.

Although tens of thousands of teachers fill the classrooms of evening sessions of graduate schools, attend in-service training programs, and take courses in adult education programs of all kinds, this passion for additional schooling is not the same as the passion for learning. It derives from different sources. Teachers attend school in order to earn credentials that pay off in higher salaries and opportunities for promotion. The motives behind the acquisition of credentials are consistent with the trade union orientation of many teachers, rather than a more intense search for excellence. Most teachers do not view their continuing education as voluntary. It is a necessary part of their professional lives —and thus ironically results in a significant prolongation of the work day. Similarly, a great deal of teacher participation in such extracurricular activities as sports and departmental clubs is accompanied by higher pay, greater prestige, and eventually higher occupational status. Thus, teachers withdraw psychologically from the classroom and contact with students, but not from the institution.

Teacher training institutions have traveled a great distance from the visions of the important philosophers and innovators of American education. The stress of Dewey, Meiklejohn, and other leaders of the progressive education movement on learning by doing as a step to critical thinking, offering a chance to the student to construct his own reality, has been debased by the emphasis put on "methods" rather than content in the preparation of teachers by teachers' colleges. This approach to the curriculum has contributed to the training of several generations of elementary and secondary school teachers whose main skill has become maintaining control over the class rather than understanding the cognitive and affective processes of learning. Moreover, thousands of young teachers suffer from intellectual ignorance; they bring few resources to their work and often fall back on policelike behavior toward students to compensate for their inability to teach.

Among the most important sources of teacher recruitment in the 1950s and 1960s was the large number of young men who avoided the draft by choosing teaching as a career. In many cases this choice proved to be a fortunate one for students. Many of the most socially conscious and critical persons among the young generation became fine and creative teachers, even if their selection of a vocation was more by default than voluntary and enthusiastic. At the same time, there were many other young teachers, deprived of a rich and varied education themselves, who fell easily into the prevailing power structure of the schools and became its instruments. Having no outlets for their own repressed creativity, and having experienced school only as a necessary step toward survival in industrial society, they expressed their insecurity about their teaching skills and need for control over their own lives and aspirations by exercising over students the power denied them within the school hierarchy.

Teacher unionism was long overdue when it swept nearly all large Northern cities in the 1960s. For decades teachers had been falling behind some categories of industrial workers, as well as behind other workers with similar professional credentials, in pay and benefits. The fragmentation of teachers' organizations into departmental groups, the subordination of teachers to administrators in the National Education Association, and the antiunion bias of boards of education had prevented unions from achieving a foothold during the first half of the twentieth century. In addition, the economic situation of the 1920s and 1930s and again in the early 1950s had been adverse to bold actions by teachers and other professionals who clung to their jobs as their most precious possessions. But in the 1960s economic buoyancy, teacher shortages, and the infusion of a large number of veterans and other young people into the schools helped revive sentiment for organization, especially in the period when the mass character of education was becoming more pronounced and school administrations more authoritarian and remote from the classroom.

Even as teachers became more organizationally independent and renounced their institutional dependency, they shed their old conceptions of public service and much of their concern for educational ideas. This contradictory development in the political socialization of teachers became one of the key issues in the struggle for community control in the late 1960s. The earlier left-wing and liberal teachers' unions had lacked collective bargaining rights even though they had a considerable membership in the mid-thirties for a time. Their embattled situation had forced them to seek alliances with parents and students. Typical teachers' union programs during the 1930s and 1940s went far beyond wages and working conditions. Often they included demands for sweeping reforms in educational practice, and revealed a keen interest in both international affairs and broad areas of domestic issues that went far beyond education. But in the 1960s the old alliances between parents and teachers were destroyed by the political thrust of Black demands for community control because of their conjunction with the emerging trade union consciousness of teachers. In the larger cities this tendency became a racial fight because the program of teachers' self-interest seemed to be antagonistic to the demands of Blacks and other parents of minority group students for a new teacher commitment to community service.

In forming new unions, teachers had taken a step away from social action without economic power. They perceived that the old ideologies that were instilled in them by professional training simply did not correspond to their actual social position. But they had never fully integrated the recognition of their working class status—and were unwilling to subordinate their job interests to the public interest that was now articulated in the rhetoric of Black Power and community control.

One of the most significant features of the changing consciousness of the service professionals has been the rise of unionism among health workers as well as teachers. Traditionally, health institutions are among the most hierarchically organized of all workplaces. At each level, there is a new set of prerequisites and credentials that allow entry. For many years, even the very lowest-level workers performing direct patient care services, such as the blue-collar occupations of laundry, housekeeping, and catering departments were suffused with the prevailing humanistic ideologies that regarded self-organization as a betrayal of the mission to heal the sick. But the conjuncture of long-term historical trends that brought millions of Black people from the South to the center cities and forced them to labor in the most exploited economic niches in the society, with the rise of the civil rights movement in the North after 1960 found its most articulate expression in the mass upsurge of hospital workers and other manual workers in public health bureaucracies within the big cities of the Northeast. The missionary claims of the large medical empires were thrown into bold relief by their resistance to the attempts of hospital workers, sanitation workers, and other municipal employees to overcome wage and working conditions that had served to maintain the economic dependency of the working poor on the state and quasi-public institutions. Invoking the old professional values, the hospital bureaucracies were unable to reverse the tide of union organization or even contain it to blue-collar categories. The impulse to collective action soon extended to a large number of registered nurses, lab technicians, and professionals, and finally to doctors who had come to the realization that they might never practice medicine outside of a large hospital or research institution and had become little more than highly skilled salaried workers. The threatened strikes of residents and interns in New York and San Francisco in 1971–72 cannot be said to constitute a definitive trend among those who labor in this most sacred of all occupations. But the indications are plain: increasingly, staff physicians are recognizing their subordination to the administration, the progressive specialization of medical arts, and the disastrous impact of this development upon the quality of medical care.

The rise of medical empires is parallel to the concentration and centralization of capital in fewer manufacturing and financial corporations. The amassing of medical capital in ever fewer hands has meant that treatment for certain diseases is only available in those institutions that can afford the modern machines and the expensive techniques. As in the defense sector, almost all research and development activities are concentrated in a few prominent elite university medical schools that have contractual affiliations with the medical empires who monopolize the results. Under these conditions, the old general practitioners and hospitals are being reduced to auxiliaries to the large institutions that permanently claim the talents of most graduate physicians. In turn, young doctors are encouraged to become specialists rather than generalists, a choice that obtains the high status of an independent professional for some, but secures the dependency of a salaried worker for most.

With few exceptions, notably in New York where the Hospital Workers Local 1199 has attempted to organize on an industrial rather than craft basis to some extent, health and education unionism has followed the historical tendency of unions to solidify the stratification rather than the unity of the work force. The old professional associations have yielded to the pressures exerted by newer, more militant formations and become trade unions. But they have preserved their professional character at the same time. Such groups as the American Nursing Association have entered the collective bargaining arena in behalf of their own credentialed constituents, the registered nurses, while the larger number of less credentialed workers in nursing have remained unorganized or join unions directed to their special places in the hierarchy. Even Local 1199, the largest of the newer hospital unions, has failed to recruit among the professional categories in the hospitals except for social workers and some laboratory groups. The ANA and the professional organization of interns and residents have organized themselves as special interest groups and cooperate only sporadically with the nonprofessional unions.

The doctrine of occupational mobility is preserved within health institutions by allowing limited movement within the hierarchy. But the separation of professional from nonprofessional, a chasm generated by ideological means, is as rigidly enforced as it is within industrial hierarchies by both unions and management. There are no battlefield promotions of nurses aides to registered nurses. Social-work assistants must attend professional schools to receive professional status and salary in social services departments. The newly arrived semiprofession of physician's assistant or assistant doctor has its own professional requirements and training that is sharply demarcated from professional medicine. In time, this new professional will discover his/her own interest and win the stability of a certain niche within the professional occupational hierarchy, and an association of assistant physicians will undoubtedly be formed; the assistant doctors will be protected from those who perform similar labor but have distinct credentials, just as they are excluded from the physician status themselves. The rampant survival of professional distinctions amid worker militancy has helped preserve prevailing authority relations, and simultaneously to suppress the potential for united consciousness and action among hospital employees.

The modifications introduced by unionism into health institutions have been substantial in some instances: wages have risen by 300 percent over 1959 levels while the general level of wages has only increased by just over 50 percent. But the general rise in the price of labor has produced new standards for employment for low-level patient-care personnel, particularly more training requirements and credentials prerequisites. This tendency is likely to become stronger as the employment opportunities for the unskilled decline and the number of high school graduates in the general population remains above 80 percent of those who enter secondary education.

Higher wages and relative labor surpluses have created other changes in hospital practice. Direct services to patients are almost totally performed by nurses aides and licensed practical nurses, elevating registered nurses to supervisory and administrative levels. The enlargement of job responsibility for the nonprofessionals has helped reduce the demand for labor in the hospitals, since most hospital unions have barely touched the sphere of working conditions, preferring instead to concentrate their energies on wages and benefits. Neither the hospital unions nor the public employees' unions have shown substantial interest in becoming instruments for workers' resistance to job enlargement without increased pay, the limited promotion opportunities defined by rigid separation of professional from nonprofessional job categories, or the structure of authority in the workplace. To the degree that wages and benefits have been the almost singleminded concern of the new public employees unions, they have followed in the footsteps of their industrial union predecessors.

Even the structure of collective bargaining has paralleled the private sector. Unions have cooperated in the codification of job hierarchies; accepted the concept that management has the unreserved right to determine policies having to do with the quality of services as well as to direct the work forces; have fought for, and obtained, central bargaining as the best means of winning substantial benefits and preventing competition among workers; and created internal union practices that leave the workers little power over union decisions. These practices include hiring large full-time staff representatives to deal with grievances and placing most of the union funds in highly centralized "district councils" or regional offices that are largely exempt from rank-and-file influence. Shop stewards or chairpersons have little autonomy in opposing management and protecting workers' interests. Typically, management will call upon the union staff members to assist it in disciplining members who are recalcitrant on matters having to do with job assignment or work load. In many cases, the unions are cooperative, not because they are blatantly company-minded, but because many believe that the best interests of the membership are served by suppressing job grievances and directing all efforts toward wage issues instead.

Unions have forfeited their interest in the quality of patient care and often join hospital administration in resisting changes in the configuration of service-delivery systems demanded by community groups because they may involve changes of existing occupational patterns. The image of hospital and public employees unions as opponents of systemic reform is merely a concomitant of the integration of unions into the institutions. This alliance is cemented by the economic rewards that hospital workers have been able to wrest from the administration on the basis of an acceptance of the prevailing order, which includes the ability of the medical empires to transfer the costs of health care to workers as consumers of that service. Just as the Steelworkers Union and other industrial organizations failed to protest the displacement of higher labor costs to prices after the Second World War, the public employees unions have become complicitous in the same development in the 1960s and hold the support of their members, even if by silence, because the gains of the past decade have meant the difference between working class economic dependency and dignity.

Hospital workers in the large Northeastern cities are rapidly escaping the underclass. Their wages by no means approach those of industrial workers in the most advanced industries. At best, they earn as much as semiskilled industrial workers in consumer goods industries such as textiles and food processing, but they are a long way from the $40 a week salaries of barely a decade earlier. This achievement is hardly an indication of genuine class mobility in the industrial sense. But it means a great deal to workers who had been obliged to depend on public assistance for part of their income, or to live their lives in unrelieved squalor. Hospital workers, like Southern mountain people who increased their annual income by as much as 500 percent by getting jobs in the auto industry, are making a slow transition to the psychological and cultural expectations of working class members, which will take as much as a generation of high wages and high levels of consumption.

Among the more significant innovations in the public sector has been the attempt of state and local governments to find ways to mechanize services among those branches that are the most labor-intensive. In New York, the widely publicized introduction of computerized methods of determining client eligibility for welfare benefits has already reduced the number of case workers substantially. At the same time, special services to clients—such as providing emergency benefits, adjusting inequities in payments, and working with families suffering particular hardships—are being performed by less credentialed lower-paid workers recruited often from among welfare recipients.

Parallel efforts are under way in schools and health care facilities. Such devices as teaching machines, information retrieval systems to trace patient care requirements in hospitals and clinics, are aimed at reducing labor costs by increasing productivity and reducing staff. Often these measures are justified in terms of efficiency of service delivery rather than cost-benefits, but it seems clear that the increased emphasis on technological means to provide social, health and education services is directly related to the higher labor costs that have resulted from militant worker activity and inflation. At the same time, the introduction of labor-saving technologies corresponds to the bureaucratization of services and the concomitant rise of the technocrat at their helm. Moreover, the concept "cost-benefit" has itself become an ideology in the public services. In part, the elevation of efficiency to the status of morality reflects the attempt by the corporate-like public institutions to solve the rising costs of public services by eliminating workers. But efficiency has its economic beneficiaries besides the taxpaying wage earner not employed by the public sector: the technological revolution in the public services is a boon to manufacturing corporations searching for new markets for their products and is an outlet as well for the technological innovations generated by the defense sector. Many professional associations are neutralized by the drive toward technology, especially when such labor-saving measures eliminate the least skilled workers, many of whom are Blacks and other minorities or women.

In the main, workers in the human services have remained divided by status within the bureaucracies, even though all subordinate strata, regardless of their credentials, have exhibited a higher level of militancy than ever before. The rise of trade unions has reinforced the hierarchical organization of the human services, particularly where they have become strong, as in the health and education industries. At this stage of the development of the struggle, the main issues that bind workers to one another have to do with the rejection of the old ideologies promulgated by both professional schools and the institutional managements that they must subordinate their own interests to those of the clients.

The direction of their struggle clearly shows the limitations of trade union consciousness. The gulf that now separates workers from one another within institutions and the whole human services working class from the rest of the working class has widened considerably because of the narrow, self-interested militancy that is more or less consciously put forward by trade unions. The success of unions and management in keeping workers apart until now has been a function of the ability of the institutions to raise funds to pay for increased wages and benefits to service workers by increases in taxes and insurance premiums levied upon the rest of the working class.

These mechanisms are reaching their limits. Public funds are become scarcer and workers are showing increased resistance against higher tax and insurance levies. Thus hospital and school managements are becoming more obdurate in their opposition to the wage claims of workers in these institutions, and strikes are more frequent despite public laws that prohibit them. At the same time, management is distributing benefits unequally among various sectors of public bureaucracies in the hope of splitting off certain sections of the labor force from other sections in order to hold down costs and maintain control. Thus, police, sanitation, fire, and teacher wages have risen faster than other sectors in the past few years, compared to health workers and those employed in sectors of government that are less powerful and visible. Yet thousands of workers in state, county, and municipal governments remain poorly paid and relatively powerless. Their interests are typically sacrificed by both union and management to those workers employed in public services considered politically "vital." The rise of ideologies that proclaim the primacy of "law and order" and education over other services has made political managers more willing to settle with these groups than with others in less crucial occupations. In the schools, for example, the rate of teachers' salary increases has far outdistanced those of cafeteria workers, clerks, and even "paraprofessionals" employed in the classroom as assistants. The same tendency can be observed in health institutions, where highly credentialed occupations have taken a relatively larger share of salary increases than the so-called "nonprofessional" categories.

Meanwhile, power in these institutions remains concentrated at the top, although some union bureaucracies have transcended their traditional role as pressure groups and become part of the administration, holding veto power over many decisions, especially those involving a reduction in the size of their own dues paying membership.

NOTES

1. C. Wright Mills, *White Collar*, New York, Oxford University Press, 1951.

2. Victor R. Fuchs, *The Service Economy*, New York, National Bureau of Economic Research, 1968.

3. Ralf Dahrendorf, "Recent Changes in Class Structure," *The New Europe: A Timely Reappraisal*, edited by Stephan Graubard, Boston, Mass., Beacon Press, 1967.

7

The Unsilent Fifties

— 1 —

The Last Picture Show, Peter Bogdanovich's film of life in a small Texas town in the 1950s, epitomizes our remembrance of the era. Daily life is suffused with boredom and frustration. The concerns of the townspeople—the prowess of the local high school football team, the desperate search for sexual pleasure even if purchased at the price of ultimate and inevitable disappointment, the brutal games played to pass the time of day—testify to the essential flatness of the everyday world. The film ends with the shattering of the last pleasures and dreams of youth. The town's lone movie house is shut down, perhaps forever, as the people retreat even further into private reveries, presumably in front of their television sets.

Bogdanovich's vision of the fifties is a graphic illustration of the more theoretical presentations of the social scientists and philosophers who have helped fashion our collective memory of the decade. The sources of Bogdanovich's images are the same as those of another Texan, C. Wright Mills, who in 1954 made his judgment of the times: "The transformation of a community of publics into a mass society is one of the keys to the meaning of modern life."[1] In Mills's definition, a "public" is a group of people who participate in the decisions affecting their lives. They give more opinions than they receive. On the other hand, mass society is a world of isolated individuals victimized by the battering of the media, more to be characterized as recipients of information from mass sources than participants in the formulating of policies. Modern society, according to Mills, had transformed people into consumers and was destroying the foundation upon which the idea of democracy was conceived: "The public is the loom of classic eighteenth-century democracy; discussion is at once the thread and the shuttle tying discussion circles together. It lies on the basis of the conception of authority by discussion, based on the hope that truth and justice will somehow carve out of society a great apparatus of free discussion."[2] In his view, the mechanisms of mass communication were destroying the self-activity of persons and converting individuals into manipulated objects of those who had concentrated economic and political power in their own hands and were able to regulate channels of public information through "centralized points of control."

Since mass society required that the working class and other political publics convert their organizations into mirror images of the "bureaucratic structures of executive power," which had themselves become "large scale and inaccessibly centralized,"[3] political discourse had been replaced by attempts to pressure those who occupied the commanding heights of power in the "economic, political and military orders": "Voluntary associations have become larger to the extent that they have become effective; and to the extent that they have become effective they have become inaccessible to the individual who would participate by discussion in their policies."[4]

For Mills, as for Bogdanovich, the fifties signaled the end of the old middle class of small shopkeepers and, concomitantly, the decline of small-town life. Mills's new middle class was the white-collar worker whose rise to numerical importance in the twentieth century typified the problem of modern times. The white-collar world was seen as preeminently a world of anonymity where work and leisure were organized by a faceless bureaucracy and where the underlying population was characteristically estranged from community and society.

In Arthur Miller's *Death of a Salesman*, the atomization of the individual in the new world of bureaucratic manipulation was again portrayed, setting the tone for the fifties. The old salesman, Willy Loman, plying his trade in a personal, eminently human style was being rendered obsolete and useless to the new, efficient sales effort, against which human traits were measured on the yardstick of profit and loss. Not only did Willy Loman suffer the disintegration of his work-world; his family also fell apart as the fissure between generations mirrored the historical changes under way.

Against the pervasive fifties images of passivity and victimization were contrasted the active forces of the times, no longer personified by plunderers, adventurers, and captains of industry who, however ruthless, at least provided visible targets against whom political debate could take place. Herbert Marcuse's world, for example, contained new executioners. For him, the triumph of organization reflected the triumph of the machine over man. He saw in the fifties the end of reason, and the formation of the unhappy consciousness which, despite itself, was trapped inside the prevailing culture. The giant apparatus created by technological domination absorbed all the forces of discontent or crushed them. Even those who declared themselves opponents of the prevailing system of power were forced to be its servants. Revolutionaries functioned to remind the apparatus that there were imperfections in the machine. Their criticisms became grist for administrative reform. All political issues, in fact, became objects for technological adjustment, and there were no social issues exempt from administrative and technical solutions.

A decade later, Marcuse carried the analysis one step further. Technology, once regarded as the cornerstone of the idea of progress, had now become an instrument of enslavement. In the course of "mastery over nature" in order to serve human needs, man's own nature was thereby transformed. Technology, originally a product of human activity, had become dominant over human will. Its requirements imposed themselves on human thought, the quality of life, and the configuration of social intercourse, so that all opposition, all critical thought, became collapsed into one-dimensionality. Human nature, now alienated from man, became his second nature; human institutions created out of man's self-activity now stood over and above him.[5]

According to both Marcuse and Mills, in the 1950s the essential conditions for citizenship were in the process of disintegration. The concentration of political and economic power, the manipulation of thought by bureaucratic purveyors of mass culture, rendered most individuals isolated and passive observers of their own lives. Both the sense of collectivity and the individuality which results from self-activity were nearly abolished. Neither critic of society held much hope for overcoming the banality of culture and the consequent debasement of the critical sensibility as mass society extended its tentacles further and further into the fabric of daily existence, destroying every source of opposition. Even the working class, once regarded by revolutionaries as the bearer of human liberation, had long since succumbed to the blandishments of consumerism.

A group of liberal, ex-Socialist theorists celebrated the end of ideology and the breakdown of classes and struggles based on ideologically wrought utopias. For Daniel Bell and Seymour Martin Lipset, the working class had, through economic and political action, achieved full citizenship in society. The apocalyptic visions of the Marxists—the breakdown of a capitalism rent with internal contradictions and the reconstruction of society by a class-conscious proletariat—had fallen victim to the successes of capitalism in overcoming its problems. According to Lipset, there remained class conflicts (such as over wages) in the America of the 1950s, but no class struggle. The workers and the corporations had differing immediate interests, but capitalism had proven its ability to solve the most pressing material problems of the underlying population. Bell held that ideologies only flourish among the masses when there is widespread belief that the system is incapable of successfully meeting their needs. Although American capitalism had unfinished business, in the view of these celebrants of its success, this business did not require a fundamental alteration of its economic or political institutions. The search for utopias, in Bell's opinion, was a problem for practical planning. While the radicals of the fifties deplored the social enslavement implied by the growing conformity of thought within the country, the liberals attributed the persistence of radical criticism to intellectual romanticism. According to Bell, the radicals expected more than the workers and their expectations were not fulfilled. Where the radicals saw nothing but conformity in the tendency to large organization, Lipset saw hope: "The growth of large organizations," he believed, "may, however, actually have the more important consequences of providing new sources of continued freedom and more opportunity to innovate."[6]

Yet, despite these differences between radical and liberal commentators on America in the fifties, there was a strange convergence of thought. Together with many others, they were convinced that America had reached a watershed. The old political rhetoric had lost its legitimacy, since America was undergoing changes which rendered the old slogans obsolete. Marcuse believed that the present indicated the future: "A comfortable smooth reasonable democratic unfreedom" in which "independence of thought, autonomy and the right to political opposition are being deprived of their basic critical function in a society which seems increasingly capable of satisfying the needs of the individuals through the way in which it is organized." Both the celebrants and the critics of mass society assumed that needs could be defined in their material aspect. If capitalism could "feed the face," in Brecht's phrase, it could impose what is right and what is wrong upon the underlying population. The implicit assumption in this idea is that the conditions for revolutionary action are present only when society has failed to overcome material deprivation. Since the system had "delivered the goods" (an apt characterization of Marcuse's), it presented its rebels with an insoluble dilemma—could they convince the workers to bite the hand that fed them?

However, many who resisted the bureaucratization and fragmentation of social life in the 1950s defined their needs in terms which transcended the opportunity to consume. Political discourse could not be circumscribed on all occasions within the bounds established by the "centers of control" because new needs were beginning to emerge as old ones were satisfied. The fifties witnessed the first outbursts against the erosion of the quality of social life generated by the expansion of capital. Ordinary people persisted in the effort to protect the measure of control over their work or their homes which they had won in previous decades.

It is a tribute to the power of bureaucratically controlled information channels that these struggles never reached public consciousness. Indeed, that capitalism had "massified" culture was the most pointed, and accurate, critique of capitalist society made by theorists whose observations in the fifties were uttered as if they were muttering to themselves.

Apart from the perception of unmistakable trends within American life, radical critics of mass society and culture derived their pessimism from two distinct sources: As social commentators who worked within a tradition that regarded the working class as the driving force of social change, they could not have failed to be impressed by the collapse of the Socialist and Communist left in the wake of working class acquiescence to the onslaught of European and Japanese fascism in the 1930s. The optimists among Socialists and liberals blamed each other for the rise of fascism rather than seeking deeper explanations. Mills and Marcuse (and even Bell) rejected the conventional wisdom according to which the failure of socialism in the West could be ascribed to tactical errors; instead they asserted a historical disjuncture in all Western societies. Mass society had replaced class society as the overarching spirit of the times. History in the old sense had somehow come to an end, since one could no longer assert with confidence that it was being made by men and women.

For the radicals the ascendancy of the repressive apparatus of the capitalist state in the late 1940s and early 1950s, particularly the victimization of outspoken critics of the new conformity, constituted an immediate second source of pessimism. Two of Marcuse's associates, Theodore Adorno and Max Horkheimer, accepted an invitation to return to Germany in 1950 rather than subject themselves to harassment and possible imprisonment. Their vivid memories of the horrors of the Nazi regime had determined their analysis of American life. They interpreted events in this country as a replay by the same underlying forces that had made for the victory of authoritarianism in Germany in the 1930s.

Indeed, the proximity in time of the fascist sweep of Europe and the rise of cultural and political repression in America made all the more plausible the constructs of those who saw in America the portent of the end of civilization. The actor, J. Edward Bromberg, suffered a heart attack in the midst of a congressional investigation and the literary critic, F.O. Matthiessen, took his own life rather than submit to the interrogations of congressional committees and the certain persecution that would follow. During the late forties and early fifties thousands were dismissed from their jobs for alleged Communist activity or sympathies. The price of acceptance was complete renunciation of one's beliefs, or worse—becoming an instrument of the repression itself by naming others who had been so foolish as to believe that the apparatus could be defied. It was only when Senator McCarthy went after the Army that the most overt aspects of political repression began to ebb. He had overstepped his bounds and was becoming an embarrassment.

Although America has never since been quite free of efforts

to persecute political minorities, by 1954 the worst of the overt terror was over. Yet its influence reverberated for years. It was another decade before those who were forced into hiding began to reenter political life. Within the unions, community groups, and political parties the ideology of anti-Communism remained an important force; only recently has some liberality in this regard been evidenced.

But it would be a mistake to regard the repression and conformity of the fifties as constitutive of the whole period or to overvalue the degree to which the homogeneity of culture and thought dominated social and political life. The early fifties were indeed years of defeat, not only for the ideological left, but for the workers, Black people, and others who engaged in segmented opposition to the prevailing social system. Yet even in defeat there was considerable movement. The characterizations of Marcuse and Mills must be appreciated with substantial reservations when it is remembered that the Montgomery bus boycott occurred in December 1955; that there were severe internal struggles throughout the late 1950s within the relatively staid NAACP between those advocating a more militant policy to obtain integration and those who would place continued reliance on legal means to achieve the association's ends; that, toward the end of the decade, the beginnings of mass activity among young Blacks were already evident.

Nor was there a lack of opposition within the spheres of high and "low" culture. Mass communications certainly took their toll in the repression of many forms of cultural autonomy, but incipient nodes of divergence from mass culture were already appearing. Foremost among these was the tiny but influential group of poets, novelists, painters, and underground film-makers who explicitly rejected the value structures of commercial art and turned away from "centralized points of control" to produce a virtual plethora of little magazines and independent art shows and, most important of all, asserted a new way of living that sidestepped the predominant symbols of mainstream culture consumption. The capacity of the cultural apparatus to absorb the "beats" by mechanically reproducing their art and disseminating it in every drugstore and airport in the land may have repeated the well-known commercialization of Black jazz forms by popular music a generation earlier, but their rediscovery of the politics of authenticity lived long after the particular actors burnt themselves and their art out.

In the area of culture, the rise of the civil rights movement in the 1950s also had its impact. Black musicians and writers received a degree of recognition from the white public. Although there is no denying the difficulty presented by the adoption of Black jazz styles by white musicians, the fact is that the syrupy, flat pop music modes of the 1940s gave way during the 1950s to the more vital, multidimensional art of an Elvis Presley or a Kay Starr, and thus mass culture itself began to express aspects of the revolt against conformity. The current nostalgia for the rock music of the 1950s is in part a reflection of the recognition that the music of the 1950s had a vigor which has been lost in the present offerings.

Even the film of the fifties expressed discontent with the decline of the hero. If Bogart was the quintessential individual who set his face against the wheel of social mores in the 1940s, the western hero, such as Shane, who projected both courage and humility, was the subterranean commentator on the contemporary depersonalization of much of the film fare of the era.

It can be said that critical art, like critical theory, is always to be found in the interstices rather than the mainstream of culture in capitalist society. There is no doubt that during the fifties hit-parade songs, banal musicals, and frothy novels predominated. It is also true that the tendency of commodity culture is always to absorb critical thought and to transform it into a commodity, shorn of its revolutionary content. But these reservations do not detract from the fact that the fifties were a time of upheaval, even in the midst of repression, and produced their share of protest and insubordination to the dominant themes of politics and culture.

The critical view of mass society that survived from the period became the basis for the radical analysis of all that was evil in American life. In the buoyant years of the rise of the student movement and the antiwar movement, Mills and Marcuse, who had both been assigned by the academic establishment in the 1950s to genteel oblivion or outright scorn, were resurrected as new left theorists. Their theories described and gave shape to the boredom and cultural poverty of suburban upper middle class life, the treachery of status hunger, and the emptiness of the substitution of the love of things for the love of persons. The deprivations of the students were not material in the old sense: they appeared postindustrial. It was the quality of life that they experienced as impoverished, not the quantity of goods. Mills and

Marcuse were the first to speak of their condition in the English language and gave it a specific historical context and political significance. The banality of existence need no longer be experienced as a private affair. The perception of the banality of existence became the core of the youth revolt of the 1960s.

Images of the fifties as a time to be rejected were promulgated by a young generation determined to reinvent the concepts of collectivity and individualism, to be self-directed rather than other-directed, to create a new culture independent of the mass media.

Our evaluations of historical events are too often informed by prefigured expectations or ideologies. For radicals and liberals whose view of politics stems from the degree to which the activities of the masses correspond to their own criteria of social progress, the fifties were clearly disappointing, since they were marked by the eclipse of a specific vintage of left-wing and New Deal politics—the heroes of the student generation, Che Guevara and Ho, Mao and Bobby Seale, represented their own break with the past. These heroes were revolutionaries, guerrilla fighters against repressive societies, individuals who conquered the passivity of the masses, who made the new world. They were the Indians challenging the hegemony of the cowboys, the farmers who defied the ranchers, the hope of the hopeless.

Notwithstanding the Vietnam War, rioting in the streets of America, murder and assassination, the 1960s were the best of times for a generation emerging from impotence. For them, there was rebirth in the demonstrations and the marches. We are just beginning to remember the defeats of that decade and some are beginning to feel the disappointment of not having changed the world completely or succeeded in creating a life sufficiently different from the past.

The criteria for judging or remembering an era can neither be taken from values superimposed from the outside upon the actual development of history nor from the perspective of the immediate results. In the first place, we must attempt to see the fifties from its own perspective. Second, we must try to look at daily life to discover its richness as well as the forces making for its disintegration.

To deny the emergence of bureaucratically determined mass society during the fifties is to deny an essential part of the times.

On the other hand, to mistake this tendency for an iron law is to pronounce the end of history and to forget that the future is always forged in the present.

I offer in the next pages evidence from my own personal experience. It is partially a chronicle of struggles among some working class people against the hardships of their own labor, not necessarily as I would have had them conduct those struggles, but as they were actually fought. It cannot be denied that most of the battles that will be described were lost, in terms of their concrete objectives. The workers who waged a war for rank-and-file control of their work and the unions representing them only succeeded in overthrowing the particular instruments of their denial, not the substance of it. Yet they acted, in C. Wright Mills's terms, as a public, dealing with bureaucracies they perceived as pernicious. The Black and white residents of the center cities who fought the "urban removal" policies of municipal governments marching to the tune of the large banks and insurance companies did not stop the bulldozer; they succeeded in slowing it down. But they were among those who did not greet the simultaneous urbanization of the rural poor and suburbanization of the white working class meekly. Black residents were fighting for their homes against these institutions as early as 1955; this fight culminated in the mass movement which struck terror into the heart of corporate America less than ten years later.

— 2 —

The year 1949–50 was a kind of turning point in American life. It was not only the man in the gray flannel suit who took the 5:30 from the center city train station back to his suburban ranch house. Increasingly, the industrial factory worker as well, formerly encapsulated in the ethnic ghettoes of large cities, was finding his new suburban dwelling a necessity. The old three-story red brick plant on the edge of the city was giving way tó a single-level white brick and cement structure set in the middle of an old cornfield in Boondocksville. The neighborhood bar as a social center was yielding to the 14-inch television set, the bowling lanes in the new shopping center, and the bar in the basement of the union hall, newly constructed a half mile down the road from the plant.

It was beginning to occur to Americans that war, admittedly no damn good, was nevertheless becoming a part of the fabric of ordinary existence. International crises were now brought into the living rooms of every family. Not that the public was invited to help determine the ways out of these crises; but thanks to the wonders of electronics, "information" was more widely disseminated than ever before and the latest sports event was no more remote than the switch on the television set.

These were the years of the first Communist trials under the Smith Act, of the beginning of the Korean War, of the deep split in the old coalition of the ideological center and the so-called "left wing" of the CIO, and of the disintegration of significant segments of the left-liberal middle class movements. The buoyancy of the early years after the war was nearly dissipated. Despite a presidential veto, the Taft-Hartley Act restricting union autonomy had become law in 1948. The restrictions on unions—particularly their freedom to strike, to elect Communists to union office, and to require union membership prior to employment—were enacted by Congress in direct response to the huge strike wave of 1946 when workers in nearly all basic mass production industries had "hit the bricks" to force the corporations to grant 18¢-an-hour wage increases. Worker militancy had been at a high level following the wartime wage freeze and the no-strike pledge. After the victory over Japan, consumer prices rose substantially following similar increases in basic material such as steel, oil, and rubber.

Meanwhile, the Truman administration was moving away from the wartime alliance with the Soviet Union and toward the establishment of an anti-Communist alliance more explicit and powerful than that which had followed the Bolshevik Revolution. Among the first tasks of the administration was to win support of the trade unions for its policies. The top leadership of the CIO was more than willing to back the Cold War aims of the President, in exchange for continuation of the prolabor policies which had been initiated by the Roosevelt administration during the Depression. The task was complicated by two factors. The first was the determination of large segments of business "to restore efficiency and raise productivity" of workers by extracting from the unions "company security" from wildcat strikes and a recognition of management's "right to manage." In other words, the corporations wished to set the pace of work, control the introduction of new techniques into the production process, and otherwise retain a free hand in directing the reconversion from wartime to peacetime production. The corporations believed the problems of conversion could be solved only by worker cooperation in holding the line on wages. Such cooperation was not forthcoming since real wages had declined during the war and were plummeting again in the first months after the surrender of Japan. The strike movement began to gain momentum during the last days of the fighting when it became evident that the war was soon to be over. And most union leaders, although sympathetic with the demand for national unity insisted upon by the Cold War–bound administration, were helpless to prevent conflict. As early as 1944 strikes had broken out in the auto industry. George Homans and Jerome Scott, two Harvard sociologists, reported that "the responsible leaders of unions were as weak as the management in dealing with 'quickies',"[7] (that is, strikes that occur without prior notice).

Even though in 1945 the top leaders of the AFL and CIO had signed a "Charter of Industrial Peace" with Eric Johnston, president of the U.S. Chamber of Commerce, the strike movement of the next two years was the largest in U.S. history. The Truman administration interpreted it as a "rebellion against the government" and proceeded to seize oil refining plants, packinghouses and coal mines on the ground that the strikes were "impeding the war effort" even though the war was already over. (It should be noted that a state of emergency under which the President assumed wartime powers to seize industry still officially existed.) In response to the national walkout of railroad workers in 1946, the President threatened to have the army draft strikers and run the railroads directly if workers refused to return to work. The railroads were seized and the strike was broken.

A second barrier to labor-administration cooperation in the pursuit of the anti-Communist crusade was this existence of divisions within the trade unions themselves. The CIO could not become a bulwark in the great patriotic effort to preserve the free world as long as its house was divided. The old alliance between the non-Communist unions and those that were built and led by trade unionists closely associated with the Communist left was fragile even in the best of times. But the Cold War era was no time for sentimentality or tolerance of the heathen. Either the left-wingers would have to be prepared to fall into line behind the resolve of the CIO leadership to give firm backing to the President's foreign policy or they would have to leave. The conflict remained unresolved in the early postwar years. Philip Murray, president of the CIO, was a man with a distinct distaste for internal squabbles. For most of his career he had been the faithful lieutenant of John L. Lewis, who ran the United Mine Workers union with an iron hand. Murray, who had been a UMW vice president, was appointed by Lewis himself to head the giant United Steelworkers and was no more liberal toward opposition than his former master. He assumed the presidency of the CIO only after Lewis, who had backed Wendell Willkie in the presidential election, resigned over the endorsement of Roosevelt by the organization in 1940 and the subsequent defeat of Willkie in the election.

But the CIO was less monolithic than the Mine Workers. Most CIO leaders believed that its task of bringing 6 million mass production workers into the ranks of organized labor demanded both the recognition of different and often divergent ideologies within the organization and the subordination of all differences to the single task of organizing the unorganized. These contradictory requirements were met by the CIO's careful avoidance of making demands on its affiliates that wanted so much outside the framework of narrow trade union concerns. Thus the principle of autonomy was preserved, except when Lewis felt constrained to appeal to his Communist friends for favors. Lewis, among other professed anti-Communists in the CIO, had enjoyed a unique relationship with the left. Even though his ruthless repression of radical opposition within the Mineworkers in the 1920s had been legendary, after the formation of the Committee for Industrial Organization in 1935 Lewis had welcomed the assistance of the Communist Party and the splinter groups that had broken away from it, and no left-wing faction had actively opposed him when he was head of the organization. The Communists did not always appreciate his ability to finesse them out of leadership of some of the most important of the new unions, but they had managed to gain a strong foothold in the mainstream of the trade union movement for the first time since the founding of the party in 1919 and were openly grateful to Lewis.

However, with Lewis gone from the scene, the pressure was mounting both from the White House and from important right-wingers such as Walter Reuther of the Auto Workers and Emil Rieve of the Textile Workers. It was evident as early as 1940 that

Murray would not be able to preserve the old arrangements. At first the anti-Communists tried to provoke a fight on abstract intellectual issues. A resolution at the 1946 CIO convention opposing "totalitarian" ideologies such as Communism and demanding CIO conformity to anti-Communist beliefs was greeted with silence by the Communist left, who refused to engage the issue on the ground that it made little practical difference in the everyday affairs of the labor movement.

But subsequent events were to prove this strategy self-defeating. The dissident unions, representing about a third of the CIO membership, were to face constant harassment from the right until 1949, when eleven of them were expelled from the CIO and another, the United Electrical Workers, walked out of the federation, decrying the betrayal by its leadership of the principle of autonomy for its affiliates on such questions as political endorsements and foreign policy issues. Murray's moderate posture had finally collapsed and the Communist left found itself all but isolated from the unions, except for some pockets of influence, notably the West Coast Longshoremen and the UE.

The bulk of the trade union movement in America has never been a center of political opposition to the corporations and the government. But the 1949 purge signaled an unprecedented era of conformity within the unions. Although the CIO was a critical battleground of the Cold War since it was an organization with enormous influence within American industry as well as a key sector of the Democratic Party's constituency, the issues that rent the labor movement resonated widely in American society.

Other sectors of American life were affected by the virulence of the anti-Communist crusade. The American Veterans Committee, for example, was a casualty of the left-right split. An organization formed by Second World War veterans who eschewed the conservative American Legion and the Veterans of Foreign Wars, it might have played an important role in postwar politics, but it never really got off the ground because of intense internal ideological conflict.

In 1947 congressional investigations of the film industry had resulted in the public discharge of ten directors and screen writers and the blacklisting of many more. A year later, government workers suspected of Communist membership or leanings were being fired from their jobs, or, worse, arrested and tried for a variety of alleged crimes. These crimes ranged from refusal to answer the questions posed by congressional committees to having perjured themselves when swearing their loyalty to the country, or, penultimately, to spying for a foreign power.

A University of Washington professor, Herbert Phillips, an admitted Communist Party member, was fired from his job for his political affiliation. Phillips's defense consisted in his insistence that he never taught Communism in the classroom. He claimed his teaching was untainted by political ideology, a symbol of the fact that the Communist Party assiduously tried to separate work from politics. Elsewhere, left-wing teachers were discharged from public schools in New York State when they refused to sign loyalty oaths and students were being denied financial aid for similar reasons.

A possible dedication for this book could have been "to Dean Mahoney of Brooklyn College without whom this work would not have been possible." Dean Mahoney was neither a close personal friend of mine nor a wise counselor. On the contrary, he was an instrument of punishment against me. Dean Mahoney sent me a letter in the fall of 1950 in which he suspended me from the college for the rest of the semester for "conduct unbecoming a student." The unbecoming behavior had to do with a sit-in of several hundred held in his office protesting the suspension of the student newspaper for having come out against the refusal of the good dean and the college administration to sanction a left-wing organization, the Labor Youth League, as an on-campus group.

The suspension of the student newspaper, *Vanguard,* resulted in one of the first underground newspapers of the modern era, *Draugnav,* and a letter signed by club presidents including myself urging our fellow students to demonstrate outside the Dean's office, since he had issued the suspension order. Our demonstration was an early version of the kind of student protest that was to become routine in the 1960s.

My suspension from Brooklyn College was a reflection of the increasingly frozen political atmosphere of the time. The college administration was certainly neither unique nor idiosyncratic in its repression of dissent that it felt, or professed to feel, was part of a worldwide conspiracy to destroy American freedom. Like many liberals, President Gideonse followed the dictum coined by Sidney Hook in a characteristic anti-Communist diatribe of the period—*Heresy Yes, Conspiracy No.* In this classic defense of political repression, Hook carefully distinguished the liberal position from the cruder varieties of anti-Communism of the traditional right. His theme reverberated throughout liberal circles and provided a major rationale for their silence during the McCarthy era. According to Hook, liberals have a sacred obligation to defend the civil liberties of those whose views are scorned by the majority. Political dissent is an integral part of the American heritage. But the Communist Party, in Hook's view, was not a legitimate representative of political dissent. It was the American branch of the worldwide Communist conspiracy to impose a totalitarian dictatorship on the whole of humanity. This conspiracy, directed from Moscow, made its American followers agents of its interests. No means were excluded from its arsenal to achieve its ends. The ends were domination, not socialism. The means could include terror if these methods served the interests of the conspiracy. Liberals beware!, admonished Hook. Just as no government can tolerate subversion of its right to rule, so no democratic society should tolerate those who would undermine its very principles by totalitarian means. The preservation of our institutions, declared Hook, demanded the rooting out of this cancer.

Although many liberals were uncomfortable with this line of reasoning, their tacit silence during the early fifties indicated not only fear, but consent as well. My own perception of the general mood of the country was that it was moving rapidly toward fascism. The liberals were true to the derisive epithet applied to them by the sectarian left: they had their feet planted firmly in midair. They were unable to decide whether to join the fascists or fight them. But at the age of seventeen I was completely out of sympathy with their struggle. It reminded me too much of the ambivalence of my parents. Because he was keenly aware of the Jewish experience during the Nazi rise to power, my father had become paralyzed by fear. At the time, he had a technician's job with the New York Port Authority. After a brief flirtation with one of the many liberal groups which sprang up after the war dedicated to the preservation of peace on the basis of "Big Three" unity, my father quietly dropped out of political activity after getting a civil service appointment. My mother had been a sit-down striker in the early days of the CIO, but it was to be some years before she got a job in a union shop again. She was sympathetic to liberals like Henry Wallace, who had run for President in 1948, but, like my father, was not inclined to stick her neck out for political pariahs. As it then seemed to me, my parents would have joined the rest of the Jews on the way to the gas chamber, clutching the few possessions they had successfully concealed from their captors.

This intemperate opinion was not the product of political analysis alone. I am certain that it was helped along by my father's frequent outbursts against my long periods of absence from the home during high school. I could never be certain whether my father objected more to my late night encounters with girlfriends or my growing interest in radical politics. I often suspected that he was angered more by the political activities. Later in life, I began to realize that my father was a fairly direct man. He fumed over my politics, but was equally threatened by my adolescent sexual adventures. My politics threatened his job security. He was certain that I was bound to cause him grief on the job, especially after my hour of political martyrdom. But I am sure he knew no simple remedy for my alleged amorous precociousness. All I wanted was privacy and license to pursue my life. That was precisely what my father could not grant, especially in view of the fact that he expected me to realize his own repressed ambitions. In December of the semester in which I was suspended my father issued an ultimatum: either I give up my suicidal radical friends and activities, or get out of his house. I decided after a New Year's Eve party to accept the offer of an acquaintance to share an apartment and quit school. My decisions to leave both home and school were so closely intertwined that for years it was difficult to sort out the motivations. My political reasons were crystal clear in my own mind. Plainly, nobody with a revolutionary sensibility could agree to remain part of the bourgeois university, in the midst of its repressive rampages. The university had become a brilliant example of the perfidy of the liberal intellectuals, as I saw it. Like the Jews in Nazi Germany who disdained to defend the Communists as long as they themselves were tolerated, the liberals were hoping that the repression would blow over, or, alternatively, were playing quisling to Truman's Attorney General and actively showing their loyalty to the master class. College was no place for a young revolutionary. The virtue of the shop was that you did a day's work and kept your thoughts free. All the boss could buy was your hands. In the university, the administration seemed to be demanding the subordination of the mind as well as the body.

Ostensibly I went into factories for the virtues of honest manual work and for the chance to help transform the unions from appendages of the Cold War to instruments of social change.

But my decision was largely in reaction to my father's hatred for his own working class way of life. I had contempt for my parents' middle class aspirations for me and resented their failure to liberate themselves from immigrant and depression fears, even though they had both grown up in America.

Another important reason I fled school was the boredom of college. After twelve years of elementary school, junior high school, and high school, I itched to get out into the world. When I was fifteen, I had spent part of the summer hitchhiking and working in a direct mail company. By the time I entered college my restlessness took over. I simply could not bear sitting in class listening to a teacher drone away. I had expected that the childish treatment accorded students in lower grades would be transformed in college. The dismal level of instruction I had suffered during high school was only bearable because of my belief that college would offer something different, an atmosphere of inquiry, or at least of intellectual excitement. I found Brooklyn College to be a combination of intellectual mediocrity and bureaucratic excellence. Since neither interested me, it was easy to leave. The most disappointing aspect of my education was that the long years of waiting for something new, different, and stimulating were never to be fulfilled.

I was searching for work that was moderately tolerable—rather than something that would lead to a career or to learning a trade. My jobs were of short duration at first, because of the recession of 1950–51 when the impact of the Korean War had not yet been felt in terms of improved employment opportunities. I had landed my first job a month after suspension, working as a helper on a fur dressing and dyeing truck. It lasted two months. I was laid off after Christmas and got a job in the head office of a textile manufacturer where I did order picking. I quit that job as soon as I got my second paycheck. Finally I landed a job I kept for a year.

After much searching, I had been tipped off that there were some jobs available through a Brooklyn local of the now-independent United Electrical Workers (UE). The local sent me to a camera factory on East Twenty-second Street in Manhattan where I learned production grinding on camera lenses. The work consisted in operating five metal disks, whose abrasive action was augmented by rouge. The action of the rouge and the electrically powered lapping machine ground the lenses to the desired angle.

My task was to keep the lenses lubricated by applying the rouge and water solution with a brush as the conical disk did the actual grinding. After they were ground, I took them off and put them in a tray, picked up new lenses, and repeated the process. It was an extremely tedious job at the beginning because until the operator had picked up the skill, he was not allowed to set up the machine. Meanwhile the foreman did this. But even after I learned how to set up the machine, there was still a great deal of repetitive work to do. The trouble was, you couldn't take your attention off the job because if the lens became dry, the angle could be ruined. The nice part of being in the shop was the friendly relations among the workers, especially since many of us were young and unmarried. Since the plant employed both men and women on the same jobs, there was a natural inclination toward social life after work and during lunch hours.

I was transferred to a new department six months after starting work and quickly was elected steward. Although I had attended a few union meetings upon completing my thirty-day trial period (a provision of the Taft-Hartley Act permitted employers discretion in hiring and firing employees up to 30 days unless a longer period was provided for in union agreement), I had not really participated in union affairs, receiving most of my information through Angelo, the shop steward on the lens grinding floor. Now, as a steward, I attended shop committee meetings and gained an enlarged sense of union loyalty.

Local 475 was made up of a large number of small- and medium-sized plants in the New York area. Unlike another large UE local which represented radio and TV workers, 475 had jurisdiction over miscellaneous metal working industries such as machine shops and manufacturers of cameras, safety razors, and aluminum cookware, and, in fact, any plant it could organize. Blacks, Puerto Ricans, and young workers were heavily represented among its 6000 members. For this reason, its fairly "progressive" stands on contemporary social issues received support among the rank and file. It was one of the strong backers of the NAACP in Brooklyn, was always ready to support the strike activity of other unions, and exhibited an unusual degree of aggressiveness in organizing the unorganized in a period when some unions were more interested in picking one anothers' carcasses or had become dues collection agencies. Yet I could never figure out from what I saw in 475 why the union had been expelled from the CIO for being Communist dominated. It seemed to me it resembled other unions much more than it differed from them. Apart from its interest in outside political affairs there were precious few aspects of the union's relationship to the shops that could be described as "radical," much less revolutionary.

When I started working in the camera factory in January 1951, my wage was 85 cents an hour, which was much lower than industrial wages for semiskilled labor in the metal fabricating industries. The top rate on the job was a little more than $1.40 an hour, but I was not scheduled to get it according to the automatic progression increase until the middle of 1952. Of course, the company was marginal in its industry and probably could pay only low wages (it actually went out of business at the end of 1952). Its low wages probably accounted for the large number of minority workers, women, and youth employed in the plant. But there was no sign that the union intended to conduct a battle to bring the wages up to decent standards. Soon I began to realize why.

Unions that represented workers in labor-intensive, competitive industries were faced with problems that transcended ideology. It did not matter whether the UE or the local's leadership favored socialism, or harbored hatred of capitalism. They were forced to make decisions in daily affairs in terms of the prevailing economic conditions. As a union within New York City, Local 475 had to deal, in the first place, with the fact that most of the employers under contract were either struggling to stay alive, like the company I worked for, or were seriously preparing to leave the city for New Jersey or the South. In the rural areas they could build larger plants, receive free water and be free of local taxes for twenty years in communities suffering the poverty caused by the agricultural crisis or the decline of the Northern textile industry. In New York, the threat of bankruptcy or runaway shops could always be used by employers to keep wages down.

Even though the local union officials were inclined toward militancy, their options were severely limited by the conditions under which they had to negotiate contracts. In the first years of the 1950s some of the most important larger plants in the industry left the city, including the American Safety Razor Company, where the membership waged a courageous and prolonged strike to call attention to the fact that more than 700 workers, many of them middle-aged, were being abandoned. Later on, when I became active in the New Jersey labor movement, I was impressed by a president of a large Westinghouse local in Bloomfield, Dick

Lynch, who often spoke of this situation. At every CIO council meeting Lynch inveighed against the shops running away from Newark and Jersey City. He became known as "Runaway Shop" Dick, because he dwelt on this theme. His speech was always the same: the big companies were running out on the workers, especially those who had no place else to go. The unions had to fight it. What labor should do was to introduce legislation similar to that existing in England. There no company was allowed to move without government license. A firm was permitted to move only to areas of substantial labor surplus, and then only provided it did not leave surpluses behind. If it was granted permission to relocate, the company was obliged to offer jobs to its former employees, who would carry their seniority with them. If the workers did not wish to move, they would receive substantial severance pay.

Everybody applauded Lynch's classic oration. When he became a Democratic state assemblyman he actually introduced a bill embodying the principles he had long enunciated. For a time, he was seriously listened to because the frequent recessions of the 1950s resulted in many plant closings. But New Jersey was not the best place to argue the case against runaway shops. More industry came into the state from New York and elsewhere than left it toward the end of the decade. Moreover, many of the plants leaving the large cities found havens within the state's own suburbs. The only people hurt by the exodus were the Blacks and older workers. And, for the time being, they could be safely ignored by both the legislatures and the unions. The industrial unions functioning in the center cities in the 1950s and 1960s had hard choices to make. If they demanded higher wages and fought against speedup and other working hazards, they stood a good chance of driving industry away. Jobs and members would be lost. On the other hand, if they failed to conduct militant struggles for decent wages and working conditions, they could justifiably be called "sellouts" by their members and the unorganized workers whom they sought to bring into the union ranks. The argument raged among trade unionists for years.

Many of my friends were young radicals who had chosen to work in factories rather than go to school. Others never considered college as a real choice, and had been attracted to left-wing politics through contact with the so-called left-wing unions or with rank-and-file workers who were members of or sympathizers with the Communist Party and other Marxist-oriented groups.

Most of us felt that the union had an obligation to fight the employers no matter what the consequences. "If a boss can't pay a living wage, let him go out of business," we reasoned. We felt that workers should not pay the price necessary to keep the cockroach bosses afloat. Since monopoly was an inevitable feature of capitalist development, it was not up to the unions to try to roll back history. We fought on the floor of shop meetings for aggressive wage demands and condemned the "social-democratic" and "reformist" labor bureaucrats who seemed more interested in saving their dues money than in representing the workers interests. Since most of us were between eighteen and twenty-one years old and were single or newly married, we felt sure that we could find other jobs. (We were right.)

Yet even our beloved UE was not sympathetic to our arguments in those years. Despite its radical reputation, it was unwilling to risk the union's existence for the sake of abstract principle. In those years, the expelled unions had a hard road to travel. Most of them were ensconced in sick or highly competitive industries, with the exception of the Mine, Mill, and Smelter Workers, West Coast Longshoremens Union, and the UE, which had been the third largest union in the CIO and had unionized virtually the entire electrical and radio industry by 1948. Although UE had made substantial inroads in the machine tool industry, it was by no means as powerful there as it was in the electrical industry. Among the former CIO unions one of the most stable was stuck in the dying fur trades, already suffering from declining employment losses inflicted upon it by changing fashions. The Fur and Leather Workers Union was the only national union boasting an avowed Communist leadership in the American labor movement. Its leather division was located in rural and small-town areas. Much of the leather membership evaporated in the early 1950s as foreign competition began to eat away at the glove crafts and other branches of the industry. But the greatest losses to the FLW as well as unions such as the UE were to come from other quarters. The expulsions were a signal for the CIO to charter competing unions, wherever possible.

Even though the CIO declared open season on the expelled unions, some of them were either not vulnerable to raiding or were not worth taking on. For example, despite constant harassment by the U.S. government, the ILWU had an iron grip on the West Coast ports. For a brief instant Harry Lundberg, the leader of the Sailors Union of the Pacific and a rock-ribbed anti-Communist, considered making war on Harry Bridges and his union. But the moment passed—Bridges was simply too strong to be challenged successfully.

The Fur and Leather Workers were in a similar position, simply because many within the rank and file were Communists or sympathetic to them. It was among the few unions in America where the Communist politics of the leadership were shared by the members. Walking through the New York fur market, one could witness sewing machine operators or cutters standing on Seventh Avenue and Twenty-eighth Street reading Communist organs such as the *Daily Worker* or the Jewish *Freiheit*. Rank-and-file workers attended Communist mass meetings and donated money to CP-supported causes. The Socialist and Liberal parties had enjoyed such support among garment and clothing workers during the first half of the twentieth century. But these political groups were never as despised as the Communists in the 1950s, which made the continuation of left-wing politics among the FLW membership even more remarkable.

Other expelled unions were not as richly endowed with a loyal membership and a similarly strong position in their industry. For example, the minuscule Food and Tobacco Workers conducted heroic strikes in the South in an attempt to force tobacco manufacturers to bargain with them. In 1947, the union waged a momentous strike against the R. J. Reynolds Tobacco Company during which several strikers were killed. The strike prefigured the civil rights upsurge a decade later. It was sparked by Black workers who emerged as militantly pro-union. Despite the attempts by the employer to divide white from Black in typical Southern style, the union succeeded in forging a remarkable degree of unity between them. The loss of the strike, combined with raids against its dwindling membership by the AFL Tobacco Workers International Union after the expulsion, forced the tiny organization to merge its remnant with New York's Local 65, a union which organized any workers it could. Local 65 also absorbed the embattled United Office and Professional Workers, which had never made a significant dent in the huge commercial and banking industries of New York, Boston, or Chicago.

Even though the CIO Steelworkers staked a claim on the Mine, Mill, and Smelter Workers, the dominant union in the nonferrous metals industry, Murray's organization had rough going at first. Mine-Mill had inherited the radical traditions of the old Western Federation of Miners and the IWW. Its avowedly left-wing leadership was no stranger to the rough-and-tumble mining communities and mill towns. Actually, the relatively staid Steelworkers were no match for Mine-Mill. The early losses of the expelled union were sustained at the hands of the more flexible and skilled United Auto Workers in Connecticut's heavily Catholic Ansonia Valley region. The UAW swept Mine-Mill out of many of the area's refineries early in the 1950s, but the Steelworkers had less success in the mines. Repeated Steelworkers' attempts to win over the large copper mines in Butte, Montana, and Sudbury, Ontario, were beaten back by Mine-Mill, which was hurt but not mortally wounded by the fierce red-baiting attacks of Murray's raiders.

In 1949 the International Union of Electrical Workers (IUE) was formed under the leadership of James Carey, who had been CIO secretary-treasurer. Carey had been deposed as president of the UE by the pro-Communist faction in 1941, and became a member of the militant anti-Communist wing of the CIO. Carey, a quick-tempered and brooding man, ached for the day when he would return as head of the Electrical Workers Union. Philip Murray granted a small group of UE dissidents a charter to form a new organization and clean the industry of Communist influence.

The dismemberment of the UE became a key component of the CIO strategy in the first years of the new decade. The IUE was to be the centerpiece of the effort to destroy the Communist Party in the labor movement and clear the way for full-throated support of U.S. foreign policy, the Democratic Party, and finally, unity between the CIO and the AFL, which had foundered on the rock of Lewis's tolerance of the Communist-led unions. William Green, the president of the AFL, and his successor, George Meany, insisted that the condition for labor unity was the success of the CIO in cleaning out the reds.

In the 1950s the big prize remained the electrical industry. Not only was the CIO interested in breaking the UE, but electrical manufacturing was a critical war industry, especially in newer electronics branches making equipment for the Korean War and the advanced weapons systems being developed by the Defense Department. The IUE drive was aided by material culled from U.S. government sources, particularly the FBI, the House Committee on Un-American Activities, and the Senate Committee on Internal Security, which held hearings in towns in which IUE raids against UE-held plants were under way.

The new CIO affiliate was actually not unified within its own ranks. In order to conduct his campaign, Carey assembled a group of unionists who were united by one theme—opposition to the "Communist-dominated" UE. Apart from this area of agreement, there was little reason for the disparate collection of Catholic trade unionists, former Trotskyists, and trade union careerists to be thrown together. As it turned out, the heterogeneity of the IUE became its undoing a little more than a decade later, when Carey was defeated once more by a former lieutenant, Paul Jennings. In the 1950s IUE was a single-minded organization that employed any means necessary to convince electrical workers to leave the UE. These means were as varied as the appeals based on the argument that defense contracts would be lost to shops represented by Communists, charges that the Communists took dues money to support subversive causes, militant tirades against the alleged company union character of UE, and straightforward evidence that some UE officers and staff members either were or had been members of the Communist Party or its "front" organizations.

By 1954, five years of raiding had produced a new union of electrical workers boasting nearly 300,000 members. The Machinists, Steelworkers, and Auto Workers also engaged in raiding with some success. In turn, UE lost about two-thirds of its half-million members, but retained some areas of strength. Although IUE had taken most of the GE and Westinghouse chains into the new union, UE salvaged contracts in some key plants of both companies. The critically important Westinghouse Lester plant remained with UE, as did the Erie plant of the General Electric Company.

In almost all cases, the success of IUE hinged on its ability to win over the local union leadership. Neither red-baiting nor such scare tactics as threats to employment were generally sufficient to displace the UE. IUE even had the unqualified support of liberal, anti-Communist politicians such as Senator Hubert Humphrey, who actually issued a public statement on the eve of several elections at GE plants. But the critical turning point usually came when local union leaders went over to the IUE. Where they stayed with UE, it was able to withstand the IUE assault in most instances. For example, IUE's success in winning over workers in the machine industry was less notable than in electrical manufacturing. Here the UE organizing director, James Matles, a former machinist, had maintained close relationships with local leaders over the years and was able to persuade them to hold the line.

A sizable group of locals quit UE after key district leaders were "exposed" as Communist Party agents by various government investigating committees or courts. UE suffered a great number of losses in the Midwest for this reason, especially in Ohio, Indiana, and Missouri. The IUE victories attributable to sheer red-baiting were particularly effective in small towns where, at great distances from major industrial centers, anti-Communism had become an effective tool to launch or maintain careers for many politicians and community power groups. Workers in these towns took great risks in remaining inside UE or any other union labeled "Communist-dominated." To openly defend such organizations one had to be prepared to bring down upon oneself the enmity of the entire community, as well as lose one's livelihood.

Finally, UE lost ground in some instances where the IUE allegations of collusion between the local or international union leadership and the company were true. In every union there are cases of cozy relationships between the union leadership and management, and UE was no exception. The UE had been among the major proponents of the wartime no-strike pledge. But many workers had resented the union for its politically inspired agreement to step up production in the shops, hold down wage demands, and prevent strike action against management. Five years after the war, some were unwilling to forgive or forget. The first chance they got to strike back, they voted for an alternative.

From the UE point of view, the most bitter pill to swallow was not the red-baiting, the jailings of some of its leaders, or the IUE raids. These were the fortunes of war which had to be accepted as part of the times. If a local leader sold out for a staff job or embraced religion, it was sad but understandable. When the Catholic Church declared a holy crusade against UE and sent a brilliant priest, Father Charles Rice, to combat the devil at Pittsburgh's Westinghouse plant or held Communion breakfasts in New Jersey for Catholic Electrical unionists at which sermons were delivered for God and against the devil's representative James Matles, the resulting losses could be absorbed. In fact, the UE leadership was prepared to withstand the blitz of government, church, and the business community. There was a distinct satisfaction in being a pariah when you felt your cause was just.

The sting came from within. In 1955, the Communist Party changed its trade union policy. Instead of encouraging the survival of the independent unions, it ordered its cadre to press for a return to the mainstream of the labor movement. On the eve of the CIO merger with the AFL the party's judgment had been that the independents could not survive the colossus that was to become the AFL-CIO. Better to make preparations for merger with mainstream unions than suffer certain extinction. In all fairness, some of the expelled unions suffered sorely from isolation. The Fur Workers, once a proud, if modest-sized, union, was facing financial insolvency in the midst of the permanent depression of the industry. The Meatcutters Union, an organization with a fairly tolerant leadership, was making overtures to the Fur Workers that were increasingly difficult to refuse. The treasury of the Mine-Mill Workers was being drained simultaneously by seemingly endless efforts to repulse raids by competing unions and by legal fees for defense against government attempts to send its leaders to prison for alleged violations of the Taft-Hartley prohibition against Communists holding union office. Besides, its growth had been halted and its membership was slowly slipping away for reasons of technological unemployment as much as interunion conflict.

The case of UE was different. After five lean years, the union was smaller, but its membership had stabilized at about 180,000. Its treasury was depleted, but by no means empty. The New York–New Jersey district, still one of its largest, had lost 60,000 members to the IUE, but had 20,000 members who constituted a hard core of resistance. Even the IUE was getting tired of continually raiding shops such as the Edison plant in West Orange, New Jersey, without success. Five large amalgamated locals, that is, locals that had a large number of shops organized, in New York City and northern New Jersey, were virtually unassailable.

But as soon as the CP issued its directives, party members inside the district organizations of UE began to make overtures to IUE officials in New Jersey. The IUE promised that no UE staff members would be fired and that the amalgamated locals could retain their autonomy. The entire district went over to the IUE. Shortly thereafter, the House Committee on Un-American Activities came to Newark, subpoenaed the former UE staff members and many were fired from their short-lived IUE jobs.

The national UE leadership was furious at the Party. From its vantage point, the CP's policy of going back to the AFL-CIO was nothing short of treachery. From the mid-fifties to the late 1960s, when the UE and IUE were allied for the first time in joint strike activity against GE, UE remained a genuinely independent union, free of all political ties, except to its sister organizations, the West Coast Longshoremen and Mine-Mill, with which it held occasional consultations on trade union and political questions. In upstate New York, the antagonism between the UE and IUE had been so strong that it was impossible to effect an honorable merger. UE leaders decided to join the Machinists Union, rather than suffer humiliation at the hands of the former enemy.

The disintegration of the independent unions was unlamented by the workers, except those who applied ideological criteria to trade union practice or identified the Independents with militant action. As for me, I learned an important lesson during the early fifties. It was taught to me by a rank-and-file UE member in the Edison plant who described his local as a "red company union," that is, one where the politics were friendly to Communist Party policies while its stance on the day-to-day issues on the shop floor was compromising and weak. I learned that there was no necessary connection between ideological politics and shop floor militancy. But I did not yet realize that the history of the left wing in the trade unions was full of instances in which ideology demanded accommodation with the employers, and that it did not matter to the workers whether the ideology was Catholic or Leninist. "A company union is a company union."

I was laid off in late winter 1952, a few months before the company went out of business. It was hard to find work in New York that winter. It seemed that the Korean War boom had bypassed New York City, even though you could always find a job pushing around hand trucks in the garment center for ten cents more an hour than the minimum wage. I was anxious to find some better-paying work by then because I had met a young woman during the previous November and we were going together seriously. We had already talked about getting married when she graduated from high school in June, so I began to look for a job in New Jersey.

The New York Times "help wanted" section was carrying big ads placed by aircraft companies for all kinds of workers, even those with little or no machine-shop skills. They promised to teach you. The ads read "trainees for turret lathe, engine lathe, and drill press." I had conflicting feelings about working for a defense plant because I opposed the Korean War, so I held back for some time. I landed a job in the early spring with another lens grinding outfit, but they stuck me on the 4 to 12 shift and I hated it. The only advantage to this job was that there was time during the day to look for another one, so one morning I took the bus out to Woodridge, New Jersey, to the employment office of Curtiss-Wright, a major manufacturer of airplane engines.

Despite the huge number of applicants in the office, they moved us through pretty fast because they had a virtual army of employment interviewers. When my turn came, one of the interviewers asked me what job I was applying for. I answered: "Trainee on machines." After glancing at my application, he instructed me to sit down again outside. Had I given the wrong answer? I guessed that in a few minutes he would emerge from his cubicle and inform me that they would keep me in mind. I was genuinely surprised when I was called in again and told to report for "processing" the next morning.

I remember thinking that there was little difference between getting into the army and getting work at Curtiss-Wright. "Processing" was a fairly complicated procedure in big defense plants. There was the same thorough physical examination given by most large employers to reduce the chance of hiring workers who might require medical treatment and would blame it on the job. Companies never hired anybody with a physical disability which might be subject to workmen's compensation and thereby increase their insurance rates. In addition, I was given a test to discover my mechanical aptitude. The company was not going to hire untrainable workers if it could screen them out. Training, after all, costs money. And if you have to fire a person for failing to measure up to production norms, it's even more expensive than the losses sustained by normal breaking-in time.

If you passed through these screening procedures successfully, there was a vital third one: the fingerprinting and photo test. When I completed these, I was told that I would be sent a telegram informing me of my starting date. I rode home on the bus with little hope of landing the job. How the hell could I expect to work for an airplane company with my nefarious record of revolutionary activity? Thrown out of school, a member of an organization on the Attorney General's list (I had finally joined the Labor Youth League, although I was a member of an industry-wide club whose membership was not as openly known as the membership of clubs based in particular shops), an active member of a "left-wing" union, I must have been crazy to believe I could slip through Wright's "processing."

Like many other radicals I either overestimated my own importance or the FBI's intelligence—or both. A week later, I got the telegram ordering me to report on the midnight to 8 A.M. shift the following day. For the next six months I drilled holes in a flat piece of metal. The job required little training except to make sure that the drill was sharp. They even put a stop on the drill so it was almost impossible to ruin the work, except when the drill broke. A setup man set the depth and width of the hole and checked the first piece to make sure it conformed to the specifications. When the drill became dull I removed it from the machine, walked over to the tool room and got another one, already sharpened.

There was no pressure from supervision for production as long as you met the required number of pieces for the night. Wright operated under federal "cost plus" contracts. It was guaranteed a profit over its costs. The company only cared for precision and sufficient production to meet delivery deadlines. My work actually took about five hours to complete in an eight-hour shift, if I did not run into trouble or was not pressed to meet some deadline.

The three free hours on the midnight shift were spent by most of us catching up on the sleep lost in the hot summer daytime hours. Like many others who worked in the plant, I lived in the middle of the city, on the fifth floor of a tenement building on West 132nd Street in Manhattan. The street noises and the heat conspired to rob me of sleep, except on rainy days. Sometimes I used my free time during the shift to read or talk to other young workers, but the world of those who work the midnight shift always seemed to revolve around the pursuit of sleep. It is a topsy-turvy existence. When everybody else in the city seems to be working, you either fight for a few hours of sleep in the morning before the sun makes your bedroom a cauldron, or go to an air-conditioned movie, where sleep can be obtained for the price of admission.

By the autumn, I was married and my 18-year-old wife, Jane, was pregnant with our first child. She worked at Woolworth's for a while, and then got a job in a television assembly plant. The only time we slept together was on weekends. Since she worked days we began to eat dinner with each other when the cooler fall weather made it possible to sleep during the daytime, but there were occasions when I ate dinner and then sacked out until it was time to go to work. Finally, we decided that even the high wages at the engine plant were not sufficient to outweigh the disadvantages of a broken marriage. I had begun to be irritable with her because of the sexual and social frustrations produced by our constant nocturnal separation. I even struck her a few times after she became pregnant, and was horrified.

Looking back at that time in my life, I realize that even though my political sense was fairly well-developed, our daily life was no different from that of other young married working class people. We reproduced the prevailing relations between men and women: I drank beer every Friday night after work with the "boys" in the plant and came home late to a cold supper and my wife's fury. Later on, while working in a steel mill, I acquired the habit of television-watching after work, especially at the end of the week when the exhaustion of factory labor made it impossible for me to talk to Jane, or to think or to read. I became furious in the early months of our marriage when Jane insisted on visiting her mother a couple of times a week. I had no understanding of her predicament. After she was six months' pregnant, she could no longer lift television sets onto the assembly line, and was forced to quit work. She had few friends of her own age who were in a similar married situation so she came to rely on her mother for companionship. I interpreted her turning there for social life as a direct threat to our marriage and an indication that she could not break the umbilical cord of childhood. I became furious when, after I had found a day job in a New Jersey steel fabricating plant, she resisted my proposal to move to Newark. I had rebelled against the bourgeois values of my parents and their attempts to emulate middle class existence, even though their work and many of their attitudes belied such pretensions. But now I heard myself yelling at my wife about money, and seemed unable to control much of my behavior generated by the pressures of bills, work, and alienated leisure. Politics notwithstanding, our life together differed little from that of other working class people.

Our main topics of conversation concerned our tight income situation and our divergent priorities as to how to spend what little we had. Jane was often angry at my propensity for taking days off from work. At the end of the week such irresponsibility would show up in my take-home pay, and when I was bringing home less than $40 a week, if I missed a day it meant we ate less well. I liked to go to the movies and eat out once in a while. Jane enjoyed these pleasures, but was far more practical about indulging in them. We fought over how to bring up Michael, our son. Like my father, I tended to favor a more rigid concept of discipline in his early years. Looking back, I wonder whether I derived my prejudices from any firm set of beliefs or simply from my work-weariness. I know that I expected my wife to keep our son from disturbing my sleep or "bothering me" after a hard day's work.

On weekends I did the shopping, and took Michael out to the park in order to give Jane a break (she spent her "free time" doing the heavy housework). The three of us went for a "ride" on Sundays, one of the favorite working class pleasures. Sometimes we visited our parents.

We moved to New Jersey after I got a job in Worthington Pump Company, one of the large employers in a geographically small, but industrially well-endowed, suburb of Newark. Harrison was known for its roster of large employers, including RCA, GM, Otis Elevator, Crucible Steel, and Worthington. It also was famous for having more bars per square block than any other town in the state. It was in Harrison that I got my first glimpse of the relationship between alcohol and labor.

There were many opportunities to imbibe liquor during the course of the working day. The younger shop workers could find a conveniently located gin mill across the street from every plant or could drink at the Veterans organizations' bars. Some workers ate lunch in the bars that served food and went back after work for more serious drinking. I knew a lot of men who simply spent all of their free time in the bars. In the 1950s the industrial tavern was a place of convivial conversation about baseball and politics or about problems in the shop. The tavern would field a bowling team in a town-wide league. Its television set, usually one with a large screen, was the inducement for sports fans to watch championship fights in the evening, important baseball games in the late afternoon or evening, and Milton Berle or other popular comedians of the time.

Most workers who used the bars for social hangouts drank beer, but consumed a lot of it. But a substantial minority drank boilermakers (a shot of rye and a beer) ever day. Some of these men were well on the way to alcoholism before they reached thirty. I have no statistics on working class drinking, but I believe it was widespread among workers of all ages in the plants where I worked. Although I was never a heavy drinker myself, I got drunk fairly regularly on Friday nights for the first year of my marriage, and certainly knew that some of the reasons had to do with the fear and insecurity of being so young and having to support a family, and the pressure to produce on the job.

The older immigrant workers in the mills did their drinking in the bars of nationality clubs such as the Polish Falcons, the Polish National Home, or the Ukrainian Home. In the 1950s Harrison and its environs had a big Eastern European immigrant population working in industrial plants. The ethnic organizations were the center of social life as well as political activities. Any candidate for either public or union office had to make the rounds of the clubs if he wanted to succeed. Although the rank and file was composed of factory workers, the officers of the ethnic clubs were either small businessmen or lawyers. Frequently a president of a Ukrainian organization was the local undertaker. I suspected that the reason business and professional people were chosen for office was connected to the awe many workers felt for the educated or for those who had successfully made it out of the working class. The immigrant workers chose leaders who were role models for their children, even if they themselves had abandoned hope of opening up a tavern or a grocery store.

Among the younger people in the shop one of the most highly held beliefs about the older immigrant workers was that the Eastern Europeans and the Italians who came to work with lunch pails and never seemed to spend money in the bars were actually wealthy property owners. Once a fellow worker of about thirty pointed out a man in his late fifties who worked in our department as a sweeper. "See that guy," he began. "Don't be fooled by the broom. He owns a shitload of apartment buildings in Kearny. He just works here to keep busy." This tale, repeated in infinite variety, seemed to perform a vital psychological function for younger people who were beginning to suspect that they might end up in the shop for the rest of their lives. It gave them some hope that factory work did not signify class position or low income. All kinds of people did factory work—not just those who needed the money to live. The legend of the rich "honkie" reinforced their own dreams of escaping the shop as well. "When I get some savings together, I'm going into business with my brother-in-law. We know a guy who can get us a liquor license in Chatham. All we need is about $5000 down payment on the saloon and a few thousand to pay him for getting the license. Then you won't see me around here anymore."

Apart from the plans for opening up a small business, there were two other talked-about avenues of escape for workers under thirty-five. A small number of them were working toward the day when the old German foremen would finally retire and they would be tapped. These workers became the "favorites" of the foremen because they were hard workers, even though they argued vehemently over piece rates and did not hesitate to call the union in when they thought the company gave them the shaft on a job.

An even tinier minority coveted union office; shop stewards enjoyed super-seniority in their departments, which meant that they were the last to be laid off. Plantwide union officials received the top rate of their job classification in addition to the average piece rate bonus for their department. Besides, they did little or no work on their regular jobs since they spent most of the time during the day on union business. Of course, not all workers who sought union leadership were impelled solely by the material rewards. But many of them viewed unionism as a career.

Everybody played the numbers in the plant. Every morning the numbers runner came around to collect the nickels and dimes from the guys at their machines. The numbers runner was usually a worker whose job assignment was bringing materials from machine to machine, so his illegal activities could be hidden behind legitimate work. Of course, everybody including the foreman knew who the runner was. But the identity of the "banker" was less obvious. I never knew who ran the numbers or the football pool until I hit the pool one week. You hit the number when you guessed the last three digits of the parimutuel take for the daily double at a certain race track. It was a matter of pure chance. But the football, basketball, and baseball pools required genuine skill. In football, you not only had to guess the winners of ten leading college games, but also the margins of victory. I rarely played the numbers except when I had a sentimental attachment to it, like my kid's birthday or some famous historical event. But I always played the football pool.

Discussions about football and baseball were serious shithouse conversation. Passions often ran pretty high, easily outdistancing raps about electoral politics or women. After all, you could not have much effect on these problems, but you could make money and earn prestige if you were lucky enough to hit the number or were smart enough to hit the pool. Workers daydreamed about sex while turning out thousands of parts on automatic screw machines, but the sense of power was more concrete about sports.

That Monday when I knew I had hit the jackpot, I immediately contacted the go-between. He told me that he did not give out the money (the odds were 150–1), so I had to wait until after work to meet the banker in the parking lot. I practically ran out of the washroom after work that day. A few minutes after I got to the parking lot the runner came walking slowly toward me in the company of the vice president of the local union. I was a steward in my department at the time, so was well acquainted with "Tex," the long stringy Southerner who worked as a maintenance man. I always had him down for a pretty good guy. He was soft-spoken, sometimes downright taciturn, but he was an effective grievance man. Tex greeted me with a mumble and took out the bills to pay me off. I was stunned. It's one thing to play the numbers; it's another to be part of the apparatus.

Later that night it dawned on me that the company had to known about Tex. I began to wonder how many other union officials were operating similar businesses in the shop. Guys would come around all the time with watches, offers of cheap television sets, and good buys on used cars. We all suspected that the merchandise was hot, but never begrudged a guy's trying to make a living. Almost everybody held down an extra job, sometimes even another full-time job. But at the time I thought it ought to be different for union officials: they should be proof against that kind of temptation, especially illegal activity. The nature of the deal was all too evident. The union leader could operate his business, the company would shut its eyes, the men would get screwed.

It was not so simple. Tex was like a basketball player who scores 20 points a game instead of 30 and makes sure that his team only wins by 4 instead of 11 points, or a boxer who knocks his opponent to the canvas in the eighth round instead of the first. But how many other union officials were in similar positions? Later on I learned that few union leaders in the large plants were so obviously corrupt, but in the medium-sized or smaller shops the union officer as businessman was the rule, not the exception. It was not so much that shop leaders took money from companies. It was more a matter of their being allowed to engage in illegal activities or, equally common, being allowed to roam the plant obstensibly on union business without having to work. It's hard to imagine a unionist selling the workers out for the price of freedom from being chained to a machine all day. But for many shop officials that freedom is worth more than money.

Unlike assembly line labor or industries like oil and some branches of chemical, where the machines do all the work and the operator adjusts dials all day, operators of machine tools such as drill presses, lathes, and milling machines can control the pace of work. There are a great many manual operations on machine tools, such as moving the cutting tool or drill into position to meet the piece of metal, setting the speed and feed of the machine to satisfy the specifications for the particular job, and changing parts of the machine itself as needed.

In the 1950s most automobile, aircraft, and appliance parts were manufactured by machine tools. At Worthington, we made generators, all kinds of pumps, meters, and motors. There were 2000 workers in the plant, many of them operators of machine tools. On the main floor of the plant, large equipment was made by huge horizontal and vertical lathes, a machine called a boring mill, which is literally a very large lathe, huge drill presses, and milling machines. The machines moved so excruciatingly slowly that operators sometimes sat for an eight-hour shift watching the machine cut a single piece. The work was not physically exhausting, but incredibly boring because the operator had to keep his attention riveted to the machine, make sure it was properly lubricated with a milky white solution of oil and other ingredients, and keep the waste material from interfering with the cutting. Each finished piece of metal was very expensive because it took a great deal of time to complete a single operation on it, so the company was as much concerned with quality as with production.

I worked upstairs in the balcony of the plant, so-called because we could look down to the floor below and see everything that was going on. Upstairs there were no cranes or big machines. We worked on the smaller parts: fittings, plates, small valves, and flanges. Here, production came first and the method of wage payment was piecework. The company measured our work in units of time. Each operation was given a time-value. The sum of the values assigned to a specific part constituted the rate for the job. For example, if our rate card called for one minute for facing, one minute to turn the circumference, 30 seconds for rounding out the edges, and one minute for drilling, the job would take 3 minutes and 30 seconds. In order to make our straight-time hourly wage we would have to produce approximately 17 pieces an hour. Theoretically, if we produced 34 pieces we could earn twice our straight-time earnings, but the job was supposed to be timed so a good operator could make about one and one half times his base rate. The central issues in the shop therefore were only secondarily the question of "time wages." Most of the workers' energies were devoted to fighting with management over piece rates. We were always careful not to "turn in" more than 150 percent every day, even if we produced more. We "banked" the remainder, keeping it aside for days when everything went wrong; when for some reason we couldn't sharpen our tools properly; when the clerk in the tool crib, where all parts for the machine itself were stored, did not have the proper-sized drill and we had to wait; or when we were given a job with a particularly difficult setup, that is, one that required a great deal of precision. Since many of the machines were old, a "tight" job calling for close tolerances went more slowly because of the need to check measurements and make adjustments after every few pieces.

The piecework system forced us to seek jobs that were less interesting, complicated, and varied. Many setups were awarded piecework values far below the actual time required to complete them. The company's argument for assigning them low value was that many were simple: the worker could make up time lost in difficult setups by "making out" on production. The most senior men and the favorites were often awarded the "long run" jobs which required fewer changeovers and less precision. After learning how to set up and operate our machines, we younger workers got to do the most precise, and, as it turned out, lower-paying jobs. I didn't mind the work, but there were many weeks I went home with little more than my base pay, which was 50 cents an hour lower than the gross pay of workers in auto plants or aircraft factories. Since I was not one of the favorites of the foreman who handed out the work I kept getting stuck with the short-run jobs carrying tolerances of less than .001 of an inch. The turret lathe to which I was assigned was always going "off" and I could never manage to get production on it.

Appeals to the steward in the department for equal distribution of the long-run jobs fell on deaf ears. He kept reminding me and some of the other younger workers that our turn for the "gravy" jobs would come some day. We just had to be patient. The older, more senior workers rarely did work requiring close tolerances except when the company was obliged to establish a rate on a new job. Then they chose an expert older worker to perform the job for rate-setting purposes, even though the contract required that the job be timed with an "average worker." The president of the local was a young, sharp-tongued Pennsylvanian who would later rise within the Steelworkers' hierarchy. I soon learned that his options as a leader of the local were severely limited by the character of its membership. A large number of workers were older and were seeking better insurance and pension benefits rather than wage increases, which only marginally affected their income. About six months after I started working there, the union held a meeting reporting a contract settlement. The two-year agreement provided only a one-cent an hour increase in the first year and a nickel in the second year, but made substantial improvements in health insurance and the pension plan.

During these years, the unions were beginning to make a sharp turn in collective bargaining goals. The strike movements of the years immediately following the Second World War were predicated on the expectation that relatively high levels of employment would make possible strike victories for wage demands. These demands were necessary to overcome the inflationary tendency of the economy and the deferred wage increases of the war years. By 1949 most unions in the mass production industries which were almost completely organized had won three major annual increases that, in some instances, approached 50 percent of the 1945 wage level.

During the Second World War workers' savings had accumulated because of the constriction of spending outlets since much of the production of auto factories and appliance makers was diverted to munitions. In the first years after the war, returning veterans and those who had remained at work wielded their pent-up buying power with a vengeance. The enormous demand for housing could not be met by home builders, and the automobile and appliance corporations had no difficulties finding markets for their goods. The expected economic downturn resulting from reconversion problems never materialized as European countries created new outlets for American commodities as well as investment capital. All over the United States, construction was being rushed on new one- and two-family frame houses clustered together on erstwhile suburban farm land which had been abandoned to the weeds during the twenties and thirties. Everybody bought cars since the new growth in suburban housing far outpaced the expansion of mass transportation. And the larger families being spawned by returning veterans were attracted to the new gadgets that promised "less work for mother" advertised in washing machine, radio, and vacuum cleaner commercials on TV.

Economic activity began to slow down in 1949. Some of the industries that had led the expansion, such as steel and machine tools, found that production capacity had been overexpanded. Soon the buying of consumer goods began to decline and the unemployment rolls got larger. The first postwar recession tempered labor's wage drive. But there were other equally important developments which signaled a shift of union contract goals.

The unexpected election of President Harry Truman to a full term of office in 1948 had given union politicos some hope that the 81st Congress would enact the first new wave of major social legislation since Franklin Roosevelt's initial administration. Previously industrial unions had concentrated on two major objectives: gaining the right to bargain with employers over wages, hours, and working conditions and actually winning some battles to bring wages up. The first really solid wage increases since the rise of industrial unionism in the 1930s had been won after the war, even if it meant letting the bigger corporations transfer the cost of those increases to consumers. Now the recession combined with the factor of the advancing age of many veterans of the early union organizing drives helped to turn the CIO's attention away from what could be won from the employer to governmental legislation. A major campaign was launched to increase social security benefits and win gains in a new field—national health insurance. As the new Congress opened, among the early measures put into the hopper was the Wagner-Murray-Dingell bill to provide national health insurance. For many labor leaders, a universal health plan was the missing link in the achievement of a welfare state in America. The CIO threw its considerable lobbying machine into the battle to support the bill, and the issue became a central theme of the 81st Congress.

From the beginning, the proposal met with fierce opposition from the American Medical Association, which led the fight against it together with such groups as the National Association of Manufacturers. The idea that all Americans were entitled to health care regardless of their ability to pay was a clear case of "creeping socialism" according to the Medical Association. The strength of the American medical system was its voluntaristic nature—particularly the confidential relationship between doctor and patient. The state should not interfere with such private matters, ran the AMA argument.

The bill's sponsors and the CIO were willing to compromise as much as possible to convince Congress to accept the principle of public health insurance. The bill was not "socialized medicine" as the opponents charged. Doctors would not be forced to subordinate themselves to the government or any other public body. Medical fees would simply be regulated by the government, which would agree to pay for services in behalf of the citizenry.

The campaign failed to convince the Democratic Congress for the same reasons that have haunted the liberal advocates of social welfare since 1938. The Congress is normally controlled by conservatives, regardless of who sits in the White House. The mean trick of American history has been that the House of Representatives has become more resistant than the Senate to even the incremental change proposed by liberals. The framers of the Constitution established a bicameral legislature as a check on the wild-eyed, radical dirt farmers who had composed the membership of the lower chamber in the late eighteenth century. The upper chamber was naturally more conservative since it had been elected by state legislatures. Thus the "third party" in the House, the coalition of Southern Democrats and Northern Republicans, exercised its majority and succeeded in burying the measure for a decade. In 1957, the principle of publicly supported health care was revived when Representative Forand of Rhode Island introduced a bill to tie medical care for the aged to social security. It was finally passed in modified form in the mid-sixties, when America's concern for poverty was at its zenith. Organized labor's dream of national health insurance for all remained as an item on its agenda into the 1970s, but no longer at the head of the list. The recent bills introduced by prolabor congressmen are even less far-reaching than the Wagner Bill of the 1940s.

Yet the seeds of defeat for labor's social program were sown long before the issues were joined in legislative combat. Much of the trouble stemmed from tendencies within the unions themselves. Foremost among these was the traditional AFL principle of voluntarism, according to which unions should not seek support from the government on issues properly belonging within the purview of the collective bargaining relationship. Old Sam

Gompers, the AFL president, fearing government interference in the trade unions, had long been an opponent of Socialist efforts to enlarge the role of the state in the industrial sphere. Consequently, many AFL unions had made provisions themselves for members' needs in health, unemployment, pension and burial benefits, and had even opposed New Deal efforts to extend coverage for unemployment insurance to all workers. But other unions, such as the Amalgamated Clothing Workers, even though forced to make provision for members' welfare needs within the framework of the bargaining relationship, were less enamored of this arrangement because it cut down funds available for wage increases in a highly competitive, labor-intensive industry like the needle trades. Most industrial unionists were eager for the enlargement of the state's role in social welfare, but the craft union leaders of the AFL were less enthusiastic. Many of them, notably the Building Trades and the Teamsters, had flourishing health plans of their own, financed by employer contributions. From their point of view, union or joint management of elaborate welfare programs served several valuable purposes. The welfare program became an adhesive for members' loyalty to the existing union leadership, which usually controlled the vital pension and health policies within the local or district union. Moreover, welfare plans were used by the leadership as a club to curb members' resistance to union policies.

Apart from anti-statist considerations that, after Gompers, had receded from AFL rhetoric, the craft unions were unwilling to surrender an aspect of union affairs which enhanced their political and economic power. Their support for significant improvements in social welfare through legislation took a back seat to the use of bargaining power to strengthen the existing welfare structure within the industry. Since nearly all union members had occasion to require the services of the health plan, pension benefits, or the increasingly common cut-rate eyeglass, dental, drug, and other retail goods sold either by union outlets directly or through special arrangements with retail stores, the function of the union in the lives of its membership extended far beyond the shop floor. Many members who had given up hope that the union would defend them on the job remained loyal to the union leadership because of the growing importance of these ancillary services.

Without the weight of the AFL, the CIO legislative program was doomed in the 81st Congress of 1948–50. Moreover, the antiunion atmosphere that had been generated in reaction to the general strikes of 1946 had by no means abated. On the contrary, it was building up toward new efforts to enact antilabor legislation. One of the provisions of the Taft-Hartley Act (the conservative manifesto enacted in the previous session of Congress in 1947), had been the leave given to the states to enact laws which prohibited the union shop from being incorporated into labor agreements. Every Southern state seized the opportunity to assure employers that it was prepared to cooperate with them to attract industry to its domain. The CIO Southern organizing drive, which had foundered in the late forties, was to suffer almost complete disintegration during the following decade. After 1948 the trade unions found themselves on the defensive. Neither the swift expulsions of the CIO's Stalinist wing, nor the election of a Democratic President was sufficient to stem the antiunion tide.

After 1949 union leaders responded to the conservative mood and the adverse economic conditions of the country by concentrating their political action on softening the blows of the antiunion forces in Congress and adopting their collective bargaining strategy to the pursuit of health benefits, pensions, and other "fringes" rather than concentrating on money wage increases. The lead in this direction was taken by the Miners. In 1950, the union welcomed the mechanization of the mines by the large operators in return for the most advanced labor-run health program in American history. Instead of relying on "clinics," like those which had been established by the needle trades unions, or simply purchasing insurance benefits from such agencies as the Blue Cross or the life insurance companies, the Miners negotiated the establishment of hospitals providing comprehensive care for union members and their families. These hospitals were financed in lieu of wages directly out of the miners' own production. At the time, the disastrous consequences of this agreement were not evident. But the principle upon which it had been made had wide implications for the future course of union bargaining. For the first time since the rise of the CIO a major industrial union was willing to transfer increases normally incorporated directly into the pay envelope to social benefits. To be sure, the Miners union secured a substantial wage increase, but the most significant feature of the contract was its health provisions.

Large corporations in mass production industries were amenable to trade union demands for substantial fringe benefit packages as part of the labor agreement. But, in contrast to the competitive industries where the union was able to dominate the bargaining process against the huge number of small employers and thus win agreement for the practice of union-run welfare plans, the larger corporations insisted that control of the fringe benefits remain in their hands. For the most part, they got their way.

Fringe benefits are awarded in lieu of wages, so union bargainers normally calculate their value in terms of percentages of the hourly wage. But this method of accounting becomes extremely tricky when some of the following factors are considered: Many contracts specify the amount of monthly pension per the number of years of service but do not specify how much the employer must contribute for pensions. In industries such as auto, where the labor force is predominantly young and the turnover is great, either the insurance company or the employer reaps enormous advantages in employer controlled pension plans. Relatively few workers will actually benefit from the "30 and Out" provisions of the Auto Workers' contract with the large companies which permits a worker to retire at any age after thirty years of service with full pension. The turnover rate on automobile assembly lines is more than 5 percent annually. In thirty years 150 percent of the labor force will be gone. The fact that the average age of workers on these lines has been falling steadily means that the employers contribution for pensions is correspondingly reduced, but the value of the benefit is calculated by negotiators as a fixed percentage of straight-time hourly earnings for all workers, not just those actually likely to retire. Unless the pension plan provides for vesting rights, that is, unless workers are able to withdraw funds that have been contributed by employers or themselves, those workers who have given up wage increases may never benefit from the program. Instead, the funds accumulate interest derived from investments over which the workers have no control.

Even in industries where the union does control the welfare plan, workers are required to work in the industry for a certain number of years before they are entitled to pension benefits. In the women's garment industry, for example, workers must have twenty years of *continuous* service before they are eligible. Workers who accumulate less than the minimum number of years are simply refused pension benefits, or, if their work is interrupted, must go beyond the twenty years in order to qualify again. From the employer's point of view, fringe benefits helped cut down turnover among skilled workers and others considered central to production and maintenance. Pension benefits tempered militancy among older workers nearing retirement age or possessing long seniority in the company, especially in mass production industries where benefits are not transferable from employer to employer or between industries.

Some pension funds have been badly invested. During periods of stock market decline, some plans have run into serious financial difficulties and have been unable to meet their contractual obligations to retirees. Other plans have underestimated the number of workers reaching retirement and making claims on the fund and have found it necessary to reduce monthly payments to retirees or face bankruptcy.

Rising costs of health benefits administered by private insurance companies or nonprofit health plans have meant that in order to hold costs down some bargaining agreements have actually reduced coverage under these plans. In some cases, workers have been asked to contribute additional funds from their wages in order to receive the same amount of coverage formerly paid by the employer. In recent years, union interest in national health insurance has been once more evident because the cost of health care is simply too great for self-financed or privately administered programs to bear.

On the whole, fringe benefits have never cost the employer as much as union bargainers have represented to the membership. The key word employed by union negotiators has been "package increase," which is the amalgam of wages and other benefits. During the 1950s and 1960s these package increases, reported in the trade union and public press as fairly substantial figures, were actually worth less to the worker at the machine than claimed and workers in many industries purchased them at a cost to money wages. Although the value of the fringe benefits was often calculated as if all workers were immediate beneficiaries, in plants where younger workers (with younger immediate families) predominated, there was much less use of hospitals, medicines, medical care in doctors' offices and surgical services than in industries where older workers predominated, like sections of the needle trades in New York or the building trades.

The proliferation of benefit plans not only reduced union enthusiasm for campaigns to enact substantial new social welfare legislation, particularly health insurance, but, in the case of the pension plans, had a negative impact on the fight for improvement of social security. Unions capable of exacting relatively high retirement benefits from employers were able to convince members that social security *and* employer-paid pensions would provide adequate funds. It was not until the organization of the National Council for Senior Citizens and the Golden Ring clubs— groups of retirees who found that inflation rendered their social security and meager union retirement benefits economically inadequate to pay for health care—that the battle for medical care under social security was taken up in earnest by a constituency capable of conducting such a struggle. There is no doubt that the AFL-CIO played an important role in making legislative victories such as medicare for the aged possible in the early 1960s, but the impetus really came from outside the labor movement.

In the 1950s many of the younger workers in the plants opposed the new trend in collective bargaining. They were interested in pressing the fight for higher wages and for improvement of their working conditions. But many of the industrial unions which had previously been willing to conduct mass strikes around these issues were now dominated by skilled workers and others with high seniority. Union meetings were sparsely attended, except at contract time, and those among the rank and file who remained active were invariably the older or more skilled workers. With few exceptions, they were preponderant in union affairs in the better paid industries. Even in the auto assembly plants the median age of workers in jobs usually filled by young men began to rise.

But 1950 was the heyday of the drive for fringe benefits. In that same year, the United Auto Workers signed a five-year agreement with the large automobile companies providing for increases in health and pension benefits as well as wage increases, tied, in part, to the cost of living. The union pioneered in the concept that workers should not lose "real" wages when prices of consumer goods went up: moreover, they should be rewarded for increased productivity. The famous escalator clause and the "annual improvement factor" were UAW's price for the long-term strike freedom that followed years of mass strikes in the industry. The five-year contract marked the explicit recognition by the union that the employer drive for more productivity was an essential ingredient in preserving the high wages of its membership, and was a response as well to the new threat of depression hovering over the American economy. The UAW was saying, "We'll go along with more production, but we want to share in that productivity."

For years, workers had conducted militant struggles inside the plant and on the picket line to limit management's right to increase production without expanding the labor force. Speedup had been one of the perennial issues of industrial workers. The fight against it was often the only means workers possessed to protest management's authority. It was symbolic of the rejection of the concept of management prerogatives. When the unions began to link wage increases to productivity improvements it was a sign that the struggle for workers' control—often conducted in the disguised form of resistance to work norms imposed by the company from above rather than negotiated on the shop floor between workers and department foremen directly—was being abandoned. Auto workers, steel workers, and others in many industries vigorously opposed the substitution of long-term contracts for one-year agreements, the substitution of pension plans for wage increases, and the acceptance of productivity increase. Rank-and-file rejections of contracts negotiated for them by union officials became more common in the 1950s than in previous decades, although they did not reach floodtide proportions for another ten years when young workers poured into the shops during the Vietnam boom, constituting a critical mass sufficiently great to force some unions to give militant voice to their demands. The sixties told a different tale than the fifties; the "package deal" over the bargaining table was exposed at membership meetings where the youth wanted to know "how much money," not "how many fringes."

The 1950–55 period was the most turbulent in the auto industry since the sit-down strikes of the mid-thirties. The wildcat movement in GM assembly plants reached epidemic proportions during these years, as the companies interpreted their new rights under the contract to mean that the pace of the assembly line could be increased by as much as 20 percent. At the Buick-Oldsmobile-Pontiac division in Linden, New Jersey, where a relative of mine was employed, the line speed was pushed from 45–50 cars an hour to 60 in 1955. On some days the pace inched up to 63 or 64 cars. Workers reacted by walking off the job often that year, especially in the summer. From this vantage point—on the assembly line—the union experiment in new bargaining tools such as arbitration to substitute for the strike weapon was a miserable failure. Workers had no intention of permitting a third-party umpire to decide whether the line was too fast. Equally significant, the arbitration phase of the grievance procedure was the final step after a long series of preliminary attempts to settle grievances.

In Harrison, New Jersey, where 1500 workers were employed by the Hyatt Roller Bearing Division of GM, the number of "major" unsettled grievances awaiting arbitration was never less than 100, and workers were forced to engage in many "job actions" or "quickie" strikes to deal with in-plant problems as it became evident that the grievance procedure was not designed to deal with issues, but instead delayed action on them. But Harrison was not unique. The number of unsettled grievances mounted throughout the country in the fifties.

By 1955, the turmoil in the auto shops was so widespread that the next agreement abandoned the five-year no-strike formula and permitted walkouts over changes in the work pace and health and safety grievances. The union was forced to come down from its devotion to long-term contracts as well. The five-year agreement had become intolerable after it was evident that the long-awaited depression was not forthcoming, even if workers did experience frequent economic difficulties over the decade.

In late 1954, I decided that the individual piecework system was not for me. Jobs were not easy to find, as the end of the Korean War brought with it a now-familiar round of layoffs in defense-related industries, especially those such as Curtiss-Wright, whose product was directly dependent on the air war in Asia. But the fact that I had a family made me determined to find work that paid more money. I was only twenty-one years old and knew that I could get another job even in the middle of the recession because I had a good employment record and more industrial experience than a lot of men my age. My cousin urged me to go out to GM in Linden, where I worked for several months in the body shop. At that time young people entered the plant and left in droves after a few days, a few weeks, or a few months because the work pace was intolerably fast and the job itself boring and repetitive. I was among those who lasted a couple of months; then I found the job I was to stay with for four more years before entering full-time union work.

The new job was with the Driver-Harris company in Harrison, a medium-sized manufacturer of steel-chromium and nickel alloy metals for the electrical industry. The plant transformed the ingot into wire, sheet, rods, and some other structural shapes. I jumped at the chance to get off machine or assembly work, even if I would have to start at the lowest-grade job—as a laborer. The union representative assured me that everybody started there in the steel mills since, with the exception of the crafts that had a separate seniority list, all other jobs were open to bidding based on seniority.

Sure enough, a few weeks after I started working in the plant, a job for a wire drawer was posted on the bulletin board, and I got it. Instead of being paid by the piece, workers in this department of the plant received a bonus for work performed above a specified number of pounds. Some workers were faster than others and made more money, but there was no comparison between this kind of work and work where you were organized by the machine or the assembly line organized you. Workers helped one another when the wire was stuck in the die, or when it was tangled on the spools. We had a department steward who fought with us for "looser rates" on new jobs and the workers were generally younger so they were ready for combat at the slightest provocation from management.

In my four years in this plant, like many other younger workers (except wire drawers, who made very big money on some jobs), I worked on six or seven different jobs. When I left the mill, I knew a lot about the steelmaking process except for the actual conversion of iron ore into steel. Driver-Harris was known throughout the district for its militancy. New local union officers had been elected a few years earlier and had won their spurs with the rank and file by leading a highly successful strike. Unlike the auto assembly plants where the right to transfer from job to job was rarely enforced, no valid bid was ever refused during the time I worked there, even though the contract gave the company the right to question whether a worker had the "qualifications" to perform the job he desired. The union forced the company to train workers who successfully bid on jobs and prevented it from trying to write a provision into the contract limiting the number of moves to one a year. Workers could transfer from job to job twice in one year, which meant that they could hold as many as three jobs in any year.

Much of the work was paid on a straight-time hourly basis, but many of the departments had a group bonus method of wage payment which, I soon learned, was every bit as ruthless as individual piecework.

For a time I worked in the hot mill. There, we heated the ingot to 1700 degrees Farenheit, took it out with tongs, and placed the almost-molten metal in a series of dies which drew it into heavy wire to be drawn down later to closer tolerances. The amount of cooperation required to perform the various operations on the job made the workers in the hot mill a very close-knit crew. We worked in intense heat, under very dangerous conditions, especially when the hot wire began to "dance" wildly out of control and chased the workers all over the shop floor.

In 1957–58 when I worked in the mill I was making close to $4 an hour, thanks to high bonus pay, at a time when most workers in industrial plants considered $2.50 an hour very good wages. The heat and the dangers of the job were so great that we had a 20-minute rest period for every hour of work. During these periods, we had time to talk to one another in the locker rooms, where some of us drank beer, others smoked a cigarette and just lounged. Discussions usually centered upon a few topics: sports, sex, and reports of accidents, which occurred with alarming frequency in the plant. In the year and a half I worked in the mill, I saw several men who failed to get out of the way of a "crazy" snake-dancing wire get a thick piece of it through a leg or in the pelvic area. Some workers received burns of varying degrees of seriousness on their arms or legs from a "pass" made too close to their body. Other workers in the plant were constantly dropping ingots on their feet. Even though we had more free time than most, our crew felt no sense of guilt for the amount of break time we enjoyed. Our working conditions more than offset the few pleasures of the job.

We made our extra money by breaking our necks to produce more pounds of wire than the norm. The disadvantage of the group bonus system was that the newer workers who were less experienced in handling the peripatetic material could get hurt badly, and did, while the more experienced workers pressed for more production and really put the heat on to get the pounds turned out. And nobody could opt out since the interdependence of the operations tied us to our mutual fate. The speed of work in the hot mill was the downfall of nearly all members of the crews. I only suffered minor burns and a badly mangled big toe. Some workers lost fingers, burned parts of their bodies permanently, and were crippled by dropped ingots or cans of wire. After a short time, I realized that the group bonus system was largely responsible for the self-imposed speedup in the department. If the workers had been paid as much money on a straight-time basis, they would still have risked accidents but the rate would have been significantly reduced.

The foreman in the hot mill became a kind of quality control technician, but did not dare to attempt to exercise authority over the men. The role of foreman as a technical assistant and expediter was entirely new to me. In almost all previous jobs, the foreman was a pusher of production. He literally "directed the work forces," putting workers on "hot" jobs, that is, work that had to be produced immediately, recommending discipline for excessive lateness and absenteeism, firing workers who came in drunk or were insubordinate to his orders, and distributing overtime work and good jobs to his favorites. In our department, the foreman was almost invisible and only emerged from his office when something went wrong with a "heat" or with a run of wire. Even then, his job was to call the engineer or the maintenance mechanic to make necessary corrections.

In the hot mill, the foreman would not dare issue an order. He requested the help of the crews and usually received cooperation. I don't think it was a question of good psychology on his part. Since much of our work pace was self-directed, and the job content was well known by all the workers on the crews, his chief responsibility to the company became delivery of production quotas and he depended on our good will.

We had several job actions in the hot mill. Some of them were precipitated by the blistering summer heat, which, combined with the furnace's temperature, gave us a practical idea of what hell was like. The others were mostly expressions of anger when nasty accidents occurred. We would simply take the rest of the day off, leaving one person to make sure that the furnaces remained lit. The workers talked about making the job "time work" instead of bonus to cut down on the dangers, but we always doubted that we could win agreement from the company to retain the high wages.

Even under conditions of severe heat spells and heavy, dirty, and dangerous work, everybody coveted overtime. The workers themselves prevented the foreman from playing favorites with overtime by exacting an agreement for workers' control over overtime assignments. The steward, who worked full time on the furnaces, would meet with the foreman on Thursday to find out if there was to be Saturday work and how many men would be required. Overtime was assigned on a rotating basis. If a worker refused a Saturday, his name would go to the bottom of the list and he would have to wait his turn again. And there were no exceptions, because the rotation list, as well as the assignment list, was posted in the locker room.

Workers accepted overtime as a means of getting out of the "financial hole" of car payments, mortgage payments. Some workers used O/T as savings, extra money for the proverbial "rainy day"; layoffs were no myth in the steel industry, which reacted to the economy like a barometer. In the 1950s workers were moving out to the suburbs in large numbers. They came to work from a 50-mile radius of the shop by car, or, in rare cases, by train. Under these conditions, to term cars "luxuries" was patently absurd.

By 1957, after four years of working in New Jersey plants, I finally knew my way around industry well enough to get active in the union. The United Steelworkers was and still is the largest union in the AFL-CIO. And 1957 was a momentous year of rank-and-file stirrings in the steel industry and in the plant I worked in. Much of the discontent among workers had to do with the structure and administration of the union as well as grievances at the workplace.

After Philip Murray's death in 1952, his right-hand man, David McDonald, had been elevated to the top union post and Walter Reuther, the leader of the United Auto Workers, became CIO president. McDonald was the epitome of the new breed of union leader become business executive. He presented himself to both the union members and to the public as a responsible, efficient trade unionist who was prepared to subordinate the immediate desires of the membership to serve the needs of the country. Espousing the doctrine of "my country right or wrong," McDonald was an ardent advocate of the policy that union members and corporations had identical interests. The strength of American capitalism, particularly its high standard of living, derived from the productivity of its labor force as much as the strength of its "free institutions." Therefore, American workers and American corporations should cooperate with each other in a great effort to preserve America's leadership in the world. While I was in the plant, McDonald went on a grand tour of the steel mills with Benjamin Fairless, the president of U.S. Steel, in order to demonstrate the union's sincerity in seeking labor-management collaboration.

The contrast between McDonald and Reuther was more than a matter of personal ties and political style. Reuther was the last great figure of social unionism in America. A staunch opponent of the Communist Party and others who challenged the Cold War road the unions traveled after 1945, Reuther remained a social reformer who voiced criticisms of the excesses of capitalism. At times, he succeeded in articulating the resentment of the underlying mass of working people against privilege. In the 1960s he even became dubious about the foreign policies he had once espoused. Reuther prided himself on his clean living. In contrast to McDonald and many other union leaders who became enamored of the good life, Reuther comported himself rather modestly. He lived in a modest home and drove an ordinary low-priced car. His Spartan habits of no smoking and drinking had been cultivated in his Socialist youth—one that was infused with a not inconsiderable dose of Calvinism. If the UAW of the postwar era was only slightly more democratic and militant than the Steelworkers, the transformation from its once proud rank-and-file brand of unionism took place almost imperceptibly. When, as a delegate to a state CIO convention, I encountered Reuther, he was giving his familiar tirade against the persistence of "poverty, hunger, and disease" in a country that had attained the pinnacle of material abundance. Compared to the flat prose of my union's tired old men, Reuther's rhetoric sounded like poetry.

Together with industry's leaders, the Steelworkers became strong supporters of federal action to deal with the importation of foreign steel. I remember attending a conference in 1957 in Bethlehem, Pennsylvania, the seat of the district union, and hearing a staff economist from the union's headquarters in Pittsburgh explain the dangers of foreign competition. The union's leadership was arguing that unless we produced more in the shops and reduced the unit labor costs so that the companies could hold down steel prices, we would lose our jobs to the Japanese and other countries where labor costs were much lower. The union had an ambivalent position on import curbs. On the one hand, it opposed tariff walls or quotas as a destructive measure, since at the time America's balance of payments was favorable and it was in the workers' interest to keep the level of exports high. On the other hand, some union members were being laid off because of the substitution of foreign steel. Thus the union's support for productivity increases in the mills was spurred by a desire to avoid becoming an all-out advocate of trade restriction.

In the mid-fifties, all labor was deeply concerned with the specter of automation. Articles began to appear in both labor and daily newspapers warning that the new transfer machines, which were capable of performing a great number of machine operations automatically and were even self-regulating to an extent, were bound to replace human labor in great numbers. In the steel industry the corporations introduced a cold-rolling process that regulated production with a panel board rather than by hand. One board could control five or six cold-rolling mills and was operated by a single worker who literally spent an entire shift pushing buttons and watching from an enclosed booth a process which formerly required two workers on each mill—a highly skilled roller and an assistant.

Unions were holding automation conferences, the most important of which was sponsored by the UAW in 1955. The main thrust of union policy was not opposition to the introduction of technological change in American industry, since unions were devoted to the idea of progress. Instead, union demands centered on "sharing in the fruits" of automation. The most prominent plan for accomplishing equity became the UAW's Guaranteed Annual Wage proposal in the 1955 negotiations. The union declared that the corporations had an obligation to assure an annual income for employees laid off for lack of work or for reasons associated with rising productivity engendered by technological improvements. Rising worker productivity would earn more profits for the corporations, and these profits would more than offset the costs of paying workers displaced by the new machines. Besides, manufacturers needed ever rising levels of consumption to maintain high sales and consequently high profits.

In the next few years unions in the auto, steel, and rubber industries won a modified version of the guaranteed income plan —supplementary unemployment benefits. The SUB program provided income additional to state unemployment benefits to laid-off workers with more than a year of service with the company. SUB was a useful benefit, but it hardly constituted an answer to the problem of automation and its permanent impact on employment.

The Steelworkers contract had provided another protection against both the unilateral introduction of labor-saving machinery and the adoption of new methods of production which would result in increased labor for workers. Section 2B of the national agreements provided that no new methods could be introduced without prior consultation with the union. In the late fifties, the effort to maintain a measure of control against corporation attempts to violate this protection was to constitute the main thrust of the steelworkers struggles.

But despite the contract he had helped negotiate, McDonald appeared to swallow the corporation line on productivity hook, line, and sinker. His ostentatious tour with Fairless, his cavorting in nightclubs and among movie stars and the very rich, angered many shopworkers. In the context of these examples of class unconsciousness, combined with the consequent boldness of the companies in ignoring their obligations under the union contract, the time was ripe for a challenge to the national union leadership.

In 1957, Joseph Maloney, the director of the important Buffalo district, declared his candidacy for vice president against a key operative of the McDonald machine, Howard Hague, the quintessential bureaucrat of the organization. This was the first internal challenge to the leadership since the founding of the union in 1942. Characteristically, it came from a member of the palace guard, supported by a significant minority of fellow district directors and presidents of large locals. The contest was the first in a series of upheavals that were to lead to McDonald's downfall less than a decade later.

The contest was instructive as a prototype of the kind of intraunion combat which swept the industrial unions in the subsequent years. Like many others who led CIO unions in the 1950s, including Murray himself, McDonald had been brought into power through appointment by a reigning monarch. Both he and Hague were administrative types lacking the flair for the rough-and-tumble of rank-and-file activity and union political struggle. In its organizational style, the Steelworkers Union had come to bear a close resemblance to the old AFL. Its blatant class collaboration rhetoric rankled many in the ranks. Maloney, who later emulated his adversaries, was the first to take his campaign directly to the locals. Although defeated, he stirred the pot sufficiently to make possible a more genuine challenge from a rank-and-file movement two years later.

Typically, Hague's victory was won by the union apparatus rather than his own appeal. Maloney supporters, at the local union level were offered union staff jobs as an inducement to support the administration candidate; staff members in pro-McDonald districts were ordered to campaign among the locals in behalf of Hague or risk losing their jobs; some of Maloney's rank-and-file supporters who resisted the blandishments of the incumbents were fired from the plants or made victims of physical attacks. These techniques of union politics were scorned by union militants who had similar experiences during AFL attempts to thwart the rise of industrial unions in the 1930s. But the stakes of power were too high to be let go without a fight.

The next challenge was more direct: the president of a Pittsburgh area local declared his candidacy to replace McDonald himself. Again, the issues were the separation of the administration from the needs of the membership, especially on the problems of speedup and the consequent dangers to life and limb. Pat Rarick was not a clear alternative to McDonald on all matters. His social attitudes prefigured the celebrated blue-collar radical rightism of the late 1960s and early 1970s. Yet, like Maloney, he symbolized the growing discontent among the Steelworkers membership with the deterioration of working conditions in the shops and the apparent helplessness (or refusal) of the union leadership to deal with their problems.

These were lean years for steelworkers. The relatively high employment levels of the early 1950s were apparently over. In 1957–58 companies began to shut down older plants and, instead of rebuilding them along more modern lines, chose the path of decentralization by moving to other regions of the country. Pittsburgh was losing its position as the steelmaking center of the nation and was being replaced by the Chicago-Gary area. Maloney's own district was in the throes of decline, and the Ohio Valley was entering a permanent state of crisis as the mills laid off thousands, many of whom were never rehired even during the boom years after the Vietnam War began.

Rarick himself suffered physical beatings at the hands of union goons, but his showing was extremely impressive. Rarick forces claimed that the administration victory was accomplished only by allowing pensioners to vote. According to the challenger, his vote was greater than McDonald's among workers in the basic steel mills. McDonald actually lost in some Pittsburgh and Chicago area districts, and in parts of the Ohio Valley. His strength was based in areas where the union represented workers in metal fabricating plants, or in steelmaking plants far from the major centers. Since workers in the basic steel sectors of the industry only represented about 60 percent of the membership of the union, McDonald's weakness among these workers was not necessarily sufficient to defeat him. On the other hand, the opposition suspected widespread fraud in the elections, a charge never proven.

When McDonald was finally toppled, it was at the hands of his own secretary-treasurer, I. W. Abel, a man with more credentials among the rank-and-file. As it turned out, Abel simply gave a more credible veneer to the union buraucracy, but provided no more sensitive leadership. In the last analysis, it was the membership that was obliged to take matters into its own hands to defend its hard-won conditions.

My initiation into the intricacies of the class struggle came in 1957. Although not part of the basic steel national agreement, the company I worked for followed its wage and benefits pattern. Our contract was modeled after the national agreement with Big Steel since many of the plants' operations were parallel. Union clearance for new work methods was a provision of the contract, and the shop committee had so far resisted labor-saving machines which promised nothing but unemployment to our members or speedup. We had a few cold-rolling panel boards already, but the company was pressing for more concessions. One day, over union objections, the company brought in a machine which would replace thirty-three men with five. The riggers, skilled craftsmen responsible for installing equipment, refused to obey a direct order to do the work. When the company demanded that work be done on penalty of discharge, they walked off the job, followed by the whole maintenance crew and the workers in the affected department. Within ten minutes the whole shop was on the street. The company immediately contacted union officials to get the plant back to work, reminding them of the no-strike clause in the union contract. The local union officers refused to comply with the company's order and were suspended from their jobs. A mass meeting was called. About 95 percent of the workers in the plant jammed into the tiny hall adjacent to the union office above a neighborhood bar. Speaking to the overflow crowd, the international union representative from the district office praised the solidarity of the membership but urged them to return to work pending negotiations with the company on the suspensions and the larger issue of mechanization.

The rep's speech was relatively effective because he did not attack the wildcat strike. Instead, he exuded confidence and support while reminding the workers of the illegality of their behavior. Even if the company had acted arbitrarily, the proper use of the grievance machinery would result in "complete victory for our side." Workers took the floor to ask questions of the representative. Should the riggers install the equipment? After all, that was the real issue. How could we go back to work unless we had the company's agreement to delay implementing their intention to bring in the disputed machine? The representative sputtered, "Ah, well the contract says we have to do the work under protest until the arbitrator renders his decision."

I had recently been elected department steward and delegate to the CIO council in the area, but was still fairly unknown in the shop. By this time, despite my trembling knees, I felt the blood rush to my neck in anger. "Mr. Chairman," I began slowly, rising unsteadily to my feet, "if the riggers do the job, the company's got us by the balls. You know goddamn well that we'll never get that machine out of there—and they'll never respect us again. Besides," by this time my voice was as high-pitched as a soprano and getting louder by the second, "besides, how can we go back in unless they reinstate our officers?" I lost my fear and reminded my fellow workers of the retreats we had already made on the question of speedup and other plant issues. As a member of the stewards council I was aware of the tales of woe recited with appalling regularity by the representative concerning the fate of our grievances. They were piling up and the company was stalling. In the past few months it had been nearly impossible to settle any problems on the shop floor. The accident rate was rising and the hot mill was pulling more "quickies" than ever in protest against the speedup. Almost shouting, I ended with a plea to reject the representative's position and to stay out until we got satisfaction. A cacophony of applause greeted my speech and a motion was made to stay out; it passed almost unanimously. A committee was appointed to escort the representative out of the hall. We settled down for a long siege.

The strike lasted for nearly six weeks. The first weeks were high-spirited and there was a great deal of joking on the picket line and in the now-crowded bars, punctuated with frequent meetings where the shop committee reported the results of negotiations with the company over the two issues. The company was holding out on principle. It insisted on the right to manage the plant free of interference from the workers, the union, or anyone else. At the end of the first week, we all picked up paychecks from the previous week's work, so the mood was still pretty militant.

By the end of the third week some workers became a little tense. Since we had pulled a walkout unauthorized by the union, we were not entitled to strike benefits. Even though the $25 a week granted by the union was not sufficient to keep anybody going, it was important symbolically as a sign of union support. The local community services committee, of which I became a member, was fairly effective in convincing merchants to skip TV or car payments for a month until the end of the strike. The local gave out a few food baskets and made mortgage and rent payments for some who really needed help, but its resources were limited since the international union took the bulk of the dues as *per capita* tax, and left it a smaller share. Black workers, most of whom worked in the lower labor grades or in the foundry, took home less money than many others in the plant and made many requests for assistance from the local. Within a few weeks the local was broke.

Fights began to break out in the local bars. One day I walked into a bar and was approached by a heavy-set young worker whom I knew from the hot mill. He had been drinking quite a bit and walked toward me in a slow weave. "It's your fault, you dirty Jew bastard," he whispered. Then his hand reached out and cracked me across the face. I stood there, stinging from the blow. I tried to fight back my own rage, because in the back of my mind I understood his predicament. He was getting a lot of pressure from home and probably had hit me to release his own fears. I decided to go to the bar. But he shoved me against a chair and my fury took over. When the other workers broke up the fight we were both bleeding from the face. Later I realized that the anti-Semitic remark was the real source of my almost uncontrollable anger, not his blow.

I had encountered Jew-baiting many times in the plants, especially since moving to New Jersey. Most of the anti-Semitism took the form of remarks like "What is a Jew doing working in the shop?" Many workers thought that all Jews had money and owned businesses, rather than having to work in them. Some workers assumed that I could not be a smart Jew if I worked with my hands. They acknowledged that some Jews were proletarian but had to be somewhat mentally defective to stay there. Others were literally in awe of me because they bought the myth that all Jews who were not rich were at least smart. I was often called on to assume responsibilities in the local because of my presumed radically inherited intelligence. The most curious form of anti-Semitism was the refusal of some workers who liked me or respected my shop floor militancy to believe that I was a Jew. No Jew could be trusted; they learned to trust me; therefore I was, at most, half-Jewish or kidding them.

I had been raised in an assimilated atmosphere. My relationship to religious Judaism was most casual, especially because I did not even have a bar mitzvah and was brought up in a neighborhood where the Jewish population was equaled by Italians and Irish and there was little distinction between our class positions to generate conflict. For this reason, my encounters with Jew-baiting were all the more startling. Even more surprising than having to suffer abuse was my readiness to deal with it by direct action. My sense of identification with Jews was so weak that I was as surprised at how I reacted as I was at having been singled out.

The fights and the general irritability were symptoms that workers were getting nervous about the chances for victory, and were buckling under the pressure of unpaid bills and family tensions. In our plant, the company did not go so far as to promote a back-to-work movement, but it did offer the union an out to settle the strike. In return for reinstatement of the suspended union officers, it proposed to submit the disputed machine installation issue to arbitration, provided the riggers agreed to install the machine provisionally. Meanwhile, the company promised not to lay off any workers until the ruling of the arbitrator. The union officers announced the proposal at a mass meeting and urged us to go back to work.

Many workers realized that the issue which had prompted the strike was not only left unresolved, but was likely to be lost in the long run. The company had fired the union officers to divert our attention from the main dispute and it was asking for a trade-off. A minority of us opposed the recommendation of the local officers, but it was clear that most workers were tired and had no confidence of ultimate victory, unless the battle was joined on a much larger scale than a single plant. Two years later, in 1959, workers in the whole industry went on strike for 116 days to protect the crucial section of the agreement prohibiting unilateral company changes in work methods. Even though the union sanctioned the national walkout, the struggle had been seething for many years; it was conducted as much against the union's policy of cooperation with management to raise productivity as it was against management itself. The long steel strike belied the beliefs of many that workers had become totally immersed in the ethic of consumption and would only strike to expand their purchasing power, but were uninterested in controlling production. For the first time since the war, they had manned picket lines on a grand scale over an issue which transcended narrow wage struggles. Steelworkers were fighting against the proliferation of accidents in the wake of speedup, against the increased pressure by steel corporations for more production, and for the right to have a voice in determining the pace of technological changes that were nearly always intended as labor-saving and profit-making innovations. The unexpected solidarity among the workers had been anticipated in thousands of job actions and wildcat strikes similar to those I had experienced in the years immediately preceding the national walkout. The apparent invulnerability of the union hierarchy had been shaken by the mounting movement to replace it. In short, the two-decade love affair between Big Steel and the union was shattered and for an instant it looked as if the rank-and-file steel workers were forging their own destiny.

The workers' victory proved to be pyrrhic, in historical perspective. Conditions in the mills were no better after the strike. On the one hand, workers were obliged to resist persistent company efforts to change work methods or to move plants away from areas of rank-and-file militancy. On the other hand, the changing of the union guard only produced temporary respite from the blatant class collaboration policies of the McDonald regime. In the wake of foreign competition that was to become a major issue within the industry in the late 1960s, the union leaders once again took to urging members to increase their productivity or risk unemployment. History was bound to repeat itself: the first time as tragedy, the second as farce.

The impact of the 1950s upon the working class was experienced as profoundly by the worker in the realm of his private life as at the workplace. The most dramatic changes had to do with the shape of the cities. The old ethnic minorities that had dominated the populations of New York, Chicago, Detroit, and Newark were dying out or moving to the suburbs in pursuit of decent housing, racial homogeneity and, probably most important of all, jobs. Even when the old people stayed in the city, their children did not remain. First-generation Americans whose parents were of Eastern and Southern European origins were determined to escape the caste markings of ethnic ghettoes. Besides, there was no way to house large families in the city and their income did not permit traveling fifty miles to the new suburban industrial plants every day.

The term "suburban mass transit" has been until this day a cruel play on words. Since the Eisenhower administration, the only "social expenditure" enjoying consistent bipartisan political support has been the federal highway program. At the President's urging, Congress appropriated $100 billion for this program in the 1950s, securing the future of the automobile as the major form of passenger transportation in this country, and helping over-the-road truck transportation make deep inroads into rail transport. There was little chance after that initiative for substantial improvements in rail transportation, the construction of new regional mass transit systems, or even the expansion of intercounty bus systems.

Similarly the actions of the postwar congresses granting loan insurance for the purchase of dwellings to veterans, and subsequently to the general public, at the expense of public housing effectively made private-home construction the major tool for dealing with the chronic shortages of working class housing. Moreover, the 1949 Housing Act introduced the idea of federal assistance for private development of the center cities, an approach to urban renewal vigorously pushed by the General Electric Company, large banks, and insurance companies. The center cities were not to be the site of housing redevelopment for working class people. Even workers with steady jobs simply could not find decent, moderate-rental urban housing.

These political and economic decisions effectively determined the pattern of industrial and residential development for the next generation. The white working class was fated for dispersal; the center cities would be reserved for the very poor and the relatively affluent. In the circumstances, durable goods purchases—cars, washing machines, one-family houses—began to absorb an increasing proportion of workers' income and had an enormous impact on work patterns.

In the place of the white working class came the Southern Blacks. In Newark within the decade, the population changed decisively as three of the five wards of the city either had Black majorities or substantial minorities that, within a few years, would outnumber the whites. At the same time, Newark was irrevocably being transformed from a major industrial city boasting substantial electrical manufacturing, packinghouse, metalworking, and light industries of many kinds, to a commercial center for banks and insurance companies and the army of professionals and white-collar workers who depended upon them. There was little large-scale manufacturing industry remaining in the city at the beginning of the 1960s. Newark had been one of the more important garment producers in New Jersey, but did little independent manufacturing. Most of its work was controlled from New York, and when the New York market was slow, Newark followed suit.

The banks and insurance companies had always been important in the city. As the large manufacturers such as GE and Westinghouse moved out, the utilities together with such giants as Prudential and the major commercial banks turned their attention to rebuilding the badly deteriorated downtown areas and preserving their own investments in it. The original plans for Newark, drafted in the late 1950s, provided for a totally refurbished core city, utilizing federal urban renewal funds to clear the central business district and the surrounding fringes, populated now by Blacks, poor residents, and a more transient group of white Southerners seeking employment in the already depleted manufacturing sector. The renewal of the downtown district would consist in erecting several plazas of huge office buildings as well as many individual buildings. The business periphery that was dominated by dilapidated residential buildings and small manufacturing and service plants would be torn down to make room for large institutional development, particularly a new medical center, an urban center for the State University, and sufficient parking facilities to accommodate workers and shoppers from the suburbs.

Major obstacles stood in the way of this grand plan. First, the city commission form of government was not progressive enough to provide efficient administrative assistance for its implementation. Commissioners dominated city government, chose the mayor from among their number, and were in charge of the various departments of the city, which they ran like private fiefdoms. In the old Newark, dominated by a few large ethnic groups, the commissioners were representative of their particular constituencies instead of the entire population, even though they were elected at large. For example, the Italian commissioner might be nominally responsible for Public Safety and Parks, but actually his chief political responsibility was to dispense patronage to the large community of Italians in the city. The commissioners were always obliged to compromise with one another in order to get jobs for their constituents, as well as to win support for their particular departments.

The business community found this situation intolerable in view of its massive plans for a "New Newark." They required a strong central administration capable of delivering substantial political and economic support to the renewal projects. The old commission had bankrupted the city. It was not even capable of taking advantage of the 1949 Federal Housing Act, which made possible urban renewal projects under private development. It had lost the confidence of the federal government and was careening Newark down the road to municipal ruin.

Thus the precondition for urban renewal was municipal reform. In 1954 business leaders spearheaded the charter reform movement. They were ready to coalesce with liberals and the growing Black population, who similarly objected to the city commission, but were interested in a city council that would be more reflective of neighborhood interests. The new charter provided for a strong mayor-council form of government. The city commission was preserved in the selection of four councilmen at large in an effort to appease the old ethnic interests and to provide a group of legislators whose concerns were not geographically parochial, but who could act on the basis of the "public interest." At the same time, five wards were created and each given one representative to the council. These ward boundaries were geographically contiguous so that the old ethnic power was not completely dissipated and Blacks could be represented in the New Newark for the first time.

However, the key change was the designation of a mayor whose powers over vital city functions were only subject to minimum influence from the council. The mayor would control all planning and development activities, as well as the ordinary operations of city departments. The alliance of liberals, corporation leaders, and Blacks assured the victory of the new form of government and the New Newark was on its way.

A second obstacle to the plan was the problem of dealing with small industry, now looming as increasingly important in the economic life of Newark. If the old plants were cleared out, there was a danger that an exodus of this sector of the economy would result. Instead, the city administration proposed to construct a light industrial center in the middle of one of the residential areas of the south ward, a district composed largely of Jews and Blacks.

The area chosen, Clinton Hill, was a site of large-scale recent influx of Black people. The renewal project would displace 20,000 people, most of them Black working class residents.

However, the third obstacle to renewal—and the one of major importance—was the resistance of the citizens themselves to the plans of the city government and the corporations. The late 1950s and early 1960s were turbulent for Newark and for many other large cities undergoing far-reaching physical, social, and economic changes. The early enthusiasm for urban renewal on the part of Black and white residents, who had become disillusioned with the corrupt city government, changed to hostility.

In 1955 the Clinton Hill Neighborhood Council was formed out of a group that had vigorously backed the charter reform during the previous year. From the beginning, the Council was dominated by the desires of an important segment of white and Black owners of small homes to preserve the neighborhood as a decent place in which to live. The newcomers to the area were former apartment dwellers, now purchasing one- and two-family homes for the first time. Older residents of both races were concerned that the transition from a predominantly white area to one where Blacks constituted a substantial portion of the population would bring a decline in city services and new racial tensions, and would result in the destruction of the community. At first the concerns of council members centered upon such issues as tree-trimming, traffic lights, and the frequency of garbage pickups. Its first neighborhood-wide issue was the fight to persuade the city to change its plan to convert an empty lot on the area's main shopping street from a parking lot to a small park.

I became vice president of the Neighborhood Council in 1957. At the time, we were only vaguely aware that the parking-lot project was only a small part of a more comprehensive citywide plan to serve the commercial and industrial needs of the business community at the expense of its residents. We were genuinely surprised at the resistance of the new city administration to the ample evidence provided by the Council that there was substantial neighborhood support for the park. The fight for the park was later overshadowed by other concerns, but in the relatively optimistic atmosphere of the early days of reform government, these were the issues from which politics was still made.

For the next few years, the overriding problem in the neighborhood was the decline in city services which accompanied the reform government's expanding power. When my son entered school in 1958, it was immediately apparent that the quality of education, to say nothing of the safety of the physical plant, was extremely shaky. Elsewhere in the city, groups such as the NAACP were demanding more Black administrators and the construction of new schools in ghetto neighborhoods, which suffered most from both dilapidated buildings and uninspired teaching. In Clinton Hill, we wanted a new school to replace the overcrowded elementary schools operating on double shifts. The overcrowding resulted from the large influx into the area of young married Black residents who had larger families and lived under more congested conditions than previous groups. The demand for the new school was generally ignored by the city officials, although we were not ignored as an important organization. The new city administration, headed by a former trade union official, was one of the first to have absorbed the governance skills associated with the concept of citizen participation. No "legitimate" group failed to receive an audience with top city officials, even when there was no intention of granting local requests. For a long time, we were charmed by the attention we received from powerful bureaucrats and elected officials. In retrospect, I am amazed how long it took before we became genuinely sophisticated about the pattern of response from government officials. It was not until 1959–60 that we changed our polite requests for a new school into the demand for the resignation of the superintendent of schools. During the same year, the city administration announced its intention to create the industrial park in the middle of our neighborhood and displace 20,000 persons. It held a series of public "planning" meetings, inviting members of the now-powerful Neighborhood Council to participate.

The Council, which had begun as a loose general group of homeowners and residents, had long-since transformed itself into a fairly tight-knit organization that boasted at least twenty affiliated block groups, and had formed committees to deal with neighborhood-wide issues. They included groups to organize tenants to fight absentee landlords, parents to win improvements in the local schools, a group to deal with the urban renewal plans of the city administration, a committee to negotiate with the police on such matters as harassment of area residents as well as the lack of police protection of neighborhood pedestrians—goals which often appeared contradictory—and a committee to work to increase the number and the quality of recreational facilities in the neighborhood, particularly to carry on the battle to get city government moving to build the combined parking lot–park area that had resulted from the long series of negotiations, demonstrations, and public meetings held in the neighborhood and at city hall.

The city knew that without the support of the Council's 500 members and block groups its industrial park was a political liability. But even after we made our opposition known to the mayor and his planning staff, it appeared that the plans were moving ahead concomitant with the progress of the renewal program downtown. We began to lose our naiveté. The more or less systematic deterioration in city services to our neighborhood had been prompted all along by the mayor's intention to build the new facility. In the years just prior to the industrial park proposal we had witnessed scare-selling by whites of one-family homes, their purchase and conversion into multiple dwellings by large real estate companies.

We had always attributed block-busting to unprincipled real estate speculation. Some of the homes were bought by Black workers interested in finding decent housing for themselves and their families. But an alarming proportion of the houses remained in the hands of absentee owners who seemed to be interested in helping the deterioration of the neighborhood along. For example, we conducted many battles against zoning variances initiated by these speculators aimed at increasing the permissible population density of the community. Even when we successfully defeated the variance proposals at the Zoning Board, we found the city unwilling to enforce the existing zoning laws. Garbage collection became irregular and it appeared impossible to get such small improvements as the installation of a new street light.

The formation of the Save Our Homes Committee of the Council was the high point of its ten-year existence. The Committee took the struggle against the renewal plan out of the conference rooms and into the streets and the political arena. Mass meetings in local churches, marches to City Hall, and packed hearing rooms where Council spokesmen and neighborhood residents kept public officials awake long into the morning hours culminated in the defeat of the industrial park. The issue became so explosive that the challenger in the May 1962 mayoralty election, Hugh J. Addonizio, pledged he would kill the plan if elected. The Council's president ran a strong campaign for City Council that year. Although he was defeated, the victor was pledged to work against the renewal plan for the neighborhood.

It soon became evident that Addonizio was no more willing to hear popular protests against the federal-corporate bulldozer than his predecessor. It was announced that a massive medical center was going to be created in the heart of the central ward, the largest concentration of Blacks in the city. Urban "removal" seemed impervious to political pressure. Neither the electoral process nor the peaceful protest of Newark's citizens was sufficient to reverse the plans of the large banks, utilities, and insurance companies who were in power at City Hall. To add insult to injury, it was not only the removal of residents that was the fruit of the "New Newark," but the decline of services as well. The exodus of large plants had deprived the city of substantial tax ratables, that is, buildings subject to property taxes, and the decision of other commercial interests to remain did not remedy the situation. In return for expansion within the city, these institutions demanded and received a 20-year amortization for taxes that would normally be paid on the new buildings constructed in the center of town. The combined loss of ratables, undervaluation of older commercial buildings, and the paucity of state aid in New Jersey, which levied no income tax and had little to offer the large cities, left Newark with few resources to combat the decay of its residential neighborhoods. The battle to retain the shreds of livability still possessed by parts of the city in the 1950s seemed endless. Every victory was followed by a new set of problems. We found that we were winning all of the battles, but losing the war.

Because of the financial crisis caused by runaway industry, Newark badly needed new sources of funds. Suggestions that the tax rate on commercial buildings be raised were greeted with threats of removal of these employment sources. However, for many Black people, the loss of companies like Prudential Life Insurance would have made little difference because most of the company's employees were recruited from out of the city. Most Blacks worked in the small shops, in city and federal jobs, or were on welfare. Their migration to north Jersey in the fifties took place in the midst of the exodus of industry precisely from those cities in which they were able to find living space. The new plants, located in suburban towns, were inaccessible to many of these people because of the paucity of mass transportation. Others were unable to take advantage of job openings in government since these increasingly required a high school diploma, a relatively rare achievement for those who had attended rural Southern schools.

To be sure, there were others, longer established in Newark's

Black community, who were beginning to find well-paid factory jobs, jobs in city and federal agencies, and a thin stratum was even being sought by the powerful local corporations to become members of public relations staffs and lower-level supervisory positions. These workers had perceived their interests differently from poor Blacks. They had constituted the solid 15 percent of Newark's population in the prewar years, had graduated from high school, and many were attending college. The older generation had already accumulated seniority from jobs acquired in the Second World War. Their children were becoming white-collar workers. They were willing to fight against the deterioration of the city. But they became bitter when they discovered that when they were able to find a decent home in a neighborhood formerly occupied by whites, the price of the house was inflated by the real estate agent and they were forced to pay it or stay in the ghetto. The Black workers who had saved enough money to get out of the central ward ghetto began to realize that new ghettoes were in the making. The whites moved out, homeowners were faced with welfare client neighbors, and, above all, a neighborhood that became predominantly Black was always stripped of conventional city services.

The Italian and Eastern European whites who remained in Newark were not very different from the working class Blacks. They had emerged just ten years earlier from their own ethnic ghettoes and were now occupying streets once reserved for the recently-departed Protestant elites or the lace-curtain Irish. The invasion of the Blacks was feared partly because the physical deterioration of the neighborhood robbed them of the morsels of comfort and status derived from recent acquisitions of steady work and good pay in brewery or construction jobs. In the 1950s the white population was in general retreat from the city, but many working class people realized they had no place to go, especially those whose jobs stayed in Newark. A surprisingly large number of younger white workers stayed in the city, but did not become politically visible until the Newark riots of summer 1967. Prior to that year, white working class people still identified themselves with the ethnic political machines dominating City Hall.

Neither white nor Black workers were at all sympathetic to the urban renewal policies of the city administration, but only the Blacks were ready to conduct a consistent battle against them. Their sense of being squeezed was greater as slum clearance invaded their neighborhoods, and the suburbs were not beckoning them, even when they could pay the price of the rapidly inflating ticky-tacky houses locked into chaotic developments in the farmlands. Blacks had to make their stand in Newark—and they did. Later, working class whites were similarly motivated, but instead of turning on the power groups they turned on the Blacks.

Newark came to symbolize the end of an era of white urban America. In the late 1950s and 1960s, a serious attempt was made by the big corporations to make room for middle management to relocate in the city. Part of the core's periphery was cleared and high-rise luxury housing was built explicitly to attract the departed middle class that had led the flight from the city in the early years after the war. Now their children were grown up and had moved to California and suburban life was dull. Besides, the railroads, victims of the greed of the bondholders and the advance of the automobile nurtured by the highway lobby, were increasingly unable to deal with the growing commuter load. Travel was becoming more uncomfortable and more expensive and the exploding real estate taxes on the white elephants purchased in better days were eating into relatively fixed incomes. But the effort to bring the middle class, middle aged, middle America back to the cities was unsuccessful outside metropolises such as New York. Instead, the apartments built close to the downtown area became dwelling places for transients on their way up the corporate hierarchy.

— 4 —

When I left New York for the swamps of industrial New Jersey, I separated myself from my left-wing organizational attachments but not my political views. I never joined the Communist Party, mostly because it virtually went underground just as I was coming of age. Besides, I began to sense that the party had become strangely irrelevant to my life and my concerns once I worked in industrial plants. Even the few CP officials I met in New Jersey appeared conservative and cautious in comparison to me. They regarded me as an intemperate hothead who would certainly be purged from the labor movement by rampant anti-Communism. I had the distinct impression by the late 1950s that my politics were well to the left of the Communist Party's, especially on trade union issues. They were trying desperately to find a way to overcome their isolation of the Cold War era. For the most part their trade union cadres worked silently in the plants or barely distinguished themselves from the mainstream of union officials. In contrast, my politics were much more public. I even organized a Marxist study group among young workers in Harrison area plants. I was associated with opposition movements within the union and in my neighborhood. I was critical of those Communists who bored so deeply within the shop or community groups that they became part of the woodwork.

In 1956 Khrushchev made his famous report to the 20th Congress of the Soviet Communist Party revealing the crimes of Stalin and the complicity of the Soviet CP leadership in them. The world Communist movement was thrown into turmoil and the American CP entered its final stage of disintegration. Faced with the loss of a good reason to stay in the plants, many Communists went back to school, entered business, or otherwise dropped out of political activity. Friends of mine who had left college in the early 1950s for reasons similar to my own, and who had been generally unable to do any constructive political work in the unions, found an excuse in the revelations about Stalin and the loosening of their political ties to pursue deferred careers as teachers and scholars. One person, now a well-known historian, worked for five years in an electrical plant and became a good troubleshooter on the production line, but acknowledged that he had been totally ineffective as a trade unionist or left-wing agitator.

I attributed some of my ability to stay in the shop and in the labor movement to my isolation from the political left in the 1950s. I was interested in the breakup of the Communist movement and the efforts by C. Wright Mills, A. J. Muste, and other independent radicals to reconstitute a new left, but it was not until the 1960s that I participated in the radical movement. For the most part, my encounters with the remnants of the sectarian left in those years were extrinsic to my daily experience. I drew my conclusions from a general radical framework and from my own practice and my observation of the actual struggles within the shops and in the unions, not from the political line of any group.

When, in 1959, at the age of twenty-six, I was laid off from the plant "for lack of work," I was able to look back upon eight years as an industrial worker, having experienced much of the dreariness of labor, as well as much of the excitement of industrial combat. Everyday life for me had consisted in the struggle to overcome the exhaustion of the worday that in the steel industry was not evoked by the monotony of the tasks as much as by sheer physical exertion. I used to read the perorations of those who proclaimed the end of arduous tasks and the dawning of the era of automation which promised more leisure time for those chained to the industrial workshop for eight to ten hours a day. The sooth-sayers of the technological revolution assured us that the days of manual work were numbered. By the early 1960s their predictions seemed to be confirmed by the fact that nonmanufacturing jobs exceeded factory jobs for the first time. Most commentators interpreting these statistics believed that nonmanufacturing jobs were all in technical, scientific, sales, or administrative areas where the manipulation of symbols, people, and ideas replaced the manipulation of things. For example, writing in 1962, Daniel Bell asserted that "The new technology changes the worker from a machine operator to a machine overseer,"[8] and that the essential prerequisites for the new society would be ever higher levels of technical and scientific education for larger segments of the population. According to Bell, the amazing advances in technology wrought by growing predominance of research and development activities over investment for the production of goods and services would radically transform the character of society. The growth sector of the new society was services, particularly recreation, education, and health, rather than the old manufacturing or agricultural industries, which were either declining or standing still in the postwar era. Later, when these confident predictions proved overoptimistic, the next generation of intellectuals issued fresh manifestoes about the "human services revolution"; even if the earlier cybernetic revolution had revealed its limitations in the late fifties, they confidently asserted that in the sixties and seventies most of the people who were formerly confined to the deadly routines of factory work would find bright new opportunities in the service sector.

Unlike some of the more ebullient theorists of the new technological and human services revolution, Bell was too acute an observer to ignore the countervailing trends in the economy. He noted that "There is very little spillover from industries involved in space development into the civilian sectors of the economy.[9] In the pre-Vietnam War years even though we were spending "almost 3.0 percent" of our gross national product on research and development, according to Bell, "only about 10 percent is devoted to the civilian sector and our growth rate is lagging,"[10] compared to that in Japan, which at the time was devoting most of its R and D expenditures to the civilian sector.

The predicted decline of manufacturing employment failed to materialize for the simple reason that technological advances were not initiated in civilian industries rapidly enough to displace physical labor. It was not surprising to me to read the *Wall Street Journal*'s revelation in 1971 that hot, dirty, and menial tasks had not been eliminated from the American workplace and that the work of the 1950s was still very much part of most people's lives, notwithstanding scholars and public relations men.

NOTES

1. C. Wright Mills, "Mass Society and Liberal Education" in *Power Politics and People,* New York, Oxford University Press, 1963, p. 353.

2. *Ibid.,* p. 357.

3. *Ibid.,* p. 360.

4. *Ibid.,* p. 360.

5. Herbert Marcuse, *One Dimensional Man,* Boston, Mass., Beacon Press, 1964.

6. Seymour Martin Lipset, *Political Man: The Social Bases of Politics,* Anchor Books Edition, 1963, p. 452. See also Daniel Bell, *The End of Ideology,* Collier Books Edition, New York, Crowell-Collier, 1961.

7. George Homans and Jerome Scott, quoted in Jeremy Brecher, *Strike!* San Francisco, Calif., Straight Arrow Books, 1972.

8. Daniel Bell, "The Post-Industrial Society" in *Technology and Social Change,* edited by Eli Ginzberg, New York, Columbia University Press, 1964, p. 54.

9. Bell, *ibid.,* p. 53.

10. Bell, *ibid.,* p. 53.

PART THREE

A Break with the Past

8

The New Workers

— 1 —

In the 1960s political opposition appeared to be defined by student activism. By then even those who had grown into their ideological majority during the 1930s and the anti-fascist forties had become persuaded that the American working class had become narrowly self-interested, just another pressure group in society. Despite the rhetorical militancy of the trade unions on civil rights and social-welfare legislation, only the most euphoric observer could defend the apparent absence of labor's legions from the political combat of the period. Workers seemed to have turned the corner from their position as an underclass, so evident in the early decades of the twentieth century. Now they had been transformed into avid consumers and patriots and appeared to have joined the American celebration.

What was forgotten in this superficial judgment was that the conditions for struggle remained a permanent feature of working class life. Unlike students in elite universities who are wont to retire from political involvement when wars end or specific movements subside, workers are perpetually aggrieved, and their opposition is rooted in daily labor. For this reason, ideologies weigh heavily on them as crucial determinants of action and the problem of their domination by the prevailing culture is always central to an explanation of their inability to transcend their immediate situation and become conscious actors in the social drama.

Hidden from surface view, there was a radical transformation of the American working class during the 1960s. The blue-collar worker of recent immigrant origins who lived his life in the shadow of poverty and unemployment did not vanish, but he was no longer a true archetypical figure in working class life. Not the least of the new currents in the working class was the rise of a generation of workers whose life experience has been radically different from that of all previous generations.

The traditional industrial working class remains a necessary condition for expanded capitalist production, and its centrality in the production of capital in most industries has been essentially unaltered despite its numerical stagnation. But the rise of the mass of workers employed in the public bureaucracies, in the distributive trades, and in the services is a striking feature of late capitalism, illustrating its capacity to feed off itself. Moreover, the relationship between mental and physical labor has altered dramatically since World War II even within the production sector, so that in several key industries knowledge has become the critical productive force.

As modern capitalism requires ever more investment outlets to absorb the tremendous output made possible by rising productivity, these opportunities for investment are provided not only by foreign markets, but by the systematic exploitation of the home market. In the 1950s and 1960s, this plunder was accompanied by the well-known devices of making the government a consumer of capital through military expenditures paid for by taxes, by expanding the sales effort, shortening the amortization of durables by lowering quality, and enlarging public employment as a partial disguise for the disutility of vast quantities of human labor and capital within the productive sphere.

The potentially revolutionary sector of the working class can no longer be sufficiently defined by Marx's famous concept of the productive labor force—that is, all who own nothing but their labor power, but are engaged in the production of profit. But in my opinion, the objective possibility for the emergence of a new revolutionary subject is in the process of formation. This subject would not be the old working class, which, as has been pointed out by Marcuse and others, was not a revolutionary class in America because it actually did become *of* society, in the sense that it was persuaded that its essential interests were tied to the prevailing social system. Nor would it be only the controversial new force of technical and scientific workers, whose absolute numbers have begun to approach the size of the skilled and semiskilled work force. Knowledge has indeed become a productive force in our society, but it is widely disseminated among the whole new generation of workers, which is better educated than any in history. The new revolutionary subject is simply this generation of collective labor that is emerging as the direct antagonist of the collective capitalist. It was created by the conjuncture of capital's own development and the struggles of previous generations of workers to limit the arbitrariness of capital. Its needs and aspirations are radically different from those of its ancestors. Its demands, not yet articulated, may be too far-reaching for capitalism to satisfy.

As has been shown, the stultification of American working class consciousness has had its roots in the basic formation of the class out of the waves of immigration between the end of the Civil War and the end of World War I. Divisions within this class, already divided culturally, were further ingrained along occupational lines by the recruiting of different nationalities not only into different industries but into categories of skilled and unskilled labor. It was not only these divisions that made trade union organization difficult, but the fact that the waves of immigration made possible some mobility within the working class itself. As long as the system kept expanding, the frontier myth could be sustained on the basis of the chance for upgrading as well as real and imagined opportunities for small-business ownership. Even if only a few workers ever left the shop or reached the exalted status of foreman, it was difficult to persuade workers that their own class solidarity was the best guarantee of change. The efforts of radicals to educate workers to the principle that they should rise with their class, rather than above it, was always countervailed by the differential access of different ethnic groups to opportunities within the system. The social division of industrial labor, combined with its ethnic divisions, was the core of the development of racist, chauvinist, and egotistical ideologies within the working class.

Equally important as cultural diversity, as a factor explaining the low level of class-consciousness among immigrant groups, was the exquisite sense of the promise of American life deeply imbedded among the foreign-born. To the extent that historians have dealt with the impact of immigration on the development of social and political life, emphasis has been placed on the importance of the frontier or Horatio Alger myths as determining the conservatism of the immigrants. But the ideology of social mobility was more than a myth. It corresponded to the real opportunities for advancement within the ranks of the unskilled created by the hierarchical organization of the labor force as well as by the rapid expansion of American capitalism at home and abroad. It should be remembered, however, that few foreign-born workers ever reached the middle class or joined the skilled labor force. Most immigrants were victims of famines or other forms of agricultural crisis, or were similarly victimized by repressive regimes. Many European peasants filled the cities of their native lands. For others, like my grandfather, a Lithuanian Jewish peasant who fled tsarist military conscription, there was no room in Amsterdam or London. The United States may not have been the promised land, but at least if offered a chance to live.

Some immigrants had been imbued with the revolutionary traditions of the old country. When they came to America they sought out the labor and socialist movements. Others were attracted to the militant and idealist movements of immigrants and native-born after some years of life and labor in the United States. Having fled from oppression, they were determined not to endure it all over again. But the majority saw a new chance in America, if not for themselves, at least for their children. And this country did provide an opportunity for some of their children. Of course, the route of higher education was not available to most first- and second-generation children of the immigrants. But a number of first-generation native-born workers found their way into the skilled trades or out of the lower-paid industrial jobs.

The irony is that both the radicals and the government failed to perceive the conservative influence of immigration. The rise of nativistic movements seeking to exclude immigrants from this country on the basis of their alleged radicalism and/or laziness was belied by the fact that American capitalism was built on the backs of Black and white imported labor. Government suppression of immigration was prompted more by the slowing growth rate of the economy and the appearance of frequent economic crises after the turn of the century than by the clear and present danger of revolution. But it is important not to underestimate the significance of the antiradical impulse behind nativist ideology. In the early 1900s, just as during the emergence of the permanent war economy in the 1940s and 1950s, the Red Menace provided the rationale for government suppression not only of radicals but of the entire working class as well. The last great waves of immigration came to our shores during the three years following World War I. After 1921, in the wake of the Palmer raids against radicals, the government clamped down on immigrants and only permitted a trickle after that.* At the turn of the century, the rapid acculturation of new Americans was a key objective of the corporate-minded liberals. Settlement houses, adult evening classes in English, public education, and the ethnic social and fraternal clubs which sprang up to help immigrants make a successful adjustment to their new environment (and to instill a patriotic orientation) were all assisted by large corporations and the government in the quest for a docile labor force.

Even though socialist-minded nationality groups were a powerful influence among some new arrivals and formed a significant part of the Socialist and Communist movements well into the twentieth century, most foreign-born workers belonged to such organizations as the Polish Falcons or the Sons of Italy, which were strongly conservative if not downright reactionary. These ethnic organizations preserved the contradictory goals of the American ruling class: on the one hand, homogenization seemed to be a strong preference of corporate and government planners; on the other, within industrial towns and plants ethnicity was an important industrial relations tool for the employers.

The Democratic Party grew in the later nineteenth and early twentieth centuries as another powerful representative of ethnic interests. Apart from its role in national politics, the party built its popular support on the basis of its links with the everyday needs of immigrants thrust into a hostile urban environment with few resources to cope with the bewildering welter of problems facing them.

The first-generation workers were often influenced by the attitudes of their parents. It was not until the second and third generations of native-born workers that the process of homogeni-

* The exceptions were to occur for victims of the fascist terror in the late 1930s, the refugees of the Hungarian uprising in the late 1950s, and the Cubans after the rise of the socialist regime.

zation was complete. Although many workers born after 1910 in the United States were already well on their way to breaking from the hyphenated-American syndrome, the Great Depression of 1929 prevented the emergence of mass working class consciousness until the postwar era.

Among the most commonly held shibboleths of radical thought is the notion that misery brings revolutionary awakening. But this has long since been proven false. There is convincing evidence that the leading forces in the rise of industrial unionism in this country were the native-born younger workers who actually did not suffer as greatly from the Depression as their elders, but rather occupied the better semiskilled jobs. The skilled-trades workers within industrial plants and the most stable of the older semiskilled workers in the mines and the largest mass production shops experienced some deterioration of their living conditions during the early years of the Depression, but were not thrown out of work. They resented the boldness of employers during the Depression in cutting wages and speeding up the work. It was the unemployed older workers who were part of the solid support for the New Deal, which offered them a life raft. The workers who conducted the mass textile, mining, and transportation strikes during the early years of the New Deal did not perceive the government as a friend, much less a savior. These mass strikes were genuine expressions of self-activity and remarkable class solidarity.

For the mass of Americans reared in the first half of the twentieth century, however, the Depression was a deeply traumatic experience which resonated long after the economy resumed its upward movement. The fear of unemployment and outright starvation haunted the working class for at least another generation. It was the quest for economic security that was to dominate their lives. There was no way their response to radical ideas could be anything more than sentimental, even when they were willing to accept the help of radicals in their struggle for social justice within the prevailing order.

My father reached his industrial coming-of-age in the late 1920s, on the eve of the Depression. In his boyhood he had helped his father deliver cases of seltzer to customers living in fifth-floor walkup apartments. He spent a year in college, but quit to work on a newspaper as a cub reporter. Since he was the son of immigrant parents, he always had one foot in the ghetto and the other in the American mainstream. The contradictory part of his

Lower East Side childhood was his inheritance of a passion for social justice alongside a gnawing yearning for economic security. The gnarled, decrepit tenements of his childhood stamped themselves on his social consciousness indelibly.

Although my father resolved to escape the ghetto, first through sports and then through journalism, these avenues proved too risky in economic terms. The newspaper he worked for folded in 1931 and after working briefly for the Associated Press, he finally left the low-paid and extremely shaky newspaper business. After some time in a textile factory and on a WPA project, he finally landed a clerical job with the city and lived most of the rest of his life in the choking confines of civil service; at the end, he went back to factory work. He died having worked and worried himself to death—but with some savings.

My father loved Walt Whitman's America, but lacked the poet's recklessness. He respected the muckrakers and the radicals, but could not summon either the energy or the courage to join their ranks. The specter of the 1930s was never far from his nightmares and so he died an angry and frustrated man, unable and unwilling to take chances to realize his aspirations.

My mother, born into a family intimately tied to the labor and Socialist wings of Jewish immigrants, was always more class-conscious than my father. Fearing the bosses but hating them even more, she worked and fought for the CIO retail union of which she was a member and participated in the sit-down strikes of the 1930s. She became angry enough—or crazy enough, according to my father—to quit her department store job in the middle of the second depression in 1938 after the defeat of a strike. Yet she was never too distant from her own harrowing childhood as the daughter of a sporadically employed garment cutter. Her own ability to achieve some degree of courage and independence was always based on the pressure she exerted on my father to seek economic security. Both of my parents lived in the shadow of the past that constituted compulsions in their behavior even when the larder was full and held no threat of becoming empty.

Even the members of my own generation, born in the thirties, were too close to the scarcity mentality of the Depression to transcend it. I rebelled against my family's lust for upward mobility, so I became a factory worker. But looking at my childhood friends in the East Bronx and the second-generation workers I encountered in my years as a shopworker and union organizer, it seems few of them went much beyond the aspirations of their parents. Among the kids on the block where I spent my childhood, a few entered college. They went to work in factories and offices, or for branches of the government by necessity. In my own case, the choice of factory labor rather than finishing college was motivated by political conviction, but even with a college education I learned later that my fate would still have been tied to wage or salary labor. As time passed, it became much clearer to me that the main difference between the factory and the office was not one of material rewards, but of dress and sanitation.

After 1940 most white kids born into the working class never experienced real hunger. The struggles for union security, health benefits, and pensions were taken for granted by this generation. They could not get hot for welfare capitalism or the guarantee of a job, because they really had no sense of what it is not to be able to find a job. Instead, they were reared on the doctrines of infinite opportunity within an expanding economic system and the expectation that they would not starve, no matter what. Just as the workers of the 1930s often took factory or clerical jobs as a temporary cushion to ride out the storm of the Depression, so many high school and college graduates took these jobs in the 1960s as an aid to finishing college, technical or professional schools. The relative freedom of this generation from the expectation that hard times are a permanent condition, interspersed with the opportunities provided by war, made the need for decent satisfying jobs more important than the goals of decent income and job property rights guaranteed by a union contract.

The older generation was often grateful merely for the chance to work. Besides the craving for security, there was also the eternal hope of escape into the middle class. The wartime and postwar expansion of U.S. capitalism revived the expectation that some workers could escape the shop into their own tavern or small construction contracting business, thanks to steady work and rising wage levels. Most of the postwar working class became quickly smitten (but also burdened) by huge mortgages, time payments for mechanical gadgets, and, finally, college tuition for their children. Thus, steady work bringing regular paychecks helped workers in the fifties to repress the realization that the distance between their rising educational levels or vocational aspirations and the routine character of their work was widening.

During the years immediately following the war, the idea of

education as a rite of passage to better jobs was widely disseminated. The early impulses behind the mass migrations from factory labor to the colleges were prompted by the leveling off of the need for new entrants into semiskilled factory work and the actual decline of the need for unskilled workers. As technical and scientific labor expanded vastly in the 1950s, workers possessing administrative skills were in great demand. Returning veterans were given the chance to go to college free of tuition and with government subsidies to defray living costs. The increasing reliance on schooling as a means of moving up the occupational ladder was prompted by the resumption of technical innovation within the production industries, particularly those which produced means of production, as well as the rapidly expanding public sector. Technicians and engineers were required by the war industries, particularly the aircraft companies, which were not really dismantled after the war because of the decision to solve many of the economic problems of conversion by perpetuating the war economy. And the baby boom following World War II created a greatly increased need for teachers by the early 1950s.

Public employee unionism began to grow in the mid-fifties as millions of new workers found jobs in state and local governments still offering salaries and fringe benefits appropriate to the prewar Depression decade. The public worker was a returning veteran who received his bachelor's degree under the GI Bill of Rights, a Black worker able to get a job in the post office or in the sanitation department, or a woman leaving her home for a job because her husband was not taking home enough or had split. These workers were no longer grateful to be working. The more plentiful, but also higher credentialed, public service employment was often received at a sacrifice in comparison to better paid industrial work. In this environment, weak, forgotten unions were able to revive. The nearly moribund State, County, and Municipal Workers Union and the equally ineffectual American Federation of Teachers seized the opportunity provided by the restlessness and militancy of the public workers. During the late 1950s, the growth of public workers unions was among the few bright spots in the already sclerotic labor movement.

Workers were still seeking jobs with more pay to offset their enormous debts, and the pay was more important than the quality of the job. The struggle for higher wages was a product of the inflationary spiral of the economy and the rise of consumerism as a way of life. In some instances in the 1950s, the speedup and stretchout in the shops were met with stiff worker resistance, but, for the most part, the Depression babies who entered the labor force from 1945 to 1955 were prepared to fight for higher wages against the erosion of their hard-won right to limit the company's ability to displace labor with machines, and for the expansion of health and welfare benefits under the union contract.

The fight for pension plans and health insurance in the 1950s was actually a sign of the aging of the industrial labor force owing to the restrictions on younger workers entering the shops. The two recessions of the 1950s and the rise of technical labor in comparison to manual labor had created this situation.

In the 1960s, the expansion generated by the Vietnam War, combined with the tremendous rate of retirement among those who had entered the labor force in the decade after the First World War—the workers who had helped build the CIO and won the right to get out of the shop at sixty-five—brought a relatively large number of young workers into industrial plants. As this generation of workers entered the shops and the public bureaucracies, the Depression-wrought issues of job security were pushed to the side in workers' struggles. In the service industries, particularly the public bureaucracies, workers possessing educational credentials entitling them (or so they thought) to work of genuine service to the community, or at least intellectually interesting to themselves, found that they had not succeeded in escaping the monotony of industrial labor—even if they were a little cleaner and less physically exhausted at the end of the day.

The new generation of workers was not prepared to endure a working life suffused with repetitive tasks performed with mindless submission. Neither the incentive of two cars in every garage, which had become a compulsion for their parents, nor the fear of plunging to the lower depths of poverty, which had propelled their grandparents, was sufficient to contain their resentment against the betrayal represented by highly rationalized factory or service work. Even those such as teachers or health workers, blessed with the chance to escape the most severe forms of rationalized labor, found the hierarchies of authority no less repressive.

Nearly all members of the present generation of wage and salary workers have jobs whose routinization bears no correspondence to the expectations generated by their educational experiences—for although the curriculum and authority relations in the schools breed submissiveness, the dialectic of schooling consists in the tension between its socialization functions and its promise of deliverance from the banality of everyday life. It is too simplistic to assert that students remain in school merely in order to obtain the credentials required by the shift from manual to white-collar and gray-collar labor. This is true enough. But the ideals of self-fulfillment sown by American education are equally powerful among the young.

Eighty percent of those entering high school now graduate. The number of college graduates exceeds the number of jobs available for which the degree is a prerequisite. The proliferation of youth who have successfully endured school has reached explosive proportions, and there is no room for them either in the teaching profession or the public bureaucracies. These youth find themselves in factories, offices, working as truck or cab drivers or as sales personnel in department stores. They are furious that they have wasted their time and have been oversold about the importance of education, which has not paid off for them in terms of getting them jobs which are significantly better than those of their parents.

The present generation of workers is qualitatively different from any in the history of American capitalism. It has shared the transcendence of ethnicity, the distance from scarcity, the partial recognition that consumerism is insufficient to overcome the alienation of bureaucratically rationalized labor, and the experience of having been incompletely socialized by the weakening of institutions and ideologies upon which capitalism relies for its survival.

Many young workers, like the young workers at Lordstown, have begun to evolve new work patterns to avoid having to do jobs which are essentially meaningless in terms other than bare survival. In many companies absenteeism is massive on Mondays and Fridays. In auto plants the huge turnover mitigates the disruptive impact of the refusal of many youth to work steadily; there is always a new crop of students looking for summer jobs or others who need money badly enough to work intensively for short periods. But in other industries, management has been forced to consider, and in some cases introduce, shorter work weeks with similar hours. The mass strikes in the postal industry and among truck drivers, as well as in the Lordstown plant of the GM company, were symptomatic of the refusal of young workers to accept boredom and monotony for five and six days a week, even at more than $4 an hour. Workers are refusing overtime work or Saturday work and resent company policies that make the longer work week compulsory.

In fairness to critics who maintain that wildcat strikes against the company and the union are not new in the auto industry or among youth, it should be stated that a similar development occurred in the early 1950s in the auto plants, but there were no mass strikes among other groups of workers, except for the big wage strikes in 1946, which could be attributed to the pent-up rage against the wartime wage freeze.

The differences this time are substantial, I believe. The old mediations are losing their force. Neither the unions nor the anti-Communist ideologies which were nurtured by immigrant fears are capable of containing the discontent. Nor are young workers willing to spend their lives in unremitting labor in exchange for high levels of consumption.

On the other hand, this generation still shares the legacy of racism and sexism—and the division of labor along racial and sexual lines. This legacy is a potent counteracting force upon the development of revolutionary consciousness. A second brake on the development of genuine political consciousness is the persistence of the hierarchical division of labor in general.

The social division of labor has been a source of persistent conflict within the working class. This division is not based on race, sex, or actual work requirements alone. The credential routes to higher occupations, the seniority system as a basis for promotion, the classification of jobs grounded in arbitrary distinctions which have no basis in job content or skill level, are important barriers to class solidarity. There are few industries where the leveling of status and skill is so complete as the automobile assembly line. The united action of the workers in Lordstown and other auto assembly plants in recent years is abetted by the relative uniformity of work assignments among the workers. There are distinctions between the grimy, heavy work for Blacks in the body shop and the fast, but clean and light, tasks, of final assembly. But the distinctions are not nearly as sharp as between foundry work and cold rolling in a steel mill or between the bedpan draining of the nurses aide's job and the quasi-supervisory tasks of a registered nurse.

The minute division of labor, whose hierarchical structure is reinforced by the seniority and bidding system within union organized industries, and by the system of educational credentials within both technical and human services industries, provides the material roots for elitism within the working class. In many industries, the so-called generation gap is produced equally by the relatively good jobs obtained by older, high-seniority workers as by cultural differences. The unions have become representatives of the older workers and guardians of the prevailing occupational differentiations which produce higher pay and less onerous jobs for their constituencies. Since the younger workers have taken for granted the real achievements of the unions, the unions are increasingly judged not by their past records but by what they have done for their membership lately. Young workers find that the unions, like the school and the family, promise more than they are structurally able to deliver. The unions have all but abandoned the fight for decent working conditions, and, insofar as they are perceived as staunch defenders of the status quo in terms of the organization of work, they are increasingly looked upon as enemies.

It would be a mistake to exaggerate the degree to which young workers have liberated themselves from the institutions of socialization or the authoritarian structures and ideologies which accompany them. The internalization of arbitrary authority within consciousness cannot be rooted out in one generation. In fact because the material supports within society for these structures remain powerful, without a convincing movement whose objectives are consciously antiauthoritarian, these structures of domination reassert themselves within the individual and the class. The struggle of workers in industry against the efforts of management to exceed the historically acceptable pace of work is not the same as the recognition of the immorality of deadening labor once the possibilities inherent in technology for the abolition of alienated labor are understood. Young auto workers have neither challenged the object of their labor (the production of cars), nor have they transcended the inevitability of submitting to the old methods of production. Their struggle remains defensive even when they have an inkling of a different vision of life and labor.

Most young workers, whether in the factory or anywhere else, take their money and run. They concentrate as little as possible on what actually happens on the job and try to live as full a life as possible during leisure hours. But lacking the elements of either an aesthetic culture or an alternate concept of work, workers have been made manipulated objects of the productions of mass culture that have been imposed from above.

The most significant characteristic of the capitalist division of labor is the transformation of the worker from an active producer to a spectator of his own labor. Workers who perform a set of discrete operations that are only a tiny part of the whole commodity and who have no real grasp of the commodity's social destiny after it leaves the work station, tend to view the production process from the outside as if it actually emanated from the ingenuity and initiative of the company. The managerial function at the workplace is often regarded with awe. Workers have even made the reification of management part of their everyday self-depreciation: "If you're so smart, how come you ain't rich?" Only in rare moments such as strikes does the understanding that workers themselves possess the real power over production make itself somewhat clear. The introjection of domination within the consciousness of the working class prevents this perception from being fully comprehended in ordinary life. To the extent that the real relations of power and initiative remain obscured in production, the masked domination extends beyond the workplace to all aspects of existence.

Among the spectacles of the marketplace, spectator sports play a unique part in replacing the traditional forms of folk or high culture. Spectator sports retain the alienated character of labor, but create the aura of participation for the observer. Emotional catharsis results from the mediation between the reality of the powerlessness of the fan over the events taking place on the playing field and the feeling of control which sustains personal involvement. The spectator appropriates the skills required to play the game symbolically. His involvement is energized by the passions of partisanship.

At the sports arena the spectators become imaginary strategists and generals and find a momentary substitute for the authority they do not enjoy in their personal lives. In the workplace and in the home, sports is a shared pleasure and obversely a field of competition among observers. It provides a way for men to establish contact with their children. The father remains the supreme authority but his power does not have the appearance of arbitrary domination. If the son is willing to share the excitement and love of the games, he can get some love from his father, since most men can only express affection in a mediated way. Like the movies, sports is an escape into total immersion, removing the observer from the banality of his own life, but creating the forms of manipulation which propel a sense of power and a vision of an alternative to the mundane.

Betting is an attempt to make the involvement with sports more tangible because it artificially creates a real stake in the game. Recently, many state governments have started lotteries replacing the Irish Sweepstakes of past decades. The lottery, like sports, is a way to perpetuate the fantasies of many workers that there is a way out of the oppression of the routines of their labor. In the old days, becoming a fighter or baseball player was a universal dream of young boys as a way to escape having to go into the factory, just as becoming a movie star served the same function for Marilyn Monroe and the millions of girls who ended up in offices. For Blacks and members of other minorities, sports and entertainment industries still serve as the "impossible dream" which is not so wild that it is completely discounted as a route to fame and fortune.

The sad thing is that many workers cling to gambling and sports as serious avocations even after the illusions of youth are shattered by the realization that they are not going to ever get out. Sports become the veil for the incapacity of workers to face the inevitability encompassing daily life. It is at once a protest against the worker's self-concept of his failure, and a means by which the ruling class is able to manipulate and channel discontent. As long as the workers can participate in the games through betting and drain their passions in heated arguments about whether Mays or Mantle was the greatest all-around outfielder of all time, the system has a few years left.

But there are better ways for workers to structure their leisure. The typical working-class barroom of the first half of the century was the place where the fraternity that was denied to workers in the isolating environment of the shop could be asserted. Drinking itself provided a refuge from both the shop and the home. But it was more important as an occasion for entering social life. The tavern was the center of political discussions, gossip about the shop and the neighborhood, and some sports activities such as miniature bowling, pinball and darts. The older working class groups did their drinking in the ethnic fraternal clubs or veterans' organizations. Later, the bowling alley and the union hall were added as places for workers to congregate.

The dispersal of industry to farmlands surrounded by nondescript housing developments or, worse, by no community or neighborhood center at all, has made it difficult for working class people to enjoy any form of social contact. This generation of workers is often confronted by an absence of opportunities for communal ways to reaffirm their experience of anger against the quality of life, particularly of their work. The widespread practice of year-round daily overtime, robbing workers of time to meet other people; the long distances traveled from home to work (which have the added drawback of taking away any sense of common experience associated with a hometown); the 24-hour operation, 7-day-week patterns of many plants and transportation industries, have helped defuse any sense of solidarity which might arise from the emerging homogeneity of experience, language, and culture.

We are witnessing the gradual disappearance of daily social life beyond the workplace in American society. The lack of social life has increased the capacity of bureaucratically organized cultural institutions to influence social consciousness, particularly through the media and mass sports. Moreover, under conditions of increasing isolation, workers reintegrate the protective function of the family which was eroded during the evolution of urban industrial society. Although Reich is right to describe the ways in which the authoritarian family structure reinforces the susceptibility of workers to the authority of the corporate and state institutions, the family is also experienced as a protection against the tyranny and the terror of the everyday world. The conflict is played out among some young people in the search for new forms of family life, through communes. Among young workers, there is a tendency to retreat into the nuclear or extended family when the whole idea of neighborhood has been rendered obsolete by the political economy.

Mass culture and mass politics developed on the ruins of the old ethnic and neighborhood ties associated with the large industrial city. Mass society, based on the fragmentation of the producers, buttressed by ideologies of consumerism, was challenged by a young generation which began to understand its objectification and develop a new subjectivity in the 1960s. The achievements of mass communications prevented the new sensibility generated by the student protest from remaining class-specific or ensconced within the universities.

The fact that most young people reject the artificially stimulated ethnic revival and have refused to respond to the slowing of the economy in traditional ways, namely, by cooling their protest against the intolerability of the work-world, is evidence that the working class is fundamentally altering its perspectives. Nor do they accept the old institutions as truly meeting their needs.

However, it is a long way from this point to significant movement for social change. There is absolutely no sign of emergent self-activity which transcends the ample evidence of defensive action against immediate injustices. What is clear is that as old needs have been satisfied for large numbers of workers, particularly the basic material requirements of survival, new needs are made. It is upon these new needs that the future will be fashioned.

— 2 —

If the idea of class implies not only an objective relationship to ownership or nonownership of the means of production, but a totality of economic, social, and cultural identity that leads to self-conscious political activity, then the American working class is at best a class-in-formation. Marked by its historical heterogeneity, it remains an object of the social process rather than a self-conscious subject to it. This book has been an attempt to root its diversity not merely in its bewildering array of social, political, and religious ideologies but within the social division of labor.

It must be recognized that the radical movement itself has reflected the inability of the workers to transcend the internalization of the social division of labor in their own character structure as well as in their organizations. Thus, invocations to class solidarity have often had a sentimental ring and have never become a program for action. Sometimes the left has even gone further toward legitimating divisions than the workers themselves. Witness the ardent support for nationalism, feminism, and the glorification of ethnicity within some radical movements of our own day. This is not to say that the elevation of the sectoral interests of the working class to a world view and political totality does not have material roots. The contradiction of working class struggle today is that it must recognize the demands of different oppressed groups who are fighting merely to be exploited on an equal basis with other segments of the class, and simultaneously strive for a unified class identity that transcends the prevailing system. On the one hand, particularistic ideologies have become useful for developing movements whose object is to secure the integration of specific groups within the larger social struggle. On the other hand, feminism, nationalism, ethnicity, and race—when congealed into rigid political identities—become deterrents to the development of class-consciousness.

On this score, it is instructive to recall the historical split within the left wing of American socialism and trade unionism at the turn of century on the subject of race. Eugene Debs's famous comment was that "There is no Negro question outside the labor question," and that therefore the Socialist Party had "nothing special to offer the Negro."[1] The underlying ambiguity here was that Debs recognized the reality of Black oppression and expressed his own horror at the bestiality of white employers; he advocated building a workers' movement on the basis of complete equality among the races but scorned attempts to recruit Blacks to the movement on the basis of their racial interests.

But Debs himself represented only one view within his own party. Many Socialists were outright racists, believing that Black people were no more than employers' tools fulfilling Marx's stern description of a "dangerous" underclass (lumpen proletariat) that could never become revolutionary. Latter-day radicals have rejected both the racist views and the color-blind views of earlier socialists. But the radicalism that panders to particularistic interests in its attempt to recognize and support specific needs that cannot be subsumed under a general class rhetoric and program is simply the obverse of racism or sexism. There was a kernel of truth in the traditional socialist view that questions of racial or sexual divisions could never be resolved short of a general social solution. Sadly, the left has failed to find the way to integrate sectoral struggles within a general framework.

It may be argued that such movements as the IWW which insisted on the concept of One Big Union were doomed to failure by the divisions within the working class. But it cannot be denied that, alone among trade unionists and socialists alike, the IWW made the attempt toward unity. Historical judgment can be made of those who proclaimed their adherence to the principles of solidarity as a matter of faith but acted within the framework of prevailing social relationships. The progressive role played by industrial unions and radical movements during the period of formation of the industrial working class within the emerging capitalist economy was confined to issues having to do with preventing the ruling classes from transferring the burdens of economic crises, wars, and exploitation entirely onto the workers. The heroic role of the militants in countless labor and political struggles cannot be underestimated. Yet to deny that these struggles failed to fashion a popular tradition of class solidarity is sheer romanticism.

In the main, the militant wing of the workers movement that insisted on more than defensive action and offered systematic opposition to employers was savagely repressed by the capitalist state. But there is nothing unusual about repression in any industrial country. The rising capitalist class could not have been expected to remain passive in the wake of agitation for its downfall. The failure of the working class in America to realize itself as a class with interests that went beyond its own immediate conditions of labor cannot be attributed to the coercive power of the state. It was its lack of a common historical culture, its lack of common language, social traditions, geographic origins, that made impossible the modes of communication that generate solidarity. In turn, this fragmentation gave rise to unique modes of corporate domination embodying both material and spiritual elements.

According to Marx, the political significance of the working class arises from its centrality to the production process. In turn, cooperative relationships forced by factory production and the concentration of great masses of workers in relatively few large production units created the objective possibility of social struggle among the underclass that was not possible in earlier modes of production that were largely based on widely scattered units of agricultural labor. But it is clear that Marx presupposed a common culture among workers almost entirely recruited from a peasantry which shared a common language and the same experience of having been expropriated from the land.

Second, Marx noted that the tendency of capitalist production was toward the formation of the collective laborer shorn of skill. The appearance of this collective worker, caused by the increasingly minute division of labor, was held to be an essential condition for the development of revolutionary consciousness since the worker was torn from both the traditional feudal agricultural bonds and the artisan skills of earlier production. In contrast to handicrafts, where the artisan performed all tasks, the division of labor in manufacture required cooperation among laborers performing only small segments of the work. Thus, the conditions of labor themselves produced the preconditions for social solidarity. The workers had to rely on one another rather than on a lord or their own self-contained independence.

Marx acknowledged the directing role of the capitalist to be a necessary function as long as the laborer lacks skill and capital.[2] At the same time that the laborer is made a dependent element in the production process, science is separated from the productive laborer and is pressed into the service of capital as well.

The actual configuration of American industrial development bears out the thesis that labor has been reduced to a function of capital and that the work process has been made relatively simple compared to earlier modes of production. Capital has organized labor both technically and ideologically. Its hegemony is buttressed by the hierarchical division of labor that invests forms of labor of the same complexity with differential status and rewards. Marx made provision to offset the reduction of the laborer to a "detail" of production by defining the machine as the agent of the reintegration of these details into a unified whole. Mechanization however, only potentially represents the overcoming of the division of labor; the division of hand operations is reproduced in the division of machine operations. The old tool-maker and machinist capable of designing and performing all machine operations to fashion a part, is now only responsible for setting up a series of operations performed by a drill-press operator, a lathe hand, and a milling-machine operator, none of whom can understand the process as a whole. But the machinist also loses his designing function, which is now assigned to a professionally trained engineer, so that even the skilled worker can no longer comprehend the totality of the production process.

Marx's belief that large-scale industry provided the social political basis for the working class to be the first exploited class in human history to take control of society was expressed in his analogy of the power of the industrial workers to the "offensive power of a squadron of cavalry."[3] Unfortunately, adherence to Marx's military analogy has prevented social theorists from understanding why the working class has failed to become a self-conscious revolutionary subject. The factory and, indeed, the entire society, is held together by military-like discipline that stands in sharp contrast to pluralistic ideologies that proclaim the individualistic character of social life. But under the hegemony of capital, industrial authoritarianism has served to perpetuate the prevailing social system, and only in the most abstract sense represents the preconditions for revolutionary consciousness. Lenin, following Marx, thought that the military-like quality of industrial labor was the best preparation for workers' power. I believe that both he and Marx were too optimistic and underestimated the alienation of workers from one another embedded in the division of labor and the factory system. Consciousness can never be the result of the reduction of the working class to so many cogs in the industrial machine. It is only when the conditions of social life permit the reintegration of knowledge in each individual as well as in the class as a whole that the debilitating impact of the division of labor and of industrial militarism can be overcome. In the workplace, the workers are not only prevented from achieving collective self-consciousness because of the alienation from their product, which appears as an independent force standing over and above them, but they are prevented from achieving independence from the capitalist by the hierarchical division of labor.

The most crippling aspect of the occupational hierarchy is the separation of mental from physical labor: a separation exacerbated by artificial divisions based on presumed skill differences. The problem of achieving united action within a single factory, much less an entire class, always revolves around the issue of how to cement an alliance between skilled and unskilled, how to prevent some technicians now called "supervisors" by the company, from operating the more technically advanced plants, and convincing the various strata of "semiskilled" workers that their interests are more or less identical with the corporation's. It is precisely the "organizing role" of the capitalist or the corporate manager in the production process and the complicity of "workers'" organizations in the perpetuation of this role that lie at the root of the political divisions within the labor force. A central feature of a new class strategy becomes the challenging of the prerogatives of the corporate management to organize production and of the unions to integrate workers into the production process under the prevailing social division of labor. Unless the workers themselves initiate actions to thwart the reproductive process on its current basis, they will remain a dependent variable with the political economy, and the particularistic ideologies of craft and profession, role, and sex will be perpetuated among them.

The development of American capitalism itself is creating the preconditions for overcoming the historical fragmentation of the working class. In the contemporary period, the fundamental new feature of capitalist development is the tremendous productive capacity of industry resulting from the replacement of human labor by machinery. As Gorz says:

> Nowadays, the tremendous increase in the productivity of labor and potentialities of automation make virtually possible the total and radical transformation of the work process, repetitive jobs could be abolished in most places; where they cannot, they could be performed alternatively, and only for short periods by everyone; multilateral training and comprehensive education could be made accessible to all; the barriers between manual and intellectual work could be torn down; rotation of jobs, collective debate on and responsibility for methods of production and the quality of production could be made the rule.[4]

But American capitalism cannot fulfill the promise of its own achievement. On the contrary, the spectacular industrial capacity of the system is ensconced within a social framework that thwarts its own development.

Twenty years ago automation was both a promise and a specter. It promised deliverance for millions from spending their lives in backbreaking, boring labor. The integration of the work process implied by advanced methods of production such as automation eliminates the technical division between manual and mental labor, since knowledge rather than human labor becomes the critical productive force. Yet automation has proceeded by fits and starts. The modern techniques that have been introduced into American industry have been distributed according to the criterion of investment for profit. The guaranteed markets for military spending have generated technological innovations in defense while some civilian sectors have remained relatively undeveloped. Such industries as auto, machine-tool manufacture, and metal fabricating have barely scratched the surface of automation. Although computers are now widely used in many office procedures —especially accounting—their application to the production of goods remains limited.

The failure of automation to spread to all corners of American industry is not a technical problem. For example, steelmaking processes have been developed that could meet current levels of output with 10 percent of the production workers that were employed in 1970. The introduction of these automated processes has not occurred for two reasons: First the modernization of the steel industry would require huge expenditures of capital that could not be amortized in less than five years, roughly the current rate of turnover upon which investment decisions for plant and equipment are normally made; second, the mass unemployment, the destruction of cities and towns and those whose economic bloodstreams are linked to the fortunes of this industry would present incalculable political and social problems to corporations and the state. Only because the American steel industry is faced with increased foreign competition and higher labor costs is technological change accelerating to some extent; but it is still confined to piecemeal measures.

The rise of worker productivity in all manufacturing generated by twentieth-century mechanization has caused a dramatic shift in the composition of the working class. The desperate demand for labor produced by the rise of industrial capitalism in the last century was eased considerably after the First World War. Indeed, the postwar perception that labor surpluses were not temporary conditions within a wider context of industrial growth, but had become a chronic feature of the economic system in periods of growth as well as of stagnation and decline, led to severe restrictions on immigration. The labor shortages that appeared from time to time were met instead by the accelerating pace of migration of Blacks from the South, Puerto Ricans and Chicanos, and the availability of women for full-time employment.

The cutting off of immigration has deprived the ruling class of one of its most powerful weapons for dividing the working class, at least potentially. The silent revival of ideologies of ethnic identity reflect the persistence of divisions within labor. But those ideologies are also artificially created in proportion to the actual decline of ethnic divisions among members of the recent generations of workers. Among youth of all groups, the separation from ancestral cultures is striking. While this indicates a tendency toward the adoption of massified cultural forms, it is simultaneously a sign that an autonomous popular culture is in the making. Young people in the workplace communicate with one another not only in the same literal tongue but in the same meta-languages, that is, modes of communication in which ordinary words contain imbedded in them a different emotional content and a meaning that goes beyond traditional meanings, evoking new symbols of self-expression and a common social experience. The incipient ability of youth to communicate among themselves a common sense of estrangement from the dominant mores as well as the values of the prevailing social order constitutes a qualitatively new stage in the development of the working class. Their capacity to translate their interior life into artistic forms as well as modes of political self-expression has also begun to invest the concept of "homogeneous culture" with a different meaning. Within the historical context in which "youth culture," in this sense, takes place, homogeneity connotes an emerging common symbolic universe as well as a common life situation among young workers that transcends both the old value of the sanctity of labor and the new symbolism of consumerism as status.

Of course, the new forms of social solidarity will not develop in a single dimension or a straight line. Racial divisions still exercise an important influence on social consciousness, and the ability of the bourgeoisie to repair the institutions that legitimate rule has been considerable. Yet even as repairs are under way, new evidence appears of breakdown. The complaints increase about the high crime and divorce rates, the indifference of the young to traditional social norms and their apathy to the old invocations to patriotism. The tenuousness of the social order is attested to by the proliferation of police work as a major new occupation that rivals education and health as a key "social service." No crevice of American life is exempt from surveillance. Not only in the population under constant scrutiny, but even the watchers watch one another. The specter of Communism has been replaced by the specter of chaos. But this chaos has been produced, it is not an act of the devil. It is produced by the awareness of the contradictory signals received about the rules of behavior and the matrix of ethical beliefs.

A rich society that demands adherence to canons that proclaim the necessity of maintaining scarcity cannot be believed. A society that promises equality but delivers hierarchy must be opposed. If capitalism has been able to contain its contradictions in the economic sphere, they have been displaced to the sphere of social life where the potentialities of technology for introducing a world of human freedom are understood by people who no longer believe that this social order can deliver freedom by its technical means even though it can produce cars with the rapidity of popcorn. The redundancy of large portions of the labor force, especially women and children, created by labor-saving technologies has led to the increased importance of institutions whose central role in society is the transmission of values and ideologies that reproduce capitalism within the consciousness of the working class in the absence of experiences in the workplace that formerly performed this function. Family, schools, churches, and mass culture now constitute the critical substitutes for the factory as instruments of the socialization of workers within the authoritarian and hierarchical structure of capitalist society.

But there are two aspects of the socialization process that constitute disintegrative factors within the prevailing structure of power relations. The first is that the prolongation of childhood, made possible by the wider technical basis of commodity production, provides space within which persons create autonomous social groups and values that are subversive to the social system. Adults too possess the objective possibility for the creation of a popular culture of their own in proportion to the amount of available time that is not bounded by the compulsions of necessary labor. The contradiction between the play element of everyday life and the requirement that each person perform a role in the reproduction of capital creates the necessity for the repressive secondary institutions of socialization. Schools and mass culture are made to occupy a central place in the daily lives of children and young adults, since they are the most effective institutions for maintaining the ideological hegemony of capital in the wake of those factors that undermine its domination.

The authority of educational institutions is maintained by their importance in the new occupations that have been created to meet the needs of modern corporate institutions. Credentials are the most important means for entrance into the work-world in modern capitalism. The ideological and labor-deferring functions of schools are masked by their apparent technical role. It is only when the student becomes a worker that these functions are normally revealed. At the workplace, the "knowledge" gained in school is rapidly demeaned by management, which eternally proclaims on-the-job training as the only real education, even as it increasingly requires credentials as an employment prerequisite. The schools are preparatory institutions for the structure of labor, not its content.

Mass culture colonizes leisure more directly. Whereas popular culture, which can only be created by the underlying population, expresses the play element in society and is usually informal and underground, mass culture draws on the creativity of children and adults and transforms the games and art forms produced by the people by mechanical means. It is produced as any other commodity but corresponds to the real needs of the masses to the extent that its sources are sex, play, and other deep socially created desires that are repressed in the ordinary work-world. The expression of these is trivialized and debased by the commodity form.

The second contradiction within the socialization process is that the key institutions upon which American capitalism increasingly relies for its social as well as economic stability cannot be successfully rationalized within the framework of the democratic ideologies that legitimate them. Schools are not only sustained by their role in the industrial order; equally, they derive importance from the fact that they represent the material embodiment of the egalitarian claims of bourgeois civilization. Even if the occupational hierarchies demonstrate the persistence of inequality, schools claim to offer equal opportunity to all regardless of class, sex, or race to enter these hierarchies on more favorable terms. In the 1960s students challenged the efficacy of the authoritarian structure of learning characteristic of public schools because unconsciously they could no longer accept the rewards of labor as a sufficient object of education. The conflict between the increasing capacity of the industrial system to abolish material scarcity in its most basic aspects and the persistence of the old work ethic that glorified self-repression and competition produced serious disruptions in the socialization trajectories of a large number of children and youth. Repression now appeared socially unnecessary. The release of the play and erotic impulses expressed in the student revolt as well as the uprisings of young workers against authority within the workplace were reflections that the democratic claims of the social order were not being successfully sustained.

To be sure, consumerism as an ideology substitutes for individualism and democracy to the extent that it resonates in the repressed needs of large constituencies among the working class and other subordinate groups. To the extent that labor becomes an instrument for individual consumption rather than a creative activity in itself, psychological alienation can be successfully repressed and displaced. Workers do not challenge their separation from determination of either the ownership, the object, or the uses of their labor under "normal" conditions. The conflict at the workplace is confined to such questions as its price or such conditions as affect health, safety, and the intensity of labor. Even the struggle against onerous working conditions remains restricted by the limitations imposed on workers by the collective bargaining agreement between unions and the employers.

Unions have remained useful to workers as instruments for negotiating more favorable terms in the sale of labor power, but they have often bargained away their members' rights to retain a voice in the determination of the conditions of labor. This has been a fundamental tendency in labor relations. Thus, the first expressions of the revolt of young workers have been for the restoration of their power at the workplace. In many instances they have been obliged to go beyond the rigid institutional framework of collective bargaining to assert their resistance against speedup, compulsory overtime, and the prevailing authority relations that appear to them increasingly arbitrary.

The infection of democratic ideology and the social legitimation of erotic needs by mass culture among this generation of young workers constitutes the permanent roots of the revolt. These impulses are the material basis for hope that a new working class strategy can transcend both trade unionism and particularistic demands.

— 3 —

The history of the working class in America is filled with evidence of an incipient and spontaneous tendency toward the transformation of struggles for the defense of wages or working conditions into struggles for control by the workers of their own labor. During the general strike in Seattle in 1919, workers actually managed the essential production and distribution of goods for the entire city. The capacity of the workers to direct commerce was again demonstrated in the Minneapolis Teamsters strike and the general strike in San Francisco in 1934.[5] The sit-down strikes that were the most dramatic expression of the rebellion of industrial workers in the 1930s were significant for the fact that the workers who participated in them invented the tactic of occupying the factory as an organizing weapon. The employment of this tactic was potentially insurrectionary, even though its conscious objective was always eminently respectable: recognition by the company of the union as a collective bargaining agent or defense against the employer's attempts to destroy existing organizations or working conditions. That the workers themselves were unable to recognize the revolutionary implications of their own acts attests to the partial and one-sided character of working class struggles in America and the persistence of the cultural hegemony of bourgeois institutions.

The employers in Minneapolis, Seattle, and Detroit were well aware of the spontaneous and dangerous quality of the strikes of the thirties, and of their further implications. They demanded that all the legal machinery of the state be mobilized to prevent the seizure of factories and transportation systems by the workers and that the strikes be suppressed by arms if necessary. Despite assurances by trade union leaders that the aims of these strikes were purely reformist, the employers knew that the workers were not entirely under the control of the unions; for a brief time, it was the rank and file who actually managed to exercise control over the course of the combat.

But those who have glorified these struggles of the past on revolutionary grounds have consistently refused to recognize the central problems that are revealed by the ultimate incorporation of the workers and their unions into the industrial apparatus. They fail to see that in our time, when social domination is highly political and cultural in character, it is impossible for any challenge to the corporations to succeed as long as it is restricted to conflicts within the industrial order.

In Western European countries, the demand for workers' control as a means of carrying the fight a step further has become an important element of trade union and political struggle. Militants in factories have demanded that employers agree to "open the books" to bargaining committees as a prelude to serious negotiations around wages and working conditions; that workers be given the right to challenge corporate investment decisions that result in technological changes and plant removal as well as the right to question the choice of the commodity that is being produced; and that in-plant conditions such as production norms, safety, promotions and transfers, discharges and layoffs, be directly controlled by the workers—who must have the absolute right to strike over all issues affecting their labor.

To a certain extent, U.S. collective bargaining agreements incorporate some of these demands. But in the bureaucratic form of the contract, as I have shown, the right of management to direct the work forces and impose its investment decisions upon them has been codified and accepted by unions. Nonetheless, workers still retain some shop-floor power on questions of working conditions in many industries. Flash strikes or "job actions" often take place within a single department or plant against speedup or violations of elementary canons of safety and health. Increasingly, workers recognize the grievance procedure as a straitjacket on their capacity to express their demands and act without authorization of the union.

"Workers' control" in the sense used here presupposes the industrial system as the framework for social struggles. As a means of ameliorating the most authoritarian aspects of corporate management of the workplace, it can be a useful short-term strategy. But there are two limitations to the concept itself that belie its radical potential. In the first place, to the extent that all collective bargaining is about the question of power within the prevailing structure of production, most of the demands that relate to this question are eminently incorporable and do not transcend the structure itself. Moreover, in workers' control the form of trade union bargaining is not changed even if its provisions are more advanced; thus the institutionalization of workers' rights that has tended to hamstring the ability of workers to act outside of formal agreements is perpetuated.

Second, one must question not the content of the demands but the circumstances in which they are made, when considering both workers' control demands that limit the power of the companies to control production and "workers' self-management" that transfers key decisions concerning the operations of the enterprise from management to workers' councils or committees. The limitations of both movements have been demonstrated in Germany and Yugoslavia. In Germany, the concept of "co-determination" expresses the complicity of the trade unions in the economic life of the nation under the general direction of the corporations. Workers assume responsibility for production norms, patterns of investment, and other important aspects of management but have no power to direct the economy in any essential way. The Yugoslav experience is admittedly more hopeful since the workers at the plant level actually exercise a considerable degree of autonomy over production. But they are constrained by requirements dictated by the central planning agency of the state that determine what is to be produced, how much capital is available to the enterprise for modernization, and the general scale of wages allocated to the specific plant or industry. As a nation earnestly trying to industrialize itself, Yugoslavia remains under the central control of the Communist League and the government at the national level as well as in each factory. The role of the workers is really advisory as long as self-management merely means the right to select from among a number of options determined from above.

Under conditions in which the criterion of capital accumulation (or profit in Western countries) remains central to production decisions, workers' freedom to allocate resources is severely restricted and workers' control becomes more of an ideological construct to win workers over to the idea that high productivity is in their self-interest than a genuine social change that provides actual self-determination. Clearly, neither in Germany, Yugoslavia, nor any Eastern European country are the workers free to cut their own hours of work, to reduce production norms, or to choose another product line.

In both Western and Eastern European countries, contemporary experience in "workers' control" within the framework of the traditional social and technical division of labor has contradicted its overt intentions. "Workers' participation" has been obtained while decision-making power has been retained by the bureaucratic state or corporate structures. In this connection it is instructive to recall the "employee representation" plans established by many U.S. corporations in the 1920s to counteract independent trade unions. Workers were invited to present their grievances to management but were obliged to accept the ultimate decisions of the company. Most workers recognized these plans as thinly veiled company unions. More recently, profit-sharing plans negotiated by companies and trade unions have been used as a means to increase productivity. Workers are asked to work harder in order to earn more wages, labeled as a share of profits. It is true that productivity increases in the Soviet Union are encouraged on the basis both of patriotism and self-interest. But the substance of these incentive plans is no different from that of similar plans in the West. Workers are asked to share in their own exploitation in both cases, since they have no real control over the outcome or the process of production.

Workers' councils or committees can only become serious expressions of working class interests when they challenge authority relations in the enterprise, are based on some understanding that the prevailing division of labor reinforces these relations, and when they possess the power and the desire to transform the workplace and society in accordance with a new conception of the relations between work and play and between freedom and authority. Workers' control demands that are instruments of trade union and bureaucratic institutions merely reinforce the powerlessness of workers because they sow the seeds of cynicism concerning the possibility of actually achieving the vision of a selfmanaged society.

During the 1968 revolt in France and again in the industrial strikes in Northern Italy during the following year, workers challenged the state and the trade unions by making demands that were truly impossible to implement within the existing bureaucratic structure of the workplace. At Fiat, auto workers demanded that the salaries of administrative and technical workers be equalized with those of production workers and that the authority of management over production be rescinded. They assumed the right to slow down or stop production without observing institutional constraints such as the union contract. In France, some workers began to produce and distribute goods within their towns. Workers' committees took control over smaller regions in scattered areas throughout the country. For a short time, important segments of the working class in both countries were able to act on their own. They created their own leadership in the plants that was dependent neither upon the trade unions nor upon the parliamentary parties that have held an iron grip on workers' movements for a half-century. In these struggles, it was possible to observe the emergence of a social consciousness in which workers were able to transcend their traditionally narrow interests framed in terms of incremental gains within the corporate capitalist structure. They began to contest the validity of the configuration of production relations themselves, and strained to create a democratic basis for authority. In the end, these efforts were defeated and the old institutions were able to repair themselves. Part of the reason for the restoration of the old order, at least temporarily, was the failure of the new forms of struggle to spread sufficiently beyond their origins. The workers were still culturally dominated by capitalism, even if they were economically in opposition to it. It was precisely the inability of the workers to transcend the fragmented economic struggle and the defensive character of their movement that enabled the state capitalist hegemony to be restored. The great libertarian slogan of the May 1968 revolt, "All power to the imagination," never became more than a slogan for the majority.

A distinguishing feature of recent working class struggle in the United States is that its militancy has not been matched by its imagination. American workers have perfected the strike weapon to a degree unknown in European countries, but it is their cultural level that prevents them from transcending corporate domination, except to win specific, and mostly defensive, demands. As Gorz has reminded us, in referring to a statement of Max Weber's, it is only by pursuing the impossible that we make what is possible come true.[6]

In both America and Britain, recent experience has demonstrated clearly that the sheer social power of workers within the factories or the offices to transform production or to challenge the rule of capital is beyond question. The degree of centralization, interdependency, and union organization of the most basic industries means that a national strike in a small number of key industries can precipitate a national crisis. For example, national strikes in coal, auto, railroad, shipping, or truck transportation can have a crippling impact on the essential flow of goods and services. In Britain, this was shown dramatically when the dock and coal strikes of 1971–72 were accompanied by visible, slow strangulation of the arteries of the economy.

Similarly, toward its conclusion, the 1970 General Motors strike in our own country began to have a marked economic effect upon the coal, rubber and steel industries and the many cities dependent upon these. This effect was quite evident to government officials as well as to the workers who were being laid off. The main feature of the auto strike was that the real issue propelling it was liberation from labor. Of course, workers were concerned with wages and fringe benefits, especially those with long seniority who wanted a contract that allowed retirement at full pay after thirty years on the job. But even this "economic demand" reflected the deep desire of workers to get out of the factory. Among younger workers the demands for less work were more explicit. The national strike had been preceded by numerous flash strikes protesting the accelerated pace of work, health and safety hazards in the plants, and the arbitrary policies of management regarding punishment for lateness and absenteeism. Work discipline had broken down because workers accepted neither the inevitability of the rationalized character of their labor nor management prerogatives in directing it. To be sure, however, the workers were not making demands that GM cease to produce cars and switch to mass transit or some other socially preferable product. Neither were they demanding significant changes in the authority structure of the shops.

Similarly, in late 1972, coal miners elected to national union office a rank-and-file slate offered by the insurgent organization, Miners for Democracy, whose leader, Joseph Yablonski, had been murdered during a previous attempt to wrest union power from the incumbent administration. The new leaders promised to rigorously enforce the existing contract and to take over responsibility for policing the federal mine safety act from the employers and the government. The increase of mine accidents and the almost universal spread of black-lung disease among working miners were issues that had been notoriously neglected by both the union leadership and the employers for years. Despite the comprehensive union-sponsored health program initiated under the administration of John L. Lewis in the early 1950s, with funds provided by means of a fixed sum deducted from the price of coal tonnage, conditions in the mines and among miners had steadily deteriorated. The new leadership has promised to democratize the internal structure of the union and to work for comprehensive improvement in miners' lives. Yet the fundamental problem of mining is not solved by ameliorative measures. Mining is not only dangerous to limb; the ecology of the mine represents the most treacherous threat to life faced by any group of workers in all industry.

A workers' movement in the mines would have to deal with the larger question of whether or not coal mining is literally viable as a way to make a living. Miners and other workers would have to question why America cannot develop other energy resources to replace coal as a major element in steel and electric power production. They would have to demand a ten- or fifteen-hour work week with no cut in pay while mining was being phased out as an industry. In order to guarantee mine safety they would have to demand the end of profiteering in coal mining. Moreover, strip mining, which is rapidly replacing pit mining as a major production method, would have to be ended, since it erodes the soil and raises the danger of flooding mining communities and their environs. In short, only the abolition of coal mining can really do away with its hazards. Technologically, this is an eminently practical proposal, since there are alternative sources such as geothermal energy that can be employed. The inherent problems are plainly economic and political. These problems cannot be solved under the present industrial structure without imposing real hardship on the workers, unless the workers assume much wider control of society as a whole. Yet the "impossible" demand that conditions that threaten human life within industry be removed, even if it means finding alternative ways of providing the means of subsistence for displaced workers, is eminently practical.

One hundred years ago, American workers accepted industrial health and safety hazards as part of the "natural order" of things. The widespread incidence of fatal respiratory and heart diseases among nearly all categories of factory workers and the frequency of industrial accidents because of the work pace or the lack of careful safety measures were viewed with a cynical fatalism by workers, since they lacked even the most elementary means of controlling their working conditions. During the last thirty years, workers have begun to become aware that these conditions are a function of the neglect and greed of the corporations and can be improved through collective action. Wildcat strikes have occurred with increasing frequency around health and safety issues. In some industries, union safety committees have worked to place restrictions on workers' exposure to unhealthy working conditions. In a few instances, notably the Oil, Chemical, and Atomic Workers and the Mine Workers, the top union leadership has become more sensitive to industrial health issues. OCAW has actually included a fairly rigid requirement for independent health and safety inspection within its collective agreements with the major oil companies. But this relatively small and fairly weak organization is almost alone among unions in basic industries in its grassroots efforts in occupational health. The OCAW has a small national staff that cannot begin to deal effectively with the problems of hundreds of plants and over a million members facing health hazards at work. Even the Paperworkers Union, representing the highly dangerous asbestos-producing plants of Johns-Manville, is fearful that a serious effort to eliminate dangerous conditions would cause the company to run away from its New Jersey locations to more hospitable environments. In most cases, union efforts have focused on legislative reforms that reduce but cannot eliminate these dangers because they do not reach down to the source of the problem—the production process itself.

Barry Commoner[7] has brilliantly argued that the general questions about insuring a healthy, safe environment are intimately bound with the configuration of our corporate and industrial structure. The question of the survival of humans cannot be separated from the development of a rational social system that removes the profit criterion from production decisions.

Production for profit rather than use has drained our resources, induced the revolt of nature against its violation by predatory industries, and destroyed the health of millions of workers forced to surrender themselves to the dangers of both factory and the ordinary conditions of life. The alienation of humans from nature and the corresponding alienation of humans from their own labor have produced a crisis that can only be remedied by swift changes in the way we produce our material life. The perpetuation of highly centralized corporate bureaucracies that exploit human and natural resources according to arcane criteria of capital accumulation rates is no longer permissible, according to Commoner.

It must be added that the human costs go beyond the damage inflicted on the lives of the workers in the mines or factories, or even the long-range pollution of the air or erosion of the soil. The predatory pattern of investment makes whole regions within our country dependent on corporate decisions. The American South became the beneficiary of the conscious choice of textile manufacturers to move from New England more than forty years ago, leaving much of that region permanently depressed economically. Although the impact of defense industries on many areas prior to the Second World War temporarily solved unemployment problems for many cities and rural areas in the Northeast, the Pacific Northwest, Texas, and California, shifts in spending have resulted in distress for many of these areas since the 1960s. Central Pennsylvania has never recovered from the widespread closing of pit mines in the 1950s. Its cities are grim, pockmarked places that have deteriorated to the point where their major export, as in New England, remains their young people.

What is striking about all the recent struggles of workers here and abroad is the enormous power still possessed by blue-collar workers, notwithstanding the ideologies of postindustrial society that claim the subordination of manual to mental labor as a critical productive force. But the potential power and militancy of the workers at GM or in the British coal mines was not matched by their ability to draw conclusions about the way in which production, or, indeed, society could be organized differently. The strikes were resolved when management made concessions on issues such as wages and fringe benefits, but did not go further to address the underlying problems that motivated them.

The disparity between the continued subordination of workers and their ability to disrupt production and show amazing courage in refusing to follow the direction of union leaders or in withstanding threats of government reprisal must be attributed to their habit of being dominated rather than to any enthusiasm for the existing systems of the factory or society. This habit of accepting domination suggests cultural bemusement in the midst of workplace militancy.

A strategy that would address the broader interests of workers—issues that go beyond collective bargaining or the limited scope of the trade unions—must include the creation of independent workers' organizations and committees at the shop level, within industries and nationally. These groups would not limit their interests or activities to the immediate demands of workers in the shops, but would also agitate for larger social demands having to do with the environment in the workplace and the community. They would generate opposition to U.S. involvement in wars, to corporate efforts to impose wage freezes, and to federal actions that limit workers' freedom to act on their own behalf. These independent workers' organizations would not be substitutes for trade unions. On the contrary. They would be their most vigorous critics. They would urge workers to strike at any time in defense of their wages and working conditions and not to accept the restrictions imposed by management through bargaining agreements; they would disseminate information about the experiences of workers in other countries in strike movements and workers' control struggles; they would argue for action on general political concerns, especially the need to go beyond reform and consider the possibility of transforming all social and authority relations in society, including ownership and control over socially productive resources.

Any self-management, either at the workplace or in society, of unbounded time has as its essential precondition the liberation from the compulsions of economic necessity. The undercurrent of the working class struggles that have occurred during the past few years and about which corporations have become deeply disturbed, is the movement toward less work and the consequent retreat of workers participation in the social system. Workers are expressing their refusal to labor under existing social conditions, but so far have only fought for this desire spontaneously and negatively. The indiscipline at the workplace represents the yearning for play as much as the refusal of larger numbers of workers to identify their life activity with that of the corporation or of the workplace.

The desire to spend less time on the job and to observe a less rigorous schedule has been observed not only by factory workers but by young workers employed in some service occupations. The search for more flexible work routines is exemplified by the preference of many New York taxicab drivers for part-time arrangements rather than the six-day week traditional within the industry. Young drivers are content to work half that time, even though they are able to bring home less than $100 a week. Some of the drivers put in a half-week in two long shifts rather than spending more days on the job.

The struggle for a shorter work week is no longer a demand for alleviating the unemployment generated by the rising productivity of labor. It corresponds to the separation of workers from the goals of the enterprise or the corporate system as a whole and to a marked decline in the mobility desires among workers as well. Recent programs initiated by some employers to improve work morale by enlarging job assignments have been met with some resistance by workers who had formerly performed more repetitive tasks. For example, when a New England appliance manufacturer broke up the assembly line and permitted a group of workers to perform a variety of operations rather than the narrow tasks afforded by assembly methods, some workers were pleased with the new arrangement because it provided a relief from boredom—but many others were more discontented than ever before. They claimed that the old methods, however boring, required only that their hands be sufficiently active to keep up with the line. The new methods required more mental concentration during the workday as well as manual dexterity. They could no longer talk to one another while working; there was no time for daydreaming. One woman complained that the job enlargement scheme meant that the company had bought both the hands and the mind and that the old system was far superior because it left the mind free for other things.

It may be objected that the demand for less work only applies to a relatively narrow range of stultifying factory jobs or those that are very dangerous such as mining, textiles, and foundry work. This view assumes that many service jobs, particularly those where the labor consists in working with people—teaching or health care for example—are exempt from the constraints of industrial labor upon the autonomy of the individual. Nothing could be further from the truth. The struggle of public school teachers for smaller classes and fewer class hours reflects their recognition that schools are nothing but another factory. The supervision is no less pervasive in teaching than in any other labor, and the teachers' autonomy within the classroom is extremely restricted. The widespread introduction of teaching machines and other audio/visual aids has relegated teachers to the role of consultants in many cases. In some ghetto and rural communities films replace class discussion and are viewed as a kind of tranquilizer for students. Many classes are held in complete darkness and the old art of instruction has essentially disappeared. Various other innovations have reduced many teachers to little more than equipment operators in the widespread use of standard syllabuses and uniform textbooks, and the recent introduction of programmed instruction into the classroom. Teachers become proctors, dispensing instructions to students on how to use the textbooks or programmed material. Teachers are partially aware that their "professional" skills have been demeaned and have proletarianized their demands. Like other workers, they want less time in the shop.

Similarly, the range of decisions made by health workers has been curtailed by the rationalization and specialization of medical care. Even doctors have powers that are severely limited by their specialties. For many younger doctors, medicine corresponds little to the old comprehensive, personal-care model that has been embedded in traditional small-town life. The performance of the same routines is boring whether the work is done on an automobile assembly line or in a hospital.

Workers' control demands in the human services could not be limited to trade union objectives for more pay in return for less work. Teachers, health workers, and others in the human services would have to demand the humanization of these services through the reintegrating of rationalized jobs. They would have to demand that their work be made more labor-intensive not less so; that distinctions based on caste be eliminated; that patients, students, and others be involved in decision-making; that the rigid hierarchical structure of supervision be broken down since it is socially destructive.

But these demands presuppose that education and health institutions would no longer serve corporate interests. They would also be predicated on a cultural revolution among workers, that is, their rejection of the ideology of professionalism that reinforces actual caste relations among human services workers and supports the present goals of these systems. The task of movements among health and education workers as well as workers in public and corporate bureaucracies would be to challenge the dependence of workers on the framework of their labor imposed by institutional power, to support short-term demands that sharpen the perception that the interests of these workers and those of the corporate government higher-ups are not the same, and that the old ethos of service can only be recovered within the framework of workers' self-management and ought to be opposed until it is possible to institute such changes.

The first step in the reeducation of workers is to help them become aware of their own biographies, that is, the ways in which they have been educated so that their character structure is harmonious with the structure of domination. The failure of socialism in the twentieth century can be ascribed to a large degree to the separation of the personal and the political that was accepted by socialist movements as the presupposition of their public activity; the task of the new radicalism has been to insist on the reunification of these two aspects of human existence. The attempt to forge links between the two has been at the center of New Left politics in the 1960s and 1970s. It is curious therefore to find some who were educated within New Left social and political movements abandoning the most valuable contribution to working class strategy when they address so-called working class issues. Here we can observe a sudden transformation among leftists from cultural revolutionaries to economic determinists. It is as if working class people lived in a different world of economic necessity while "consciousness-raising" was an appropriate activity for middle class students and women; factory workers and Black people obviously are unable to afford the luxury of self-examination and can only be "reached" with bread-and-butter appeals, according to this view. Radicals who insist on reliving the horrific errors of the past are not merely irrelevant to the new contradictions that propel working class action; they become coconspirators with the corporations in the cultural impoverishment of the working class.

The second task of an educational movement is to combat the influence of school, the workplace, and mass culture in destroying the critical sensibilities. Capitalism requires a labor force that is only literate enough to do the job and to assimilate the ideologies and commercial messages of mass communications. Recently, "labor education" has been trivialized to the limited function of supporting and enlarging the influence of the trade union bureaucracies. Shop stewards and local union officers attend classes at universities that are mostly of technical interest. They are "trained" in the administration of the union contract, and are indoctrinated in the political and economic policies of the union. Those who participate in union-sponsored education programs are frequently potential full-time officials or candidates for local union office.

The contrast between the pragmatic orientation of contemporary labor education programs and the tradition of workers' education that began as a radical cultural enterprise is symptomatic of the degeneration of all traditions within the trade union structure. Samuel Gompers, in his autobiography, *Seventy Years of Life and Labor,* described the most basic historical form of workers education: the employment of a "reader" in the cigar trades who read to workers in order to divert them from their repetitive labor. The reader would draw his texts from socialist literature, classical poetry, and the workers' press. Gompers himself became familiar with the work of Marx while plying his trade. Later socialist and trade union organizations formed night classes for workers in subjects such as economics, political science, trade union principles, and English language and literature. Although part of the function of these classes was intimately linked to the effort to gain citizenship for union members and win workers to the labor and socialist causes, the concept of workers' education itself was a specific political struggle aimed at preventing the drudgery of alienated labor from destroying workers' minds. The ideological character of these programs is no better expressed than in a line of the famous labor song: "We want bread, but we want roses too."

Workers' groups would have to deal with problems of family, education, and mass culture, since these are the significant institutions that influence working class consciousness. The struggle of workers' self-management at the shop level cannot be waged successfully as long as corporations and the government have cultural hegemony over the workers. The central mechanism of this hegemony is the control over unbounded time and its consequent rationalization analogous to the rationalization of industrial production. Consumerism, mass media, spectator sports, and educational institutions prepare workers to view themselves as objects of manipulation, to view their lives as outside of themselves, to surrender their subjectivity to the spectacle and to destroy their imagination. The central task of a New Left among the working class is to create the conditions for the separation of popular culture from mass culture. Independent workers' groups would have to help recover the elements of autonomous popular culture as a conscious aspect of the everyday lives of workers. Workers would have to be encouraged to create their own educational institutions, sports organizations, and arts activities as political expressions of their opposition to cultural colonialism. In this way they would learn to take control of their own "leisure" as well as demand power over their labor.

It is impossible to stress this point excessively. Spontaneous efforts among workers toward recapturing their leisure are incessant. The proliferation of hunting, fishing, camping, golf, and other leisure-time activities among men is an expression of their yearning and striving for personal autonomy. Yet these activities are no less infiltrated by consumerist ideologies and practices than other leisure-time activities. Hunters and campers in particular are obliged to purchase clothes, massive amounts of equipment, licenses to practice their sport, and a multitude of publications. These activities are not primarily social in character. They assert the individuality that is denied in social labor, but they enforce a sense of separation of the person from others. Hunting expresses the aggressions that individuals experience because of their social and personal powerlessness within the plant and in other aspects of the social world. Although hunting is a sublimated form of personal self-management, it represents a retreat from, rather than a deeper involvement in, the world.

For millions of Americans, the desperate search for vocation is only found outside the workplace. "Work" for them is sharply separated from "labor" and is only achieved in the private realm. The colonization of leisure by commodities that prevents private life from becoming truly autonomous also prevents the development of a self-conscious, popular working class culture. Since the cultural institutions of the dominant society are not subject to popular control but are influenced by ordinary people only indirectly, the creation of self-conscious alternative cultural institutions has equal importance with the creation of autonomous political and economic forms of workers' struggles. The history of the American working class, indeed the history of the working class in all advanced capitalist countries, is marked by the gradual replacement of popular culture by mass culture. Unless the workers themselves are able to go beyond the "manipulation of the manipulators" and control their own destiny, they will remain the objects of history, not its subjects.

The movement of young workers toward the creation of an autonomous culture is more than a programmatic hope. Literally tens of thousands of young working people have tried to participate in making, rather than observing, art. For example, the proliferation of rock groups among young adults is not only characteristic of high school and college campuses; playing musical instruments, composing songs, performing at parties and bars, or simply playing for enjoyment is widespread as leisure-time activity among working class youth. Often, members of these groups even become interested in "classical" music as they become aware of the technical and musical issues imbedded in contemporary rock music.

Unfortunately, the dissemination of popular musical culture is often imitative of commercial forms that, in turn, have arisen as simulations of indigenous creations. Thus, the awareness of the popular roots of music is mediated by its mechanically reproduced products. Moreover, many small rock groups that are composed of youths who work in factories or offices seek out ways to sell their music to promoters, record companies, and commercial clubs and become unwitting sources of their own domination. Similarly, rejection by young people of high fashion by adopting proletarian dress became a new fashion that provided a vast market for the previously small work-clothes industry; the deep concern with nutrition among young people that produced a rejection of mass-produced foods that contained harmful chemicals was debased by the rise of a multimillion dollar "organic foods" industry.

Yet the recognition by young workers that the prevailing cultural norms are corrupt is acute. In New York City, subways, trains, and stations are filled with graffiti that express both the imagination of the young and their awareness of the banality of the official advertising. The graffiti are poetic, humorous, irreverent of commercial culture, and often political in content. The subways are a gallery of popular art and literature that has no legitimacy in the organs of high culture. The art is as anonymous as it is individual. The streets of the *barrios* of New York are equally grim in their physical architecture and festive in the murals that adorn the fading brick façades of the tenements.

Children and youth are constantly inventing new languages to express their separation from the dominant public idiom. Each new colloquialism finds its way into mass cultural forms, but the incorporation evokes a new set of expressions that represent the private communications of the young. Mass culture finds itself straining to catch up with these popular speech forms in order to hold its audience. The struggle goes on without ultimate victory for either side.

One of the most characteristic expressions of the attempt at individuation through language has been the ascription of opposite meanings to words as ordinarily understood. For example, the words "bad" and "outrageous" mean "good" and "exciting" respectively to young people. Young people attempt to enrich communications by devising these descriptive modes; but they are also straining to find ways to create a unique idiom.

The conflict between the creation of popular culture and its mass production illustrates a central feature of late capitalism: having created the material preconditions for the abolition of scarcity, that is, having met the base material needs of the vast majority of the working class, it has generated new needs. Workers can no longer be contained with a surfeit of commodities because the new generation has never experienced systematic deprivation. New needs for cultural and social autonomy from industrial institutions that appear increasingly irrational and oppressive have come into being. Thus the cultural struggle becomes a primary focus and takes the form in the factory of release from the compulsions of industrial labor. Lacking the social and political expressions of protest, workers have historically sought private means of alleviating the sense of frustration they experience at the workplace. Workers employ alcohol and drugs to help them get through the day. In the early textile mills, drugs were made available by employers to children and youth to overcome boredom and exhaustion. The defensive use of drugs among young workers is even more widespread today. This does not signify a cultural revolution in the factory or offices; the use of drugs on the job is merely a symptom of the failure of workers to make political their acute experience of alienation in work.

The struggle against the cultural domination of capital is rendered more difficult by the fact that consciousness is rooted in several generations of working class experience. A still substantial segment of the work force remains locked into the scarcity mentality of the prewar era. The compulsiveness of its quest for job security, its habit of submission to the domination of corporate, trade union, and national political leadership is rooted in the sense of powerlessness that is generated by the economic vicissitudes of the social order. Another segment celebrates deliverance from abject poverty but is manipulated by the colonization of its needs by consumerism. The surplus repression represented by life styles that are defined by the variety of commodities workers possess becomes a chain that prohibits autonomy, and makes this segment of the working class still dependent on the corporate order.

The process by which children are made into relatively obedient adults is fraught with considerable difficulty in the modern era because the patterns of capital accumulation tend to disrupt everyday life and traditional customs and social relationships, and thus undermine the authority of traditional institutions, particularly the family. Even though children are withheld from participation in the labor force for considerably longer than ever before, they tend to leave home earlier. This trend, evident among college students and technically trained workers, has also become more pronounced among children of working class families. The significance of mass culture as a control mechanism has grown in proportion to the decline of neighborhood and family life, and its role has become important in maintaining the habits previously formed by traditional interaction processes. Yet the contradictory images of freedom and authority imposed by mass culture and schools both encourage and suppress "deviant" political behavior.

A growing minority of workers has brought to consciousness the irrationality of prevailing social relations, has rejected the commodification of culture, and refuses to participate in the compulsive mobility or consumerist life modes of previous generations. They define themselves as radicals or deviants even as they work in factories and offices and are engaged constantly in a struggle against regression to the psychological and political subordination of their parents. Within this generation, as in all others in the working class, the three moments of historical sensibility exist simultaneously both in individuals and social groups and are in constant conflict with one another.

Even though there is no articulate force within the working class that possesses an understanding of the fundamental contradiction between the industrial structure and its containment of the liberatory possibilities that it has generated, the material and the spiritual basis exists for its emergence. The trenchant critiques made by Black workers groups that have acted outside the official trade unions, the women's groups that are attempting to fuse a feminist with a class approach to politics, and the incipient rebellions of young workers against the reified ideologies of compulsive labor and individual advancement are all indications that the objective possibilities are straining for actualization.

Reich has defined class consciousness as:

1. Knowledge of one's own vital necessities in all spheres;
2. knowledge of ways and possibilities of satisfying them;
3. knowledge of the obstacles that a social system based on private property puts in the way of their satisfaction;
4. knowledge of one's own inhibitions and fears that prevent one from clearly realizing one's needs and the obstacles to their satisfaction (the "enemy within" is a particularly true image of the physical inhibitions of the oppressed individual);
5. knowledge that mass unity makes an invincible force against the power of the oppressors.[8]

The task of a radical movement among the workers is to help create a new working class "public," in the classical sense of the term, that is, a group that participates in public life in accordance with its self-conscious interests. Radicals must carefully avoid "vanguard" politics for three reasons: first, the working class in America does not need such a vanguard because it has the objective possibility of comprehending its own experience and leading itself. Second, the left has no credentials for assuming the role even if it were needed; its contributions to working class struggle, however considerable, have never transcended the level of consciousness of the workers themselves, and have often seriously impeded that consciousness. Third, it is not the job of the left to reproduce authoritarian social relations in the workers' movement. Instead, its first responsibility is to help create a movement that prefigures a nonauthoritarian society—a movement that is aware of the dialectic of domination and subordination within the structure of society as well as the character structure of the workers themselves and tries to transcend these syndromes, even as it simultaneously struggles every day in the workplace against the assault of capital on working conditions. Admittedly, the reasons to hope for the creation of such a movement are countervailed by opposing tendencies.

I have argued that neither the revolutionary cheerleading of every strike for higher wages nor ominous predictions of impending economic and social catastrophe will bring about social change or even deepen the understanding of the forces that can lead to a new political movement among the working class. The great socialist Rosa Luxemburg has reminded us that the left can only speak clearly and honestly among workers—not lead them. Historians, sociologists, political theorists, psychologists, and activists have a grave responsibility to separate their wishes from their observation of the actuality of the working class movement and its position in society. The chief method of our work ought to be to discover the roots of the revolt, while at the same time facing up to the obstacles presented by the social order. We are obliged to courageously reexamine every article of faith and be prepared to abandon it. If social theory does not remain critical of itself, it is sure to ossify into dogma. Of course there is no need to jettison a fundamental commitment to social change. Equally dangerous however, is a commitment to political judgments that have been surpassed by history.

NOTES

1. *Eugene V. Debs: Writings and Speeches*, edited by Arthur M. Schlesinger, Jr., New York, Heritage House, Inc., 1948, pp. 65–66.

2. Karl Marx, *Capital*, Vol. I, New York, Modern Library Edition, 1936. See chapter 13, pp. 353–68.

3. *Ibid.*, p. 357.

4. Andre Gorz, "Workers Control Is More Than Just That" in *Workers' Control*, edited by Gerry Hunnius, G. David Garson and John Case, New York, Random House, 1972, p. 338.

5. See Harvey O'Connor, *Revolution in Seattle*, New York, Monthly Review Press, 1964, and Jeremy Brecher, *Strike!* San Francisco, Calif., Straight Arrow Books, 1972.

6. Gorz, *op. cit.*, p. 342.

7. Barry Commoner, *The Closing Circle*, New York, Alfred A. Knopf, 1971.

8. Wilhelm Reich, *Sex-Pol*, New York, Random House, 1972, p. 358.

Short Bibliography of Works Not Cited in Text

Peter Henle. "Organized Labor and the New Militants" in *Monthly Labor Review*, Vol. 92, No. 7, July 1969

James Weinstein. *The Decline of Socialism in America 1919–1925*, New York, Monthly Review Press, 1967

Technology and the American Economy. National Commission on Automation and Economic Progress, Washington, D.C., 1966

William Preston, Jr. *Aliens and Dissenters: Federal Suppression of Radicals 1903–1933*, Cambridge, Mass., Harvard University Press, 1963

Wayne G. Broehl, Jr. *The Molly McGuires*, Cambridge, Mass., Harvard University Press, 1964

Loyd D. Easton and Kurt H. Goddat, eds. *The Writings of the Young Marx on Philosophy and Society*, New York, Anchor Books, 1967

Karl Marx. *Economic and Philosophical Manuscripts of 1844–* , translated by Martin Milligan, Moscow, Foreign Languages Publishing House (no date)

U.S. Department of Labor, *Handbook of Labor Statistics, 1969*, Washington, D.C., U.S. Government Printing Office, July 1969

Hugh D. Duncan. *Symbols in Society*, New York, Oxford University Press, 1968

———. *Communications and Social Order*, New York, Oxford University Press, 1962

Daniel Bell. *Marxian Socialism in the United States*, Princeton, Princeton University Press, 1967

———. *The Coming of Post-Industrial Society*, New York, Basic Books, 1973

Lewis Corey. *The Crisis of the Middle Class*, New York, Coivici-Friede, 1935

E. W. Andrews and M. Moylan. "Scientific and Professional Employment by States," in U.S. Department of Labor, *Monthly Labor Review*, Vol. 92, No. 8, August 1969

Michael F. Crowley. "Projected Requirements for Technicians in 1980," U.S. Department of Labor, *Monthly Labor Review*, Vol. 93, No. 5, May 1970

Robert Michels. *Political Parties*, New York, Collier Books edition, 1962

H. L. Nerburg. *In the Name of Science*, Chicago, Quadrangle Books, 1966, 1970

Alain Touraine. *The Post-Industrial Society*, translated by Leonard F. Mayhew, New York, Random House, 1971

John C. Leggett. *Class, Race and Labor: Working Class Consciousness in Detroit*, New York, Oxford University Press, 1968

U.S. Department of Commerce. *U.S. Industrial Outlook 1972 with Projection to 1980*, Washington, D.C., U.S. Government Printing Office (no date)

Georg Lukacs. *History and Class Consciousness*, Cambridge, Mass., MIT Press, 1971

Herbert Marcuse. *Eros and Civilization*, Boston, Mass., Beacon Press, 1955

————. *Negations*, Boston, Beacon Press, 1968

————. *An Essay on Liberation*, Boston, Beacon Press, 1969

Eleanor Flexner. *Century of Struggle*, Cambridge, Mass., Harvard University Press, 1959

Karl Korsch. *Marxism and Philosophy*, London, New Left Books, 1970

————. *Karl Marx*, New York, Russell and Russell, 1963

Mary-Alice Walters, ed. *Rosa Luxemburg Speaks*, New York, Pathfinder Press, 1970

Wilhelm Reich. *Mass Psychology of Fascism*, New York, Orgone Institute Press, Cleveland and New York, 1946

William Appleman Williams. *The Contours of American History*, World Publishing Company, 1961

J. David Greenstone. *Labor in American Politics*, New York, Alfred A. Knopf, 1969

Max Horkheimer. *Critical Theory*, New York, Herder and Herder, 1972

Max Horkheimer and Theodore Adorno. *Dialectic of Enlightenment*, New York, Herder and Herder, 1972

Ronald Radosh. *American Labor and U.S. Foreign Policy*, New York, Random House, 1969

Gregory Bateson. *Steps to an Ecology of Mind*, New York, Ballantine Books, 1972

Gregory Bateson and Jurgen Ruesch. *Communication*, New York, W. W. Norton, 1951 and 1968

Antonio Gramsci. *Selections from the Prison Notebooks*, New York, International Publishers, 1971

Murray Bookchin. *Post-Scarcity Anarchism*, Berkeley, Calif., Ramparts Press, 1971

Jurgen Haberman. *Knowledge and Human Interests*, Boston, Beacon Press, 1971

Henri Lefebre. *Everyday Life in the Modern World*, New York, Harper Torchbooks, 1971

Oscar Handlin. *The Uprooted*, Boston, Little, Brown, 1951

Harold Underwood Faulkner. *Politics, Reform and Expansion, 1890–1900*, New York, Harper and Row, 1959

Thorstein Veblen. *The Higher Learning in America*, New York, Hill and Wang edition, 1957

Work in America—Report of a special task force to the Secretary, U.S. Department of Health, Education and Welfare, Cambridge, Mass., MIT Press (no date)

Jules Henry. *Culture Against Man*, New York, Random House, 1963

Lloyd C. Gardner. *Architects of Illusion*, Chicago, Quadrangle Books, 1970

———. *Economic Aspects of New Deal Foreign Policy*, Madison, University of Wisconsin Press, 1964

Jacques Ellul. *The Technological Society*, New York, Alfred A. Knopf, 1964

Juliet Mitchell. *Woman's Estate*, New York, Pantheon Books, 1971

Stanley Aronowitz. "Is There a New Working Class?" in George Fischer, ed., *The Revival of American Socialism*, New York, Oxford University Press, 1971

———. "Law, The Breakdown of Order and Revolution," in Robert Lefrant, *Law Against the Reader*, New York, Random House, 1971

Index

About the Author

Born in New York City in 1933, Stanley Aronowitz, who holds no advanced degrees, was educated in the public schools. A factory worker in the steel, auto, and electrical industries from 1951 to 1960, Aronowitz became an organizer for the Amalgamated Clothing Workers of America in 1960 and from 1964 to 1967 was International Representative for the Oil, Chemical, and Atomic Workers. He subsequently worked as a community organizer on the Lower East Side of New York and as a Director of the Joint Planning Committee of Park East, a public experimental high school. He now teaches at the New School for Social Research and in the experimental college of Staten Island Community College, CUNY.

Mr. Aronowitz was an editor of *Studies on the Left*. His articles and essays have appeared in the *Village Voice*, *Social Policy*, *Liberation*, *New Politics*, and the *Guardian*. He is currently writing a book on mass culture and social learning.

Catalog

If you are interested in a list of fine Paperback
books, covering a wide range of subjects
and interests, send your name and address,
requesting your free catalog, to:

McGraw-Hill Paperbacks
1221 Avenue of Americas
New York, N.Y. 10020